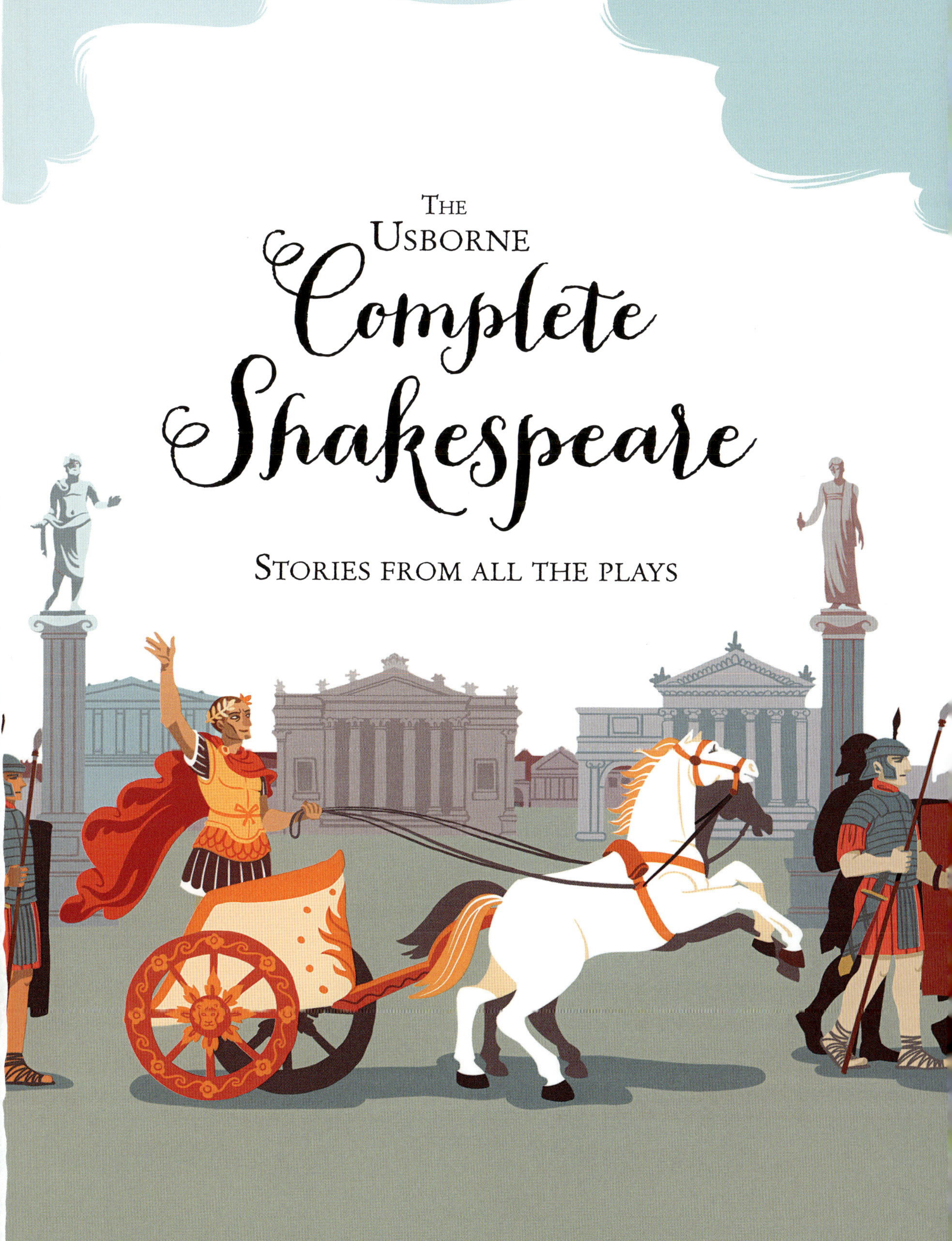

The Usborne Complete Shakespeare

Stories from all the plays

The Usborne Complete Shakespeare

Stories from all the plays

Stories written by Anna Milbourne,
Jerome Martin and Megan Cullis

With Henry Brook, Mary Sebag-Montefiore, Rachel Firth,
Sarah Courtauld, Susanna Davidson, Ruth Brocklehurst,
Matthew Oldham and Laura Cowan

Illustrated by Maria Surducan
Designed by Hayley Wells

 Contents

Shakespeare's plays are divided into the following categories. All the story titles have been marked with symbols to show which category they belong to.

- Comedies (with happy endings)
- Tragedies (with sad endings)
- Histories (based on English history)

Stories

A Midsummer Night's Dream 6

Twelfth Night 20

Romeo and Juliet 40

Coriolanus 58

Love's Labour's Lost 78

Richard II 92

Much Ado About Nothing 108

The Merchant of Venice 128

Hamlet 146

As You Like It 166

Henry IV 184

Julius Caesar 200

Two Gentlemen of Verona 214

Othello 228

The Merry Wives of Windsor 244

Macbeth 262

The Winter's Tale 278

Antony and Cleopatra 296

The Taming of the Shrew 314

Henry V 332

King Lear 348

Pericles 368

The Comedy of Errors 386

Timon of Athens 402

Richard III 414

Troilus and Cressida 430

The Tempest 446

Stories told in brief

Henry VI 464

Measure for Measure 466

King John 468

Cymbeline 470

Titus Andronicus 472

Henry VIII 474

All's Well That Ends Well 476

William Shakespeare: Life and Times 478

Pieces of text like the one below are quotations
taken from the original Shakespeare plays.

" We are such stuff
As dreams are made on; and our little life
Is rounded with a sleep "

The Tempest, Act 4, Scene 1

A Midsummer Night's Dream

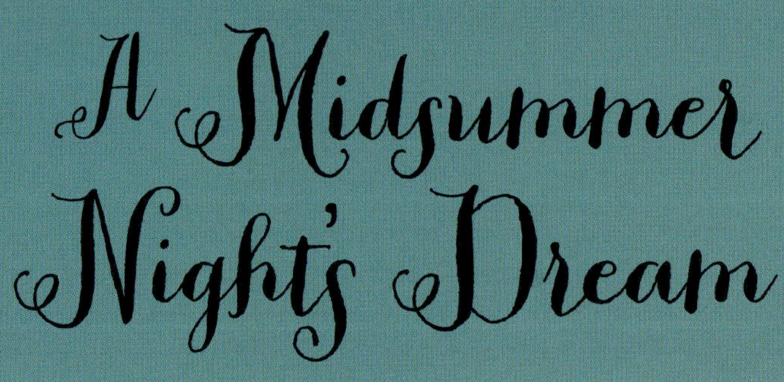

In the lead up to the duke's wedding, a group of hilariously bad actors are rehearsing a play. Lovers pursue lovers into the forest, where fairies run riot and magical things happen.

Theseus

The Duke of Athens. He's about to marry the Queen of the Amazons.

The Players

A group of amateur actors who are rehearsing a play called *Pyramus and Thisbe* for the wedding celebration.

Bottom

One of the amateur actors who finds himself comically mixed up in magic…

Titania

Queen of the fairies who, by some magical mischief, falls in love with Bottom.

Oberon
A spiteful fairy king. Annoyed with Titania, he asks his servant Puck to make mischief in the forest.

Puck
Naughty little sprite who sprinkles flower juice into people's eyes and uses magic to cause havoc.

Hermia
In love with Lysander but promised by her father to Demetrius. She flees with her beloved into the forest.

Lysander
Elopes with Hermia into the forest but magic meddling changes his mind…

Demetrius
Initially wooed Helena but is more interested in Hermia now. He pursues her into the magical forest.

Helena
Desperately in love with Demetrius, she chases after him. In the magical forest, strange things begin to happen…

LYSANDER, ACT 1, SCENE 1

FLOWER GARLANDS FESTOONED THE STREETS OF ATHENS. It was almost Midsummer's Day, and everybody was making ready for the city's annual festivities. This year there was even more reason to celebrate, for their noble duke, Theseus, was about to marry the Queen of the Amazons, Hippolyta.

Theseus and Hippolyta were relaxing in his cool marble palace away from the glare of the sun. "Our wedding day is almost here!" the duke exclaimed. "I can hardly wait for the days to pass."

Hippolyta smiled. "Those days will quickly melt into nights, which we will dream away in no time."

Just then, the door burst open and Theseus's friend, Egeus, marched in with his daughter, Hermia, and two rather anxious-looking young men.

"What's the news, Egeus?" Theseus asked.

"My noble lord, I have chosen this man, Demetrius, to marry my daughter, Hermia," Egeus began, pointing at one of the men behind him. "But this man, Lysander," he continued, pointing at the other, "has bewitched Hermia, and stolen her heart. My gracious duke, please make Hermia marry Demetrius."

Theseus looked at Hermia, who was staring sullenly at the floor. "What do you say, Hermia? Demetrius is a worthy young gentleman."

"So is Lysander," Hermia protested.

"According to the law of Athens, if you do not do as your father wants, you must become a nun," Theseus warned.

"Relent, sweet Hermia—" Demetrius began.

"My love for Hermia is greater than his," Lysander interrupted, frowning. "Demetrius has been courting another girl, Helena, and she is still in love with him. He is a fickle man!"

Theseus sighed. "Demetrius, come, and come Egeus. Hermia – you must do as your father says." He took Hippolyta's hand, and beckoned Demetrius and Egeus to follow them.

Once they were alone, Hermia fell weeping into Lysander's arms. "The path of true love never did run smooth," Lysander murmured, stroking her cheek. "Hear me, Hermia. Tomorrow night, let's run away into the forest. There we can get married, where the strict laws of Athens cannot touch us."

"You're running away?" came a voice from behind them. Hermia looked up – it was her best friend, Helena.

Brushing away her tears, Hermia explained the problem to her friend. When she had finished, Helena sighed.

"Teach me how to look as beautiful as you do, Hermia!" Helena exclaimed. "How did you manage to capture Demetrius's heart?"

"I frown at him, yet he loves me still," Hermia replied. "Take comfort, Lysander and I will flee this place tomorrow."

Lysander took Hermia's hand. "We must go. Goodbye Helena. I hope Demetrius comes to love you as you love him."

Helena watched sadly as the young lovers hurried away. "Why do I still love Demetrius, even when it's plain to see that he dotes on Hermia?" she thought, biting her lip. "Love looks not with the eyes, but with the mind. But what can I do? I know – I'll tell Demetrius all about Hermia and Lysander's plan. Perhaps when they are gone, he'll choose me."

Not far from the palace, a motley band of amateur actors had gathered at the house of a carpenter, Peter Quince. They were there to rehearse a play for the duke's wedding.

"Is all our company here?" Quince called out. "The play I've chosen is *Pyramus and Thisbe*. It's a sad play about a man called Pyramus, who kills himself for love."

Nick Bottom, a weaver, nodded keenly. "A very good play, I assure you," he said to the others. "I like comedies."

Quince sighed impatiently – Bottom clearly wasn't listening. "Bottom, you are to play the role of Pyramus."

Bottom beamed. "I will move the audience to tears," he declared, turning his head to gaze heroically into the distance.

"Francis Flute, you'll be his lover, Thisbe," Quince continued.

"A woman!" Flute was horrified. "But I have a beard coming!" He pointed to a few meagre wisps of hair growing on his chin.

Quince squinted to see them, then shook his head in despair. "You can play it in a mask. Now, Robin Starveling, you are the Moon. Tom Snout, you are the wall. And Snug, you will play the lion's part."

Bottom was dancing with excitement. "Oh, let me play the lion too!" he said. He bared his teeth and roared his best roar.

Quince jumped. "You'll frighten the queen away!" he said, scowling, and started handing out scripts. "Here are your parts. We'll meet in the forest tomorrow night to rehearse."

Deep in the forest, in the silvery dark of night and away from human eyes, a fairy king and queen were having an argument.

"Titania, I beg you, give me that servant boy of yours," the fairy king, Oberon was saying. "You have plenty of servants, and I need a pageboy."

The fairy queen shook her head. "Not for the whole of Fairyland," she declared. She flicked her silken hair and flew away, her wings shimmering in the moonlight.

Oberon stamped his foot. "Puck, come here!" he said, beckoning his cheeky, tangle-haired sprite. "Fetch me that flower, the one they call love-in-idleness."

Puck's green eyes twinkled with mischief and he nodded.

"I want to play a trick on Titania," Oberon explained, grinning wickedly. "I'll drop the juice of this flower on her eyelids when she is asleep. When she awakes, the next thing she looks upon – be it lion, bear, wolf or bull, she will fall madly in love with it."

"I'll search around the Earth in forty minutes!" Puck promised, before darting off into the starry sky.

Oberon's ears pricked up as he heard the sound of bracken cracking nearby, and he sank into the shadows to see who was coming… It was Demetrius, searching the forest for Hermia. Helena was following close behind him.

"I do not love you. Stop following me," Demetrius groaned. "It makes me sick to look at you."

"And I am sick when I *don't* look at you," Helena insisted.

Demetrius rolled his eyes and carried on walking. Poor Helena hurried after him.

Oberon gazed after her, full of pity. "Don't be unhappy," he murmured. "Before the night's end, he will love you."

A merry tinkle filled the air, and Puck appeared with the flower.

"Welcome, wanderer." Oberon smiled, taking it from him. He squeezed the purple petals, dripping the precious juice into a tiny, shining bottle. "Here, take this juice," he said, giving the bottle to Puck. "Find the young man who just left here, and make him fall in love with his companion."

"Fear not, " Puck said with a wink. "I shall do as you ask."

Oberon swept through trees searching for Titania. He found her asleep on a bed of violets, the air around her thick with their sweet, flowery scent. Oberon dripped flower juice onto her eyelids. "What you see when you awake, you will for your true love take," he chanted softly into her ear.

"What thou see'st when thou dost wake,
Do it for thy true-love take"

Oberon, Act 2, Scene 2

Puck looped around branches and over tree stumps, searching for the young man. When at last he came upon a couple asleep on a mossy bank, he swooped down and dropped flower juice onto the young man's eyelids. "Upon your eyes do I now throw all the power this charm does owe," he sang.

Little did Puck know, but the sleeping couple was not Demetrius and Helena, but Lysander and Hermia. Puck had cast his magic spell over the wrong man…

Nearby, Helena was stumbling around in the dark. Demetrius had stormed off without her, and she had been left frightened and alone. Luckily, she spotted Lysander asleep on the ground. "Lysander!" she cried out in relief. She hurried over and shook him awake.

Lysander woke up with a start. When he opened his eyes, the first person he saw was Helena peering down at him. The charm worked its magic at once, and he gasped in wonder – he'd never seen a beauty more enchanting. "Helena, I love you!" he cried.

Helena stared at him in utter disbelief. "But you love Hermia!"

Lysander shook his head. "It's not Hermia but Helena I love," he insisted, gazing up at Helena in awe.

Helena scowled. "You must be mocking me!" she cried, and dashed off into the forest.

Without a moment's thought, Lysander leaped up and chased after her. He had forgotten all about sleeping Hermia.

Moments later, Hermia stirred. Opening her eyes, she looked around for Lysander, and realized she was alone. Crying out in panic, she hurried into the trees to look for him.

Puck had no idea of the trouble he'd caused. He flew deeper into the forest, looking for fun and mischief. Hopping across toadstools and splashing through streams, he slowed down when he came to a clearing where a group of men were rehearsing a play. Smiling to himself, he perched on a high branch to watch.

"Thisbe," Bottom bellowed. "Your breath smells as sweet as flowers!" He clutched his heart dramatically, then retreated behind a bush to wait for his next scene.

Flute, who was playing Thisbe, looked confused. "Am I supposed to speak now?"

Quince groaned. "Yes!" he shouted.

Flute coughed, and began to speak in a high, squeaky voice. "Most radiant Pyramus! You're as beautiful as a rose, and as true as a horse that never tires!"

Puck raised his eyebrows. "I've never seen such a silly play," he thought. Then, an idea popped into his head. He darted behind the bush, and whispered a magic charm into Bottom's ear.

Bottom didn't suspect a thing, but Puck, hiding in the branches, doubled up with silent laughter as he watched his spell take effect. Bottom's ears shot up, with hair sprouting all over them. His nose grew long, and bristles spread all over his face. Within seconds, his head had been changed into that of a donkey.

Unaware that anything at all had happened to him, Bottom crashed back into the clearing and ran towards Flute with open arms. "Hee-haw… If I were fair, I would be… hee-haw… yours!"

Flute took one look at the donkey-headed brute hurtling in his direction and let out a blood-curdling scream. "Help! A monster!" Tripping over his own feet, he fled in the opposite direction, with the other terrified actors hot on his heels.

Bottom was confused. Was this part of the play? What on earth had made them run away? He looked around, wondering what to do. Deciding he should probably try to head back home, he lumbered off through the bushes, braying a tune as he went.

Nearby, Titania the fairy queen was sleeping on her bed of flowers. At the sound of Bottom's braying, Titania lifted her head.

She took one look at his long, bristly nose as he emerged through the trees, and fell instantly in love.

"What angel wakes me from my flowery bed?" Titania breathed. "Sing again, beautiful stranger!"

Bottom grinned at the fairy queen, revealing a set of enormous front teeth. Sitting down next to her, he brayed out another tune.

Titania stroked his long, furry ears. "Feed him apricots and dewberries, with purple grapes, green figs and mulberries," she commanded her fairy servants.

Puck, who had been watching the curious scene from above, covered his mouth to stifle a giggle. Mischief had been made! He darted off to tell Oberon.

"In love with a donkey?" Oberon roared with laughter. "This has worked out better than I could have planned!"

The fairy king fell quiet when he saw Hermia marching through the trees below, with Demetrius in hot pursuit.

"Where is Lysander?" Hermia demanded, pushing through the branches. "I fear you have killed him in his sleep!"

Demetrius looked hurt. "I am not guilty of Lysander's blood. Why are you so cruel to me when I love you so?"

Hermia scowled and marched on.

Sighing, Demetrius hung back, exhausted. It was no use – Hermia would never love him. Yawning, he lay down on the mossy ground, drew his cloak around him, and closed his eyes.

Oberon looked at Puck in confusion. "Did you cast a spell on this man as I asked?" he whispered.

Puck shook his mop of curly hair. "Not this one."

"What have you done?" Oberon groaned, realizing Puck's

"Lord, what fools these mortals be!"

PUCK
ACT 3, SCENE 2

mistake. "Fly through the forest, swifter than the wind," he whispered. "Find the other girl and bring her here."

As Puck disappeared, Oberon crept over to sleeping Demetrius and sprinkled flower juice on his eyelids. "Flower with your purple dye, sink into this sleeper's eye," he chanted. He flew back into the trees, where Puck was already waiting for him.

"Helena is nearby with Lysander," Puck whispered. "Lord, what fools these mortals are!" he laughed.

Just then, Helena and Lysander came into view below. "Why do you think I'm teasing you? I love you!" Lysander declared.

"You should be saying that to Hermia!" Helena pouted. She stopped abruptly when she saw Demetrius lying on the ground. "Demetrius!"

Demetrius, who had been fast asleep, woke up with a start. Seeing Helena, he jumped up and held out his arms. "Oh Helena, goddess, perfect, divine! I love you!"

Helena stepped backwards. Previously, nobody had loved her, and now everybody claimed they loved her. She could see only one explanation. "I see you are all teasing me!" she said bitterly.

Lysander scowled at Demetrius. "You are unkind, Demetrius. Do not be so. You love Hermia."

"You can keep Hermia, for I love Helena," Demetrius replied.

As the two men began bickering, Hermia appeared.

"Why did you leave me?" Hermia cried, running to Lysander.

Lysander shrugged, looking away. "I love fair Helena now."

Furious, Hermia turned to shout at Helena. "You thief of love! I'll scratch your eyes out with my nails!"

Before long, a terrible argument had erupted. In a fit of fury, Lysander challenged Demetrius to a duel.

Oberon rubbed his temples as he watched the disaster unfold. This was not how things were meant to be working out. "Follow them," he said to Puck, pointing at the men. "Keep them apart until you've cured Lysander. I'll find Titania and release her from the charm."

Puck leaped into the air. "As you wish, my fairy lord!"

Luckily for Puck, the two young men had plunged so rashly into the forest that they had lost one another already. "Where are you, Demetrius?" Lysander growled.

"Here, villain, drawn and ready," Puck replied, in a perfect imitation of Demetrius's voice. "Follow me this way."

Lysander stumbled off after the voice.

Demetrius plunged through the shadows behind him. "Where are you, coward?" he cried, pointing his sword into the trees.

"Follow me!" Puck called in Lysander's voice, flitting in the opposite direction. Demetrius dived after him.

He led the two young men a merry dance through the trees, going round and round until they were dizzy. Try as they might, they simply could not seem to find one another. Finally, they gave up. Neither realized it, but they were almost in the same spot where they had started. Without any idea how close they were to each other, they both sat down to rest.

Helena and Hermia, who had grown weary of following them and trying to stop them fighting, settled down nearby. Before long, everyone was fast asleep.

Puck breathed out a sigh of relief. "On the ground, all sleep sound," he whispered. Swooping down, he dropped some flower juice on Lysander's eyelids. "When you wake, you'll delight in the sight of the lady you once loved."

Puck flew off and found his master watching over Titania, who was fast asleep with her arm around Bottom's hairy neck. "I met Titania in the woods earlier, draping this fool's hairy head with flowers." Oberon laughed. "When I teased her, she begged me to leave her alone and promised to give me the servant child. Now

I have what I wanted, I will release her, I think."

Oberon squeezed the flower, dropping the last of its juice on Titania's eyelids. "Titania, wake, my sweet queen."

Titania yawned and opened her eyes. Seeing her husband, she smiled. "Oberon, my love, what dreams I've had! I thought I was in love with a donkey!" Her laughter was like the tinkle of bells.

Oberon pointed at Bottom. "There lies your love."

Bottom was snoring so loudly the leaves around him trembled. Titania gazed at him in amazement. "What an ugly face!" she said.

"Gentle Puck, change him back," Oberon told the sprite. Then he took Titania's hand and looked at her fondly. "Come, my queen." Oberon chuckled. "Tomorrow we'll dance at Theseus's wedding and bless the happy pair."

Puck watched them flit away, and then bent and whispered into Bottom's ear. The charm was undone and, in an instant, Bottom's head was back to normal.

Dawn broke, and a warm glow filtered through the tangled trees. Then a horn blasted – Theseus, Egeus and Hippolyta had come out hunting.

"What creatures are these?" Theseus said, pulling his horse's reins. On the ground below were four young people, all fast asleep.

Egeus gasped. "My lord, this is my daughter, Hermia, and this is Lysander, Demetrius and Helena!" he cried in surprise.

With another blast of the horn, the four sleeping lovers awoke.

"My lord!" Lysander said, scrambling to his feet.

"Explain yourselves – I thought you two were sworn enemies," Theseus said, nodding at Lysander and Demetrius.

"I cannot say how I came here," Lysander admitted, looking around in confusion. "All I know is I came here with Hermia."

Demetrius nodded, looking equally unsure. "I don't know why, but my love for Hermia has melted like snow. The object and pleasure of my eye is only Helena."

Egeus turned pink with indignation – Demetrius was meant to be in love with his daughter, Hermia. He opened his mouth to speak, but Theseus held up his hand to silence him.

"Wonderful!" Theseus smiled. "Come with Hippolyta and me, and we can all be married." Taking Hippolyta's hand, Theseus led the two couples back to his palace.

Nobody noticed Bottom waking up. "I've had the strangest dream," he thought, rubbing his face sleepily. "I thought I was a donkey!" Clambering to his feet, he looked around. "Now, where is everyone?"

That day, three weddings took place in the city of Athens. The duke married his queen, Hermia married Lysander, and Helena married Demetrius. They were all as happy as could be.

To close the day's events, there was to be a performance of the play *Pyramus and Thisbe* in their honour.

Bottom had found his way to the palace just in time, and Quince, faint with relief, staggered on stage to announce the start of the play. "You will see a beautiful lady, Thisbe," he said, pointing at Flute who, anxious not to be taken for a real lady, was flexing his muscles in the wings. "And a handsome man, our hero Pyramus…" Bottom gave a cheery wave. "They are in love, as you shall see."

Snout waddled on stage, dressed rather cumbersomely as a wall. "I, Snout, am a wall," he announced. "Through this chink, Pyramus and Thisbe whisper often."

Bottom dashed forwards. "Thisbe, kiss me through the hole of this wall," he said, smacking his lips against Snout's armpit.

"I kiss the wall, not your lips at all," Flute squeaked as daintily as he could, tripping over his dress.

Then Snug clambered on stage, baring his teeth. "Ladies," he said, addressing the audience. "I'm a fierce lion, but don't be afraid.

I'm Snug, really, underneath the costume!" He gave his most fearsome roar, and chased the screaming Flute offstage.

The audience tittered. The play was far better – and far worse – than they had expected.

In the next scene, Bottom reappeared on stage. "Thisbe, eaten by a lion?" he sobbed. "Oh, she was the fairest dame ever to live. Now I must die." He pulled out a fake dagger and pretended to stab himself.

As Bottom collapsed in a heap on the floor, Flute reappeared as Thisbe. "Dead, my dove?" he wailed, waggling Bottom's limp head as he cradled it in his arms. "Come, trusty sword." He dropped Bottom's head, picked up the dagger and pretended to stab himself too.

As Flute flopped down on top of Bottom, there was a long pause. Then the audience stood up, clapping and cheering with delight, and some measure of relief that it was all over.

Bottom crawled out from underneath Flute's leg. "Now, do you want us to dance for you?" he said, with a broad grin.

"No more," begged the duke, chuckling. "It was a fine play, thank you."

The audience whooped, and Bottom and Flute clambered to their feet and broke into a merry dance.

Floating in the air above, unseen, the fairy king and queen had been watching everything. "Hand in hand with fairy grace, we will sing and bless this place," Titania sang. She took her husband's hand, and they flitted about, their wings twinkling like stars.

Puck flew through the palace, sprinkling everyone with fairy dust. "Good night to everyone," he whispered. "And may all three couples live happily ever after."

Twelfth Night

Shipwrecked and alone in the world, Viola disguises herself as a boy to earn a living. Soon, she finds herself with the job of wooing a lady on behalf of a man she's fallen in love with. Unfortunately, the lady she's wooing for him has fallen in love with *her*!

Orsino

A duke who says he is in love with Olivia, but is he really just in love with being in love?

Olivia

Doesn't love Orsino. Claims still to be in mourning (but is she wallowing a little?). Finds herself falling for the duke's pageboy 'Cesario'.

Feste

The wise fool is the only one who sees things clearly.

Viola / Cesario

Viola dresses up as pageboy 'Cesario' to work for Orsino, leading to the awkward position of her courting a lady on behalf of a man she loves.

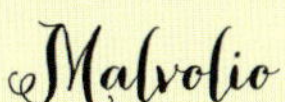
Malvolio

This normally dour servant is tricked into thinking Olivia loves him. Dressing up and smiling to please her, he becomes a laughing stock.

Maria

Olivia's servant plots with Sir Toby to bring Malvolio down a peg or two.

Sir Toby Belch

Drunken old uncle of Olivia's, and a bit of a practical joker.

Sir Andrew Aguecheek

Sir Toby's friend and a ridiculously unsuitable suitor to Olivia.

Sebastian

Viola's twin brother, supposedly drowned at sea. He appears just in time to resolve the tangled plot.

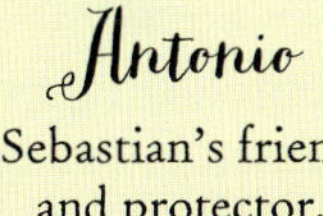

Antonio

Sebastian's friend and protector.

"IF MUSIC BE THE FOOD OF LOVE, PLAY ON!" Duke Orsino urged his musicians. He sank back into a pile of velvet cushions and sighed, "Give me so much that my hunger fades... Oh, play that part again! It was as sad as the breath of violets." But when the musicians obliged, he snapped, "Enough! No more. It's not so sweet as it was before." Waving the musicians away, Orsino got to his feet and went to stare out of the palace window.

A servant entered. "Sir, Lady Olivia would not let me in. But her maid gave me this answer: not even the sun will see her face for seven years more. She will stay in mourning for her dead brother."

The duke groaned with disappointment. "I'll go and lie down in the flowers. They'll suit my dreams of love..."

On the coast of the island, not far from the duke's palace, the sea sparkled, betraying no sign of the terrible storm that had wrecked a ship the night before. On the beach, survivors had gathered: the captain, a few sailors, and a young lady named Viola.

"My poor dear brother," Viola sobbed. "Do you think there's any chance he did not drown?" she asked the captain. Her brother, Sebastian, was her twin. They loved one another dearly, and were as alike as two halves of an apple.

"It was only by chance you were saved," the captain replied.

"So, by chance, might he be," said Viola.

"After our ship split in two, I saw him tie himself to the mast," the captain volunteered. "He stayed afloat as long as I could see."

"Here's gold for saying so," said Viola, pressing a coin from her purse gratefully into his hand. "Do you know where we are?"

"Aye," said the captain. "This is Illyria. I grew up three hours from here. It's ruled by a noble duke called Orsino."

"I have heard of him… He's a bachelor, isn't he?" Viola asked.

"That he is, and a noble ruler," the captain said.

"Perhaps I should ask him for employment until I can work out what to do," Viola pondered. "But – oh, it would be easier if I were a man… I've had an idea – I'll disguise myself as a gentleman, and ask the duke if I can work for him. Captain, you seem a trustworthy fellow. Will you help me?" Viola asked.

"Aye, that I will," replied the captain.

Disguised as a young man and calling herself 'Cesario', Viola was willingly employed by the duke. He warmed to the fresh-faced youth immediately, and, within days, had confided all his feelings for Olivia. "Will you call on her on my behalf, Cesario?" the duke asked. "Stand at her door until she lets you in!"

Viola agreed. "But what shall I say if she does let me in?"

"Unfold the passion of my love!" exclaimed Orsino. "She'll believe you, Cesario, with your honest face. You are so fresh-faced, and so young, you are not quite a man…"

Viola blushed – little did the duke realize how little a man she actually was. "I'll do my best," she said in her gruff boy's voice, and hurried away. But her mind was in turmoil. "I'm sent to woo on his behalf, but I myself would rather be his wife." The sorry fact was, in the space of the past few days, she had fallen in love with the duke.

At Olivia's house, her uncle, Sir Toby Belch, was sitting in the kitchen drowning his hangover with a mug of ale. "What a plague that my niece is taking her brother's death like this. Caring too much stops you getting on with life, I'll tell you that."

Maria, Olivia's maid, bustled around him, wiping his spills from the table. "My mistress doesn't approve of you coming in so late at night, Sir Toby," she tutted. "All that drinking will be your downfall. My lady was complaining about that silly knight you brought here to court her, too.”

“Who? Sir Andrew Aguecheek? He’s as tall as any man in Illyria!” proclaimed Sir Toby.

Maria couldn’t help but laugh. “What use is that?”

“He is rich too!”

Maria snorted. “He’s a fool!” she said. “Not only that, but he’s drunk every night in your company!”

“We are only drinking to my niece’s health,” Sir Toby said mildly. “Here he is, look. Sir Andrew *Agueface*, my dear fellow!”

“Good morning, Sir Toby Belch!” Into the kitchen trudged a skinny knight with a face as long as his bandy legs and a head of hair that resembled a well-used mop. He slumped down next to Sir Toby, who poured him a drink from the jug, slopping ale all over Maria’s freshly wiped table.

Maria rolled her eyes. “I think I’ll leave you to it,” she said, and bustled out of the kitchen.

“I’ve never seen you so miserable,” Sir Toby said to his friend.

“Never!” agreed Sir Andrew. “I think I’ll go home tomorrow. Your niece won’t even see the duke, so what chance have I?”

“She doesn’t want anyone as rich as the duke, I heard her swear it,” Sir Toby said persuasively. “You’ve definitely got a chance.”

“Alright, I’ll stay a month longer,” said Sir Andrew.

Meanwhile, Maria had found someone else to scold. It was Feste, the jester, a clown employed to fool around for people’s entertainment – lots of rich houses had them. He had been absent for a few days, just when Olivia most needed cheering up. “Where have you been? The mistress will hang you!” Maria told him.

The jester just shrugged, the bells on his costume jingling. “Many a good hanging has prevented a bad marriage,” he said. He eyed Maria up and down. “You’d make Sir Toby a fine wife, if only he'd sober up to see as much," he said cheekily.

Maria hid a smile. "Hush, you rogue. No more of that!" As she bustled away, Feste went out to the garden to find Olivia.

She was with her sour-faced servant, Malvolio. He was as black and gloomy as the jester was bright and jolly, and suited her sad mood better. As soon as Olivia saw the jester, she frowned. "Take the fool away!" she told Malvolio.

"You heard," the jester said to Malvolio. "Take away the lady."

"What? Why do you think I am the fool?" said Olivia, her interest piqued. Feste had always been a witty one and, although the jokes he made were often a little close to the bone, it amused her to see how cleverly he made them.

Feste grinned. "You'll see. So tell me. Why are you mourning?"

"For my brother's death," Olivia replied.

"Ah, so his soul must be in Hell," said the fool.

"No, his soul is in Heaven, fool," she bristled.

"How foolish of you to mourn his soul being in Heaven!" concluded the jester. "As I said before: take away the fool!"

Olivia smiled. "What do you think, Malvolio?"

Malvolio didn't smile. Fools were beneath him. "I marvel that you take such delight in such a rascal," he said haughtily.

"You shouldn't take everything so seriously!" Olivia laughed.

At that point Sir Toby staggered by, already thoroughly drunk. "There's a *gennelman* at the gate!" he informed her, before burping and sitting down in a bush.

Olivia sighed. She'd better send Malvolio with a message. Hopefully his solemn air would counteract any bad impression left by her uncle. "If Duke Orsino sent him, tell him to go away," she told him. Eyeing Sir Toby with distaste, Malvolio nodded and stalked off to do as she asked.

"Look after my uncle," Olivia told her jester. So Feste hauled Sir Toby out of the shrubbery, and they wandered off together.

Malvolio was soon back. "Nothing I can do will shake that messenger from his post at the door," he reported irritably.

"Really?" said Olivia. The others had been easy to turn away. "What's he like?" she asked.

"Scarcely old enough to be called a man," Malvolio answered.

"I suppose I'll see him. Call Maria to accompany me…"

When Viola came in, with a manly stride to match her disguise, she found two ladies, rather than one. One was veiled and dressed in black, the other in brighter clothes. In her deepest voice, Viola asked, "Which is the lady of the house?"

"Talk to me, I'll answer for her," Olivia answered.

"Most radiant, exquisite lady of matchless beauty—" Viola began, then she stopped. "Please tell me if you are the right lady. I spent a long time on this speech. I don't want to throw it away on the wrong person."

Olivia laughed out loud. "Are you a comedian?" she asked, and was amused to see the young man blush.

"No," Viola answered. "Tell me if you are the lady, though, so I can get on with my speech. It's very poetic."

Olivia waved her hand. "I'm not interested in flattery. I only let you in because you were so cheeky at my gate, and I was curious. If you have a reason for being here, then get on with it. Be brief. Otherwise, be gone."

"It's a message from Orsino, straight from his heart!"

"In that case, I've already heard it," said Olivia dismissively.

"May I see your face?" Viola asked abruptly.

The request took Olivia completely by surprise and she looked curiously at the young man standing in front of her. "I think you are straying from your orders, but still…" She drew back her veil.

She blushed under the intensity of the young man's gaze. "Is it not well made?" she ventured.

There was a pause. "Yes," said the young man. "You are far too proud, but even if you were the Devil, you would still be beautiful. Anyway, my lord and master loves you."

Olivia softened. "How does he love me?" she asked.

"With sighs and tears," the young man replied.

"Your lord knows my mind," Olivia answered honestly. "I know he's noble and gracious and so on, but I simply do not love him. He should have accepted it long ago."

"If I loved you as my master loves you, I couldn't take no for an answer," Viola declared.

"What would you do about it?" asked Olivia.

Viola was filled with thoughts of the duke. If she were pleading on her own behalf for him, there would be no stopping her. Filled with passion, she declared, "I would make myself a cabin so I could sit at your gate day in and day out; I'd call upon you, my soul, within the house; I'd write songs of unrequited love and sing them even in the dead of night. You'd at least have to pity me!"

Viola fell silent. Olivia was staring at her and she suddenly felt very awkward about her passionate outburst.

"You might do a lot," Olivia said, moved by the strength of feeling she'd just seen. "Go back to your master, and tell him I cannot love him and not to ask again. But…" she hesitated. "You can return, if you like, to tell me how he takes it…"

"Fairwell, fair cruelty!" Viola said, and hurried away under Olivia's gaze.

"Make me a willow cabin at your gate,
And call upon my soul within the house,
Write loyal cantons of contemnèd love
And sing them loud even in the dead of night"

VIOLA, ACT 1, SCENE 5

Olivia found herself quite taken with the young man. She had never met anyone like him – so direct, so passionate, so honest. She had to see him again. On an impulse, she pulled a ring from her finger and called to Malvolio. "Take this to that boy," she said. "He left it here. Don't take no for an answer!"

Malvolio preferred a slow, stately pace, suited to his position as the highest servant in the household, and hated having to hurry. He scurried along in an ungainly half-run, and by the time he caught up with the young man, he was thoroughly annoyed. "You left this," he sniffed thrusting the ring into Viola's hand. He stalked away with his nose in the air, leaving her staring at it.
"What could this mean?" Viola wondered. "I didn't leave a ring…" A sudden realization dawned on her. "Oh no. I hope she hasn't fallen for me!" Now she thought about it, Olivia had stared so much that Viola had thought she'd lost her tongue. What's more, when *Viola* had stared at *her*, she'd blushed. "Oh dear. Poor lady, she would be better loving a dream," Viola thought. "What a mess! My master loves her dearly; and I, poor monster, am fond of him; and she, mistaken, dotes on me. What will become of this? Time will have to untangle this mess – it's too difficult for me."

On the coast, some distance from where Viola had come ashore, two more survivors were sitting on the beach: Sebastian, Viola's twin brother, and a captain named Antonio.
"I wish I had drowned with my sister," Sebastian sobbed. "She was so beautiful, and so clever. She is drowned already with salt water but here am I, drowning her memory with more."

"O time, thou must untangle this, not I. It is too hard a knot for me t'untie."

VIOLA, ACT 2, SCENE 2

"I'm so sorry. If I can help you in any way, I will…" Antonio promised. He had saved this noble young man from the savage waves, and now felt responsible for looking after him.

"I suppose I'd best go into the city, and see if I can make a living somehow," Sebastian told him.

Antonio had been in trouble with the duke's officers last time he'd set foot in the city. "I have enemies there, so I'll keep a low profile," he said. "But I'll come with you."

At Olivia's house, Sir Toby and Sir Andrew were still drinking long into the night. The jester was there too, paid to sing songs for them. "If we don't go to bed at all, at least we'll be up early in the morning," said Sir Toby, seizing the jug to pour them all some wine. But the jug was empty. "More wine, Maria!" he roared.

Maria rushed in crossly. "What a caterwauling!" she said. "My lady will send Malvolio in a minute to throw you all out!"

"She can't throw me out, I'm family," Sir Toby guffawed, and started bawling out another song of his own.

Sure enough, along came Malvolio. "My lady said to tell you that while you may be family, she's not related to your drinking habit. Give it up or bid her farewell," he ordered haughtily.

Sir Toby fixed him with a bloodshot glare. "Do you think, just because you're so prim and proper, that we'll have no more cakes and ale?" he said.

Malvolio rounded on Maria. "As for you, I shall let the mistress know that you are encouraging their behaviour!"

"Oh, go shake your ears," grumbled Maria as he marched away. She'd always despised Malvolio, with all his airs and graces.

"Dost thou think, because thou art virtuous, there shall be no more cakes and ale?"

Sir Toby, Act 2, Scene 3

He lorded it over her, more concerned with his standing in the household than with lifting a finger to do any work.

Sir Andrew and Sir Toby were indignant too, and had started muttering about sword fights and challenges.

"Be patient," Maria soothed. "Leave Malvolio to me. I'll find a way to make a fool out of that silly puritan. He's so full of himself he must think everyone adores him," she continued crossly. Then she paused – a mischievous gleam had come into her eye.

"What will you do?" asked Sir Toby, smelling a plan.

"I know, I'll drop a love letter in his path, with lines praising him in it – his silly walk, his snooty face… my handwriting is almost identical to your niece's…" Maria said, grinning.

"Excellent!" cried Sir Toby. "He'll think my niece wrote it, and that she's in love with him!"

"Exactly," Maria said. "Then we can hide and watch what happens. I'll let you know when."

Maria whisked out of the room. "She's a true beagle, that one," Sir Toby said admiringly. "And I do believe she's fond of me…"

The following day, Maria was in Olivia's garden, clutching the love letter and waiting for Malvolio to pass by. She tiptoed down the path as Sir Toby and Sir Andrew waited in a giggling huddle. "Hide," she hissed, racing back. "He's coming!" She dropped the letter on the ground, and they all dived behind a box hedge just as Malvolio came strutting around the corner.

"It's all down to fortune," Malvolio muttered to himself. "I hold a lot of respect in this household, but it's not as much as I deserve. Now, if I were *Count* Malvolio… "

The box hedge trembled with the indignation of the three people hiding, but Malvolio was too steeped in his daydream to notice. "I can see it now," he continued, "calling my officers to me, having left my wife Olivia sleeping… Sir Toby bowing to me…"

MALVOLIO, ACT 2, SCENE 5

At this, the hedge nearly exploded. Sir Toby was having to be restrained behind it.

Luckily, it was then that Malvolio noticed the letter. "What's this?" he said, bending to pick it up. "It's my lady's handwriting… 'To the unknown beloved' it says. Why that might well be me!"

He opened the letter and read, "'No man must know that I am in love with M… A… O… I…' It's a riddle! Now, what could it mean… By Jove I have it! They're letters from my name!"

He read on: "'In my stars I am above you; but be not afraid of greatness: some are born great, some achieve greatness, and some have greatness thrust upon them. If you love me, send a sign: wear yellow stockings, crossed garters, and appear before me smiling…'"

Malvolio looked up with a smug grin, and his chest swelled like that of a scrawny cockerel. "My lady loves me," he crowed. "I have here every proof of it!" And he rushed off to change his stockings.

The crowd behind the hedge collapsed and out burst Sir Toby, Sir Andrew and Maria, holding their sides with laughter. "Oh, I could marry you for this!" Sir Toby cried.

"Me too!" said Sir Andrew.

"Little does he know," said Maria, "but my lady detests yellow, and can't stand crossed garters. This will be too good to miss!"

Despite her best attempts to dissuade the duke from sending her back, Viola had returned to Olivia's house to plead once more on Orsino's behalf. She was shown into the orchard, where Olivia was sitting among the blossom. "Give me your hand," Olivia said to her sweetly.

Viola did as she asked, noting Olivia's tender glance in dismay. It was as she feared… the lady was besotted with her. "What is your name?" Olivia asked.

"Cesario," Viola replied, taking her hand back. "I have come to try again – for my *master*."

"Cesario," Olivia breathed the name as though it would break. "I'm not interested in your master… I sent a ring to you after you were last here. I wonder – I am a little afraid to ask – what did you think?"

"I feel sorry for you," Viola answered honestly.

"Pity is nearly love," Olivia said.

"No, we often pity our enemies," Viola contradicted.

Olivia sighed. It was clear this young man did not have feelings for her. "What do you think of me?" she asked mournfully.

Viola thought about it. The lady thought she was in love with a young man, but there was no young man, just a girl in disguise. Was the lady then really in love? "I think – I think you aren't what you think you are…" Viola said.

"Well I think the same of you," Olivia pouted.

"Then you're right," Viola laughed. "I am not what I am."

"I wish you would love me back," Olivia said wistfully.

"I can swear to you," Viola told her, "that my heart will never love a woman. And so I will leave you. Goodbye, good lady."

"Do come again," pleaded Olivia.

"I'll not stay a jot longer," Sir Andrew declared to Sir Toby.

"Why ever not?" Sir Toby cried.

"Your niece shows more fondness toward the duke's messenger than she does to me! I saw them just now in the orchard holding hands," Sir Andrew complained.

"She must be doing it to make you jealous!" declared Sir Toby. "There's only one thing you can do. You must challenge the youth to a duel. Olivia will be impressed by your bravery."

"You think?" Sir Andrew said doubtfully.

"Of course! Go and write him a manly challenge. I will deliver it myself," Sir Toby urged him. He chuckled to himself, thinking that Sir Andrew and that youth Cesario would make hilarious duelling partners – each as meek as the other.

As Sir Andrew left, Maria burst into the room, crying with laughter. "Come quickly! Malvolio's in yellow stockings!"

Olivia had asked Maria to fetch him, thinking his solemn air would suit her sad mood. Maria announced his arrival with, "Something is wrong with Malvolio, Mistress…"

Olivia stared as Malvolio sidled into the room, kicking his legs oddly as he walked to show off his lurid yellow stockings with fashionable crossed garters holding them up. Not only was he oddly dressed, but, to her dismay, he was smiling.

Malvolio's face was about as suited to smiling as a china vase was suited to bouncing. His lips stretched tight over his bared teeth, and a map of lines spread across his features, cracking his normally dour face into a maniacal grin.

"I sent for you on a *sad* occasion," the lady said faintly.

"Sad? I could be sad if you like," Malvolio told her through gritted teeth. "Cross garters such as these cut off the circulation somewhat, but if some special ONE likes them, then I will bear it."

"What on earth is the matter with you?" said Olivia.

"It was well written, the note," Malvolio hinted. "'Be not afraid of greatness…'"

"What?"

"'…some have greatness THRUST upon them?'" Malvolio said suggestively, waggling one yellow leg.

Olivia winced. "Have you gone completely mad?"

A servant appeared at her elbow. "The young man you sent for has come – the one from the duke's court. Shall I show him in?"

"Do," said Olivia, hurrying away. "And someone please look after Malvolio. He's not right in the head."

Sir Toby strolled into the room, trying to keep a straight face. "Malvolio, are you not well?" he asked.

"Get him to say his prayers," Maria advised drily. "I think the Devil's taken hold of him."

"I am above you all now," Malvolio said, his grin slipping a little. "Soon you'll understand." And he stalked off.

"Olivia already thinks he's gone mad… Let's put him in a dark room to calm his madness," Sir Toby said mischievously. Chuckling, they followed after Malvolio.

Viola had traipsed back to Olivia's house, having been summoned this time by the lady herself for another fruitless attempt to gain her love. She cut the visit short, saying her master needed her. She was just leaving, when she came face to face with a round, tubby knight and a long, thin, gangling one, who was apparently being dragged there against his will.

The round knight was Sir Toby, and the man he was stopping from fleeing the scene was Sir Andrew. Sir Toby waved a letter under Viola's nose. "Young man, I bring you a challenge from this bold knight whom you have gravely offended."

Viola took the letter and read it, looking terrified. "But I have done nothing. There must be some mistake."

"You'd best draw your sword and defend yourself, for he is a fierce knight and is leaping to attack," said Sir Toby, pushing Sir Andrew forward, who was struggling to escape.

"I'm not a fighter!" Viola wailed, backing away.

Just then, Antonio, the captain, happened to stroll by. He was on his way to an inn where he'd agreed to meet Viola's twin brother, Sebastian, later. He'd lent Sebastian his purse to see the sights of the city in the meantime. Of course Viola, dressed as a boy, was the absolute image of her brother. Taking her for Sebastian, Antonio leaped to her defence yelling, "What's all this?

I'll answer on this young man's behalf!"

Sir Andrew would have bolted altogether had Sir Toby not seized him by the scruff of the neck. They were just about to draw swords, when a group of armed guards came around the corner.

Seeing Antonio, the guards cried out, "Seize him!" They recognized him from the time he'd been in trouble with the duke, and they'd been looking to arrest him ever since.

As they grabbed his arms, Antonio said to Viola. "Could I have my money back? If I pay up, I won't have to go to prison."

Viola looked at him blankly. "Money?" she said. "Well, I can lend you a little…"

Antonio's face crumpled. "Would you deny me my own money in my time of need? After I saved you from drowning too?" he asked. As the guards dragged him away, he cried, "You ought to be ashamed of yourself, Sebastian!"

Viola froze. *Sebastian*? Her twin brother? It could mean only one thing – her brother was alive! Forgetting all about Sir Andrew and Sir Toby, she rushed off back to the duke's palace. If he could free this man, perhaps he could tell her where her brother was.

Seeing the young man flee, Sir Andrew felt a wave of bravery come over him. "I'll teach that villain a thing or two," he declared.

"Right you are, just don't draw your sword," said Sir Toby, hurrying after him to make sure he didn't hurt himself.

But by the time Sir Andrew and Sir Toby rounded the corner, Viola had long gone. It just so happened that Sebastian was ambling along instead. "Ha!" Sir Andrew cried. "This is for you!" and he cuffed Sebastian around the head.

He got the shock of his life when Sebastian cuffed him back, knocking him flying. "Are you mad? What did you attack me for?" Sebastian demanded angrily.

"Hold it there," said Sir Toby, leaping to his unfortunate

friend's defence. "Or I'll have to come to blows with you myself."

Hearing all the commotion, Olivia came out of her gate. "Sir Toby, what is the meaning of all this?" she said sternly. Taking Sebastian for her dear Cesario, she turned to him and said, "My love, accept my apologies. Please come with me inside."

"Am I mad? Or is this a dream?" thought Sebastian. "If it's a dream then I hope I don't wake up!" Completely smitten with the beautiful young woman, he followed Olivia into the house.

Olivia was delighted to find the young man she loved had apparently had a change of heart and now welcomed her affections. So delighted was she – not to mention terrified he might change his mind again – that she proposed marriage that very afternoon.

For his part, Sebastian could think of no better fortune than spending the rest of his life with this delightful lady, and he happily agreed to marry her.

They were wed that very day. When they came out of the church, the sun was low, throwing grand shadows along the streets. "I must find my friend Antonio," Sebastian told his new bride. "I have his purse and he'll be needing it. But I'll be back in an hour." Kissing her tenderly, he strolled cheerfully away to find the inn.

Olivia walked home with a dreamy smile on her face, and found herself crossing paths with the duke. She was surprised to see Cesario, the very young man she had just married, at his side!

Of course, she was mistaken – it was Viola, taking the duke to find Antonio. As fate would have it, the guards came marching past with the man right at that moment. "There he is – that's the man who saved me!" Viola cried. "Won't you free him?"

The guards heard her and stopped. But the duke had eyes only for Olivia. "Gracious Olivia…" he began.

But Olivia's eyes were on Viola. "Cesario, my love, what are you doing with the duke?" she asked.

"So cruel!" cried the duke. "So you love this boy? I can see why… I love him too. Although right now I could sacrifice him gladly… Come on, let's go."

As Viola turned to follow the duke, Olivia called after her. "Where are you going?"

"With the man I love," Viola replied.

"Husband, stay!" cried Olivia.

"Husband?" said the duke, whirling around to glare at Viola. "Are you her husband?"

"No!" Viola protested, confused.

Olivia was heartbroken. Her beloved had turned against her once more.

To add to the confusion, Sir Andrew came limping along, his arm around Sir Toby. "You did this to me, villain," he said to Viola.

"What?" said both Olivia and Orsino together, neither believing gentle Cesario capable of hurting so much as a fly.

"I didn't touch you!" Viola cried.

Just when everything seemed tied in unfathomable knots, along strolled Sebastian. He was happy and carefree, apart from the fact that he had not been able to find Antonio at the inn. Not noticing Viola, he walked up to Olivia. She was staring at him so oddly, he assumed she was upset about the fight. So he confessed immediately, "I'm sorry I hurt this man," he said, nodding at Sir Andrew. "But he attacked me without warning."

Olivia gawped, thinking she was seeing double.

"One face, one voice… in two people," the duke murmured.

Viola could say nothing; she was speechless with hope. Could this be her brother, returned from the dead?

Still not noticing her, Sebastian saw his friend Antonio next. "Antonio!" he cried. "I've been looking for you."

"Is that you?" Antonio said, looking from him to Viola and

back again. "One half of an apple is not more like the other than these two people. Which one is Sebastian?"

Sebastian turned and, at last, saw Viola. It was like looking in a mirror. "But – but I never had a brother…" he stammered in confusion. "A very dear sister though… who are you?"

"I am Viola," came the reply.

The twins fell into each other's arms, crying tears of joy. "I disguised myself as a boy to seek my fortune," Viola admitted. "It's led to some confusion…" She looked guiltily at Olivia.

"Oh, now I understand," Sebastian said. "So that's why you were so in love with me, Olivia. You fell for this one first." He took Olivia's hand. "But it's me you are married to, thank goodness."

The duke, meanwhile, was looking tenderly at Viola. He had loved this boy all along, trusting him with his deepest feelings, never suspecting this could be his perfect match. "You've said a thousand times you could never love a woman as much as you love me, and all along…"

"I stand by my words," Viola said quietly.

The duke laughed. "Let me see you in your woman's clothes. From now on, you could be mistress of your former master."

"Tell Malvolio to bring the girl some clothes!" Olivia ordered. Then she remembered, "Oh dear, but he's gone mad, hasn't he?"

While the duke saw to Antonio's release, and Viola went to change into her own clothes, Olivia went to see her poor servant.

Malvolio was in a sorry state. He had been locked in the cellar and teased mercilessly by Sir Toby and the jester, who'd pretended to be a priest to get him to confess his sins. He was brought out now and stood blinking wretchedly in the evening light.

"Madam, you have done me wrong!" he said, handing her the love letter. "First you write this, then I am treated as a madman for acting upon it."

Olivia read the letter, her mouth twitching despite herself as she understood the joke. "Poor Malvolio," she said sympathetically. "This is not my handwriting. It's Maria's. You have been tricked…"

Feste the jester interjected. "Sir Toby and I played along too. And so the whirligig of time brings in his revenges…"

Malvolio was outraged. He turned white, and then red, and then a sort of puce. Then he burst out, "I'll be revenged on the whole pack of you!" and stormed away.

But it had been Malvolio's pride, not his heart, that had been hurt. And that kind of injury is never grave. Still, feeling sorry for him, Olivia went after him to soothe and make amends.

That evening, there was much merriment on the island of Illyria. Happy voices rang out of the windows at Olivia's palace as the couples all dined together. The duke had found a sister in Olivia, and turned his doting gaze upon Viola as he realized how true love felt. Viola and her brother, glowing images of one another, were delighted to be reunited. And Olivia, at last, had changed her black gown for a brighter one. Even Maria had left off scolding for one night, as Sir Toby had asked her to marry him.

When they all went off merrily to their beds, only Feste the fool remained. He sat in the moonlit garden, humming a little song to himself. There was a rumble overhead. Rainclouds were gathering.

Feste looked up and smiled as the first few drops hit his face. "With hey, ho, the wind and the rain," he sang. "It's important to fool around and have fun while you can in this life," he mused. "Another bout of bad weather will always hit you soon enough."

Feste smiled. Everybody called him a fool, but in all truth he was the wisest of them all.

Romeo and Juliet

In the city of Verona, where this story takes place, an ancient feud divides two families, but love unites a soul from each. Can a pair of star-crossed lovers overcome such deep-seated hatred?

Romeo

A passionate, idealistic teenager. Popular with friends and searching for love.

Lord and Lady Montague

The heads of a rich family of Verona. Romeo's parents.

Benvolio

Romeo's thoughtful cousin.

Mercutio

Romeo's cynical and hotheaded best friend.

Juliet

A passionate young girl who lives a protected life but believes in true love.

Lord and Lady Capulet

The heads of a rich family of Verona. Juliet's parents.

Nurse

Juliet's faithful nursemaid – her carer and confidante.

Count Paris

Juliet's suitor. Juliet's father has promised him her hand in marriage.

Friar Laurence

Friend and advisor to Romeo and Juliet.

Tybalt

Juliet's quarrelsome cousin who loathes the Montagues.

IN VERONA, A BEAUTIFUL ITALIAN CITY of flowers, sunshine, good food and fine houses, lived two families who hated each other with a fury. All Montagues and all Capulets were bitter enemies, and had been since anyone could remember.

One day, Tybalt Capulet was strolling down the street when Benvolio Montague accidentally bumped into him. "This means death for you," cried Tybalt, drawing his sword.

Instantly, a gang of Montagues shot out of the side streets, ready to fight, and at the same time a gang of Capulets appeared from nowhere, daggers pointed at their enemies.

The noise was deafening as the gangs fell upon each other. Screams, insults and the clash of steel on steel brought the ruler of Verona, Prince Escalus, from his palace to see what had disturbed the peace of his beloved city.

"They are at each other's throats again," he fumed. "This must stop. "Enough!" he commanded. "Your rage explodes from your veins like purple fountains. Montagues and Capulets, this must stop. If there is any more fighting, the culprits will be punished by death. Now go home, everyone. At once!"

And they had to obey. Everyone went home. But Lord and Lady Montague lingered, along with their nephew, Benvolio. Lady Montague was anxious about her son, Romeo, who was still missing. "Oh, where is my Romeo?" she asked Benvolio.

"He wasn't at the riot," Benvolio assured her. "He's not a fighter. He's a dreamer. He's in love, with Rosaline. He wants to be alone all the time, to think about her."

"He's far too young for love," his mother laughed indulgently.

But Benvolio was right. And later that evening, when Romeo

whistled to Benvolio to coax him out of the house, he wasn't surprised to hear Romeo's plans.

"The Capulets are giving a party tonight. Come with me, Benvolio. I might see Rosaline there. No one will know who we are; it's a masked ball. I dreamed of it," Romeo told him, brimming with the thrill of his new idea.

"Dream on, you fool!" Benvolio scoffed.

"I feel something…" Romeo whispered. "Something important that is hanging in the stars…"

"You really want to go?" Benvolio saw how eager Romeo was. "Then we will. We'll take our friend Mercutio, too."

Juliet Capulet was excited. She'd never been considered old enough to attend a ball before. Her mother and her nurse, who had looked after her since she was a tiny baby, helped her to get ready. They combed her long, shining hair, winding it with flowers, and threaded ribbons around the waist of her dress.

"My ladybird," said her nurse. "Just think! Your first ball! Only thirteen… well do I remember the day I came here to look after you, the sweetest baby I ever did see."

"Nearly fourteen," corrected Lady Capulet. "And time you thought about marriage, Juliet. There's a young man coming tonight, Count Paris, who is interested in you."

"My lamb is wise, but too young to marry," interrupted the nurse.

"I have not yet thought of it at all," said Juliet.

"Then think about it now," ordered her mother. "Younger girls than you are already wives and mothers here in Verona. I was not much older than you are now when I gave birth to you. Come down and meet Paris… try to like him."

"I'll look at him," Juliet conceded. "I'll give him one glance," she thought to herself, "for the man I love is my choice alone."

ROMEO, ACT 1, SCENE 4

That night, Romeo, Benvolio and Mercutio, all disguised in masks, went to the party at the Capulets' house. No one guessed they were Montagues. Lord Capulet was at his most benevolent, welcoming his guests, offering them wine, and ordering the musicians to play.

Romeo's eyes flitted round the room. Lit by the flickering flames of torchlight, he saw a girl more beautiful than all his dreams, more lovely than any girl he'd ever seen before. She was dancing – so gracefully – with some gentleman or other. She caught his eye, and he felt his blood surge all over his body with desire and worship and warmth and, in that heart-stopping moment, he fell in love.

"Who is she?" Romeo demanded.

Benvolio and Mercutio shrugged.

"No idea," said Mercutio.

"Aren't you forgetting Rosaline?" asked Benvolio.

"She's history," said Romeo, unable to take his eyes off Juliet. "I did not know, till now, what true beauty is…"

Tybalt overheard him. "That's a Montague!" he roared. "I can tell by the way he speaks. An enemy, a *villain* come to mock us. I'll kill him now!"

"Peace," soothed old Capulet. "I'm not having any killing at my feast. The boy is Romeo and, to be fair, Verona speaks well of him."

"Huh!" muttered Tybalt furiously, striding past Lord Capulet to gulp down a goblet of wine.

Romeo, seeing Tybalt temporarily silenced, seized his moment. The beautiful girl had left her dancing partner, and he slipped through the crowds after her. "You have taken my breath away," he told her when he caught up. "I don't know who you are, but…"

He held out his hand to her, palm upright, and the girl held out hers, so their two palms fitted together.

"I want to kiss you," he whispered.

"And I you, too," she whispered back.

They clasped each other's fingers, both wide-eyed. Both were equally spellbound, sharing the feeling of being swept away, as if they were the first and only people alive to enjoy it… as if "Don't" meant "Do", and "Be careful" meant nothing at all. They couldn't let each other go…

Until Juliet's nurse bustled by and interrupted them. "Your mother wants you, lamb," she said, eyeing Romeo.

"Who is her mother?" asked Romeo.

"She is the lady of this house, of course," the nurse replied.

Romeo froze. "So this girl…"

"…is Juliet Capulet," confirmed the nurse, bustling Juliet away.

"The daughter of my enemy," thought Romeo, turning away in despair. "I must leave this house at once."

"Who is that man?" Juliet asked the nurse as they hurried along to her mother.

"Romeo. A Montague. The son of your great enemy," Nurse told her.

"How cruel," Juliet whispered to herself. "My only love has sprung from my only hate."

She couldn't endure the party any more; it felt meaningless to her, so she excused herself as soon as she could and crept upstairs, to lie on her bed and think of Romeo, his fingers interlinked with hers, the kiss hovering on his lips, the expression in his eyes.

Romeo did not go home that night. Instead, he hid under the vines in the Capulet garden, unable to tear himself away.

Juliet couldn't sleep either. She tossed and turned, and at last, she went to her balcony, to quieten her turbulent thoughts in the cool stillness of the night air.

"What's that light?" breathed Romeo, seeing the glow from her window and creeping out. And there, above him, he saw his love. "Oh," he sighed, "it must be the east. There's Juliet, the sun."

Juliet did not know how close he was, but her thoughts were so full of him that they spilled out of her lips, and she cried out, "Oh Romeo, Romeo… why do you have to be Romeo, a Montague? Oh Romeo, give up your name, be someone else; be my love! And I'll no longer be a Capulet. After all, what is a name? A rose would smell just as sweet if we called it a different name… The name Montague means nothing to me. Oh, Romeo, take off your name – be just yourself – and in return take all of me."

Romeo emerged from the undergrowth beneath her window, smiling as if he could never stop. "I am a man, not a name. Call me love, and I'll be yours."

Juliet gasped. "If my family see you, they'll murder you!"

"I wouldn't care. My life is not worth living, unless I am with you," Romeo declared. "Marry me, Juliet. Tomorrow. Why should we wait a moment more?"

Juliet's feelings soared as she looked down at Romeo. "A thousand times: yes!" she replied, her mind reeling. But how ever would she escape the house to come and see him? "I'll send my nurse to meet you in the market square tomorrow morning, and she can tell me what you've planned."

Voices inside the house called Juliet's name. Juliet turned to go, whispering, "Goodnight… goodnight…" But, unable to tear herself away, she turned back. "Parting is such sweet sorrow that I shall keep saying goodnight until tomorrow…" she smiled ruefully. Finally, she slipped away into her bedroom.

"*That which we call a rose*
By any other word would smell as sweet"

Juliet, Act 2, Scene 1

At first light, Romeo raced to Friar Laurence, a priest, and a good friend he had known all his life.

"Good heavens," exclaimed Friar Laurence. "How come you're here so early? You look as if you have not slept all night! What's the matter?"

"I'm in love," Romeo explained rapidly. "With Juliet, daughter of my enemy. We want to be married, *today*. Please, help us. I know you are wise."

The Friar pondered the news. This was a match doomed to failure… or was it? "Your love may just be able to stop the hatred of Montague and Capulet for one another… and so be for the good of your families, and for all Verona," he mused. Within a minute, he had decided. "I will help. Yes. I will marry you in secret this very afternoon."

"Thank you," breathed Romeo, and he ran to the market square where he was to meet Juliet's nurse.

"Tell her…" he panted. "This afternoon… two o'clock… at Friar Laurence's… our wedding…"

The nurse looked carefully at the man her beloved nursling had fallen in love with. "Handsome, long-limbed, eager…" she thought approvingly. But she wanted to be sure of him.

"Can I trust you?" she asked. "If you lead my Juliet into a fool's paradise, I'll never forgive you, for she is the sweetest lady."

"Yes, trust me, for I adore her," Romeo assured her sincerely. "And tonight, when she must return home, bring a rope ladder to her balcony, and hide it there, so that I can climb up to her in secret."

"I'll remember," the nurse nodded, plucking a sweet-smelling sprig of leaves from a bush and sniffing it. "Here's rosemary for remembrance… and Rosemary and Romeo both begin with an 'R'. I won't forget." She put her posy in her pocket and hurried back to the Capulet house.

"What did Romeo say?" demanded Juliet, pouncing on her nurse the moment she returned.

"Oof," panted the nurse, sinking into a chair. "I'm too old for all this running about."

"Tell me…" urged Juliet. "Speak! Oh, please get on with it!"

"At two o'clock this afternoon you are to hurry to Friar Laurence's cell. There your love will be waiting to make you his wife," the nurse said at last.

Juliet hugged her until she gasped for breath. "And if your parents want you while you are gone, I'll make excuses for you," the nurse promised.

Juliet nodded, her thoughts still on Romeo. "How did he seem?" she asked.

"He's as gentle as a lamb. Kind. He looks honest. Not as rich as Paris, and your parents won't like it, but young blood knows what it wants. Ah, my little nursling. You can hide nothing from me. You're blushing, Juliet. Your cheeks have gone pink!"

That afternoon, Mercutio and Benvolio were strolling in the streets when they met Tybalt with a bunch of Capulets.

"Aha!" drawled Tybalt. "Montagues! You came to our party uninvited, didn't you? Villains! I'd like a word with one of you."

"Just one word?" Mercutio sneered. "Double it. Make it a word and a blow."

"And here comes another of you villains," Tybalt continued, spotting Romeo hurrying along the road.

Romeo had just come from Friar Laurence, who had secretly carried out the marriage. He and Juliet were now husband and wife. Luckily, no one had seen them, and Juliet had gone home before her parents realized she'd been out.

"I am no villain," Romeo informed Tybalt. "In fact, the name of Capulet is as dear to me as my own."

"Liar," hissed Tybalt, drawing his sword.

"Who are you calling a liar?" Mercutio said furiously, pulling out his dagger. "You rat-catcher, you king of cats."

"Don't!" cried Romeo. "The prince has forbidden brawling in the streets."

But no one listened. The clash of weapons echoed fatally in the cobbled street. Death was swift and ruthless. In a moment, Mercutio lay still, and Tybalt's sword dripped with blood.

Seeing his friend lying dead on the ground, all reason deserted Romeo. Red-hot anger flooded his mind, and he leaped forward and plunged his own sword into Tybalt's heart. Tybalt slumped to the ground, and Romeo's sword clattered from his hand.

Numb and horrified, Romeo staggered away from the scene.

The noise of the scuffle brought people rushing to the scene, including the prince and Juliet's parents. There they stood, staring sadly at the two murdered men, their short lives wasted. Benvolio, the only man left, had to answer the prince's questions.

"Tybalt began it... Tybalt killed Mercutio. Romeo didn't want anyone to fight at all. He was trying to stop them..." he explained.

"But then Romeo killed Tybalt? Romeo must die," snapped Lady Capulet. She began to cry. "Poor Tybalt. He was my brother's child."

"Enough!" said the prince. "Hear my decision. I pronounce Romeo exiled. Never shall he show his face here in Verona again, on pain of death."

Juliet buried herself in her bedroom, waiting for the slow hours of afternoon to turn into night, when Romeo had promised to come to her. She'd asked her nurse to leave her alone, so she was very surprised when she burst in, tears pouring down her cheeks.

"Tybalt, your cousin, is dead," sobbed the nurse. "Romeo..."

"Not dead too?" Juliet gasped.

"Dead to you, or as good as dead. He is banished…" The nurse closed her eyes, as if to shut out the terrible violence of her news, "…because he killed Tybalt," she whispered.

Juliet couldn't believe her ears. "Oh God, did Romeo's hand shed Tybalt's blood?"

"It shows you can't trust any man," said the nurse. "Romeo should be ashamed."

"I won't listen to you," Juliet burst out. "Shame and Romeo have nothing to do with each other. Tybalt would have killed Romeo, and for that, Romeo is banished. Oh, what shall I do? I've only been a wife for three hours." And she flung herself on her bed, sobs wrenching her whole body.

"Hush! Don't cry," comforted her nurse. "I know he's hiding in Friar Laurence's cell. I'll bring him to you in secret."

"Quickly," sobbed Juliet. "Where are my parents? They mustn't know."

"Downstairs, wailing over Tybalt. Do you want to go to them?"

Juliet shook her head.

"I'll stay here," she gulped, struggling to hold back her tears. "Let them cry. I must keep my tears for when my Romeo has gone. Hurry, Nurse, bring him to me, before we must part forever."

Romeo was with Friar Laurence, pacing up and down his cell, bitterly regretting the way he'd let himself be overcome by anger. When he saw Juliet's nurse, he fell on her like a child seeking comfort. "Tell me how Juliet is. Does she hate me? I killed her cousin, her childhood playmate…"

"She wants you…" the nurse assured him.

"But I must leave her," Romeo sobbed. "I have to go; I've been banished."

"You can't let yourself collapse in a heap," advised the friar. "Be positive. Look at it this way. You're alive; Juliet's alive. You love each other. Go on from there. Soon, you'll be able to ask the prince for pardon, and announce your marriage to the world, and Montague and Capulet will be reconciled. All will be well."

Romeo sighed. "You're right."

He left with the nurse, slinking unseen through the quiet back streets to the Capulets' garden. There, he found the rope ladder the nurse had hidden in the vines, and climbed up to Juliet's balcony, and into her bedroom.

Little did he – or Juliet – know that downstairs in the Capulet house, Juliet's parents were busy making plans that would destroy their fragile happiness.

"Poor Juliet is so unhappy about Tybalt," her mother was saying. "She hasn't left her bedroom. Let's marry her quickly to Paris. That'll take her mind off her grief… What day is it today?"

"Monday," said Lord Capulet.

"Then we'll have the wedding day on Thursday. We'll leave her alone tonight and tell her tomorrow," Lady Capulet decided.

Satisfied with their plan, they went to bed without the slightest suspicion that, across the corridor, Romeo and Juliet were together.

Morning came far too soon for Juliet. "Are you going? It's not yet near day. That was a nightingale that sang, not a lark."

Romeo smiled sadly and tucked a strand of hair behind her ear.

"Believe me, it was," Juliet insisted, her arms around his neck.

Romeo couldn't bear to leave her, though he knew – as Juliet did – that to stay meant certain death for him. "I'd rather stay than go. I'll welcome death…" he began.

"No, love, live!" cried Juliet, kissing him.

As dawn lit the sky with a treacherous sun, Romeo climbed down from the balcony to leave his new wife and Verona forever.

"I must be gone and live or stay and die."

ROMEO, ACT 3, SCENE 5

He'd left just in time. Lady Capulet bustled into Juliet's bedroom, like a tidal wave of information.

"I'm not well, Mother," Juliet parried, turning away.

"This will cheer you up. You're to be married on Thursday to Count Paris," her mother declared. "Oh, you'll be so happy! He's young, rich, handsome; what more could you ask for, you lucky girl?"

"I can't," gasped Juliet.

"You're still grieving for Tybalt, I know," said her mother smoothly, "but rest assured, we Capulets will find out where that villain Romeo is hiding, and we'll have him killed in revenge!"

Juliet shook with horror. Her father came in, eager to see how the conversation was going, but when he saw how Juliet had received the news, he was angry.

"You should be grateful to us," he snapped.

"Please," she begged, throwing herself on her knees. "Don't do this to me…"

"A daughter must do as her parents say!" he shouted, and with that, he and Lady Capulet marched out, slamming the door behind them. Juliet was left alone, feeling like an animal in a trap. How could she marry Paris when she was already married to Romeo?

"I need to see Friar Laurence," she thought. "He might be able to think of a way to save me. I'll tell my parents that before I can marry, I must make my confession. I know they'll believe me, and will let me see him."

The next day, Tuesday, Juliet ran to Friar Laurence's cell.

"I've already heard you're to marry Paris on Thursday," he told her. "I know how to solve your problem."

Juliet held out her hands eagerly. "Thank God. I'll do anything you say. Ask me to lurk in a pit of snakes, or chain me to roaring bears, or ask me to lie in a new grave, hidden by a dead man…"

The friar laughed. "Nothing quite so drastic. Nevertheless, you will need courage, which I don't think you lack." He showed her a tiny glass bottle, with dark green liquid inside.

"I have a potion here in this bottle, made of strong herbs. Swallow it tomorrow night, and there'll be no wedding for you on Thursday. This drug will make you sleep. Better than that, it will make you seem dead. You'll be cold, pale and still, and your parents will take you to the family vault, where you'll be laid out on a marble tombstone. But don't worry. The drug will last only for twenty-four hours. Then you'll wake as refreshed as if you've just had a good night's sleep. I'll get a message to Romeo; he and I will watch you wake, and then you can run away with him. How does that sound?"

"Wonderful!" said Juliet. She whispered to herself, "Love, give me strength," because she was indeed frightened. What if the potion was really a poison? What if the friar regretted marrying them in secret, and thought it was better to have Juliet out of the way? What if, shut in the fetid, stale air of the vault, she suffocated? But she could see no other way to help herself. She took the bottle, hid it in her pocket, and went back home.

Tuesday passed. And Wednesday. That night, Lady Capulet kissed her fondly. "Go to bed. You need your rest, for tomorrow you will be a bride," said Lady Capulet. "Would you like your nurse to stay with you till you sleep?

"No. Let me be alone," Juliet replied, though part of her longed to have them both with her to comfort her. What fate awaited her? "God knows when we shall meet again," she thought.

But she was determined to grasp the only chance she had to be with her love. And so, after they left, she held the bottle to her lips – and drank. "Romeo, I'm coming! I drink to you…" she gulped down the potion, and sank back onto her pillow.

LORD CAPULET, ACT 4, SCENE 4

On Thursday morning, the Capulet house was a-buzz with wedding preparations. Servants ran to the market to buy the best meats, fruit, dates, almonds and marzipan; wine was brought up from the cellar; the tables were laid and decorated with flowers; the cook was busy making a large cake.

And Juliet's nurse went to rouse her, but could not wake her up. The friar's potion had done its work. "This is the worst day of my life!" screamed the nurse, racing downstairs. "Juliet is DEAD!"

The household rushed to Juliet's bedside. She lay still and cold, her limbs stiff, her lips blue.

"My darling child," sobbed Lady Capulet. "My only child!"

Lord Capulet put his arms around his wife. "Her wedding flowers must decorate her coffin," he moaned. "Death lies on her like frost on a flower. Death is my son-in-law; death is now my only heir."

Romeo, meanwhile, had fled from Verona to Mantua. It was there that he heard from a stranger the news of Juliet's death. Mad with grief, he decided on a dark course of action. He persuaded a chemist to sell him a fatal dose of poison. "I cannot live without her," he thought. "Better to die by poison at her side. Juliet, I will lie with you tonight." And he began to make his way back to Verona.

Friar Laurence had written to Romeo, telling him that Juliet was not really dead – but Romeo wasn't in Mantua to receive the letter. When Romeo failed to answer, Friar Laurence realized to his horror that the message had never reached the young Montague.

"Oh dear!" agonized Friar Laurence. "Juliet's due to wake in three hours. I'll write again. The boy has to know it's all a pretence, so they can be together."

But as the messenger made his way to Mantua, Romeo was already galloping on horseback to Verona. He was going to break into the Capulet family vault. Nothing, he swore, was going to stop his last, terrible act; nothing would come between him and his beloved Juliet.

When he arrived, the door to the vault was wide open and, standing by the marble tomb on which Juliet lay, Romeo saw Paris. Solemnly, reverently, he was strewing her body with flowers. When he heard Romeo enter, Paris turned in fury.

"This is *your* fault!" he roared. "You murdered her cousin, and now she's died of grief. How dare you come here, to this most holy place? You vile Montague. You must die…"

"I must indeed," Romeo replied. "Listen, Paris, I need to stay here alone. Go. Please. If not it will be the worse for you."

"Never!" Paris said, drawing his sword.

Romeo tried to keep his temper in check this time, unlike in his fatal encounter with Tybalt. He implored Paris: "Be gone, and just say a madman made you run away."

"You admit you're mad? Then why should I listen to your ravings?" sneered Paris, lunging at Romeo. Romeo drew his own sword and they fought until Paris fell, mortally wounded.

Summoning all his strength, Paris uttered his last request: "If you are merciful… lay me beside Juliet." Then he slumped to the floor and closed his eyes.

Romeo stared at him in sorrow. Then he went to Juliet and gazed at her body. She looked as though she was only asleep. He drank in her beauty, her stillness, mourning all that might have been, and the cruelty of fate that had killed their love.

Slowly, he lay down beside her. "Eyes take your last look," he thought to himself. He opened the vial of poison, and drank every last drop. Then he kissed Juliet one last time on the lips. "And so, with a kiss, I die," he breathed.

The poison flooded through him, turning his body cold, and he lay down beside Juliet, and died.

An hour passed before the door of the vault opened again. Friar Laurence, true to his promise, had come to be with Juliet as she awoke. At once, his eyes fell upon the unmistakable, red-spattered stains that told a hotly violent tale.

"Blood!" exclaimed the friar, deeply shocked. First he found Paris's body, and then he saw Romeo, lifeless, next to Juliet. "Was it all my fault?" he asked himself, clutching his chest in anguish. "I wanted to help young love and end the hatred between their families… and now… Oh, now Juliet awakes…"

Juliet's eyes fluttered open and she smiled. "I feel so comfortable seeing you, Friar Laurence," she said, yawning and sitting up. "I remember everything. Where is my Romeo?"

Friar Laurence found it hard to say the words. But he had no choice; the truth lay starkly before them both. "Dead. And Paris too," he choked. "Flee, Juliet, while you can. I'll find a place for you in a convent, where no one will ask any questions. Quick. I dare not stay here any longer; it's not safe…"

Juliet gasped. Romeo… and Paris… love had played her false, and there was only one way to redeem it. But not in front of the friar. She had to be alone.

"No, I will stay here," she said, clutching the sides of her tomb till her knuckles turned white. Did she have the strength for what she wanted to do? She had to. "Go!" she shouted at the trembling, pale-faced friar. "I will not leave this place!"

To her relief, Friar Laurence stumbled out of the horrific vault as fast as he could.

Now she could begin to piece together what had happened. A vial was clasped in Romeo's hand. Poison, then. Suicide. She'd follow him, of course. Death was the only answer. But the vial was empty. "Oh, you drank it all and left no drop to help me?" she thought. "Perhaps if I kiss your lips. Some poison might still be on them…" She pressed her lips on his – they were still warm – and waited for the end.

It did not come. Death was not going to be so easy.

A last choice awaited her. "Yes," she whispered to herself. "I think I do have the strength." She found Romeo's dagger, pulled it out and plunged it deep into her side. Her body fell lifeless over his, and the rose of her blood slowly bloomed over them both.

Sad news filters fast through the storylines of life. Before very much longer, the vault was full of people: Romeo's parents, Juliet's parents, her nurse, Friar Laurence and the prince. They were all shocked and devastated by the sight of the two young people clasped together on the tomb, and of Paris lying in his blood on the floor, flowers and petals scattered wildly about them all. Friar Laurence explained how it had happened and begged forgiveness for his part in the tragedy.

"I know you are, without question, a holy man," said the prince. "We are all punished by these deaths. Capulet! Montague! See what hate has done to you? I should have done more to try to stop it. And so should you…"

"Oh, brother Montague," wept old Capulet, a broken man. "Give me your hand."

"Willingly," replied old Montague, equally moved.

The old sworn enemies finally clasped each other by their children's tomb, drawn together in grief.

Outside, the sky was dark with clouds as if, that day in Verona, the sun could not bear to shine.

Coriolanus

When Rome goes to war with the Volscians, it's
Caius Martius whose skill and daring win them
victory. But with political tensions rising between
the rich and poor of Rome, can this headstrong
warrior provide the leadership his city needs?

Caius Martius (Coriolanus)

A haughty Roman,
who earns the name
Coriolanus by defeating
the city of Corioles.

Tullus Aufidius

A Volscian general,
and Coriolanus's
sworn enemy.

Cominius

One of the Roman
generals who leads
the campaign against
the Volscians.

Menenius Agrippa
A nobleman and a shrewd politician. Friend and supporter of Coriolanus.

Brutus and Sicinius
Elected representatives of the people. They despise Coriolanus and want to stop him from gaining too much power in the Senate (government).

Volumnia
Coriolanus's mother. She is as fierce and tough as he is, but a little wiser.

Virgilia
Coriolanus's wife.

Young Martius
Coriolanus's son.

T HE FIELDS OF THE ROMAN REPUBLIC lay brown and bare under
a scorching sun, and grapes shrivelled black on the vines. It
was a time of famine. Every day, the city's bakers had less
bread to sell, and their prices were rising. The poor were going
hungry. Rumours of revolt spread in the crowded streets.

One afternoon, as the senator Menenius Agrippa left his house
to attend a government meeting, he came face to face with a mob
of angry citizens. They were armed with clubs, rakes and hoes, and
were heading towards the main square of the city.

"What's this, my countrymen?" Menenius asked mildly.
"Where are you off to with your sticks and clubs?"

"Menenius," a bricklayer replied, "you've always been a friend
to the people. But you and all the Senate should know what's
afoot. You've had plenty of warning!"

"That's right," cried a street sweeper, shaking a cudgel. "We're
hungry for bread, and the rich nobles don't care one bit. Their
storehouses are crammed with grain, and all they do is pass laws to
make the poor even poorer. It's time to make them pay! People are
rising up all over Rome."

"Please, my honest neighbours, don't listen to this folly,"
Menenius said. "It is the gods who cause famine, not the ruling
class. You slander the heads of state but, in truth, they care for you
as they care for their children."

Before the people could respond, a broad-shouldered nobleman
shoved his way into their midst. "What's the matter, you mutinous
rogues?" he demanded, glaring round at them.

"It's Caius Martius," hissed the bricklayer, "the famous
warrior! He's the worst of them. He's always insulting us."

"Do you expect me to praise you, you idle curs?" Caius Martius retorted. "You commoners are cowardly in war and brave in peace. Whoever deserves praise receives only your hate. Whoever trusts you swims with leaden fins to their doom. You're no more dependable than a hailstone in the sun. Why are you railing against the Senate?"

"They want cheaper grain," Menenius explained, "and they say the Senate's laws are unfair to them."

"Hang 'em," growled Caius Martius. "The pack of slaves! I wish the Senate would lay aside its mercy and let me use my sword. I'd wipe out this rabble myself."

There was a flourish of trumpets, and a messenger came running from the direction of the Senate house, where the Roman government sat in session. "Hear me, Menenius, and all you Romans," he cried. "The senators have considered the protestors' demands. They've granted the people free grain and political powers. They hereby appoint new tribunes – politicians who will be your special representatives in the Senate."

The commoners cheered, but Caius Martius only scowled. "No good can come of this," he warned.

"Wait, that's not all," the messenger continued. "The generals have received news that our old enemies, the Volscians, are raising an army. They're sure to march against Rome."

"I'm glad of it," Caius Martius declared. "They have a noble leader, Tullus Aufidius. He is a lion that I'm proud to hunt."

Menenius addressed the would-be rioters. "You see, your voices have been heard, and you can all go home. Come, Caius Martius, let's be off as well. General Cominius will be drawing up his battle plans, and I'm sure he needs your help."

News of the coming war spread quickly through the city. Soldiers sharpened their swords and buffed their shields to a gleaming finish. Cominius, with Caius Martius and the rest of his captains, debated strategy and tactics long into the night.

At Caius Martius's house, his wife Virgilia paced up and down, nervously awaiting the outcome, while his mother, Volumnia, sewed with steady hands in the firelight.

"Please, calm down!" Volumnia said at last, "Rejoice in this new war. If my son were my husband, I'd be happy to let him seek danger where he could find fame. Remember, when he was little more than a boy, I sent him to a cruel war, and he came back loaded with honours."

"But what if he had come back dead?" Virgilia asked.

"Believe me, if I had a dozen sons, and they were all as dear to me as Martius is, I'd rather eleven died nobly for their country than one stayed safely home."

Virgilia shuddered. "I can't think like you," she said firmly. "I have just one husband – and just one son – and neither my boy nor I will leave this house until Martius returns from the war."

The Romans decided to launch an attack immediately, and Cominius's army marched to the Volscian city of Corioles. There, they set up camp and besieged the city. For three days, the gates held strong against the Roman onslaught. Then, from the high walls of the city, the defenders heard a distant blast of trumpets. "Listen!" someone cried. "It's Aufidius and his army! They're coming to save our city."

Indeed, Tullus Aufidius and his men had marched through the night to support Corioles. Now, they attacked the Romans from behind and the city's defenders, seizing the opportunity, unbarred the gates. They poured out, hoping to overwhelm the Romans.

At first, the Roman battle line gave way, but one man alone refused to retreat, hacking left and right with furious blows. It was Caius Martius. "Come on," he roared to his fellows. "Where are you going, you shames of Rome, you souls of geese? Victory is ours if you stand fast. The gates are open – follow me!"

So terrible was Caius Martius in his battle rage that the Volscians faltered, and he stormed straight into Corioles. But not a single Roman soldier followed him, and the great gates creaked shut behind him.

"He's doomed," cried one of his companions. "It's him alone against an entire city!"

"Oh, noble Martius," another mourned, "you dared to stand straight where even swords would bend. You made your enemies shake as if the very world were feverish and trembling."

The Romans felt sure that their champion was lost. Then, suddenly, the gates of Corioles creaked open once more. Two red hands appeared in the gap, slowly wrenching it wider. There stood Caius Martius: covered in blood, but victorious.

"He lives! Caius Martius is alive," the Romans cheered. Rallying to his aid, they stormed through the gates into the city.

Corioles was defeated – but outside the city walls, on the other side of the battlefield, Aufidius and his army were still pressing the Romans hard. Ignoring his wounds, Caius Martius raced back into combat, soon coming face to face with the Volscian general himself.

"I'll fight with none but you!" Caius Martius swore as he battered Aufidius's shield. "I hate you more than treachery."

"We hate alike," replied Aufidius, striking a glancing blow at Caius Martius's helmet. "Let's settle this here and now! Whoever flees, let him die the other's slave."

The two heroes circled one another, thrusting and parrying

"O noble fellow!
Who sensibly outdares his senseless sword,
And when it bows, stand'st up! Thou art lost, Martius"

with brutal skill – but, before the contest could be decided, three of Aufidius's men dashed between the glittering swords. They blocked Caius Martius's blows with their shields and, despite his curses and protestations, dragged their leader away from the fight.

"Our army is retreating," the Volscian soldiers explained as they bundled Aufidius onto a horse. "Rome has won the day."

"Curse you, Martius!" Aufidius cried. "Five times we've fought, and every time you've had the upper hand."

"He's the Devil," one soldier said.

"He's even bolder, though not so subtle," observed Aufidius. "Now nothing more will stand between my hate and Martius. No bond of hospitality or mercy can protect him, and I swear some day I'll wash my fierce hands in his heart's blood."

After the battle, the victorious Roman troops formed a wide square around their general, and Cominius called for Caius Martius. The warrior, still covered in grime, his arm in a sling, reluctantly stepped forward.

"If I told you everything you'd done in battle, you yourself would disbelieve your deeds," Cominius told him. "We thank the gods that Rome has such a soldier."

"Please, say no more," Caius Martius said. "It grieves me to be praised. I did what you have done: just what I can. And I did it for the same reason as you: for my country."

"All Rome will recognize your worth," insisted Cominius, "and I decree that you may have one tenth of all the treasure won today in Corioles."

"Thank you," Caius Martius said, "but I cannot take a bribe to pay my sword. I refuse it. I'll take only my fair share like any common soldier."

Cominius nodded. "Very well. But one gift you must accept: a new name. To honour what you did, alone inside the city, from

CominIUS, Act 1, Scene 9

now on you shall be known as Coriolanus – defeater of Corioles!"

The Roman soldiers cheered and, beating their spears on their shields, they chanted Caius Martius's new name: "Coriolanus!"

When Cominius's army returned to Rome, news of the great victory spread rapidly from street to street. Flags flew from public buildings. People rushed out with garlands of flowers to greet the soldiers, and thank them for countering the Volscian threat. Everyone joined in the celebrations – all, that is, except for two men.

Brutus and Sicinius were the new tribunes, chosen to represent the common people. They watched grimly as the crowd surged past. "The citizens speak of nothing but Coriolanus," complained Brutus, "and bow to him as to a god."

"I fear he'll be elected consul," Sicinius added. "And then, as the highest Roman official, he'll hold power over us."

"Whatever authority we have would then be hollowed out," Brutus said. "We can't let that happen."

"Fear not," said Sicinius. "You know he'll never be able to show enough humility to beg the common people for their votes. And without those votes, he cannot succeed."

"That's right," agreed Brutus. "We'll use his pride to stop him. Sooner or later, his soaring insolence will irk the people. Then, you and I can kindle a blaze in the dry grass of the common folk…"

"And blacken his name forever," finished Sicinius.

Soon after, the senators and tribunes gathered to consider who should be elected consul, and hold the highest office in the Republic. Coriolanus was the favoured candidate, and Cominius rose before the white-robed senators to speak on his behalf.

"The deeds of Coriolanus should not be uttered feebly," Cominius said. "All his life, he's fought for Rome. We've never seen a more valiant or terrifying warrior. In this last battle, he smashed into Corioles like a wayward planet. Covered from head to foot in blood, alone, he entered the city's gates, and there alone he fought, and never stopped until the city was ours. He covets no treasure, seeks no praise, and for his deeds asks no reward."

"He's a worthy man," agreed Menenius, placing a friendly hand on Coriolanus's shoulder. The senators gave a murmur of approval.

Coriolanus winced. "I'd rather have my wounds back," he muttered, "than hear how I got them."

"Caius Martius Coriolanus," Menenius announced, "the Senate is pleased to make you consul. All that now remains is for you to speak to the people, and receive their votes."

"Thank you," Coriolanus said, "but can't we overlook that custom? I don't have the stomach to brag and pander, to show the wounds I've won in battle, praise myself and beg for votes. I cannot bring my tongue to such a place."

At this, Sicinius sprang to his feet. "Sir, the people must have their say," he said sharply, "and they won't accept one jot less of ceremony."

"From face to foot
He was a thing of blood, whose every motion
Was timed with dying cries: alone he entered
The mortal gate of th' city"

COMINIUS, ACT 2, SCENE 2

"Don't defy them, Coriolanus," Menenius advised. "This is the custom. You must speak to the people, and win their votes."

Later that day, Coriolanus went down into the Roman marketplace. There, among the honking geese and vegetables and bustling tradesmen, the would-be consul stood awkwardly. Soon, two citizens – a baker and a potter – approached.

"You know my purpose here," Coriolanus said, greeting them.

"We do, sir," said the baker, "and we know your reputation. You have been a scourge to Rome's enemies."

"And yet," added the potter slowly, "you have not loved the Roman people."

"Nor have I flattered them," Coriolanus said. "I do them the honour of speaking honestly. Tell me, what is the price of your vote for the consulship?"

"The price is to ask it kindly," said the baker.

Coriolanus grimaced. "Kindly, sir, I ask you, let me have it."

"I think you've earned it with your deeds," admitted the baker.

"Yes, you'll have my vote," promised the potter.

So, throughout the day, in groups of two or three, Rome's commoners met with Coriolanus and gave him their votes. At last, the sun began to dip in the sky and, with obvious relief, Coriolanus left the marketplace.

The Roman custom had been observed. However, as the tradesmen cleaned up their stalls and discussed the day's events, they weren't all that sure about what they'd done.

"It's true," said the baker, "he's fought and suffered for our country, and we should show him our gratitude."

"And yet," said a blacksmith, "he seemed to mock us when he begged our votes."

"He spoke scornfully," the potter agreed.

"How now, citizens," said Sicinius, appearing with Brutus at the entrance to the marketplace, "have you chosen Coriolanus?"

"We have," the baker affirmed, rather uncertainly, "although he was a little too proud when he spoke to us."

"We pray that he'll deserve your votes," Brutus said. "But don't you think that his contempt will bruise you when he, as consul, has the power to crush?"

"He boldly mocked you for your votes," Sicinius said in seeming disbelief, "and yet you gave him what he asked?"

"Well, he hasn't got it yet," the potter said stubbornly. "He hasn't been confirmed in the Senate."

"But time is running out," Brutus said urgently. "Go now, and tell all your friends that they've chosen a consul who will steal away their liberties."

"Tell them to gather tomorrow in protest," Sicinius added, "and remind them of his pride, and how he hates the poor."

"We will," promised the blacksmith and the potter, and they hurried from the marketplace.

The next day, Coriolanus made his way toward the Senate house with Menenius and Cominius. However, as they neared the building, they found the street blocked by Brutus and Sicinius, along with all the tradesmen from the marketplace.

"Go no further," warned Sicinius.

"What do you mean?" demanded Cominius. "Coriolanus has been elected consul."

"It would be dangerous to go on," said Brutus. "The people are enraged, and have withdrawn their votes for him."

"Withdrawn their votes?" Coriolanus exclaimed. "This sounds like a plot. You tribunes are the people's mouths – do you control their teeth too? Have you set them against me?"

"Let's all stay calm," Menenius urged.

"Don't call it a plot," Brutus said hotly. "The people say you mocked them, and when grain was given to them during the famine, you cursed the poor and their supporters."

"You bring that up again? I said it then, and I'll say it now—"

"Not now, not now," pleaded Menenius.

"Yes, now," insisted Coriolanus. "That rank-smelling multitude, I say again, deserves no free grain. Feeding them, we nourish only insolence and rebellion."

"Yet you think they should vote for you?!" snapped Sicinius.

"The noble Romans caved in to the rabble," Coriolanus continued, "and in so doing we debased ourselves, broke open the locks of the Senate and let in crows to peck at eagles. Yes. And I'll tell you something more that many dare not say: if we loved Rome, we'd pluck out the people's tongue, which they would use to lick the poisoned sweet of politics. We'd throw their power and their tribunes in the dust."

"That's treason! Spoken like a traitor!" Sicinius cried.

"You all heard him insult the people," added Brutus, turning to the crowd who muttered their agreement.

"Officers! Arrest this man," Sicinius ordered, grabbing Coriolanus by the arm and waving to the guards on the steps of the Senate house.

"Get off me, Sicinius" growled Coriolanus, batting away the tribune's hand, "or I'll shake your bones out of your toga."

"On both sides, more respect," Menenius urged. "Brutus, Sicinius, think about what you're starting here!"

But the quarrel was boiling over. "This violence deserves death!" Brutus declared. "We do here pronounce, on behalf of the people, that Coriolanus is worthy of death."

"Seize him," shouted Sicinius to the crowd. "Throw him from the highest tower!"

"No, I'd rather die here," said Coriolanus, and with an easy motion he drew his sword. "There are some among you that have seen me fight. Come, now try me for yourselves."

Coriolanus swung his sword in a lazy arc, and the tribunes and commoners scrambled back, tripping and shoving one another in fear and anger. Brutus was knocked to the ground, and Sicinius took an elbow to the stomach. "Bring weapons! We need weapons," he gasped.

But before anyone had a chance to recover, Menenius and Cominius pulled Coriolanus into an alley and hustled him away.

"Please, noble friend, go home," urged Cominius, "before the rioters can rally, and sweep over us like a tide."

"On fair ground, I could beat forty of them," Coriolanus spat.

"I could myself take on a few," said Menenius, "but let me speak to them instead. I'll see whether my wit can work on those who have none. The best you can do now is go."

Coriolanus nodded, leaving his two friends behind.

"Why couldn't he just speak to them kindly?" sighed Cominius.

"His nature is too noble for the world," Menenius said sadly. "He wouldn't flatter Neptune for his trident, or Jove for his power to thunder. Whatever his heart feels, his tongue must vent — and when he's angry, he forgets he ever heard the name of Death."

After a long day of negotiations with the tribunes, Menenius went to Coriolanus's house to report what had been decided.

Coriolanus's mother, Volumnia, showed the senator in. "Welcome, Menenius," she said. "What's the news? Can we still make peace with the tribunes?"

"Make peace?" Coriolanus growled. "I'm surprised at you, Mother! You hate them as much as I do. Why do you wish me to be milder? Would you have me be false to my nature? I play the man I am."

"Oh, Son, I'd wish to see you wield your power before you've worn it out. You are too stubborn, and too absolute."

"Your mother's right," said Menenius. "Listen: the people and the tribunes are still enraged. Violence could break out again. But if you would return to the marketplace and repent the things you've said…"

"To them? I couldn't do it to the gods!"

"Son, you must speak to them," urged Volumnia. "Speak not what you feel, but use your tongue as you would a strategy in battle. Win with gentleness what otherwise would cost you blood."

Menenius nodded. "If you act humbly," he said, "speak fairly, and answer their accusations mildly, you may yet win their hearts."

Coriolanus groaned. "Shall I use my throat of war to lull babies to sleep? Shall my knee, which never bends except in stirrups, bow like a beggar seeking charity?"

"Do what you want, Coriolanus," Volumnia said angrily. "I won't beg you to do this. If all comes to ruin, so be it. I'm not afraid. Your bravery you got from me: you sucked it in your mother's milk. But your pride – your pride is your own."

"Oh, don't scold me, Mother," Coriolanus replied. "I'll go to the marketplace. I'll go, and beg their pardon, and I'll come back loved by all the poor of Rome – or never trust my tongue again to flatter."

The next day, Coriolanus and his noble supporters stood again in the marketplace before the Roman people. The tradesmen's stalls had all been cleared away, and a crowd of commoners filled the space. Their anger had been whipped up overnight by the words of the tribunes – and now, two rows of soldiers struggled to hold them back.

"Why did you wish me milder? Would you have me false to my nature? Rather say I play the man I am."

Coriolanus, Act 3, Scene 2

Sicinius stepped out to address Coriolanus. "I do demand," he said, in a voice that carried to the back of the crowd, "that you submit to the Roman people and their officers, and that you suffer any punishment the law shall lay upon you."

"I consent," replied Coriolanus. "But tell me, why have you denied me the office of consul even though I was fairly elected?"

"We charge that you intended to take power, and make yourself a tyrant of Rome, for which you are a traitor to the people."

"Traitor?" said Coriolanus sharply. "How, 'traitor'?"

"Softly! Remember your promise to your mother," whispered Menenius at his side.

"No more," Coriolanus growled. "Let them pronounce what death they will. I wouldn't buy their mercy at the price of one fair word."

"This man," continued Sicinius, addressing the crowd, "has cursed you, beat your officers and defied the law. For this he deserves to die!"

"Yes!" roared the crowd.

"But," said Brutus, joining Sicinius, "because he once did service to his country, we do this instant merely banish him. He is banished! Let him never more enter the gates of Rome."

"It shall be so," the Romans chanted.

Coriolanus shrugged off the consoling hands of his friends and faced the crowd. "You pack of yelping curs," he said, "whose rotten breath I hate, whose love I cherish less than the stench of unburied corpses, *I banish you*. Despising Rome because of you, I turn my back. There is a world elsewhere."

Then, pursued by the jeering crowd, pelted with filth, Coriolanus marched through the city and out into the countryside.

Weeks later, far from Rome, as dusk fell on the Volscian city of Antium, a traveller approached the gates. The stranger, wrapped in a stained cloak and limping slightly in his worn-out sandals, asked the gatekeeper for directions to the house of Tullus Aufidius.

"There it is," said the Volscian, pointing. "He's hosting the nobles of Antium tonight."

The stranger thanked him and proceeded to Aufidius's door. His knock was answered by a haughty servant.

"Who are you?" the servant demanded.

"A gentleman," the stranger replied.

"You look like a marvellously poor one."

"True, so I am. But please, call your master. I wish to see him."

"Go away," said the servant, aiming a kick at the stranger.

"Now you're being troublesome," the stranger warned. He dodged the kick and with a single blow knocked the servant down.

"What's that racket?" called a voice from within. A moment later, Aufidius himself came into the hallway to find the stranger standing on his threshold. "What's all this? Who are you?"

"Do you not know me?" the stranger asked, straightening his back and throwing off his hood. "My name sounds harsh to Volscian ears. I'm Caius Martius, known as Coriolanus."

The servant gasped in horror and scrabbled for his sword, but Aufidius held up his hand. "Let's hear him out," he said.

"Yes," the Roman continued, "I'm Coriolanus. But now, despite all the blood I've shed for Rome, that name alone remains. The cruelty and envy of the people have devoured the rest. A pack of slaves has chased me out of Rome. So if you want revenge, I'm here, and you can easily cut my throat. But otherwise my life may be of use. For, if you let me, I'll fight with you against my former country with the fury of a demon."

Tullus Aufidius opened his arms to his old enemy. "Oh Martius! Every word you speak pulls a root of ancient envy from my heart. Let me embrace the body I so often struck at with my sword. Why, don't you know, I've been raising a new army, and every night I've dreamed of fighting you again, man to man. Now, instead, take half my army under your command. You know your country's weaknesses, and how best to destroy it. Come in, and meet the Volscian nobles. A thousand welcomes! You're more a friend today than you ever were my enemy."

So began another Volscian war. Together, Aufidius and Coriolanus launched their attack on the Roman territories. One by one, cities and towns fell to the invaders. Coriolanus fought more fiercely and relentlessly than ever before, and he soon won the trust and admiration of his troops. Before long, the Volscian armies had pushed within striking distance of the Roman capital.

News of Coriolanus's approach made the Roman citizens tremble. They knew better than anyone what cause Coriolanus had to hate them.

"I hope you're proud of what you've done," Menenius said to Brutus and Sicinius.

"He'll shake down Rome like ripe fruit from a tree," said Cominius in despair.

Tullus Aufidius also had cause to regret Coriolanus's success. He began to wonder if sharing his command with the Roman warrior had been such a good idea. "He behaves more proudly now – even to me – than I ever thought he would," the Volscian general mused. "But that's true to his nature, and I must excuse what cannot be changed. And, for better or worse, our war will soon be at an end."

The Volscian army set up camp on a hill within sight of the walls of Rome, and began preparations for a final siege. The desperate Romans sent one ambassador after another to plead with Coriolanus. None were admitted. Even Cominius and Menenius were turned away.

The two generals were preparing their plans for the attack when they heard a commotion from the entrance to the camp. A moment later, the Volscian guards appeared, escorting Volumnia, Virgilia, and young Martius. Coriolanus hadn't seen his family for months, and despite himself he felt tears welling in his eyes.

"Honoured mother, dearest wife," he said, embracing them, "and my brave boy! Oh, forgive my tyranny, but please don't ask me to forgive the Romans."

"We have nothing else to ask," said Volumnia, "except what you deny already. And yet we will ask. Think of what we've gone through. You've made your mother, wife and child watch their son, husband and father tearing his country apart. Now, either you'll be led in chains like a traitor through the streets of Rome, or you'll win glory at the cost of your family's blood."

Now, the tears were rolling down Coriolanus's cheeks. He tried in vain to turn away, but Volumnia held his hand. "Oh, my great son," she said, "what honour do you hope to gain by conquering Rome? The act will wipe out your nobility, and make your name a curse in ages to come. We beg you – make peace between the Volscians and the Romans."

Volumnia and Virgilia both kneeled before Coriolanus. Even proud young Martius bent his little knee and bowed his head before his father.

"Mother, Mother, what have you done?" Coriolanus groaned. "You've won a happy victory for Rome – but for your son, believe it, your arguments are most dangerous. But so be it. Aufidius," he said, turning to the Volscian, "I cannot wage the war I promised, but I'll make a suitable peace. If you were in my place, could you do any different?"

"I, too, was moved by their appeal," admitted the general. But although Aufidius could understand the Roman's decision, he could not excuse it…

"Dear ones," Coriolanus said, picking up his son and pulling his wife and mother close, "all the swords in Italy could not have made this peace."

A few days later, Tullus Aufidius and Coriolanus led their troops through the gates of Corioles. They were met by cheering crowds – but although they were undefeated, many of the Volscian soldiers felt that victory had escaped them. For them, the blame lay squarely on Coriolanus.

"He turned my own charity against me," Aufidius muttered between clenched teeth. "I welcomed him, made him my equal and gave him my best and freshest men. Then, with victory in sight, for a few women's tears, he sold the blood and labour of our war."

In the great square of Corioles, the returning generals dismounted to greet the nobles of the city. "Hail, my lords," said Coriolanus. "I have led your wars even to the gates of Rome. We've brought home spoils and riches, and an honourable peace."

"My lords," said Tullus Aufidius, "don't listen to this man – but tell the traitor how he has abused your trust."

"Traitor?" Coriolanus exclaimed. "How now?"

"Ay, traitor, Martius."

"Martius?! Why do you call me by my old name?"

"Yes, Martius, Caius Martius," Aufidius repeated. "Do you think I'll grace you with that robbery, your stolen name 'Coriolanus' in Corioles itself? My lords, he has betrayed you and, for a few drops of salt, given up your victory. At the first sight of his mother's tears, he broke his oath – and like a little boy he cried away your claim to Rome."

"False hound," Coriolanus roared. "You call me a little boy? Remember, it was here I fought, in this very square, and like an eagle in a flock of doves I fluttered your Volscian troops. I alone did it!"

"That's right," cried a voice in the crowd, "you killed my son!"

"He killed my cousin," cried another.

"Kill him! Kill him!" the people shouted.

"You insolent man," Aufidius snarled. He drew his sword to attack Coriolanus – but he was already too late. The crowd of angry Volscians surged forward, and the Roman was stabbed and trampled under their feet. By the time the nobles had restored order, the mighty warrior was dead.

When they saw what they had done, the Volscians' anger soon gave way to shame and sadness. "Let's carry away his noble corpse," said one of the Volscian lords, "and mourn him."

"My rage is gone," said Aufidius, and he let his sword fall to the ground. "Lift him up, and lower the flags, and beat the drum. Though in this city he has left many widowed and childless, still he shall have a noble memory."

So, led by Tullus Aufidius, the Volscians carried away the body of their greatest enemy and fiercest friend.

Love's Labour's Lost

The King of Navarre and his noble friends have promised to devote themselves to their studies, avoiding love and merry-making for three whole years. But just as they swear this binding oath, the Princess of France arrives with her three beautiful companions...

King Ferdinand

Ruler of Navarre, in Spain. Vows to give up his frivolous ways and devote himself to study.

Longaville, Dumaine and Biron

Three witty and playful lords, and the king's closest friends.

Dull

A constable.

Costard

A peasant.

Holofernes
A schoolmaster.

Sir Nathaniel
A curate.

Boyet
Advisor to the princess,
known for his courtesy
and clever wordplay.

The Princess
of France
Wise, practical princess sent
by her father on a diplomatic
mission to Navarre.

Maria, Rosaline and Katherine
Three clever and lively ladies,
and the princess's dearest companions.

Jaquenetta
A country girl.

Armado
A boastful
Spaniard.

Moth
Armado's
clever page.

"The mind shall banquet though the body pine"

FERDINAND, KING OF NAVARRE, was young, handsome, rich and clever. Fate had showered him with gifts. But he wasn't satisfied; his life was too easy. So he decided to set himself a challenge. He would dedicate himself to learning, giving up all other pleasures for three whole years.

He persuaded his three favourite courtiers, Biron, Longaville and Dumaine, to join him in this noble aim. They all promised faithfully not to see any women, and to limit themselves to one meal per day. They'd sleep for no more than three hours a night, and devote the remaining hours to their books.

The king thought it was such a good idea, he made the rules into law and had them written out on a scroll of parchment. With the scroll under his arm, Ferdinand called his friends to a meeting.

Longaville tried to look on the bright side. "It's only three years. Our minds will banquet, though our bodies pine…"

Dumaine tried his best too: "Love, wealth, pomp… who wants these? Mere idle thoughts, which are dead to me."

Only Biron was bold enough to moan. "It will be too hard! Not to see ladies, or sleep or eat… just to study all the time."

Ferdinand tried to convince him. "It's like this," he explained. "When people die, they're dead, buried, forgotten. If we can add to the world's knowledge and understanding, we'll be remembered forever. We can cheat death, don't you see? We can live on for all eternity!"

"What actually *is* the point of study though?" Biron mused.

"That's easy. To know things we would otherwise not know, of course," replied Ferdinand. "Just think, the kingdom of Navarre will be a wonder of the world! Our court will be like an academy!"

"I'm not sure I agree with you that study by itself is a good thing," said Biron. "The more you study a book – the more you immerse yourself in it, the more you become blind to everything else. It's like wearing blinkers. You strive for the sun, but find yourself in darkness. It's wrong to put everything else aside."

"If you're so against learning, Biron, then off you go. Goodbye!" said Ferdinand, deeply disappointed.

But Biron wasn't really going to desert his friend. "I'm just arguing about it for fun. I'll keep my word, I swear."

"Thank you. You've saved yourself from shame – just," the king grinned. "Everyone sign here. That makes it final."

Trustingly, Longaville and Dumaine signed the end of the scroll. But Biron unravelled the beginning and began to read it. "Good gracious, Ferdinand. Do you realize what this actually says?" Biron asked. He read aloud: "'No woman shall come within a mile of my court, on pain of losing her tongue.' Whoever suggested that?"

"I did," Longaville admitted.

"In heaven's name, why?" asked Biron, aghast.

"To frighten women off," Longaville replied.

Biron glanced over the rest of the document with growing alarm. "This isn't going to be easy," he said. "Has this actually been declared, Ferdinand?"

The king nodded. "Four days ago."

Biron read aloud again. "'If any man talks to a woman within the term of three years, he will be publicly shamed.' Well, Ferdinand! You've dug yourself into a hole here. Don't you remember the Princess of France is arriving any minute now?"

It was true. The King of France was old and sick and was sending his daughter in his stead to discuss Navarre's claims to a region in France. King Ferdinand would have no choice but to talk to her. "Oh dear," said Ferdinand. "I'd forgotten about that."

"Beware the dangers of study," Biron said with a wry laugh. "It makes you forget stuff of great importance."

Ferdinand was looking thoughtful. "Obviously, we can't keep entirely to this decree. Necessity forces us to ignore parts of it…"

Biron doubled up laughing and took out his pen. "I'll happily sign then, since my oath can be broken by mere 'necessity'." He added his name to the bottom of the scroll. "So, what sort of entertainment have you arranged for us, during these three long years of study, Ferdinand?"

"I've invited this fellow Armado, from Spain. He's vain, boastful and full of fine phrases; we'll get a lot of amusement just listening to him." the king replied.

"Oh, three years will fly by," Longaville remarked drily. "Look who's coming: Costard the peasant and Dull the constable. Our entertainment starts right now."

The constable, Dull, strutted before the king and bowed, full of importance. "Villainy is around us! I have a letter that the king must see!" he announced, and handed the letter to Ferdinand.

"It's from the magnificent Armado," said the king as he read it. "Just as we were talking about him."

"It's about me," Costard informed him. "And Jaquenetta."

"Who's she?" asked Biron.

"A village girl. I was seen talking to her in the park."

"Don't you know that's now a crime?" asked the king sternly.

"But I was attracted to her…" Costard wailed. But Ferdinand was busy reading the letter, laughing at Armado's high-flown words… "I did encounter that obscene and preposterous event in the west corner of your garden. There I did see that lowly swain…"

"*Me?*" asked Costard indignantly.

Ferdinand nodded and continued: "that ignorant soul…"

"*Still me?*" asked Costard.

"…that shallow slave…"

"Me *again*?" Costard felt wrung out.

"Costard was with Jaquenetta," Dull announced dully, cutting through the flowery language, "and now I've brought him to you."

"Here's his punishment," said Ferdinand. "He shall eat nothing but bran and water for a week."

"I'd rather pray for a month with roast lamb and porridge!" protested Costard. "Is it such a crime to like a pretty girl?"

"Be quiet," ordered the king. "Armado shall be your guard, and Jaquenetta can be a servant at the park lodge. Off you go."

Armado was walking in the park with his pageboy, Moth. "I've promised to spend three years studying with the king," Armado told him.

"What use are three years of learning to a three-minute mind?" Moth asked cheekily. "A thimble doesn't hold a deeper drink when you fill it from the sea."

"You're as quick as an eel," Armado remarked. "Now here's a secret. The minute I saw Jaquenetta, I fell in love with her, even though she's only a village girl. Look! Here she comes with Dull!"

As Jaquenetta passed, Armado whispered to her, "Wherever you are, I'll visit you... I love you!"

Jaquenetta was unimpressed. "So you say," she sniffed.

Armado was silenced by the snub, but undeterred. "I need pen and paper," he thought. "I can feel a rhyme coming on. Poetry, sonnets, the written word... I am whole volumes in love."

The Princess of France and her three companions, Rosaline, Maria and Katherine, were on their way to see the king. They wore their best clothes; their jewels glittered; their hair shone. They all looked entrancing. The princess had sent her advisor, Boyet, ahead, to sort out their accommodation, while they strolled down a flowery path through lush green fields towards the palace.

"I hear the king and his courtiers have vowed not to receive women at court. I wonder how this will work out," the princess said, sounding amused. "Do any of you know his courtiers?"

"I've met Lord Longaville," said Maria. "He's intelligent, nimble with a sword. Somewhat sarcastic, perhaps…"

"I once saw Lord Dumaine at a party," Katherine volunteered. "He was good-looking and good-natured."

"Lord Biron was at the same party," added Rosaline. "He's the wittiest man I've ever met."

"Are you all in love?" the princess teased. She spotted Boyet returning across the field. "So? Will the king let us stay in his palace?" she asked when he reached them.

Boyet shook his head. "He won't allow you any closer. He says you must camp in this field. But he's on his way to greet you."

Ferdinand and his lords were indeed approaching the princess and her ladies. They tramped across the field in their magnificent outfits: rich velvet, and gold brocade.

Ferdinand's voice rang out, "Welcome, fair princess, to the Court of Navarre."

"How can I be welcome? You are receiving me in a field," the princess retorted.

Ferdinand faltered, "You – you *shall* be made welcome."

"Then take me to the palace," said the princess.

"I can't. I made an oath," the king said feebly.

The princess raised her eyebrows, and Ferdinand blushed. He wasn't used to feeling humiliated by a beautiful woman. Normally he was the one who impressed everyone, but now, it seems, the princess was impressing *him*.

Rosaline was having the same effect on Biron. Biron was being his usual charming self, but his approach wasn't working. "Did I not dance with you in Brabant once?" he asked smoothly.

"Did *I* not dance with *you* in Brabant once?" Rosaline replied.

Biron flashed her a winning smile. "I know you did."

"Then why did you need to ask?" Rosaline asked sharply.

Biron, for once, was silenced, but somehow enthralled.

Dumaine, meanwhile, couldn't take his eyes off Katherine; Longaville was captivated by Maria; and Ferdinand was increasingly smitten by the princess.

"I will visit you tomorrow," said Ferdinand. "Fair princess, you may not come inside my gates, but you are lodged in my heart. I beg you to excuse me. Farewell."

He bowed; the other lords bowed, and they returned to the palace, leaving the ladies in the field.

"The king clearly adores you, Princess," said Boyet, as the servants began to set up tents for the royal party to camp in. "His eyes showed it, shining like crystals; his tongue stumbled as he tried to speak. He's yours if you want him."

Armado's infatuation for Jaquenetta was increasing by the hour. He'd written her a letter declaring his love, and had enlisted Costard to deliver it. Costard was in his custody, after all, and had to do what he was told. "You'll have a moment of freedom," Armado informed him. "And remuneration."

"What's remuneration?" asked Costard. He liked collecting new words. As a peasant, he'd never had any education.

Armado put three small brown coins in his hand.

"Ooh," crowed Costard. "Three farthings. If that's remuneration, it's a beautiful word."

He seized the letter and ran to the park, to the house where Jaquenetta was staying. On the way he met Biron.

"Costard!" exclaimed Biron. "How fortunate! Take this letter and deliver it to Rosaline, the princess's beautiful friend. I hear they're riding in the park this afternoon. Here's remuneration."

He put a shining gold coin in Costard's hand. Costard's eyes almost popped out of his head. "Remuneration," he gasped, "means not three farthings, but much, much more. I like it!"

Costard scampered off and found the ladies out riding. He delivered a letter to Rosaline, telling her it was from Biron, then raced away to deliver the other to Jaquenetta. Unfortunately, he had got the two letters mixed up.

"Wait," Rosaline called after him. "This isn't for me. It's addressed to someone named Jaquenetta!"

But Costard was long gone.

"I'll look at it anyway," Rosaline said, breaking the wax seal. She started to giggle as she read aloud: "You are fairer than fair, more beauteous than beauteous and truer than truth. Shall I command you to love me? I could. Shall I beg your love? I shall…" There was a whole lot more besides.

"What rubbish!" exclaimed Rosaline. "Who wrote it? Ah, he signs himself, 'I am yours, Armado.'"

"He's the strange Spaniard who's here as part of the king's three-year plan," said Boyet. "So he's in love with Jaquenetta, is he? And so she must be reading the letter meant for you. If she knows how to read. She's only a village maiden…"

Jaquenetta was no fool. She couldn't read, but she'd found a schoolmaster who read the letter to her. It was addressed to 'the snow-white hand of Lady Rosaline' and signed 'Biron', and its contents declared love for Rosaline. Unlike Armado's grandiose language, the words soared with poetry. "Though forsworn, to you I'll faithful prove," it promised.

"What a mess and a muddle," Jaquenetta declared, tucking the verses into her apron pocket.

Biron was wandering about in the park, wondering what Rosaline thought of his letter, when he saw Ferdinand coming

FERDINAND, ACT 4, SCENE 3

towards him. Not wanting to be discovered in his lovestruck mood, he quickly shinned up a tree to hide in its leafy branches.

"Ay me!" Ferdinand groaned.

Biron was surprised. These agonized words, plus the king's desperate expression, could only mean one thing: love! Who was he in love with? And what had happened to his vow to give up women?

Biron watched as Ferdinand unfolded a piece of paper. The king cleared his throat, and then read out a poem in praise of the princess. The poem finished with a love-struck couplet:

'Oh queen of queens! How much do you excel,
No thought can think, nor tongue of mortal tell.'

When Ferdinand looked up from reading, he saw someone else coming up the hill. "It's Longaville, with a piece of paper, looking very serious," he mused. "What's he up to? I'll hide and find out." And Ferdinand scrambled up another tree.

Longaville was clutching a love poem to Maria, but he had somehow managed to convince himself that he was not actually breaking his vow. He may have forsworn women, but he had not forsworn Maria the goddess.

Before he'd finished reading his poem, Dumaine strolled up, equally ripe with poetry. Longaville spotted him coming and clambered up yet another tree. Biron grinned from his own leafy bough: now there were three men hidden in three trees.

Dumaine's poem was just as telling as the others, comparing Katherine to a rose he was forbidden to pick:

'But, alas, my hand is sworn
Never to pluck you from your thorn'

Longaville jumped down from his tree in a rattle of twigs and torn leaves, and tapped Dumaine on the shoulder. "I'd be blushing if I'd been caught reciting love poetry like you!" he said accusingly.

Dumaine stared, but before he could answer, the king sprang down from his tree. "You should *both* be ashamed," he announced. "Not only have you both broken your oath; you've been spouting the most terrible poetry."

Dumaine and Longaville hung their heads in shame.

Unable to bear it any longer, Biron slid down his tree trunk too. "What a hypocrite!" he exclaimed. "You've been exposed as well!"

Ferdinand stared at him in horror.

With smug superiority, safe in the knowledge that none of them knew about the love letter he himself had written, Biron sneered, "I'd *never* sink as low as you!"

Unfortunately, at that very moment he was interrupted by Jaquenetta and Costard. "My lord, I've brought you this," said Costard, waving the very love letter Biron had written to Rosaline. "Jaquenetta got it by mistake. It contains *treason!*"

"Oh, really?" Ferdinand said. "Read it to me."

In a panic, Biron snatched the letter, tore it into tiny pieces and flung them away.

But Dumaine collected the scraps, examining the smitten words that covered them. "Biron!" he said, "This is your handwriting!"

It was time to draw the whole foolish thing to a close, Biron thought. They'd all found the oath impossible to keep. "Let us forget the silly oaths and go back to being ourselves," he suggested. "It's not natural to try to give up women. Anyway, being in love teaches us things that books never can. It sharpens our senses; it makes us better men."

"You're right," Ferdinand nodded, much relieved. "So now we've decided, let's go to the ladies. Straight away. We'll have a party. Revels, dances, masks and merry hours…"

Longaville and Dumaine agreed instantly. "We can give them

presents," suggested Longaville. "I'll give Maria a necklace."

"A pearl for Rosaline," murmured Biron.

"A diamond for the princess," smiled Ferdinand.

"And a fine pair of gloves for Katherine," said Dumaine. "That's all I can afford. Let's send a servant to their tents with the presents right away."

The ladies couldn't stop laughing as they unwrapped their gifts. Each one was accompanied by a lengthy verse, declaring fervent passion. "So much for these men swearing off love!" they giggled. "Now they're all in love with us."

"We should be careful with our mockery," said Rosaline. "Remember, Katherine, your sister died of love."

For a moment they were sobered by the thought. But then Boyet arrived with some news: "The king and his courtiers are coming to visit you this evening…"

The ladies burst into fits of giggles again.

"…in disguise," Boyet added. "They'll be dressed as Russians. They're bringing musicians. Armado and his page, Moth, are coming as well, and Costard. They'll be dressed as Africans."

"Then we'll disguise ourselves too," said the princess. "We'll wear masks so they can't see our faces and, to muddle them even more, Rosaline can wear my diamond. Katherine can have the necklace, Maria the gloves and I'll have Rosaline's pearl. Those noble lords deserve a taste of their own medicine."

That evening, the tent in the field rang with merriment. For the ladies, the little party was a great success: they didn't for a moment stop teasing the men, their words and wits as rapid as crossfire.

"It's like a great feast of language," said Moth, awestruck.

Costard was eager to keep up, with the longest word he knew. He'd kept it stored in his head for just such an opportunity. "I marvel that your master has not eaten you, as you aren't even as big as the word 'honorificabilitudinitatibus,'" he declared proudly to a confused-looking Moth.

Ferdinand clung to diamond-bedecked Rosaline, believing her to be the princess. "I want to dance…" Rosaline murmured, fluttering her eyelashes at him.

"Will you dance with me?"

"Dance? Certainly not. I change like the moon!"

"Not dance…?" Ferdinand was flummoxed.

Maria and Katherine, meanwhile, were tying up Dumaine and Longaville in verbal knots, and the princess was making eloquent Biron speechless.

At the end of the night the men left, puzzled and humbled.

"Let's carry on teasing them," Rosaline said. "When they come back, we'll tell them four silly Russians were here."

Sure enough, the men returned, their disguises removed. Rosaline's comments embarrassed them even more. "I have a confession," Ferdinand said, squirming. "We were those Russians."

"Then we must also confess," said the princess. "We disguised ourselves too."

The men were even more embarrassed to realize they had failed to recognize the ladies they had professed to love.

"I apologize," said Ferdinand, "for everything. Please, please accept my hospitality now. Come and stay at my palace, as though our foolish vow had never existed."

"I'm not sure I like men who are prepared to break their vows," said the princess archly. "We're perfectly happy in this field."

"Please, Rosaline," Biron begged. "I've been arrogant, stupid… I am a fool. I am yours — and all that I possess."

"A fool and all mine?" Rosaline teased.

But before they could go any further, a messenger galloped up. He leaped off his horse and bowed to the princess. "Madam, I'm sorry for the news I bring," he said, a look of real anguish on his face. "The King of France, your father… he is dead."

"Dead?" The princess's merriment fled in an instant. She turned to Ferdinand, her voice trembling. "We must leave at once," she said. "I apologize for our behaviour. I'm sorry, I can't think of anything else to say. A heavy heart does not have a nimble tongue."

"No matter," said the king, his eyes full of sympathy. "But is it too much to hope that, before you go, you could say whether you return our love?"

The princess hesitated. "We took it all just as a merry jest…"

"But we meant what we said," Biron protested. "I suppose plain, honest words are best in the end… I really love Rosaline…"

"Do not let the cloud of sorrow blur our sight," Ferdinand pleaded. "Say you love me too."

"Not yet," replied the princess, all gentleness. "There's too little time to make world-without-end promises now. Wait a year. If you still feel the same then, and if I do too, then I am yours."

"Agreed!" said Ferdinand beaming.

"What about me?" Biron asked Rosaline.

"You?" she wondered. "I think you should spend the next twelve months visiting the sick in hospital. You could do wonders with your wit to cheer up the poor wretches."

"I'll do it," Biron promised.

"What do you ask of me, Katherine?" asked Dumaine.

"And Maria, from me?" echoed Longaville.

"Wait a year," said Maria.

"Yes, we'll return then," Katherine nodded. "And we shall see."

Biron sighed. "So that's how our story ends. Our romance has no happy-ever-after. Jack did not get his Jill."

The king grinned ruefully. "Well… not for a year anyway."

Richard II

Richard believes God has chosen him to be king, but his subjects think he's letting the country fall into ruin. If they rise up against him, will they be going against God's plan?

Richard II

Richard has lost touch with reality. He believes he's invincible because he's been chosen by God to rule England.

"Not all the water in the rough rude sea Can wash the balm off an anointed king"

Aumerle

The Duke of York's son is King Richard's cousin and most loyal supporter. He defends the king, even when things go wrong.

The Bishop of Carlisle

The Bishop is honest and honourable. He also thinks God chose Richard to be king.

Bushy, Bagot & Green

The king's yes-men who disappear at the first sign of trouble.

Sir John of Gaunt

Henry Bolingbroke's father and King Richard's uncle. Thinks Richard has failed as a king. On his deathbed he finally speaks his mind.

The Duke of York

Another of Richard's uncles, and Aumerle's father. He reluctantly joins the rebels after losing faith in the king.

Henry Bolingbroke

Richard's cousin, who rebels when Richard steals his land. He's popular and gallant, but is that enough to defeat a king?

Northumberland & Henry Percy

The Duke of Northumberland and his son Percy support Bolingbroke, and are ready to challenge Richard.

KING RICHARD II SAT ON A GOLDEN THRONE, facing his many courtiers. They had assembled in the grandest room of his grandest palace. Lavish tapestries hung from the walls, proudly displaying the great victories of Richard's ancestors.

The king presented an impressive spectacle. His slender frame was draped in gleaming silk, embroidered with golden thread and edged with plush fur. As he held up a bejewelled hand to speak, the buzzing room fell silent.

"Call forward my cousin, Henry Bolingbroke, and the Duke of Norfolk," he commanded.

The crowd parted and two men approached the throne. They kneeled solemnly before their king.

"Stand up, Henry Bolingbroke," Richard said. "Explain why you have come here today."

"The Duke of Norfolk is a traitor!" Bolingbroke answered. "He murdered your loyal subject, the Duke of Gloucester."

"That is a serious charge," mused Richard. "What do you say to this, Norfolk?"

"Bolingbroke spreads nothing but lies and I am willing to prove it," Norfolk replied. He threw down his glove. "I challenge Henry Bolingbroke to a duel."

"On my honour, that's a challenge I will gladly accept," Bolingbroke shot back, stooping down to pick up the glove.

Richard asked the two men to reconsider, but they would not listen. Tired of listening to their quarrel, the king decided to act. "Wrath-kindled gentlemen, be ruled by me!" he shouted. "You leave me with no choice. I will arrange a duel. There will be a fight to the death! Let the Heavens decide which of you is a traitor."

As Bolingbroke's father, Sir John of Gaunt, watched the two men being led away, his eyes narrowed. Sir John was certain that Norfolk had murdered Gloucester, most likely at the king's bidding. Richard's lavish ways had left him desperately short of money. Perhaps he was resorting to murderous methods to replenish his coffers. However, Sir John would never presume to question the king. A king was given his position by God. He was anointed by Heaven. If Richard had caused Gloucester's death, then it was up to Heaven, not him, to avenge it.

On the day of the duel, a long procession of knights entered a grand arena. Flags flew and drums rolled. Norfolk and Bolingbroke strode in carrying shields emblazoned with their coats of arms.

The crowd roared. The two knights faced each other. All that remained was for Richard to give the signal.

Suddenly, a trumpet sounded. This was not usual. A servant stood up and announced, "His Majesty has cancelled the duel."

The disappointed crowd groaned.

"I cannot bear to see bloodshed on English soil," Richard declared. "But I will not tolerate this quarrel either. I am sending you both into exile. You must leave England today."

Norfolk and Bolingbroke waited for the king to address each of them in turn. "Norfolk," said the king, "you are never to come back again, on pain of death."

Norfolk kissed the king's ring and turned sadly to walk away.

"Bolingbroke," said the king, "you are banished for just six years. Your sentence is gentler because of my love for your father, my uncle and loyal advisor, Sir John of Gaunt."

Although Bolingbroke accepted the king's judgment, his heart wrenched at having to leave his father. Sir John was old and frail. They wept as they parted, wondering if they were embracing for the last time.

Some weeks later, Richard sat in his private chambers, consulting his closest advisors, Bushy, Bagot and Green. Behind closed doors, the king did not attempt to conceal his delight at Bolingbroke's exile. "I am not sorry he's gone," Richard gloated. "He was becoming too popular and too dangerous."

"How can he be dangerous when he wastes his time being kind to commoners?" Bushy sneered.

"He would smile at poor craftsmen and even raise his cap to oyster sellers in the street!" scoffed Bagot.

"But some say my people love him more than they love me," Richard said thoughtfully.

"Bolingbroke is gone, and with him go these thoughts," said Green, changing the subject. "Now we must discuss the Irish rebellion. Suppressing it will come at large cost to the royal purse."

"How troublesome," the king groaned, twirling his heavy ruby necklace. "We will have to raise some more taxes – it's the only way we will be able to pay the soldiers."

As he said this, his loyal cousin, Aumerle, rushed in. "I come with news from Sir John of Gaunt!" he cried. "The old man is dying. His final wish is for an audience with you."

"I will grant Sir John his request," Richard said. "Perhaps this is a blessing in disguise. When he dies, I could use his money to pay for this Irish war…"

In a dark palace, on the other side of London, Sir John of Gaunt lay on his deathbed. The Duke of York watched over him, holding his frail hand. They looked wistfully out of the window. Outside, the houses had fallen into decay. The dirty roads were cluttered with waste and debris. Beyond them, the fields lay barren.

"This country is nearly bankrupt and it is the king who is to blame," Sir John sighed. "I must talk to him."

"He is young and reckless," said York. "He won't listen.

I wouldn't waste your breath."

"But this is too important!" cried Sir John. He seized York's arm, and leaned forwards, his eyes burning brightly in his pale face. "Richard has to change. For the sake of this blessed country, this precious stone set in the silver sea, this earth, this realm, this England…" he broke off, coughing.

Before York could answer, the king marched in, surrounded by his advisors. "How are you, Sir John?" Richard asked.

"I am dying, as well you know," replied Sir John. "But God knows, you're suffering from a worse sickness than me. The whole world can see your reputation lies in ruins, just like our once-great country. You behave as if you are a landlord of England, not her royal king."

Richard bristled with indignation. "Be careful what you say," he snapped. "You may be close to death, but one word from me can bring you much closer." He stormed out of the room and paced angrily up and down outside. How dare anyone speak to their king like that?

Shortly after, York came to see Richard with his cap in his hand. He looked pale and drawn. "Sir John of Gaunt has died," he said softly. For a while, the only sound came from the crackling fire.

Richard broke the silence. "His time is spent," he said coldly. "So much for that. Now he's gone, I'll claim his property."

York's mouth gaped in disbelief.

"Take his gold and silver for now," the king ordered his men, "We will return for the rest."

Richard noticed York's expression. "Noble York, whatever is the matter?" he asked.

"Your Majesty, these valuables belong to Bolingbroke now.

He's Sir John's son."

"Bolingbroke's in exile," Richard retorted. "These things are mine to take."

"Forgive me, but it is only by the laws of inheritance that you yourself are king," York warned. "It would be dangerous to ignore Bolingbroke's lawful right to *his* inheritance… if you do this, you will bring a thousand dangers upon yourself and lose a thousand well-disposed hearts—"

"I do not have time to discuss it," Richard interrupted. "I must go to Ireland to fight the rebels. However, my dear, loyal uncle," he continued, "in my absence, I would like you to act as my deputy. Perhaps this honour will bring some cheer to your heavy heart?"

York could find nothing to say, and so he watched as the king and his followers left, carrying heavy sacks full of Sir John's glittering possessions.

The king's actions caused rumblings of dissatisfaction around the country. One day soon afterwards, the Duke of Northumberland and his son, Henry Percy, were sitting in a tavern, mourning the death of their friend, Sir John of Gaunt.

"This is a sorry day indeed for Henry Bolingbroke" said Northumberland. "Not only has he lost his father, but it seems he's also lost any chance of inheriting his wealth."

Percy nodded. "I hear it was stolen by the king himself," he said in a low voice.

"The king's behaving like a common thief!" Northumberland agreed. "What's to stop him from doing the same to others? What if he were to steal your inheritance from you?"

"He must be stopped," said Percy. "But how?"

"I have some good news," Northumberland told him. "Bolingbroke is sailing to England at this very moment. He comes furnished with eight tall ships and three thousand men of war. We can help him right England's wrongs!"

The next day, Bolingbroke's ships arrived on the Yorkshire coast. Northumberland, Percy and their allies had gathered a crowd of supporters, who cheered as they docked. When Bolingbroke disembarked, he embraced Northumberland and thanked him for his support.

"My lord," said Northumberland. "England welcomes you with open arms, but we do not have a moment to lose. The Duke of York has learned of your return and he's not pleased…"

"Then we must march to Berkeley Castle immediately," Bolingbroke agreed. "It is vital that we make our case to him. He will see that we only wish to do what's right."

As Bolingbroke travelled from village to village, his forces grew stronger and stronger. The people were growing increasingly unhappy with their king, and in Richard's absence more and more of them joined the rebel camp. By the time Bolingbroke reached the Duke of York's home, Berkeley Castle, he seemed like an unstoppable force.

York, however, stood firm in his duty as Richard's deputy. The old duke was in a furious mood as he greeted them from the battlements. "You have no right to come here bearing arms," he told his nephew.

"My lord, I have only come to claim what's rightfully mine," Bolingbroke insisted.

York wavered. "I'm not so sure," he said uneasily. "As Englishmen, we are all duty-bound to support our king. But then, my power is weak and I am old. I have no choice but to step aside. I invite you and your men to dine in the castle."

Out on the wild Welsh coast, a hundred miles to the west of Berkeley Castle, a lone figure stood looking out to sea. The king's loyal cousin, Aumerle, was waiting anxiously for his return from Ireland. He had gathered the king's remaining forces and they were awaiting instruction.

An old army captain approached Aumerle cautiously. "What tidings have you of the king?" he asked. "We have been here for ten days without a word from him. The troops are growing restless. They are preparing to disperse."

"Please stay for one more day," urged Aumerle. "The king has put all his confidence in you."

"The men are saying the king is dead already," the old captain replied. "The bay trees in our country are all withered and the pale-faced moon looks red and bloody. These things foretell the death of kings… I'm sorry, but I cannot persuade the soldiers to stay in the face of such omens."

He and his army departed, leaving Aumerle standing on the cliff's edge, still waiting for a sign of the king's return.

Early the next morning, Richard's boat finally drew in to the Welsh shore. "Your Highness, Bolingbroke has gathered an almighty army against you," Aumerle told him as soon as he had stepped off the boat. "The situation is grave."

The king was unmoved. "Don't worry, dear cousin," he said haughtily. "All the water in the rough sea could never wash the royal balm from an anointed king. Mere men cannot depose a king like me. I'm a deputy elected by God himself."

"Not all the water in the rough rude sea
Can wash the balm from an anointed king"

"But Your Highness," Aumerle said hesitantly. "You have no men to support you."

"What about my loyal advisors, Bushy, Bagot and Green?" Richard asked.

"They have fled, my lord," Aumerle said. "Your army has done the same. Everyone thought you were dead."

"What about your father, the Duke of York?" he asked. "I left him as my deputy."

"I believe he has given in to Bolingbroke," Aumerle replied.

On hearing this, the king became deathly pale. "Then all is lost," Richard lamented. "I see no option but to go to Flint Castle and await my doom."

The news that Richard had returned from Ireland travelled quickly. When Bolingbroke heard the king had taken refuge in Flint Castle in North Wales, he rallied his army and set off for the Welsh coast.

Richard watched anxiously as the army approached. Dressed in his most regal gown, he climbed the castle's tallest tower to face them. As he reached the top, the evening sun streamed out from behind the clouds. The troops all gazed up. Their king stood there looking down, bathed in golden light.

"See," Bolingbroke cried. "King Richard himself appears, as does the blushing, discontented sun! It is almost as though he knows the clouds are coming to dim his glory..."

"He looks every bit a king," York remarked. "His eyes are as bright as an eagle's."

Northumberland approached the castle cautiously, looking up at the king. "Henry Bolingbroke wishes you no harm," he called. "He humbly requests to kiss your hand!"

"He does, does he?" Richard asked. "Well in that case, please ask him to join me up here in the castle."

Northumberland shook his head. "No, my lord. Bolingbroke is waiting for you to come down."

For a moment Richard held his head high. Then, under the gaze of all the watching soldiers, he descended. "Down, down I come!" he muttered.

When the king emerged from the bottom of the tower, Bolingbroke kneeled before him, and his army did the same. "I'd rather feel your love than watch your courtesy," the king told him.

"Gracious lord, I have only come to claim what's mine," Bolingbroke said.

"What's yours is yours, and I am yours too," Richard answered. "How can I argue with a man and his army? I suppose you would like me to give myself up?"

The Duke of York's eyes filled with tears. "Give me your hand," Richard told the old man, and he raised him to his feet. To Bolingbroke, he said, "I will give you what you want, and willingly too, for I must do what force would make me do. So, are we going to London?"

"Yes," said Bolingbroke, without hesitation.

"Then I must not say no." Richard nodded, and two guards led him away. In a single moment, he had gone from being a mighty king to a pitiful prisoner.

The country was in a state of unease. Richard was still the king in name, but Bolingbroke was in control. He had the love of the people and the respect of the noblemen. And yet, there were those who questioned his right to claim the throne.

"What subject can rule his king?" the Bishop of Carlisle protested, as the court assembled around Bolingbroke. "And who sits here that is not Richard's subject, Henry Bolingbroke included? If we force Richard to step down, so much English blood will spill, we'll use it to water our crops! Future ages will forever

RICHARD II, ACT 4, SCENE 1

regret this foul act."

Northumberland ordered the guards to arrest the bishop on the spot. When Carlisle had been taken away, all eyes turned back to Bolingbroke.

"Fetch Richard to this court," Bolingbroke said stonily, "so that he may surrender his crown to me in public. It's vital that we proceed without suspicion."

The court waited uneasily until Richard was escorted into the room, wearing a simple, white smock. Stripped of his finery, the king looked thin and frail. His eyes darted around before they finally rested on Bolingbroke. "Is this what you want?" Richard demanded, pointing to his crown. "Do you want to take this heavy weight from my head?"

He removed the crown from his head and held it out to Bolingbroke. But as Bolingbroke took hold of the crown, Richard did not let go. And so, for a moment, both men stood holding it.

Eventually Bolingbroke let his hands fall to his sides. "I thought you were willing to give me the crown," he said.

Richard stumbled forward, holding out the crown again. "I am willing now," he said, and tears began to roll down his cheeks. "With these tears, I wash away my royal balm," he said. "And with these hands, I give away my crown. Here. Take it."

"This isn't good enough," Northumberland whispered to Bolingbroke. "People will still say his hand was forced…"

Northumberland turned to Richard and produced a piece of paper. "My lord," he said, "will you read these words to make it known that you act of your own free will?"

"I'm not your lord," Richard snarled. "Nor any man's, now I'm no longer king. Without my title, I am lost. I have no idea who I am. I don't even know my name." He paused for a moment, staring blankly ahead of him. Then an idea took hold. "Bring me a mirror so that I may see my face!" he cried.

None of the servants moved. "Go and fetch a looking glass," Bolingbroke ordered.

A servant quickly disappeared and came back with a silver-framed mirror, which Richard peered into.

"Is this my careworn face?" Richard asked after a moment or two. "Where are the wrinkles? This glass flatters me. Just like my fair-weather friends in better times. I can't bear to look any more."

With a cry, Richard threw the glass to the floor. It smashed into tiny pieces. "See," he said, looking at his broken reflection in the scattered shards. "My sorrow has destroyed my face."

"You mean a reflection of your sorrow has destroyed a reflection of your face," Bolingbroke said softly.

Richard paused as he considered this. "You are right," he said. "My outward expressions of grief are nothing but a poor reflection of the torment and anguish that darken my innermost thoughts. I am in a sorry state, in need of help. Perhaps you might allow me to beg one favour from you?"

"Name it," said Bolingbroke. "And you shall have it."

"Give me leave to go," Richard begged.

"Where?" asked Bolingbroke.

"Wherever you would like," said Richard. "So long as it's away from here."

Bolingbroke nodded. He needed to get Richard as far away as possible. "Take this man to Pomfret Castle," he commanded.

As Richard was led away, Bolingbroke felt deeply disturbed. Even though Richard was being taken to the far north of England, he still had powerful supporters. The Bishop of Carlisle's earlier outburst confirmed Bolingbroke's worst suspicions. Some men would never accept him as their new king.

Bolingbroke was right to be worried. Only a few hours later, Aumerle visited the Bishop of Carlisle in his prison cell.

"It was a terrible sight," Aumerle sobbed. "Our once-great king was led away, weeping. They treated him like a vicious criminal."

Carlisle seethed with anger. "Richard may have had his faults, but he is God's chosen king. He needs our support."

Aumerle leaned forward. "Perhaps, my lord, other people feel the same way. We must hatch a plan to save Richard. All is not yet lost…"

Aumerle rallied the support he could. Back in London, he received a letter with good news: Richard's supporters were ready to fight back. Aumerle was so pleased, he didn't notice his father, York, approaching. "What have you got there?" York asked.

Aumerle tried to hide the letter, but York snatched it from him. His face fell as he read, and Aumerle flushed with shame. "Father," Aumerle pleaded. "I have only tried to do the right thing. But I know you disagree. I realize it was wrong to plot against Bolingbroke. Can you forgive me?"

But York was a man of principles. Treason was treason, even if it was committed by his own son. "It's not up to me," he said grimly. "I have no choice but to let the king know at once."

After his father left with the letter, Aumerle felt panic rising in his chest. He would have to beg the king for mercy. It was his only chance. He hurried to saddle his horse and chased after his father as fast as could.

Aumerle arrived at the palace first. He ran straight to the throne room. "Your grace!" he pleaded. "I need to speak with you! I have a terrible confession to make."

Bolingbroke sat down to listen, but before Aumerle had a chance to continue, York burst in. "My son is a traitor," he shouted. "He has been plotting to kill you!"

Bolingbroke leaped to his feet and drew his sword.

"My lord, you have no cause to fear me," Aumerle cried, dropping his own weapon to the ground. "I've come here to throw myself at your mercy!"

Bolingbroke slowly sheathed his sword. "I believe you," he replied. "And you shall have my forgiveness. But you must let me know who else is plotting against me. I'm in grave danger from these men. They will not stop as long as Richard lives."

After Aumerle and Bolingbroke left the room, a dark figure walked out of the shadows. It was Exton, the king's servant, and he had heard everything.

"The king said he will never be safe until Richard is killed," he thought, rubbing his hands. "Perhaps if I'm the one to kill him, I shall be rewarded. I will ride to Pomfret Castle immediately."

Exton made haste to fulfill his deadly mission. He rode through the night without stopping. When he burst into Richard's cell at Pomfret Castle, he was shocked to see how frail the old king had become. His face was drawn and gaunt. But, although he looked feeble, Richard sprang into action as soon as Exton drew his sword.

He wrestled a guard to the ground, seizing his blade from him, and the two men fought fiercely, the clash and clank of the weapons echoing off the stone walls. Richard's eyes shone once more as he defended himself and, soon enough, Exton found himself cornered. Wrong-footed, he dropped his sword. Richard swung at him with all his might, but missed. Exton didn't waste a second. He dropped to the ground to snatch back his weapon and leaped up again, sinking his blade into Richard's chest. Richard fell to ground and, with his dying breath, cursed his assassin's name.

For some time, an eerie silence hung over the cell. Staring at Richard's dead body, Exton was suddenly filled with doubt. He had committed a terrible crime. "I will never be thanked for this foul task," he shuddered.

Exton was right. When he returned to court with Richard's body, he was met with horror. "Exton, with your violent hand, you have stained the king's land with his blood. You've brought a curse upon this land," Bolingbroke declared. "Even though I wished Richard dead, I can never forgive you for murdering him. England will suffer the consequences of these actions for many years to come."

Bolingbroke stood over Richard's coffin, his heart heavy. Any good he could ever achieve as a king would forever be overshadowed by this terrible murder. He was starting his reign with blood on his hands…

He turned to look outside. On the horizon, storm clouds were gathering.

RICHARD II, Act 5, Scene 5

Much Ado About Nothing

One pair of lovers won't be parted, another pair
won't be united. But in this game of love
and hate, is anything as it seems?

Leonato

Governor of Messina, Hero's father and Beatrice's uncle.

Verges

Night watchman, who stumbles across a dark plan.

Dogberry

Constable in charge of the Watch. A bumbling fool.

Don John

Don Pedro's illegitimate brother. Jealous of his brother's power, he plots to undo the prince's matchmaking.

Conrad

Don John's friend.

Borachio & Margaret

Borachio is Don John's friend. He uses Margaret, Hero's servant, in a plan to sully Hero's reputation.

EONATO, THE GOVERNOR OF MESSINA, was strolling in his garden with his daughter, Hero, and his niece, Beatrice, when a messenger arrived with a letter. Leonato read it. "The war is over!" he reported happily. "The prince, Don Pedro, and his troops are returning. They'll be here any minute. We'll have a party this evening to celebrate."

He turned to the messenger. "It says here that Don Pedro has awarded a medal to one of his soldiers…"

"Yes, sir. To young Count Claudio. He looks like a lamb but he fought like a lion," the messenger replied.

Hero and Beatrice were listening intently. "Is Sir Cut-and-Thrust returning too?" Beatrice asked innocently.

The messenger was confused. "I don't know the name…"

"She means Benedick of Padua," Hero explained, laughing.

The messenger smiled. "Oh, then yes. He's as well as ever."

"There's a kind of merry war between him and my niece," Leonato said. "There's a skirmish of wits whenever they meet."

"Last time, four and a half of his wits went limping off, so he's only a halfwit now," Beatrice quipped. "Tell me: who's his new best friend? He changes them as often as his hat."

"He is often with Count Claudio," replied the messenger.

"God help Claudio then," Beatrice laughed. "Benedick's like a disease. If Claudio's caught a Benedick, it'll cost him a pretty penny before he's cured."

As they were speaking, a group of men strode into the garden. It was the prince, Don Pedro himself, along with his two best soldiers, Claudio and Benedick.

Leonato strode over to welcome his friend. "Welcome back.

Come, tell me all your news…" Leonato urged. The two friends walked away chatting, leaving the ladies and soldiers together.

Benedick bowed to Hero. "Lady Hero, you take after your father – well, except for his beard of course!" he joked.

Beatrice cast him a withering glance. "Are you still here?"

"My dear Lady Disdain," said Benedick with a grin. "Still alive and kicking yourself, I see."

"Indeed. How could Disdain possibly die when she has such sweet food as you provide?" Beatrice replied with an acid smile.

Benedick grimaced. "It's strange, most ladies love me, apart from you. Not that I love any back, mind you…"

"That will make women very happy," Beatrice retorted. "Oddly enough, I agree with you for once. I'd rather hear my dog bark at a crow than a man swear he loves me."

"Let's leave it there," said Benedick, who had seen the prince and Leonato coming back. "Although I wish my horse had the speed of your tongue."

Don Pedro and Leonato each offered an arm to the young ladies, and the four began to walk towards the house. Claudio and Benedick stood gazing after them.

"Did you see Leonato's daughter?" Claudio whispered. "She's the sweetest lady I ever laid eyes on."

"Really? I didn't notice," Benedick said carelessly. "Her cousin outstrips her in beauty as May outstrips December. Shame she's so furious all the time…" Then he looked at his friend's dreamy face and realized what was going on. "Hold on," he cried, "you aren't going to abandon me for a woman, are you?"

"I know I swore not to, but Hero…" Claudio mooned.

"I'd rather hear my dog bark at a crow
than a man swear he loves me."

BEATRICE
ACT 1, SCENE 1

Benedick elbowed him in the ribs. "Watch out. Here comes Don Pedro."

"What secrets are you two discussing?" the prince asked cheerfully as he joined them.

Claudio flushed bright red and Benedick said slyly. "I couldn't possibly tell – unless you *ordered* me to, of course."

Don Pedro chuckled. "Very well. As your prince, I demand you tell me what you were talking about."

"He's in love!" crowed Benedick, slinging his arm around Claudio's neck. "With Hero, Leonato's daughter!"

Don Pedro smiled at Claudio. "She's very worthy."

Claudio flushed. "You're just trying to get me to admit it."

Benedick rolled his eyes impatiently.

"You always were a denier of beauty," the prince scolded him.

Benedick shrugged. "I respect women – one gave birth to me and brought me up, after all… but I won't ever marry one."

Don Pedro gave him a knowing glance. "I'll see you pale with love before I die," he said.

"Pale with anger, sickness, or even hunger, but never with love," Benedick insisted. "If I ever end up like that, just shoot me."

"We'll see," Don Pedro laughed. "Anyway, Benedick, can you go and tell Leonato I'll be there in time for supper?"

Benedick bowed and went off up the garden to the house.

When they were alone, Don Pedro asked Claudio, "So is it true? Are you in love with Hero?"

Claudio answered earnestly. "When I met her before, we were on our way to war and, although I noticed her, my head was full of the battle we were about to fight. Now that's behind us, I find my mind full of her. She is so pretty. And… and…"

"Well, I'll speak to her and her father for you," Don Pedro said. He looked at Claudio's increasingly pink cheeks. "Wasn't that the reason you began this whole story?"

"Yes, I just… I wanted to tell you everything in case my declaration sounded too sudden to be genuine," Claudio said.

"No need," laughed Don Pedro. He looked at Claudio thoughtfully for a moment. The lad was so shy, would he ever be able to tell Hero he loved her? "I have an idea," he said. "There's to be a masked ball tonight. In disguise, I'll tell Hero I am you, and find out how she feels. I'll win her for you, then tell her father. By the end of the night she'll be yours!"

That evening, the grand house was filled with light and chatter as Leonato treated his guests to a grand dinner before the ball. But upstairs, in a quiet room, one man sat staring gloomily at his feet.

It was Don John, Don Pedro's half brother. Don John had been born out of wedlock. Because of this, he was not treated as the prince's equal. It was Don Pedro who would inherit everything; Don Pedro everyone looked up to; Don Pedro who had the power to grant or deny him a place at court. The very thought of it made Don John seethe with resentment.

His friend Conrad patted his shoulder. "Why so sad?" he asked. "Your brother seems to have taken a shine to you lately. But this new situation won't bear any fruit for you unless you're a little – well – sunnier…"

"I'd rather be a fungus in a hedge than a rose in his garden," Don John spat. "I refuse to sing in my cage."

They both turned as the door opened. It was only their friend Borachio, his face flushed with drink. "What a great supper!" he said. "There's talk of a marriage! It's Claudio…"

"Who does he want to marry?" demanded Don John.

"Leonato's daughter, Hero! I was in a side-room after dinner, when the prince and Claudio came in. I slipped behind a tapestry – you know – so I could listen. Your brother is going to win Hero on Claudio's behalf at tonight's ball!"

"That young upstart," muttered Don John. He hated Claudio. Claudio was his brother's right-hand man, his protégé, his shining glory – and that was enough for Don John to want to see him ruined. "If I can cross him in any way, I'll be happy. Will you help?"

Conrad and Borachio nodded.

Don John grinned coldly. "Then let's get ready for the ball…"

Before long, masked revellers filled the hall. There were feathered fans and rustling silk dresses. Every single person wore a mask – there were glittering masks with jewels and plumes, strange masks with long, crooked noses. It was difficult to know for sure who anyone was…

A masked gentleman asked Hero to dance. Her father watched as she took the gentleman's arm, and they followed the other pairs around the room. A little later they slipped away, deep in conversation.

Beatrice found herself paired with someone she suspected was Benedick. But when she asked, he just replied, "Who is this Mr. Benedick?"

"Oh, just the prince's dull jester," she responded archly, glancing at her partner's face as she twirled around. She swallowed a smile as he winced a little. "He's here somewhere, I'm sure. I wish he had shown himself," she added innocently.

"I'll pass the message on if I meet him," her partner replied.

"Do, do. I'm sure he'll fling an insult or two in my direction," Beatrice laughed. The pair in front of them danced away and, hand in hand, they followed suit.

On the edge of the crowd, watching the dancing, was a black-masked fellow, dour and cold even in fancy dress. It was Don John. His friend Borachio was pointing out a young man nearby. "That one's Claudio," he hissed in Don John's ear.

Don John began talking in a loud voice to Borachio. "Oh, yes, my brother adores Hero. In fact, he is asking for her hand in marriage this very minute." He turned to Claudio, "Excuse me, is your name Benedick?"

"Er – yes," Claudio lied, sounding crushed.

Don John smirked. "Tell my brother not to marry Hero, would you? She's beneath him."

"H—how do you know he loves her?" stammered Claudio.

"He told me himself," Don John said.

Claudio stumbled away, bursting out of the crowded hall into the garden. "So the prince is stealing her for himself," he thought miserably. "Friendship is loyal until it comes to love."

Benedick appeared at the door. "Claudio, is that you?" he asked urgently, pushing up his own mask.

"Yes," Claudio answered listlessly.

"I just heard the prince has won your Hero for himself," Benedick hissed. "Did you suspect he would do such a thing?"

"Leave me alone," Claudio groaned, and stormed away into the darkness of the garden.

"Poor thing," thought Benedick, staring after him. Then his thoughts turned to Beatrice. He was certain she had been his dancing partner – he'd know her sharp tongue anywhere. "The prince's jester am I?" he thought hotly. "She'll pay for that!"

"Excuse me," said a voice. He looked up to see Don Pedro, Hero and Leonato, all looking rather pleased with themselves. "Have you seen Claudio?" the prince asked.

Benedick narrowed his eyes. "He was here, until I told him of his schoolboy error."

"What schoolboy error was that?" asked Don Pedro.

"That of a boy who finds a bird's nest, and is so excited he shows a friend, who promptly *steals* it!" said Benedick.

Don Pedro glanced at Hero. "His friend didn't steal the nest," he said meaningfully. "He only wanted to teach the bird in it to sing, and then return it!"

"Ah!" said Benedick. So the prince hadn't betrayed his friend after all. He was most relieved to hear it.

Don Pedro said, "Anyway, Beatrice has a bone to pick with you. She heard you'd spoken badly of her."

"*I* have spoken badly of *her*! That woman!" Benedick spluttered with indignation. "Her words are like daggers. I wouldn't marry her if she was the queen of paradise!"

"Nobody asked you to," the prince remarked, amused. "Look here she comes now," he added, looking past Benedick down the garden. Sure enough Beatrice arrived, with Claudio in tow.

"Have you some urgent errand for me, say in the Antipodes?" Benedick hissed at the prince. "Do you need a toothpick from Asia...? Anything! Send me away from here!"

"No, I like your company," Don Pedro replied impishly. To Beatrice he said, "It seems you've lost Benedick's heart..."

Beatrice glared at Benedick. "Indeed," she said bitterly. "He lent it to me once, and I gave him double in return. But it seems he won mine from me with fake dice..."

There was an awkward silence, while everyone wondered what had happened between the two to make them so prickly with one another. Could they have been in love before?

Meanwhile, Hero was smiling shyly at Claudio, but Claudio was still looking bereft.

The prince put his hand on Claudio's arm. "My friend, I have spoken with Hero and she has agreed to marry you."

"Yes, and we all agree it's a fine match," Leonato confirmed.

Claudio was speechless. He stared at Hero who was glowing with happiness.

Beatrice nudged him. "Speak, that's your cue."

"My silence shows my joy perfectly," said Claudio after a moment. "I feel more than I can possibly express..."

CLAUDIO, ACT 2, SCENE 1

He took Hero's hand, "Lady, as you are mine, I am yours. I give myself to you."

Beatrice looked just as delighted as Hero. "Well, go on, say something," she urged her cousin. "Or else just kiss him!"

"Goodness, you are cheery!" Don Pedro remarked.

"Ah yes, always on the carefree side, me," breezed Beatrice. "But look at me celebrating my cousin going off into the world, while I sit here and sing for a husband."

"I'll find you one," Don Pedro volunteered.

"He'd have to be as decent as you, my lord," Beatrice said.

"Will you have me, my lady?" asked Don Pedro.

"Only if I can have another for normal days. You're too pricey to wear every day," Beatrice joked. Then she bit her lip and looked at him guiltily. Had she gone too far? "Please pardon me, I was born to speak all mirth and no matter."

But Don Pedro didn't mind in the least. "If you were silent I'd be more offended," he said. "Being merry suits you best."

With a grin, Beatrice excused herself and went back into the ballroom to join the next dance.

"What a pleasant lady," Don Pedro remarked.

"Yes," Leonato agreed fondly. "Always laughing."

"But she won't hear of a husband?" the prince asked.

"No," Leonato said. "She mocks all who approach her."

"She sounds a good match for Benedick…" Don Pedro said thoughtfully. Meanwhile, Claudio was whispering sweet nothings with Hero.

"So when are you getting married?" Don Pedro asked.

"As soon as we can!" Claudio replied.

"I'll need a week to arrange everything," Leonato said.

"The time will fly by with what I have in mind," said the prince. "I am planning on bringing Beatrice and Benedick together…" Everyone looked shocked. "…A Herculean task perhaps. Will you help me?"

Claudio and Leonato nodded, and Hero said, "I'll help too. My cousin deserves a good husband."

"He is a good man," Don Pedro assured her. "He is noble, valiant and honest. I'll show you how to get your cousin to fall for him and we will do the same to Benedick. If it works, we'll put Cupid out of a job. Come and I'll tell you how we'll do it…"

The following day, Benedick was strolling in the garden, alone, thinking about Claudio. "It's so strange that one moment he's laughing at what fools people become when they fall in love, and the next moment he's one himself… Could that ever happen to me? I can't tell; I think not. Until I find everything I love in one woman, I'll never fall in love." He sighed.

Footsteps approached through the orchard. It was Don Pedro, Leonato and Claudio, coming to carry out their plan. Too muddled by his thoughts for company, Benedick dived into a flowery arbour to hide. Don Pedro winked at the others and began. "Did you say Beatrice was in love with Benedick?" he said, in a particularly loud voice.

"I didn't think she would ever fall in love," Claudio said.

"Especially not with Benedick," added Leonato.

There was a rustle nearby as Benedick fell over in shock. The three men swallowed their mirth and continued.

"Has she told him yet?" Don Pedro asked.

"No, and she swears she never will," Leonato replied.

"But she writes to him – twenty times a night – only to tear the letters up," said Leonato. "She's in torment, poor girl."

"We should let Benedick know," Don Pedro said firmly.

"Why? So he can make fun of her? No," answered Claudio.

"You're right. She is too good for that," Don Pedro said.

"And so sweet and clever…" continued Claudio.

"…in everything but falling for Benedick," added the prince.

"We'll just have to hope she gets over him," said Claudio.

"Yes, I agree. Benedick would never see how lucky he was to have her anyway," Don Pedro said.

"I think dinner will be ready. Let's go in," said Leonato, and the three walked off down the garden path, trying not to laugh.

Benedick was left behind, his head spinning. "Can it be true that Beatrice loves me? Everything they said about her was true: she is good, sweet, clever… and beautiful. And – oh – and I think I might just love her back." He paced to and fro, feeling more and more excited. "I'm sure everyone will make fun of me, having sworn never to fall in love, but what do I care? Things change…"

He emerged from the arbour, only to see Beatrice coming down the garden from the house. In a panic, he sprang back into hiding. "I wonder whether I will be able to tell she's in love with me…" he thought.

Beatrice stuck her head into his hiding place. "I've been sent – against my will – to fetch you for dinner," she said ungraciously.

"Beautiful Beatrice, thank you for going to all that trouble," Benedick replied with a pleasant smile.

Beatrice frowned. "If it had been any trouble, I wouldn't have done it," she snapped.

"So you were glad to come?" Benedick asked.

"About as glad as if I had a knife at my throat," Beatrice replied with a snort, and she flounced off back to the house.

Benedick followed, a ridiculously dreamy look on his face. "It's proof beyond doubt," he thought. "She obviously didn't want to ask me to dinner as she would rather be *alone* with me. I'd be a villain if I didn't love her…"

A day later, Hero and her two maids, Margaret and Ursula, were carrying out their part of the plan. Margaret had told Beatrice to hide in the arbour and listen because Hero and Ursula were talking about her. Burning with curiosity, she hastened to oblige.

Hero and Ursula walked up and down in the orchard nearby, talking loudly. "No, Ursula, if anyone let her know that Benedick loved her, she'd only mock him senseless," Hero was saying.

"Doesn't he deserve to be happy?" Ursula asked.

"Of course he does!" exclaimed Hero. "He is clever, noble, brave and handsome too. But my cousin thinks so highly of herself, I don't think she's capable of falling in love."

"That's true," agreed Ursula.

"I'd rather go back to Benedick and tell him to hide his feelings. Even if it consumes him, it would be better than death by Beatrice's sharp tongue," Hero said.

"She would be mad to refuse him, though," Ursula said.

"I know," Hero said sounding regretful. "Benedick is the best man in Italy, save for my Claudio of course…" With a wink to Ursula, she added. "Still, I've a wedding to prepare for. Come and see my dress."

The two ladies hurried off to the house, trying to hide their giggles, leaving Beatrice agog in the garden.

"My ears are on fire. Can this be true?" she wondered. "And am I really so awfully scornful and proud? I'd better mend my ways." Her cheeks flushed as she thought on. "But Benedick – I think I love you too! From now on I'll be so kind that you'll be able to confess your love, and… maybe we'll get married!" Hugging herself in excitement, Beatrice rushed back to the house.

Benedick was with Don Pedro, Claudio and Leonato in the library, being teased mercilessly. "You look pale," Leonato said. "Are you ill?"

"I do have a kind of an ache…" Benedick began awkwardly.

The prince sniffed. "Are you wearing cologne?"

"Has he shaved? Look, I think he might even have washed his face," Claudio chuckled. "Is he in love, do you think?"

"In love!" crowed Don Pedro.

"I need to speak to you, in PRIVATE," Benedick said, seizing Leonato's arm. Claudio and Don Pedro burst out laughing as Benedick dragged Leonato away to confess his love for Beatrice.

But their laughter was short-lived. There was a knock at the door and Don John appeared. His dour expression was enough to sap anyone's levity.

The news that Claudio and Hero's wedding plans were going ahead despite his attempts had enraged him. He and his friends had been racking their brains to find a way to stop the marriage ever since. Borachio had come up with a cunning and evil plan, and so here came Don John, to set that plan in motion.

"Good day, dear brother," he said to the prince. "May I speak to you both? It concerns Claudio… He may think twice about his marriage when I tell you this…"

"Tell us what?" Claudio asked.

"The lady – she is disloyal," Don Pedro said solemnly.

Claudio was stunned. "Who? My Hero?" he said in disbelief.

"Yes, your Hero, well, anyone's Hero it seems… disloyal is a generous way of putting it…" Don John said.

"It can't be true!" Claudio choked.

"No, I won't believe it either," said Don Pedro.

"I know you might not want to believe it – especially coming from me… so come with me tonight, and see for yourselves." Don John said.

Later that night, the three men gathered beneath Hero's window and saw something which led them to a terrible conclusion. Borachio had persuaded Hero's maid, Margaret, to play a game and, being rather besotted with him, she had agreed. She was to put on her mistress's dress and pretend to be Hero for him. "Oh, Hero, kiss me," he moaned, leading her to the window where he knew they would be seen. "Oh, darling, I will," Margaret giggled, playing along. She didn't realize anyone was watching their silly game. Silhouetted in the light from the window, the pair kissed passionately.

The men below drew the conclusion they were meant to and silently left the garden.

Gradually all the lights went out in the grand house. Inside, Claudio lay awake in bed, sick to his heart. Don John fell asleep with a smile on his face. And Hero was dreaming innocently of her new life as sweet Claudio's wife.

As for Borachio, he invited Conrad out on the town with a generous sum of money he'd earned from Don John for his little trick. They marauded around, drinking in every tavern and laughing about how well the plan had worked, until behind them a voice bellowed, "In the prince's name, stop right there!" They were dragged off to the constable's office for questioning by the night watchmen who had overheard their talk.

The following morning, everyone was gathered in the gardens for the wedding of Claudio and Hero. Friar Francis stood at the front of the congregation with a sparkling Hero and a drawn, troubled-looking Claudio.

The friar began. "Do you, Claudio, come here to marry this lady?"

"No," said Claudio.

The congregation tittered, thinking it was a nervous mistake.

"Correctly speaking, you are marrying them, Friar. He is here to be married to Hero," Leonato said.

"Lady, do you come here to be married to the count?" the friar continued.

"I do," Hero confirmed.

Claudio turned to Leonato and demanded, "Do you give me your one, good and pure daughter?"

"As freely as God gave her to me," Leonato smiled.

"Take her back; she's a rotten orange. She's not what she seems. Her blushes are from guilt not modesty!" Claudio cried.

Leonato gasped. "Whatever do you mean?"

"Let me ask your daughter one question, and let her answer truthfully," Claudio said. "Hero, who was the man you were with between twelve and one last night?"

"I was with no man," she whispered, horrified.

"Liar! I saw you with my own eyes!" Claudio raged.

"I saw it too," Don Pedro added sadly. "Leonato, I am sorry you must hear all of this. I was mistaken about the match…"

The whole congregation stared at poor Hero. Her blush faded, and she fainted into Beatrice's arms.

"Let us go," said Don John, quickly ushering his brother and Claudio away.

Benedick gently picked Hero up and carried her inside, followed by Beatrice, Leonato and the friar. He took her to her bedroom and laid her on the bed. She was as pale as wax. They all stood there looking at her in great bewilderment.

Then Hero's eyelids flickered and gradually began to open. "How are you feeling, Hero?" Beatrice said softly, taking her cousin's hand and stroking her hair off her forehead.

"Is she alive?" Leonato asked. "Oh the shame, the shame. It's as though she's fallen into a pit of ink, and the wide sea isn't enough to wash her clean. She may as well die. She's ruined. A prince called her unfaithful in front of everyone. If it's true… she may as well never wake up."

Leonato, Act 4, Scene 1

"Don't be too hasty," Beatrice said sharply. "We don't know what happened yet."

"I'd say the lady is innocent," said the friar.

"But she didn't deny what she was accused of," said Leonato.

Hero spoke up. "Father, if someone can prove that I was with a man at that time, you can disown me."

Leonato sat beside her, twisting his hands together. "I don't know. If they are lying about you to dishonour you, I shall have nothing more to do with them."

"Let me suggest something," the friar broke in gently. "The princes and the count left Hero for dead. Let Hero stay in her room and rest awhile to get over her shock. Let us put about the rumour that she is in fact dead. Instead of her slander being passed about, people will feel pity, so it will stop the damage to her reputation. If this count ever loved her, he may feel sorry for having so wronged her name. If Hero has indeed acted wrongly, she might then be protected from public condemnation, and allowed to live quietly, away from the public eye. But if there has been some foul play or deception, it may give us time to find it out."

Everyone agreed. Leonato left with the friar, while Beatrice settled Hero in her bed. Benedick waited outside until she finally emerged. "Have you been crying all this time?" he asked when he saw her tear-stained face.

She nodded sadly. "And I'll cry some more yet."

"For what it's worth, I believe your cousin has been wronged too," Benedick told her.

"If someone could right her again, I'd give them anything," Beatrice vowed.

"Beatrice, I could try. I love nothing in the world as much as you – isn't that strange?" Benedick said.

"I love you too – with so much of my heart that none is left to protest," Beatrice confessed.

"Ask me to do anything for you and I will," Benedick promised fervently.

"Kill Claudio!" Beatrice cried.

Benedick looked horrified. "Not for the wide world!"

"Oh, it's easier to declare love for me than fight my enemy, isn't it?" said Beatrice bitterly. She turned her back on him. "Goodbye, Benedick."

"Is Claudio your enemy?" Benedick asked after a moment.

"Someone who slandered, scorned and dishonoured my cousin, so openly and cruelly, and on her wedding day…" Beatrice raged. "Oh, I wish I were a man! I'd do it myself. I'd tear out his heart and eat it!"

"Then I'll do it. If you think Count Claudio has wronged Hero, I will challenge him," Benedick said. "Go back and comfort your cousin." He left, and Beatrice dried her eyes, and went back into Hero's room.

The rest of the house was in turmoil. Leonato, now convinced of his daughter's innocence, told Don Pedro and Claudio that his daughter had died. They were shaken by the news, and did not know how to answer him. Benedick stormed in and called Claudio a villain, and challenged him to a duel. In all the commotion, nobody noticed Don John quietly leaving the house…

Then there came a knock at the door, and two hapless men were shown in: a huffing constable named Dogberry and a night watchman named Verges. They brought with them Conrad and

Borachio, and were shown into the library where the others were gathered.

"What's all this. What have they done?" asked Don Pedro.

Dogberry counted their crimes off on his fingers: "They have made false reports, spoken untruths, slandered a lady and are, in short, lying knaves!"

None the wiser, the prince demanded Borachio enlighten him. Having heard of Hero's apparent death, Borachio was racked with guilt and fear. He confessed everything: the deception he'd enacted at Hero's window, the money Don John had given him for it, and Don John's whole plan to split up Claudio and Hero.

As he spoke, Claudio grew paler and paler. "Poor, sweet Hero," he murmured.

"Take the plaintiffs away," Leonato told the constable.

Claudio turned to Leonato. "I— I don't know how to beg your forgiveness," he stammered. "But name your revenge, and I will gladly accept it."

Leonato looked at the sorry young man. Claudio was inexperienced and impressionable, and he had certainly learned his lesson. Leonato believed he really did love Hero after all. A plan began to form in his mind, and he said, "Hero had a cousin, and she needs a husband. You shall marry her instead."

The following morning, a smaller wedding party gathered in the garden. The bride, veiled, stood by Beatrice's side; the groom looked subdued and sad.

Only Benedick and Beatrice looked truly merry. Benedick was so relieved not to have to challenge his best friend to a duel, and Beatrice was happy because she knew that all was to be well for her cousin. And both had admitted to themselves and each other that they were deeply, sparklingly, wonderfully in love.

Claudio said to the veiled lady, "Give me your hand before this holy friar, and I will be your husband."

The lady gave him her hand. Then she drew back her veil. "You already were – nearly – when you loved me before."

"Hero," gasped Claudio. Not believing his luck at a second chance, he took her other hand in his and could not say another word, apart from 'I do' when the friar married them.

"Beatrice," said Benedick. "Do you love me?"

Beatrice smiled. "No more than reason. Do you love me?"

"No more than reason," Benedick answered. "Then I suppose I'll marry you, but only out of pity."

Beatrice laughed. "I will marry you but only to save your life – they told me you were sick with love!"

"Peace!" Benedick cried. "But you and I are too clever to fall in love peacefully, aren't we? So I'll have to stop your mouth instead." And he kissed her.

Don Pedro smiled to see the two young couples being wed. But, when the ceremony was complete, he couldn't resist teasing his friend a little: "How does it feel, Benedick, the married man?"

"A college full of wit-crackers could not bring down my good mood!" Benedick told him blithely. "It's the only thing to do – don't be sad, Prince, get yourself a wife!"

A messenger arrived, with news that Don John had been caught and was being brought back to Messina under an armed guard. "Let's not think about him until tomorrow," Benedick told Don Pedro. "For now let's do nothing but dance."

There was music and merrymaking in the grand house that evening. This time, there wasn't a mask to be seen. Everyone knew who everyone else was. Two happy couples were very happily married, and all was well.

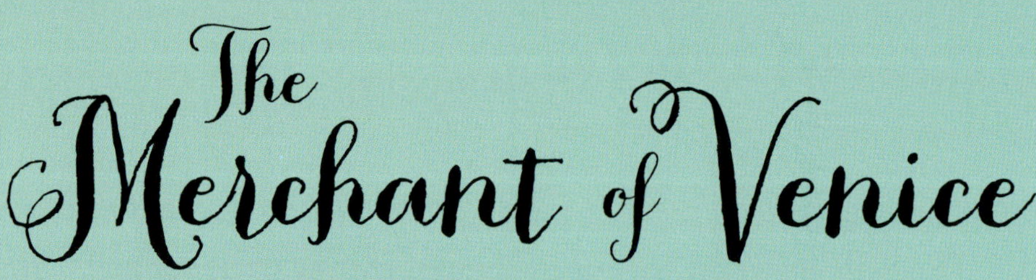

The Merchant of Venice

When a merchant borrows money from his enemy,
he agrees to an ominous contract: if he forfeits the loan,
he must pay with a pound of his own flesh. Will this
dreadful agreement lead to tragedy?

Bassanio

Rather a spendthrift, he needs
money to be able to ask Portia
to marry him. So he asks his
friend Antonio for a loan.

Portia

A rich, clever heiress with
lots of suitors. Her father
left three unopened
boxes with riddles when
he died. Only the man
who chooses the right
box may marry her.

Nerissa

Portia's maid,
confidante and friend.

Gratiano

Bassanio's friend,
who has his eye
on Nerissa.

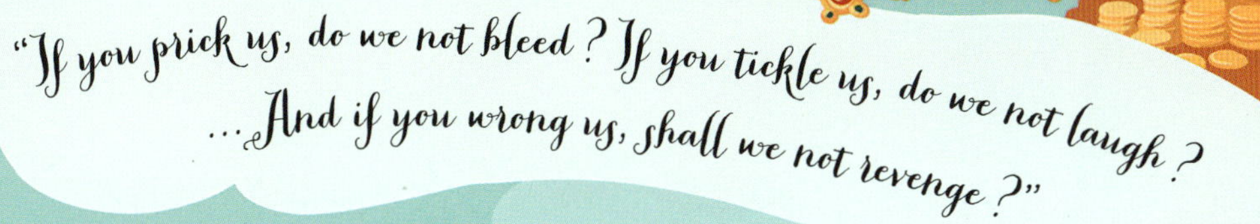

Antonio

A rich merchant whose ships are all at sea. He borrows money for Bassanio, and makes a terrible agreement with Shylock…

Shylock

Jewish moneylender. Insulted and oppressed by Christians, including Antonio, he takes a merciless view of revenge.

Tubal

Shylock's Jewish friend.

Jessica

Shylock's daughter. Fed up with her strict father, she falls in love with a Christian boy and runs away, taking her father's gold with her.

Lorenzo

Friend of Bassanio. A Christian boy in love with a Jewish girl, whose father would never agree to the match.

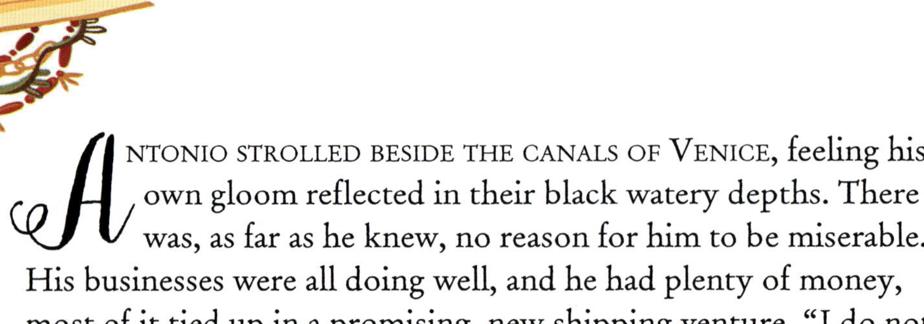

ANTONIO STROLLED BESIDE THE CANALS OF VENICE, feeling his own gloom reflected in their black watery depths. There was, as far as he knew, no reason for him to be miserable. His businesses were all doing well, and he had plenty of money, most of it tied up in a promising, new shipping venture. "I do not know why I am so sad. How wearisome…" he mused.

By chance, he met his friend Bassanio with his cousin, Gratiano. "You don't look well," Gratiano remarked.

Antonio sighed. "I feel, somehow, that the world's a stage where every man must play a part, and mine's a sad one…"

"Perhaps my problems will distract you," Bassanio smiled. He'd looked up to Antonio ever since they were schoolboys. He'd always given the best advice. "Listen, Antonio. I'm in love with a wonderful girl, who lives in Belmont. Beautiful, clever, rich… she's perfect. Her name is Portia. The problem is, I'm not her only suitor. Everyone would like to marry her. And I'm short of money. I've already borrowed rather a lot…"

"I've lent you rather a lot too," Antonio reminded him. "I had a hunch something was worrying you. Perhaps that's why I was feeling low."

"If I had more, she might consider me," Bassanio continued. "What can I do to help myself?"

He waited hopefully.

"I'd lend you more money if I could," Antonio said. "As you know, I've got plenty, in a manner of speaking. But it's all tied up in shipping, and I can't get hold of it." After a moment's consideration, he said, "Here's the answer, Bassanio. Try Shylock, the moneylender. My name is enough to guarantee any sum you want from him."

"Good idea," Bassanio replied. "If you really don't mind me relying on your name. All moneylenders are mean old moneybags. Let's go and relieve Shylock of a few of his ducats right now."

"You'd better go alone, just at first," advised Antonio. "Shylock and I are old enemies. I'll come along and join you a bit later."

So Bassanio went and called on Shylock, and asked Shylock to lend him three thousand ducats, to be repaid in three months.

"And Antonio is bound by this debt?" the moneylender said thoughtfully. "He has money to secure it. But it's not as straightforward as one might wish, is it? All Antonio's money is in his ships. Anything can happen to ships: pirates, disease, storms, shipwrecks… not very reliable. Ah, here comes the man himself."

"Good day, Shylock," said Antonio. "So you're going to lend Bassanio the money?"

Shylock's thoughts whirled around his head. "What is going on here? I know very well that Antonio hates me because I'm a Jew. He is a Christian; he hates all Jews. He lends money himself charging no interest, just to undercut us Jewish moneylenders, who must make a living from it…" The law at that time in Venice prevented Jews from earning a living in any other way. They had to live where they were told, wear what they were told and were not allowed to get jobs like other people. They were despised, for nothing but their religion. Antonio despised Shylock, and Shylock despised Antonio, and all Christians like him.

"I thought you never lent or borrowed with interest," he said to Antonio. "You don't believe in it."

"That's right. I don't," said Antonio.

Shylock answered, "I think of the Bible; how Jacob lent lambs to Laban, and the lambs turned into sheep, and became much more valuable… Earning interest is just like that."

"Look how the old devil quotes the Bible to his advantage," Antonio hissed to Bassanio. "An evil soul using holiness is just the same as a villain smiling to hide his misdeeds."

Shylock heard him plainly, as Antonio had intended, and the slur stung him. "You have insulted me about my moneylending before," he said. "You have called me misbeliever, cut-throat dog, and spat upon my Jewish cloak. But I have borne it all with a patient shrug – suffering is the badge of my tribe. Well then, it now appears you need my help. What should I say to you? Why should I lend you money?"

Antonio hardly took in Shylock's passionate outburst. He laughed, saying, "I'm quite likely to do all that again! Let's make this clear: if you lend the money, it won't be a bond between friends, but between enemies."

"I'd prefer to be friends. I'd like to have your respect. I'd be willing to forget the shame you've stained me with…"

"Very kind," Antonio drawled sarcastically.

"…so I'll lend the money and charge no interest."

"Unbelievable!" Antonio exclaimed. "What's got into you?"

"Instead of interest, I propose a forfeit," Shylock said. "If you don't pay the money back in three months, to the day, I'll take a pound of your flesh. Deal?"

Bassiano gasped, but Antonio just shrugged. "Deal," he agreed.

"Not on my behalf," cried Bassanio. "I'd rather be penniless!"

"Don't worry," Antonio assured him. "All my ships will have come in by that time. I'll have money flowing out of me."

To Shylock, he said, "It's a deal. I'll repay you within the time limit, and without interest. Very kind. Now hand over the money."

Portia, the unwitting cause of this odd moneylending deal, was sitting at her dressing table in her large, elegant house. Nerissa, her maid, was combing her hair.

"It's all so difficult," Portia confided. She always told Nerissa everything. "You wouldn't think that I, rich heiress of my dear dead father, could be stuck in this predicament, but I am! I'm totally trapped by the terms of his will."

"You're lucky to be weighed down by too much money," Nerissa chided her. She always spoke her mind to her mistress. "There are many who fret because they have too little."

"You're right," Portia sighed. "Yet I cannot choose my own husband. You must admit that's hard on me, for all my riches."

"Your father's idea was ingenious. And I have no doubt it will, in the end, lead to the right man winning your hand," Nerissa assured her.

"Perhaps." Portia wrinkled her nose. She wasn't so sure. Her father had left three sealed caskets, made of gold, silver and lead, when he died, with the firm instruction that any suitor to his daughter must choose the correct one to win her hand. Each casket bore an inscription on the outside, but only one contained her portrait.

"But so far, all the suitors are dire," Portia said. "I don't like any of them. Not the Neapolitan prince, who drones on about horses, nor the French lord, who hasn't an original thought in his head. As for the English baron: he's so badly educated, he doesn't know a word of Latin, French or Italian."

"What about the young German?" Nerissa asked her.

"Drunk. He's like a sponge. God help me if he chooses the right casket."

"But they've all told me they're going home. They don't like the casket idea. You're safe, Portia."

Portia just groaned. "I'll die an old maid, at this rate, if all men are put off by my father's will…"

"Maybe it's protecting you. Do you remember Bassanio, a scholar and a soldier, from Venice? He liked you…"

"And I him…" murmured Portia.

A servant knocked at her door.

"What is it?" called Nerissa.

"The Prince of Morocco is downstairs, Madam. He wants to choose one of the caskets… "

"Safe, did you say, Nerissa?" wailed Portia. "On the contrary, the ordeal is just beginning…"

Shylock's daughter, Jessica, was at home in Shylock's house, dreaming of her own wedding plans.

"I hate being my father's daughter," she thought. "Everyone here hates Jews; everyone hates *him*. I want to escape from it all; I can't bear being different. I want to be a Christian, like most of Venice, not an outsider. That way I'll be safe. And Lorenzo and I love each other. He's a Christian… and he wants to marry me. We can elope, and I can leave this house and my father and my religion… and all fear and anxiety… behind me."

"Jessica," Shylock called, interrupting her thoughts. "I have to go out tonight. I'm anxious about you, and about the house. I hear there's to be a carnival tonight, so there'll be lots of louts staggering about. Mind you lock the door, and don't stick your head out of the window."

"Of course, Father," trilled Jessica obediently. However, the minute he'd gone, she slipped upstairs, changed into boy's clothes, stuffed handfuls of her father's money into a bag, and waited, full of hope. The carnival meant confusion in the streets. If Lorenzo kept the promise he'd made, then he'd come for her tonight. Dressed as a boy, no one would recognize her.

Sure enough, as dusk fell, there came a furtive knock at the window. It was Lorenzo. His head, too, was full of dreams of their future life together. He was thinking how much he loved her — how, in their secret, whispered conversations, he had learned to

admire her beauty, her character and her courage in choosing
to change herself to be with him.

Moments later, they were slipping away together into the
milling crowds. Just like that, Jessica left her old life behind her
without a single pang of regret.

Meanwhile, in Belmont, Portia's suitors were trying for her
hand. First came the Prince of Morocco, with a grand procession
and trumpets blaring. He faced the three caskets and read the three
inscriptions on them.

The first, made of lead, read: 'He who chooses me must give
and hazard all he has.' The prince rubbed his beard, "Give what?
For lead? That one is not for me."

The second, made of silver, read: 'He who chooses me shall get
what he deserves.' He thought for a moment. "By birth I deserve
all I have and I deserve the lady too, do I not...?"

The third, made of gold, read: 'He who chooses me shall gain
what many men desire.' The prince smiled. "Well. All desire gold
and all desire the lady here. That much is clear."

With a nod to Portia, the prince opened the gold casket. His
face dropped when he saw what was inside. No picture of the lady,
only a silly rhyme that read:
'All that glistens is not gold;
Gilded tombs do worms unfold.
Fare you well, your suit is cold.'
Portia heaved a sigh of relief as she waved him goodbye.

Her second suitor to try was the Prince of Arragon. He sniffed
when he read the inscription on the leaden casket. He didn't like
risk – or the look of dull lead. He went for the bright silver casket.
"I deserve nothing but the best!" said he.

But when he opened it, he found a puppet's head to mock him.
"Is this what I deserve?" he said, with stiff dignity. Clearly he

thought the puppet beneath him. He left with his nose in the air.

Each suitor was sworn to secrecy before they opened the casket, so there was no chance of anyone else finding out the answers and cheating. Portia waited anxiously to see who else would come.

Back in Venice, Shylock had discovered that his daughter Jessica had run away, and taken all his money with her. He was beside himself with grief and rage. "My daughter! Oh my ducats! Oh my daughter!" he wailed, pacing the streets. He looked mad, and all the little boys in Venice followed him, giggling.

Poor Shylock was in a terrible state. Not only had his only daughter left home, but by all accounts, she had gone off with a Christian named Lorenzo. As far as Shylock was concerned, she'd betrayed him and the whole history of their people. "My own flesh and blood," he wept to his friend, Tubal. "No one knows where she is. I almost wish she were dead. No one understands…"

"The word is, she's spending your money like water," Tubal told him. "She seems to be having a fine old time. I heard she exchanged that turquoise ring of yours for a monkey."

Shylock clutched at his heart. "My dear, dead wife Leah gave me that ring when we first met," he said hoarsely. "I would not have exchanged it for a whole wilderness of monkeys."

"You're not the only one to have bad luck," said Tubal. "What about Antonio? I heard all his ships have been lost at sea. That means he's completely penniless. What are you going to do about the money he owes you?"

Shylock's grief turned to rage, and his brow darkened. Suddenly all the insults and degradation he had put up with from people like Antonio weighed down on him. He'd had enough. "I'll get my pound of flesh off him!" he muttered.

"Why? What's the good of that?" asked Tubal.

"If nothing else, it will feed my revenge," Shylock replied.

SHYLOCK, ACT 3, SCENE 1

All the hurt stored up in him over the years poured out in a torrent of words. "He has laughed at my losses, mocked my gains, scorned my nation; and what's his reason? I am a Jew. Has a Jew no eyes? Has a Jew no hands, or senses, or passions? Are we not fed with the same food and hurt with the same weapons as Christians? And subject to the same diseases, and healed by the same means as Christians? If you prick us, do we not bleed? If you tickle us, do we not laugh? If you poison us, do we not die? And if you wrong us, shall we not revenge?" If Christians could hate, so could Jews. Prejudice and hatred can consume a man, whatever religion he is.

Shylock glared at his horrified friend. "I will not let Antonio off," he declared, "for I know full well he would not hesitate to do the same by me."

Bassanio, who had not heard about Antonio's lost ships, was worried about losing the only chance he had of winning the love of his life. He was on his way from Venice to Belmont to see Portia. When he arrived, Portia was delighted to see him, and led him before the three caskets to choose.

"Be careful," she implored. "I could teach you how to pick the right one, but I'm not allowed to."

Bassanio bit his lip with nerves, and studied the three caskets before him. "Gold is gaudy. Not for me," he began. "Not silver either, for that's what goes round the shops as coins, and my love for you is above that."

He read the inscription on the lead casket. "He who chooses me must give and hazard all he has." He would give anything to marry Portia. He would risk everything for one chance at a happy life with her. "I'll go for the lead one. It doesn't seem to promise anything, and in that way, it's the most eloquent," he said.

He opened it. Inside was a portrait of Portia and a note which read simply:

'Turn to where your lady is,
And claim her with a loving kiss.'

Bassanio turned to Portia, who was waiting with her heart in her mouth. "Will you be my wife?" he asked. "I love you more than words can say, even though I have nothing to offer you."

"I always prayed it would be you," Portia answered earnestly. Suddenly, looking at Bassanio standing before her with nothing, she felt embarrassed by her wealth. She knew it put her outside the normal run of everyday life – did people see her for her money or for herself alone? And yet, for his sake, she would wish herself far, far better off. Her heart surged with love for him. To her, he deserved the world. "For myself alone I would not wish to be any better; yet for you I wish I were a thousand times more beautiful, ten thousand times more rich… Everything I have, this house, servants, money… shall be yours," she declared. "In proof of that, I give you this ring. Do not ever part with it, or that will be the end of our love."

Bassanio took the ring, beaming with joy, and slipped it onto his finger. "Thank you," he said.

Portia and Bassanio turned happily to Nerissa and Gratiano, and found them hand in hand. "What's all this?" Bassanio asked. Between them, Nerissa and Gratiano explained that, while Portia and Bassanio had been falling in love, they had developed a fondness for each other, too. "I've promised to marry him," Nerissa beamed. All four of them gazed at each other in delight.

Just then, a servant came in, bearing a letter addressed to Bassanio. When he opened it, the joy drained from his face and he turned deathly pale. "This is the worst possible news," he faltered. "I said I had nothing – well, now I have less than nothing. This letter is from Antonio. His ships are lost. The money owed to Shylock cannot be paid and the time is up. Now Shylock is demanding his forfeit: a pound of Antonio's flesh. There will be a trial in a court of law; Shylock against Antonio, with the Duke of Venice as the judge."

"I can give you enough money to pay this paltry debt twenty times over," Portia cried. "Don't worry, Bassanio. I'll think of some way around this."

While Bassanio and Gratiano rushed away from the house to be by Antonio's side, Portia ran upstairs, calling to Nerissa. "Quickly, find some men's clothing. I have a plan. A secret. Don't tell anyone. You and I are going to Venice, disguised as a lawyer and his clerk."

The trial was that very afternoon. The atmosphere was solemn in the court of law, heavy with the weight of bitterness and hostility. The Duke of Venice, dressed in heavy, red velvet, sat in a great carved chair, and in front of him stood Shylock, Antonio and Bassanio.

"Shylock," the duke began, "the world thinks, as do I, that you will give up this strange cruelty of yours at the last moment. You will forgive this poor merchant. Come now, we expect a gentle answer from you."

"You're not going to get one," said Shylock.

"That's not a good answer," said the duke.

"I am not obliged to please you with my answer," Shylock replied haughtily.

Bassanio thought he had the solution. With Portia's money, he could pay Shylock back with interest. "You are owed three thousand ducats. I have six thousand. You can have it all," he announced before the court.

SHYLOCK, ACT 4, SCENE 1

But Shylock shook his head. "No," he replied grimly. "The time is up. I will have the forfeit I was promised. Nothing else."

Poor Antonio gasped.

"No, don't worry, Antonio. Shylock can have my flesh, not yours," Bassanio told him.

Antonio shook his head. He felt as though his life was already lost, like his fortune at sea. He had given up all hope. All his fight was snuffed out like a cold, white, spent fire. He murmured, "…the weakest kind of fruit drops earliest to the ground; and so let me."

"How can you do this, Shylock?" Gratiano burst out.

"Why should I change my mind?" hissed Shylock. All the hatred he'd endured from Antonio had honed itself into this one, appalling moment. He took out his knife and sharpened it.

"Look at yourselves," he growled to everyone in the courtroom. "A lot of you are slave owners. Shall I say to you, 'Let your slaves be free? Let them marry your children, sleep on soft beds?' You will say, 'No! The slaves are ours. We bought them.' Likewise I say: 'I bought that pound of flesh. It cost me much. It is mine and I will have it.'"

Antonio looked as if he would faint away.

At this point, Nerissa, dressed as a lawyer's clerk, slipped into the courtroom. "May it please your honour," she said, bowing before the duke. "A lawyer has just arrived on behalf of Antonio. May he speak?"

Everyone looked around in surprise.

"Show him in," replied the duke.

A handsome young lawyer strode in confidently to take his place in the stand. "Are you Shylock?" he demanded.

"I am," said Shylock.

PORTIA, ACT 4, SCENE 1

"Are you Antonio?" the lawyer asked Antonio.

"Yes," Antonio replied.

"Do you agree that Shylock made a bond with you, that you are unable to fulfil, so you must pay with a pound of your flesh?"

"That is correct," said Antonio.

"Will you show mercy, Shylock?" asked the lawyer.

"Why should I?" Shylock sneered.

The smooth-cheeked lawyer's eyes blazed with sincerity. "Because mercy is the greatest virtue of all. It blesses both the giver and the receiver."

But Shylock was adamant. "I will have what the law demands. There'll be no mercy from me," he said.

"Can the debt not be paid?" asked the lawyer.

"I offered twice the sum, but he won't take it," said Bassanio. "Can't you make him?"

"No. There is no law that says he must," said the lawyer. "Antonio, take off your shirt. Prepare yourself for the knife. Have you anything to say?"

Antonio spoke up. "Do not grieve for me, Bassanio. Know I have always loved you. Commend me to your Portia."

The court fell silent. Horror filled the air and every breath was stilled with disbelief.

The lawyer pronounced his solemn words: "Shylock, a pound of that same merchant's flesh is yours: the court awards it, and the law gives it. *However*," the lawyer paused and everyone waited, hanging on his every word, "you are permitted to take no single drop of blood. The words of the bond state 'a pound of flesh' – no more, no less. And so if one, single drop of blood should fall when you cut that flesh, the law states that you will lose everything you own. Your lands and goods will belong not to you but to Venice."

"Is that the law?" stuttered Shylock. How could he hope to cut flesh without spilling blood?

"It is."

"Then I'll take the offer instead. Pay me the money and Antonio shall go free," Shylock declared.

But the young lawyer was inexorable. "No. That you have already refused. You cannot go back on your word. You must cut your pound of flesh. But be careful. If you cut more, even the tiniest bit, or less, even the difference in weight of one single hair, you will die, and all your goods will be confiscated."

Shylock hesitated.

"You do well to pause," continued the lawyer. "The law has yet another hold on you. If a Jew plans to kill a Christian citizen, as you do, the victim receives half of all that Jew's possessions; and the other half goes to the state. I suggest you get down on your knees, and throw yourself on the mercy of the duke."

"He will be hung! He will die!" Gratiano crowed.

"No," said the duke. "I will show mercy, Shylock, though you did not. I will pardon your life, but you will lose all you possess. Half to Antonio; half to Venice."

"I'd rather die," said Shylock hoarsely. "For I've lost my life anyway. Take my life. Do not pardon that. If you take everything that sustains my life then you take my life anyway."

"What mercy can you show him, Antonio?" asked the young lawyer quietly.

"I would like the duke to agree to set aside the fine for half his property," Antonio replied. "The other half I'll take on trust, to give to Jessica and Lorenzo. Two more things: firstly, we'll make Shylock sign a deed to leave all his property to them when he dies. Secondly, we'll force him to become a Christian."

The duke nodded his assent. "Do you agree, Shylock?" he

asked. "If not, I'll cancel the pardon I gave you, and you must die."

Shylock was a broken man. "I agree," he said. His dreams of revenge were over. Antonio had won, and he was disgraced. The hatred of his religion would continue. His own hatred of Antonio had ended in failure. He'd lost everything: his daughter, his dignity, his riches, and now his religion too.

The jeering triumph of the courthouse was unbearable to him and all he wanted was to slink away to nurse his shame in private. He muttered piteously: "Let me go from here. I do not feel well. Send the deed after me, and I will sign it."

The duke nodded and Shylock shuffled out of the courtroom.

The duke smiled at the young lawyer, well satisfied. "Antonio and Bassanio, you should thank this young man," he said. "You owe him a lot."

"Indeed," agreed Bassanio. "Let me pay you the three thousand ducats that Antonio owed to Shylock," he said to the lawyer.

"You have my love and gratitude for evermore," Antonio added.

The lawyer shook his head and laughed – a tinkling, pretty, noticeably unmanly laugh. "I did not do this for payment," he said. "Perhaps a token of your gratitude would not go amiss, though. Give me the ring you are wearing and that will do for payment and gratitude together."

Bassanio was horrified. The young lawyer was pointing to the ring Portia had given him – the ring which she had told him never to part with, or else their love would be over.

"I— I can't," he stammered. "Anyway, it's a mere trifle. Not valuable. I'll buy you the most valuable ring in Venice instead."

"Just let him have the ring," said Antonio. "Portia will understand. And let us both go now to Belmont, to Portia; we'll take Gratiano too; I know he wants to see Nerissa."

Reluctantly, Bassanio handed over the ring.

PORTIA, ACT 5, SCENE 1

They parted ways with the young lawyer and travelled to Portia's house. As they reached it, music floated out of her open door, and her windows glowed with warm, yellow candlelight.

Portia loved light. She always had the hall candle, a tall one, burning in welcome. It was like a symbol to her of goodness overcoming the dark. "It shines like a good deed in this wicked world," she would often say.

Seeing the light flicker in the window panes, Bassanio was filled with longing to see her again and to introduce her to Antonio. Running into the house, he fell into Portia's open arms and told her everything: how Antonio was free from his fearful forfeit, and how the debt he owed Shylock need never be paid. "We had an incredible lawyer who dropped into the courtroom like a gift from Heaven," he explained.

"Astonishing," replied Portia, with a strange smile on her face.

"It really was," said Bassanio. "Unfortunately, he insisted that I give him the ring you had given me. I didn't want to, but…"

"You gave away my ring?" Portia looked furious. She put her hands on her hips and glared at him. "I gave my love a ring, and made him swear never to part with it; and here he stands!"

Bassanio buried his face in his hands, ashamed of himself as her tirade continued… "If you had known even half the worthiness of she who gave you the ring, or how honoured you were to have that ring, you would not have parted with it…"

"But I had little choice," Bassanio protested. "I owed that lawyer everything. My honour would not let ingratitude besmear it. Pardon this fault, my love, and by my soul I swear I will never again break an oath with you."

To his surprise, Portia smiled, and then burst out laughing. "I was that lawyer," she said, drawing the ring out of her pocket.

"Look. I have the ring here as proof."

"Were you indeed the lawyer, and I did not know you?" asked Bassanio, staring at her, trying to trace in her beautiful features the strong, steady countenance of the young lawyer. Now he admired her more than ever. She was lovely, brilliant and daring… he had to be the luckiest man in the world.

"I have a letter too, which was delivered just before you arrived," Portia said. She handed it to Antonio. "It's for you."

Antonio broke the seal of the letter, and read its contents. When he looked up, his face was shining with relief. "My ships have come safely in to port. I've not lost my fortune after all!"

That night, in the house in Belmont, there was much feasting, celebration and happiness. Antonio looked around himself contentedly. "Everything has ended happily," he said. "Bassanio and Portia are together. Lorenzo and Jessica will live happily ever after. And Gratiano… where is he? Ah! Gone to find Nerissa. That's everyone accounted for. All's well with the world."

But not everybody shared his contentment. Somewhere, in the shadows of their happiness, Shylock was grieving.

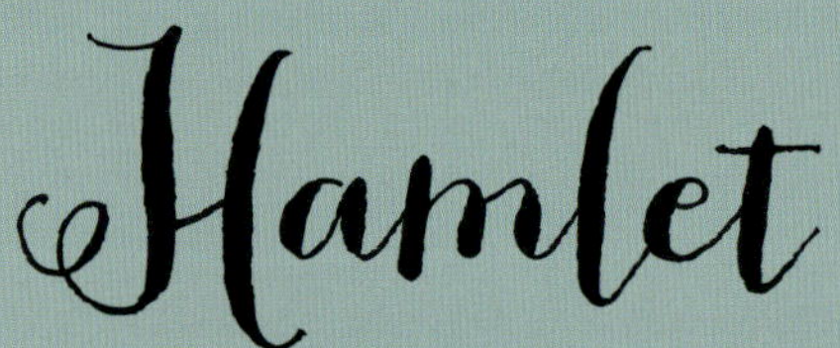

Hamlet

Danish Prince Hamlet's situation is dire. His father is dead, his mother has speedily remarried his uncle, and now a ghost of his father has appeared, demanding vengeance. The pressure is getting to him. What should he do?

King Claudius

Hamlet's power-hungry uncle. Did he murder Hamlet's father to take the throne?

Queen Gertrude

Hamlet's weak but caring mother. Worried about Hamlet's behaviour, but not sure what to do.

The Ghost

Looks like Hamlet's dead father and tells Hamlet he was murdered by Claudius. But is a ghost a trustworthy witness?

Hamlet

Sensitive, thoughtful student, prone to melancholy. Ponders the meaning of life – and death. Paralysed by intense feeling, he finds it difficult to act.

Polonius

Advisor to the king. Pompous, controlling father of Ophelia and Laertes.

Ophelia

Delicate young woman constrained by all the men around her. In love with Hamlet, she's heartbroken when he appears to reject her.

Laertes

Rash and eager to act, unlike Hamlet. Away for most of the story, but returns when trouble strikes his family.

Horatio

Fellow student of Hamlet, and his best and most loyal friend. Rational and reasonable, he is not sure he believes in ghosts.

Rosencrantz & Guildenstern

Childhood friends of Hamlet, and appointed by Claudius to keep a close eye on him.

On the misty battlements of a castle, two guards peered into the darkness. Footsteps approached, and their knuckles whitened on the grips of their spears – until at last a familiar figure emerged from the mist, wrapped in a warm cloak. It was a young man named Horatio.

Horatio greeted the guards. "Marcellus, Barnardo, I have come as you asked. Has the thing appeared again tonight?"

"There's nothing stirring yet," replied Barnardo.

"I know you think we imagined it," Marcellus added, "but now, if the apparition comes again, you'll see for yourself…"

"Hush, hush, it will not appear," Horatio said sensibly.

"Shhh! Look… here it comes," Marcellus hissed.

Along the battlements, drifting out of the mist, came a ghost. It was dressed in armour, with a crown on its head, a grizzled beard and a grimly frowning face.

"It looks like the dead king, Horatio!" whispered Barnardo.

"Very," Horatio breathed, harrowed with fear and wonder.

The ghost stopped and turned to face them. Horatio found his voice and spoke up. "What are you? In Heaven's name, speak!"

But the ghost merely drifted on, and was lost in the night.

Barnardo turned to Horatio, who was pale and trembling. "See? It is not just our imagination! What do you think now?" he urged.

Horatio weighed his words for a moment. "I would not have believed it, had I not seen it with my own eyes," he admitted at last.

A crowing cockerel broke the eerie silence, and they looked to the east, where a russet dawn was creeping into the sky. The night watch was over. "Let's tell Prince Hamlet what we have seen," Horatio said. "If the spirit speaks to anyone, I bet it will be him."

Later that morning, all the noblemen – including Hamlet – were in court, summoned by Claudius, the new King of Denmark. Hamlet's father, the previous king, had died very recently while Hamlet had been away studying in Wittenberg. He had been bitten by a snake while sleeping in the gardens, so the story went. But not long after, his mother had married Hamlet's uncle, Claudius, who had then been crowned king. All this disruption was causing unrest in nearby countries, let alone at home…

After dispatching messengers to calm the unrest, King Claudius turned to the next matter in hand. The son of his advisor, Polonius, was waiting to speak to him. "What would you like, Laertes?"

"Your leave, my lord," the young man replied, "to return to France. I came willingly to Denmark for your coronation. But now my duty's done, my thoughts turn back to France."

"If your father, Polonius, agrees, then go," Claudius nodded. Laertes bowed and took his leave, and the king turned to another young man sitting near him, his face turned away. It was Prince Hamlet. His face was pale and shadowed, and he was dressed all in black, in mourning for his dead father.

"Hamlet, my nephew, and now my son," the king said, raising a scowl from Hamlet, "how come the clouds still hang on you?"

"Yes, Hamlet, stop dwelling on your father's death," said the queen. "It's the way of things – everything that lives must die."

"Yes, Mother, it is the way of things," Hamlet agreed.

"Well then, why does it seem so particularly difficult for you?"

"Seems?" Hamlet's eyes flashed. "It IS. I don't know about 'seems'. My grief is not just my black cloak, or an expression on my face. I'm not just showing it – I feel it too."

"It's good and dutiful to mourn your father," said King Claudius smoothly. "But to carry on with it for so long is wrong. Leave your grief. Think of me as a father now: you are, after all, the successor to my throne. Your plan to go back to your studies at

Wittenberg is against my wishes. I ask you to remain here."

"Yes, Hamlet. Stay here with us," the queen echoed.

"I shall do my best to obey you, Mother," Hamlet bowed.

"That is a fair reply," said the king. "Madam, let us go." Standing, with the queen at his side, the king swept out of the room, followed by his advisors and courtiers, leaving Hamlet alone.

The young man, who had risen to his feet as they left, now sank back down with a cry of despair. "Oh, I wish I could dissolve into nothing. Oh, God, that it should come to this! Only two months dead: no, not even two…" He winced as he remembered how his mother used to dote on his father. "…And yet within a month, she married my uncle – wickedly quickly. It cannot come to any good: but though my heart breaks, I can do nothing but hold my tongue."

Horatio and the two guards found him there, with his head still in his hands. Hearing them, he looked up. A smile touched his sad face when he saw his friend Horatio. "What brings you from Wittenberg?" he asked.

"Your father's funeral," Horatio replied.

"Not my mother's wedding?" Hamlet joked bitterly.

"It did follow very soon afterwards," agreed Horatio.

Hamlet barked a laugh. "Thrift, Horatio! The food from the funeral was used up at the wedding feast." Then his expression clouded once more. "I would rather have met my worst enemy in Heaven than have seen that day, Horatio."

"He was a good king," Horatio said sadly.

"I shall not see his like again," Hamlet sighed.

"My lord…" Horatio hesitated. "I think I saw him last night."

"Saw who?"

"The king, your father," replied Horatio. Together with the guards, he told the prince all about the ghostly apparition.

Hamlet was agog. "I wish I had seen it," he cried, when they were finished. "I'll come and keep watch with you tonight;

perhaps it will come again. I'll meet you around midnight on the battlements. Until then."

That afternoon, down at the port, Laertes was saying goodbye to his sister, Ophelia. "Make sure I hear from you," he urged, taking her hands in his. "And about you and Hamlet…" His sister's eyes sparkled at the very mention of the name. "…I think you should treat his affections as no more than a trifle."

Ophelia's pretty face fell. "No more than that?" she breathed.

"No more," her brother said firmly. "Remember, his will is not his own. The whole state depends on his choice of wife. He would not be able to marry you despite his declarations of love."

"I will remember," Ophelia promised sadly.

Their father, Polonius, bustled in. "Still here, Laertes? Your ship is waiting! Before you go, let me give you some words of advice." He took a deep breath. Laertes and Ophelia, who knew their father well, exchanged amused glances as he launched into a lengthy list. "Listen to all but speak to few; take criticism but do not judge too quickly; be neither a borrower nor a lender. This above all: be true to your own self, and it follows, as night follows day, you cannot then be false to anyone."

"Goodbye, Father. Goodbye, Ophelia, and remember what I said." Laertes embraced them and ran down to his waiting ship.

"What was that about?" Polonius asked.

"Oh, just something about Hamlet," Ophelia said quietly.

"Ah yes," said Polonius. "He's been spending a lot of time with you lately. What is going on? Tell me the truth, now."

"This above all: to thine own self be true,
And it must follow, as the night the day,
Thou canst not then be false to any man."

POLONIUS, ACT 1, SCENE 3

"Lately, he has told me he loves me," Ophelia admitted, looking down as a blush rose in her cheeks.

"You are naive!" her father exclaimed. "Do you believe him?"

Ophelia faltered, "I— I do not know what to think."

"Then I'll tell you. You're a baby in such matters. You've taken tender words for truth. But they aren't real."

"But he vowed by Heaven he loved me!" Ophelia protested.

"Yes, but such vows are just traps to catch an unsuspecting bird. Do not believe his vows. They are not serious. From now on, I will not have you spend time with or talk to Prince Hamlet."

Ophelia looked crushed. "I will obey you, Father," she said.

That night on the battlements, four figures huddled, waiting, their breath making white clouds in the cold air. "What time is it?" Hamlet asked the others.

"Nearly twelve," Horatio said, and then he gasped, "Look, there it comes!"

The ghost had appeared. It was the image of Hamlet's dead father, with a grim, pale face and a grizzled beard. Slowly, it raised its hand and beckoned to Hamlet. The prince stepped forward.

"No, my lord – don't go," said Marcellus.

"What if it beckons you over a cliff, or draws you into madness?" Horatio warned, holding Hamlet back. Marcellus grabbed him too.

"Unhand me," Hamlet ordered. "My life's worth no more than a pin to me." Breaking free from their grasp, he followed the ghost.

"What can it mean? Where will this end?" Horatio fretted.

"Something is rotten in the state of Denmark," Marcellus said. "I think we should follow him." And so they did.

A little way along the battlements, away from the others, Hamlet had stopped. "Speak; I'll go no further," he told the ghost.

The ghost turned and, in a solemn, hollow voice, said, "Mark my words. I am your father's spirit. Hamlet, if you ever loved your dear father… revenge his foul and unnatural murder!"

"Heavens!" Hamlet cried.

"It is said that when I was sleeping in my orchard, a serpent came and stung me. But know this: the serpent that stung away your father's life now wears his crown."

"You mean my uncle!"

"Your uncle poured poison in my ear while I slept, and it curdled my blood. Avenge me. But do not harm your mother. Leave her for Heaven to deal with, and the thorns of conscience which prick and sting her. Adieu, Hamlet: remember me."

Fading, the ghost drifted away.

Horatio and the others rushed out of the dark and surrounded Hamlet. "My lord, my lord! What happened?"

Hamlet looked strangely giddy, his eyes two glittering stars in his pale face. "I can't tell you. Only, grant me one request: never make known what you have witnessed here tonight."

"Swear!" came a chilling voice from beneath them. They all jumped with fright. It was the ghost's voice.

"Swear it by my sword!" Hamlet cried. And they all swore.

"Oh, this is wondrous strange!" Horatio declared.

"There are more things in Heaven and Earth, Horatio, than we can even dream of!" Hamlet replied. "From now on, however strange or odd my behaviour, you are not to comment in any way that reveals you know something of its cause."

They all swore not to reveal a thing. The men trooped back inside, and Hamlet followed, his thoughts weighing on him heavily.

From that moment, Hamlet was much changed. He wandered around the castle corridors, one moment joking and laughing, the next frowning and muttering wild, whirling words. He stared into space, and jumped when he was spoken to. Sometimes he didn't even seem to recognize people. Polonius tried to talk to him, but Hamlet first called him a fishmonger, and then asked whether he had a daughter. Of course everyone knew Hamlet and Ophelia had been close… Rumours spread that the prince had lost his mind.

The king and queen were worried. Claudius summoned two of Hamlet's childhood friends, Rosencrantz and Guildenstern, and asked them to keep an eye on the prince. If they could, they were to find out what was troubling him.

When they found him, Hamlet gave his old friends a warm welcome. "Friends," he cried. "What brings you to this prison?"

Rosencrantz and Guildenstern exchanged glances. "Prison?"

"Denmark's a prison," Hamlet explained.

"Then the world's one too," replied Rosencrantz.

"Yes," Hamlet agreed blackly, "with many dungeons inside. Denmark being one of the worst. So what are you doing here?"

"Visiting you," said Rosencrantz.

"Thank you," said Hamlet. "Did you come of your own free will or were you sent for?"

One look at their faces told him the answer.

"I see," said Hamlet with a grimace. "Well, I'll tell you *why* you were sent for. I have of late – I do not know why – lost all joy in life. In fact, my heart is so heavy that this whole beautiful Earth seems to me like a barren rock; the heavenly sky like a foul cloud of smoke. And man – how angelic, how godlike – nothing but a pile of dust! Nothing delights me any more…"

He stopped, noticing Rosencrantz squirming. "What is it?"

"We met a theatre troupe along the way, and told them to come. We had hoped to cheer you up," Rosencrantz replied.

Hamlet gave him a bright, brittle smile. He had always loved theatre, and he asked about the group. They were still discussing them, when the actors themselves were shown in by Polonius.

"Welcome!" Hamlet cried, rushing to shake their hands. As he listened to their plan to perform a play at court that evening, an idea came to him. "Could you, if need be, learn an extra scene that I will write to put in the play?" he asked.

"Yes, my lord," said the lead actor.

Hamlet nodded. "I'll give it to you later."

The actors continued into the castle, and Hamlet took his leave.

Once alone, his seemingly cheery mood drifted away. "I must be a coward, or I'd have avenged my father's death by now," he thought bleakly. "Yet how can I act on a ghost's word alone? It might have been the Devil come to tempt me to do evil. But now I have a plan. I'll have these players do a scene that is like the murder of my father, right in front of my uncle. I'll watch him closely. If he so much as turns pale, I'll know what I have to do. The play's the thing. That's how I'll catch the conscience of the king."

When the king quizzed Rosencrantz and Guildenstern, they admitted that they hadn't found the cause of Hamlet's turbulent moods. But old Polonius was convinced he had the answer. A few days earlier, Ophelia had come to him quite shaken. She had told him Hamlet had burst into her room. Pale and trembling, he had seized her arm, stared at her face as if to fix it in his memory, then edged out of the room without saying a single word. "He is clearly mad with love," Polonius concluded to the king.

So Claudius decided to test out Polonius's theory. They told Ophelia to walk around reading a prayer book, until Hamlet should come by. Then she should return the love letters he'd given her. They would hide and watch his reaction. Reluctantly, Ophelia took the prayer book thrust into her hands, while her father and the king rushed off to hide.

When Hamlet came along, he was so lost in thought, that he did not notice Ophelia. Paler than ever and agitated, he ran his fingers through his hair, pacing up and down.

Hamlet was thinking grave thoughts indeed. He was thinking about suicide. "To be, or not to be, that is the question. Is it better to soldier on and suffer whatever fate brings, or fight against it, and end all your troubles? Oh, to die – to fall asleep, that's all it is. Perhaps to dream. Ah, there's the problem. For what kind of dreams come, after this life? The fear of what comes after makes us suffer the ills we have, rather than fly to those we know nothing of…"

He looked up, and saw Ophelia looking anxiously back at him.

"My lord," Ophelia said gently. "How are you?"

"Well, well, well, thank you," Hamlet said.

She held out the sheaf of letters. "I have some keepsakes which I want to give back. Please take them."

Hamlet stared at the letters, his face a blank. "I never gave you anything," he said starkly.

"My lord, you did, with such sweet words." Ophelia hesitated. She had believed the words he'd written. But now her father, and her brother had both told her that those words were meaningless, and so she held the letters out to Hamlet. "They have lost their charm. There, my lord."

"Ha!" Hamlet laughed bitterly. "I did love you once."

"You made me believe so," Ophelia said, her voice trembling.

"You should not have believed me," Hamlet snapped, his attack hiding his hurt. "I did not love you."

"Then I was mistaken," Ophelia said, her voice barely audible.

"Go live in a convent," Hamlet said, his voice rising. "Or else marry a fool; wise men know what monsters you make of them. Farewell." He rushed away, leaving Ophelia still holding the letters.

Ophelia broke down in tears. What was happening to Hamlet? He seemed so preoccupied, so desperate, so strange. She couldn't

"To be, or not to be, that is the question:
Whether 'tis nobler in the mind to suffer
The slings and arrows of outrageous fortune,
Or to take arms against a sea of troubles,
And by opposing end them?"

HAMLET, ACT 3, SCENE 1

bear to see it. "Help him, sweet Heaven! His mind is overthrown…"

The king and Polonius emerged from their hiding place, scarcely paying attention to poor Ophelia. "I do not think that was love," the king told Polonius. "It sounded more as if he's brooding on something, like an egg. I think to let it hatch would be dangerous." He rubbed his beard. "I will send him to England. Perhaps the journey will dispel whatever has settled in his heart."

That evening, the acting troupe was to perform a play for the whole court, including Hamlet's extra scene. "Don't overplay it. Don't underplay it either," he had told them nervously.

As he joined the gathering audience, he spotted Horatio. Horatio was a steady man. He took whatever came his way, good or bad, with equal cheer. That was why Hamlet needed him now. In this dangerous sea of emotion, Horatio could be his anchor.

Hamlet confided in his friend. "The play is going to contain a scene which shows something like my father's death," he told him. "When that scene comes, please watch my uncle closely. If his guilty conscience does not reveal itself, then the ghost we saw was just a devil, and my imagination is running away with me."

Horatio nodded. "I'll watch him," he promised.

With a flourish of lighted torches and trumpets, the king and queen entered the hall. They took their seats and the play began.

The actors played a king and queen who embraced lovingly. Then the king lay down and went to sleep, and the queen left him. In came another man, who took the king's crown and poured poison in his ear.

At that point, King Claudius sprang to his feet. "Lights, away!" he cried, and swept out of the room, hurriedly pursued by attendants carrying flaming torches. The queen followed with her servants, and soon the room was almost empty.

The play ground to a halt, the actors bewildered. "Play some music instead," Hamlet ordered them, rushing over to Horatio. "I'll take the ghost's word for it. Did you see?"

"I saw very well," his friend affirmed.

Before they could speak further, Rosencrantz and Guildenstern came rushing back to find Hamlet. "The king is in a temper," Guildenstern told him, "And your mother wants a word with you."

"I'll come, I'm on my way," said Hamlet.

His blood roared in his ears as he made his way along the dark shadowed corridors. Finally he had *proof*... Proof that his uncle had killed his father. Proof of the truth of the ghost's words. Proof that he must now take action. He could put it off no longer.

The king's door was ajar. Peering through, he saw the king inside. "I could do it now," he thought, gripping his sword. But as he watched, the king flung himself to his knees in prayer. "If I kill him while he's praying, his soul will fly straight to Heaven," thought Hamlet. "Better catch him while he's sinning, so he goes straight to Hell." So he hurried away to see his mother.

In fact, the king had not been praying. He had been trying to, but now he sat back on his heels and sighed. "I cannot," he thought. "My words fly up to Heaven, but my thoughts remain below. My crime is awful: a brother's murder... Yet I cannot repent while I still hold onto the gains from it – the queen and crown."

In her chamber, the queen twisted her hands as she waited for her son to appear. Polonius was there, advising her what to say. Hearing Hamlet's footsteps, he slipped behind a curtain. "I'll stay here and watch."

"Mother, what's the matter?" Hamlet said, striding in.

"Hamlet, you have offended your father," came the reply.

"Mother, *you* have offended my father," Hamlet retorted.

Queen Gertrude's lips trembled. "If you will not listen to me, I'll have someone else speak to you," she said, turning away.

Hamlet seized her and sat her down in front of her mirror. "You will not budge, until you've taken a good look at yourself."

The queen looked at his grim face in the mirror. "What are you doing?" she wailed. "Are you going to murder me?"

Polonius squealed behind the curtain and Hamlet swung around and thrust his sword into the velvet, crying, "What's that, a rat?" There was a thud as Polonius's body fell to the ground.

"What have you done?" screamed the queen.

"I don't know," Hamlet cried. "Is it the king?"

The queen drew back the curtain and they both stared in horror at the dead body. "What a rash, bloody deed," the queen gasped.

"Almost as rash and bloody as killing a king and marrying his brother," Hamlet spat.

His mother's face turned as pale as paper. "What? Killing a king?" she said.

"That's what I said," Hamlet replied. "Mother, sit down and let me wring out your heart… you've married a murderer."

"Don't!" cried the queen, sinking back down. "These words are like daggers!"

But then Hamlet stopped, swinging around to look behind him. "What do you want?" he cried hoarsely. "Have you come to chide me for not carrying out your command?"

Alarmed, Queen Gertrude turned too, but saw nothing.

"Hamlet you're talking to empty air!"

But Hamlet could see the ghost of his father. "Do not forget," the ghost said grimly. "Remember what you should do."

The ghost disappeared, and Hamlet turned back to his mother. She was staring at him askance, her trust slipping away once more. "Do not flatter yourself that it was my madness rather than your sin talking," he said desperately. "Repent your sins."

He left her there and, muttering to himself, dragged Polonius's body out of the door.

The king came in to find the queen weeping. She told him what Hamlet had done. "He's mad," she sobbed. "Mad…"

"We must ship him off, Gertrude," said the king. "It's not safe to keep him here, after this vile deed…" He called Rosencrantz and Guildenstern and asked them to fetch Hamlet.

"Where is Polonius?" he demanded when they brought him.

"At supper," Hamlet replied. "Being eaten by worms."

"Where is he?" insisted the king.

"If he's in Heaven, send a messenger to see. If he's in Hell, look for him yourself," Hamlet answered wildly. "But if you don't find him within the month, you'll smell him in the hallway."

The king sent people to fetch the body. "Hamlet, for this deed, you must go away. You must leave for England."

That very night, a quiet ship took Hamlet away from Denmark. Rosencrantz and Guildenstern accompanied him, carrying a sealed letter from Claudius, addressed to the King of England…

A few days later, another ship arrived. It brought Laertes, who had heard the news of his father's death. Bent on revenge, he burst in to see the king, demanding to know what had happened. "Why was he not charged with the crime?" he said furiously once the king confirmed Hamlet's guilt.

"His mother and the public dote on him," Claudius said. "But do not think I take it lightly. This matter is not at an end…"

At that moment, the door opened and in came Ophelia, her arms full of flowers. Singing distractedly, she went to her brother Laertes, but hardly seemed to see him. Her father's death had had a terrible impact on her. For the last few days she had been wandering around the castle, alternating between weeping and singing – like a sad, broken bird.

Laertes's heart wrenched as she started handing him flowers, one by one. "There's rosemary for remembrance, and pansies for thoughts. There's rue…" She stared sadly out of the window. "I would give you violets, but they all withered when my father died."

Laertes took her pale hand and touched her pale cheek.

But Ophelia pulled away, raising her sweet, heartbroken voice in song once more, and drifted out of the door.

As she left, a messenger arrived with a letter. "From Prince Hamlet, my lord."

"How can that be?" snapped the king. "Hamlet is on a ship to England…" He broke open the seal and read: "'High and mighty, I have come back to your kingdom. I beg leave to see you tomorrow to explain my sudden and strange return, Hamlet.'"

Claudius was alarmed and confused. "What can this mean?"

"Let him come," Laertes said grimly. "It warms my heart that I will be able to face him and say: 'This is how you shall die.'"

A gleam came into the king's eyes. "It would be better – for his mother's sake – if it looked like an accident…"

Laertes met his eyes. "I will put poison on the tip of my sword, so if it even scratches him he will die," he said vehemently.

"You can challenge him to a duel," said Claudius. "And I'll prepare a drink, a poisoned chalice. Your fight will make him thirsty. When he calls for a drink, I'll give it to him…"

There came a cry, and Queen Gertrude burst in. "Laertes! It's your sister – she is drowned!"

"No! How? Where?" Laertes cried.

"The workers in the fields saw her float downstream. Her skirts billowed out, buoying her up. But before they could reach her, the water seeped into the heavy fabric and dragged her down. She was found, under a willow in the stream, her arms still full of flowers…"

Preparations for poor Ophelia's funeral were set in motion, and the gravediggers began to dig her grave. Unaware of this, Horatio was on his way to the graveyard to meet Hamlet. He had received a letter from the prince too. It said Hamlet's ship had been attacked by pirates at sea. As his own ship fought them off, Hamlet had slipped aboard the pirate ship and sailed away with them. After the promise of a handsome reward, they had delivered him home. He wanted to meet Horatio in the graveyard.

Horatio found his friend staring at the skulls that a gravedigger was unearthing as he dug the fresh grave. "That one had a tongue in it and could sing once," Hamlet said mournfully.

"See this one? It was Yorick, the old king's jester," the gravedigger said, handing him another.

Hamlet took the skull sadly and stared at it. "Alas, poor Yorick! I knew him, Horatio. He always had a joke to tell… He must have carried me on his back a thousand times when I was little… Where are your jokes and songs and merriment now?" he said to the skull, and then set it gently back down.

"Alas, poor Yorick! I knew him, Horatio"

Hamlet, Act 5, Scene 1

"Who's this grave for?" he asked the gravedigger.

"A young woman who died," the gravedigger replied. "Here comes her coffin now."

Over the hill came a funeral procession. Laertes led the way along with the king and queen. Hamlet and Horatio retreated from the grave, hiding behind a cluster of trees to watch.

Laertes spoke, "Lay her in the earth, and from her fair and unpolluted flesh may violets spring!" As the attendants lowered the coffin into the grave, he leaped in after it with a loud cry.

"Ophelia?" Hamlet choked. Before Horatio could stop him, he raced out of the trees. "You think your grief would stop the stars! Well, here I am." He too leaped into the grave, crying, "I loved Ophelia! Forty thousand brothers' love could not equal mine!"

Laertes dived at him, raining blind, furious punches down on him. Hamlet held him off, saying, "I loved you too. Why are you treating me like this? But no matter." Pushing Laertes aside, he stumbled out of the grave and ran off into the trees.

"Be patient," the king told Laertes. "Remember the plan…"

Horatio followed Hamlet and, once Hamlet was calm, asked him to explain what had happened at sea. "I could not sleep," Hamlet told him. "So I slipped into Rosencrantz and Guildenstern's cabin. I found the letter to the English king, and I opened it, Horatio… inside was a command that my head should be chopped off as soon as I reached England!"

"Is it possible?" Horatio gasped.

Hamlet handed him the letter. "See for yourself. But there's more: I replaced the document with one of my own. Mine said that when Rosencrantz and Guildenstern delivered it, they should be executed on the spot. I sealed it with my father's ring. The next day, as you know, I escaped… Horatio, don't you think I should kill Claudius now? He's murdered my father, taken my mother *and* tried to have me killed?"

"He will soon hear of what's happened in England too! But wait a moment," said Horatio, "someone's coming."

It was a messenger, with a message that Laertes had challenged Hamlet to a duel…

The king and Laertes were waiting for them in the hall. Hamlet went straight to Laertes, "Please forgive me. I've done you wrong," he said. "In my madness, I have hurt my friend."

"I understand," Laertes said stiffly. "But I cannot let this go. I must still fence with you."

"Very well," said Hamlet. "Give us the swords."

Wine was brought in, which the king directed to the table. Swords were brought and the fencing began.

The two young men lunged and parried. "A hit!" cried Hamlet.

"A hit," the umpire confirmed.

Claudius took a sip from one of the goblets, and then slipped a pearl of poison into it. "Hamlet," he called. "Take a sip of wine. You must be thirsty."

"Let's finish this round first," Hamlet said, fighting on.

"Another hit," he cried again, moments later.

The queen entered the room to watch the duel. "Hamlet, I'll drink to your health," she called. Then she picked up the poisoned goblet of wine and put it to her lips…

"No!" cried the king. But it was too late. She had already drunk from the cup. He gritted his teeth and fell silent.

"Come on, Laertes. You're toying with me," Hamlet said.

Laertes lunged at him and there was a scuffle. They dropped their swords and Hamlet picked up Laertes's sword. "Another hit," he cried, nicking Laertes's arm. But Laertes had cut him first…

"They're both bleeding," Horatio called.

There was a cry and the queen collapsed. "She's fainted because of the sight of blood," Claudius said hastily.

"No, no!" came a faint cry from the queen. "The drink – oh, my dear Hamlet – the drink! I've been poisoned."

"Lock the doors!" cried Hamlet. "Find the traitor!"

Laertes fell to his knees, gasping, "I am a traitor. Hamlet, the sword, now in your hand, was poisoned. My foul plan has backfired and I'm about to die… You will die from it too… Your mother is poisoned… The king's to blame…" He collapsed onto the floor.

"This sword has poison on it?" Hamlet cried. "Then let it work on this!" He lunged at Claudius and plunged the sword into his side.

"Help!" Claudius cried.

But Hamlet took the poisoned cup, and forced it between his lips. "Here, you murderous Dane, drink your own potion."

Claudius gulped, choked, and fell to the ground, dead.

Hamlet sank back, gasping from his own poisoned wound, and Horatio rushed to catch him.

"Hamlet," Laertes whispered faintly, "exchange forgiveness with me now. My father's death was not your fault…"

Hamlet nodded. "And may Heaven free you of any guilt for mine!" he whispered. Poor Laertes lay his head down and died.

Hamlet turned back to his friend. "Horatio – I'm going to die… but you will live on."

Horatio sobbed, "No, I can't," and seized the chalice.

With the last of his strength, Hamlet wrested it from his grasp. "Horatio, if you ever held me in your heart, then live. Live in this harsh world, if only to tell my story. The rest is silence."

Horatio bent over his friend as Hamlet closed his eyes for the last time. "Now cracks a noble heart. Goodnight, sweet prince. May flights of angels sing you to your rest!"

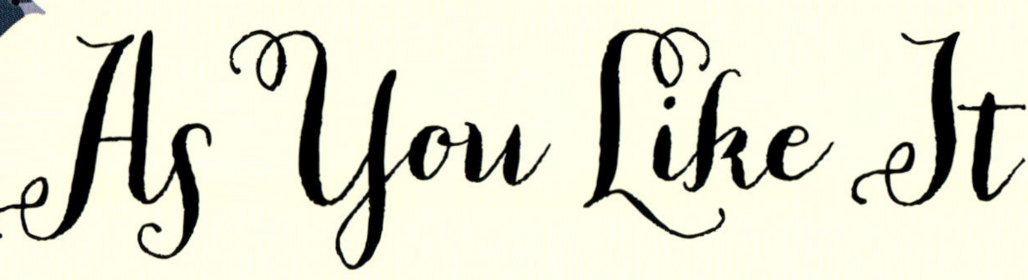

When she is exiled from her uncle's court, Rosalind flees into the Forest of Arden disguised as a boy, along with her best friend, Celia. In the forest she discovers a new freedom and falls headlong in love.

Duke Frederick

Seized the throne from his brother, Duke Senior, and banished him to the forest. Years later, he banishes the duke's daughter Rosalind as well – but in doing so he loses his own daughter, Celia.

Touchstone

A grumpy court clown who goes with Rosalind and Celia to the forest.

Rosalind

Clever, witty and independent, Rosalind falls for Orlando, but spends all her time with him disguised as a boy.

Orlando

Driven into the forest by Duke Frederick's suspicions. Besotted with Rosalind, he befriends a boy who reminds him of her…

Celia

Duke Frederick's daughter. Celia is Rosalind's cousin and best friend. She flees with Rosalind, disguised as a shepherdess.

Phoebe
A country girl.

Silvius
A shepherd.

Oliver
Orlando's jealous older brother, who hates him and wants him dead.

"All the world's a stage,
And all the men and women merely players"

Adam
Orlando's faithful old servant, who uses his own savings to support his master.

Duke Senior
The rightful duke, and Rosalind's father, who has been banished to the forest by Duke Frederick.

Jaques
Cynical and philosophical friend of Duke Senior, who lives with him in the forest.

"**I** SHOW MORE MIRTH THAN I AM FEELING,**"** Rosalind grumbled to her friend Celia, "and you tell me to be even merrier? Unless you can teach me to forget a banished father, you should not expect me to be merry at all!"

As Rosalind walked through the palace gardens with Celia, her cousin as well as her dearest friend, merriment wasn't uppermost in her mind. Her father, Duke Senior, had been banished from the court for treason by Celia's father, Duke Frederick. While Rosalind lived in her uncle's palace, she could not forget what he had done.

"What my father has taken away from yours, I will give you back," Celia told her, smiling so sweetly that it was impossible for Rosalind to feel completely miserable. "Therefore, my sweet Rose, be merry."

"I will," Rosalind promised. There was no point dwelling on her father's banishment. "We just need a distraction," she said, as a messenger came racing into the garden.

"Three brothers!" he announced, panting. "The wrestler Charles has just broken the ribs of three brothers! I doubt they'll live to see tomorrow. And now another man has challenged him! Come and see the fight!"

"I learn something new every day," said Touchstone, the court jester, who had strolled into the garden behind the messenger. "That's the first time I've heard breaking ribs described as a sport for ladies."

"Me too," admitted Celia.

"Isn't there anyone else who longs to see it?" said Rosalind, convinced it was just the distraction she needed. Celia could never say no to her best friend. Soon the two women were sitting beside the ring, their eyes on the wrestler Charles – a man built like a minotaur – as he warmed up. Outside the ring stood the challenger, a mild, lean-looking youth who was surely about to lose his life.

"I tried to persuade the young man not to fight," Duke Frederick told Rosalind and Celia, as he swept in to take his seat. "He won't listen to me. Speak to him, ladies. Perhaps you can change his mind."

So Rosalind called him over. "Young man, do not fight," she begged him.

"If I die," the young man replied, "I shall do my friends no wrong, since I have none. I shall do the world no injury, for I have nothing."

Rosalind was taken aback, both by his melancholy confession and his handsome face. "Then I hope you do well," she said. "The little strength I have, I wish it were with you…"

"Come on!" roared Charles, beating his chest. "Where's this young man who's so eager to die?"

The challenger, Orlando, walked into the ring, his head held high. He took a run at Charles. But the giant lifted him up and tossed him over his shoulder. Rosalind gasped as he crashed to the ground. A few feet away, a man in the audience smiled.

That man was Oliver, Orlando's older brother. He was taking great pleasure in the thought of his brother's imminent death. Oliver had always loathed Orlando. He didn't know why he hated him so much. Oliver had grown up with wealth, education and anything else he could want. After their father had died, Oliver had made sure his younger brother had had none of these things. But there was still something about Orlando that set his teeth on edge.

Soon, he consoled himself, Orlando would be gone. The previous night, he had made Charles promise that Orlando would not survive the fight. He had had to tell a few white lies to persuade him, but it was worth it…

Now he watched as Charles lunged towards Orlando, and frowned as Orlando dodged him and jumped up onto his back. Rosalind cheered as the two men grappled. Charles roared, his face flushed purple, unable to shake Orlando off. To everyone's astonishment, the giant toppled and crashed onto the ground.

The crowd roared. It was impossible! Orlando had defeated Charles. When the applause had died down, Duke Frederick asked the challenger who he was.

"Orlando, the youngest son of the late Sir Rowland de Bois," Orlando replied, when he was able to speak.

"I wish you were someone else," the duke said coldly. "Your father was my enemy when he was alive. Anyway, I commend you for your valour."

As the crowd dispersed, Rosalind approached the young man.

"Sir, you did well," she said softly. "You have overthrown more than your enemies."

Orlando wanted to reply. Instead, he stared at Rosalind. "Say something," he thought. "Anything!" But no words would form. Then Rosalind placed her necklace around his neck.

"Wear this for me," she said. Once more, Orlando tried to reply. His mouth was opening and shutting like that of a fish, but no sound came out.

"Erm… shall we go?" said Celia.

"You FOOL!" Orlando berated himself, when Rosalind had gone. "Something stronger than Charles has overthrown you…"

Back in her room in the duke's palace, Celia discovered that Rosalind had fallen madly in love.

"Is it possible that you love him so suddenly?" Celia asked.

"Why not?" said Rosalind. "My father loved his father dearly."

"And so you love his son?" Celia frowned. "But my father hates Orlando's father. It doesn't follow that I hate Orlando!"

"You have to love him, because I do," Rosalind insisted.

They would have gone on talking about the merits of Orlando for several hours, had they not been interrupted by Duke Frederick, who marched in and barked at Rosalind: "Be gone from my court at once. You are not wanted here!"

Rosalind gaped at her uncle in astonishment. Hours ago – no – minutes ago, he'd been perfectly polite to her. "Tell me what I've done to offend you, dear uncle!"

"You are your father's daughter – that's enough!"

"Treason is not inherited, my lord!" she replied.

"If Rosalind is a traitor, then so am I!" Celia declared. "Father, all our lives we have played together, eaten together…"

"Her silence and her patience both speak to the people, and they pity her," Frederick told his daughter. "You will seem more virtuous when she is gone."

"You'll have to banish me too," Celia cried, "for I cannot live without her!"

"You are a fool," Frederick replied. Then he turned to Rosalind. "Unless you leave, you die."

When her father had gone, Celia said, "Shall we leave together? Let my father find another heir! Cheer up. If you go, I go. And if we go together, we'll be going to freedom, and not to banishment!"

"But where would we go?" Rosalind asked desolately.

"To see your father, in the Forest of Arden," said Celia. And just like that, it was settled. They made a plan to flee to the forest, where Rosalind's father was living in exile. Better still, they would go in disguise.

Rosalind grinned. She would dress as a shepherd. "An axe upon my thigh, a boar spear in my hand!" she said. "Whatever woman's fears are in my heart, I'll still look every inch a gallant man. As, in fact, many cowardly men do, who hide their fears beneath their outfits."

"What shall I call you when you're a man?" Celia asked.

"Ganymede!" Rosalind replied, suddenly inspired. "And you?"

"I'll be Aliena," said Celia, "a simple shepherdess."

They agreed to ask Touchstone, the court jester, to help them on their journey, and waited until it was dark to make their escape.

The following day, Duke Frederick turned purple with fury when he discovered they were missing. A maid had overheard Rosalind talking about Orlando, and the duke was soon convinced that he was somehow behind it all. He sent for Orlando's brother Oliver, and commanded him to find the women – and to bring Orlando to him, dead or alive. "Dead," thought Oliver. "I'll bring him dead."

That afternoon, when Orlando walked home, he found his father's old servant, Adam, standing outside his door. "You can't stay here!" Adam warned him. "Oliver's going to burn your house to the ground tonight, with you in it!"

"Then where should I go?" asked Orlando. He had nothing in the world. No plans, no money, no refuge. Perhaps he should just stay and face his brother's spite.

"Let me go with you," the old man said. "I have five hundred crowns. I saved the money years ago, when I served your father. It will help us on our way."

Orlando was astonished. "So, there are still some kind souls in this cruel world," he thought. He took Adam's hands in his. "Let's go along together," he said. "And when the money's spent, we'll find some simple way to live, and be content…"

So they set out together, not knowing where they'd end up.

Rosalind plucked one piece of parchment off a tree trunk. And another, and another. The trees were covered in poems. Someone must have spent all night writing them.

The first one read:

    'From the east to western Ind.
    No jewel is like Rosalind.
    Let no face be kept in mind
    But that of fairest Rosalind.'

She showed Touchstone who didn't think much of it. To him, poetry was a pastime for fools with more love than talent.

"I found them on a tree!" she grinned.

"Then the tree is yielding bad fruit," said Touchstone.

But Rosalind didn't care. She knew they weren't great poems, or even good poems. But *someone* had written them. Someone who was in love with her!

"I remember when I was in love," said Touchstone, ruefully. "I broke my sword, attacking a stone that I mistook for a lover visiting my mistress at night. I even kissed the cow's udder that her pretty hands had milked." He sighed. "We who are true lovers certainly do some strange things."

Ever so casually, Celia mentioned that she had seen the poet hanging the poems on the tree.

"Who is it?" Rosalind shrieked.

Celia laughed. "You don't know?"

"WHO?" demanded Rosalind.

"Come on, you must know. You gave him a necklace…?"

"Who? Is it a man?" said Rosalind.

"This is incredible," giggled Celia, shaking her head.

"Tell me!" Rosalind shouted. "Why is your mouth stopped like a corked bottle! Pour the knowledge out!"

Celia took a deep breath. "It was Orlando, the boy who tripped up the giant and your heart in a single instant."

" We that are true lovers run into strange capers "

"No!" gasped Rosalind.

"Orlando," Celia repeated.

"Orlando!" breathed Rosalind.

Then she began to speak very, very fast. "But – what shall I do with my men's clothes? Did you see him? How did he look? Where did he go? Where is he now? Did he ask for me? When will you see him again? Answer me in one word!"

Celia creased herself laughing. "Even if I had a giant's mouth, I could not begin to answer you in one word…"

Then, just as Celia began to describe how she had seen Orlando, the man himself appeared, strolling through the forest with another man who was dressed from head to foot in black.

Orlando had found Duke Senior and his friends in the forest. They had given Orlando and Adam food and shelter. Now Orlando was deep in conversation with Duke Senior's friend Jaques, who was the most melancholy man in the forest, if not the entire kingdom.

"I beg you, ruin no more trees with your verses!" Jaques was telling him exasperatedly.

"*I* beg *you*, ruin no more of my poems by mocking them so cruelly!" Orlando replied.

"Rosalind is your love's name?" asked Jaques.

Orlando nodded.

"I do not like that name," said Jaques.

"I do not think that anyone was thinking of you when she was christened!" Orlando fumed.

Jaques took a good look at the young man. "The problem you have is love," Jaques told him.

"I would not change it for any blessing you have," said Orlando curtly. "I am weary of you."

Jaques shrugged. "I was looking for a fool when I found you."

"Go and look in the river," Orlando retorted. "You'll see him!"

"I'll see myself," said Jaques.

"Precisely."

Jaques decided he'd had enough of this young man. "Adieu, Monsieur Love!" he said, and tramped off through the forest.

"Adieu, Monsieur Melancholy!" Orlando called after him.

Once Orlando was alone, Rosalind cleared her throat, and tried out her best impression of a man's voice. "Forester, come here!"

To her amazement, Orlando obeyed. To Rosalind's further astonishment and delight, they were soon deep in conversation. Her disguise was working!

But Orlando knew there was something not *quite* right about this young man. "Your accent is very fine for someone who lives in these woods," he said.

"An old… religious… uncle taught me to speak," Rosalind improvised. "He taught me many things. Such as – not to fall in love. You know, there is a lovesick youth haunting this forest. He keeps writing poems on the trees. If I met him, I'd tell him…"

"I am he!" Orlando admitted.

Rosalind looked Orlando up and down. "Hmm, no," she said. "My uncle taught me how to recognize a man in love. You're not showing the signs."

"The signs? What signs?" Orlando spluttered.

"You should have sunken eyes, a neglected beard, untied shoes, unbuttoned sleeves… Everything about you should show careless desolation. But you look as if you love yourself, and not another."

"I am that unfortunate!" Orlando replied. "I wish I could make you believe it. Neither rhyme nor reason can express how much I love Rosalind."

Rosalind pretended to disapprove, although hearing those words made her almost dizzy with happiness.

"Love is a madness," she said. "But I can cure it."

"Go on."

"I once knew a lovesick man," said Rosalind. "Every day, I told him to woo me, as if I was his love. One day I'd smile, then I'd weep, then I'd ignore him. I'd love him, hate him, smile at him – and so I drove him from the madness of love, to living madness. Finally he decided to become a monk," she said, with satisfaction.

"I don't want to be cured," Orlando said emphatically.

"I'd cure you, if you would woo me every day…" Rosalind said.

Orlando considered the matter. He did not want to be cured. But this young man had a very fair face, an appealing manner, a sweet, teasing smile and such bright eyes, they reminded him somehow of his beloved Rosalind. Perhaps, he could learn to woo Rosalind, by wooing Ganymede…

"Very well, I will," he agreed.

That night, Rosalind, Celia and Touchstone stayed in a pretty little cottage in the forest. It was a delightful place, although Touchstone still managed to find things to complain about. Rosalind, on the other hand, couldn't keep the smile off her face. But the next morning, as she waited for Orlando to arrive, the smile faded fast. He was late. By a whole three minutes.

"He said he would come and he didn't!" she cried.

Celia shrugged. In her experience, love's eternal oaths didn't usually last that long.

When Orlando did finally appear – four minutes later – Rosalind was short with him. "You are slower than a snail. In fact, I'd rather be wooed by a snail."

"Why is that?" Orlando asked.

"At least he'd bring his house with him."

But Rosalind couldn't stay angry with him for long. "What would you do, if Rosalind said she would not have you?" she asked him playfully.

"I would die," Orlando replied, utterly serious.

ROSALIND, ACT 4, SCENE 1

Rosalind burst out laughing. "Men have died, and been buried for the worms to eat — but not for love."

"Even Rosalind's frown would kill me!" Orlando protested.

"It would not kill a fly," she laughed. "Come. I'll play Rosalind in a lighter mood. Ask me something, and I will give it to you."

"Love me," begged Orlando, pleading as sincerely as if the real Rosalind was standing before him.

He trembled as he gazed at Ganymede. Those luminous eyes, that fair skin, the sweet voice, the joyful laugh — as the youth stood before him, Orlando could almost imagine that Ganymede *was* in fact Rosalind.

"I will love you on Fridays and Saturdays," Rosalind said cheekily. "I'll love you — and twenty others like you."

"What?!" said Orlando, jolted out of his haze of happiness.

"Well, can you really have too much of a good thing?" Rosalind said. Then she called Celia over. "Come, cousin! We are going to be married!"

A few minutes later, Celia was playing the part of the priest, and Orlando was married to his Rosalind.

"Now you've married Rosalind, how long will you love her?" Rosalind asked Orlando.

"Forever and a day," said Orlando.

"Try a day, without the ever," said Rosalind. "For I'll be as jealous as a pigeon. I'll squawk like a parrot, I'll be as lusty as a monkey. I'll weep when you want to be merry, and I'll laugh like a hyena, just when you want to go to sleep."

"But... Rosalind is wise," Orlando said, tormented by this youth's words. He knew the real Rosalind would be pure and perfect in every way.

"Oh, she will do much the same as I do," Rosalind said casually, with utmost confidence. Eventually, the bamboozled Orlando left Ganymede, to visit Duke Senior. Far from being cured, he felt more intoxicated by his love than before. But was it love for Rosalind, or for Ganymede? He didn't even know. He only knew that he was deeply in love. He felt as if he could drown in it.

As she watched Orlando go, Rosalind sighed. "My love is like the bay of Portugal. No one knows how deep it is…"

"You should have your disguise plucked right off, so the world could see what you've done to that poor boy!" Celia scolded.

"You don't know how much I love him," Rosalind replied. "I'll go and find some shade to sit in, and sigh till he comes back."

"Sounds *fascinating*," thought Celia. "I'll go to sleep."

But when it was time for Orlando to return, a different man appeared, brandishing a bloody handkerchief.

"This is from Orlando," he told the two women. Then he began to relate a strange tale. "When he left you, Orlando came across a man asleep under a tree. A snake was wound around his neck. As Orlando crept closer, he saw that this man was his own brother – Oliver. As he approached, the snake slid away into some bushes, where a lioness was hiding, about to pounce on the sleeping man."

"And then?" said Rosalind, her heart in her mouth. Orlando had told her about his hateful, murderous brother. "Did Orlando leave his brother to the lioness?"

"He tried – twice. But kindness, stronger than revenge, made him battle the lioness. He killed the beast. As it fell, the man awoke. Or rather, I should say, I awoke."

"You are his brother?" said Rosalind.

" *My affection hath an unknown bottom,
like the Bay of Portugal.* "

ROSALIND, ACT 4, SCENE 1

"I was. But I'm not the wretch I was before," Oliver replied humbly. "Orlando's love has changed me. We are reconciled."

"But the handkerchief? Whose blood is that?" asked Rosalind, staring fearfully at the dark red stains.

"Wounded by the lioness, Orlando sent this handkerchief…" Oliver said. He gasped in surprise as the young shepherd he was talking to fainted onto the floor with a thump.

"Ganymede!" hissed Celia, prodding Rosalind to wake her up.

"Lots of people faint when they see blood," Oliver said reassuringly when Rosalind's eyes fluttered open. "You're a man. You just lack a man's heart!"

"I was – erm – only pretending to faint!" protested Rosalind. But she remained very pale, and only really revived when Oliver went on to tell her that Orlando had only suffered a wound in his arm, and that she could visit him later that day.

When she did, she had some surprising news to share with Orlando. Over the course of that afternoon, 'Aliena' and Oliver had fallen in love. "No sooner had they looked, than they sighed. No sooner sighed, than loved," Rosalind told Orlando. "In short, they're getting married tomorrow!"

Orlando was happy for his brother. So long his enemy, now his friend. And yet… "How bitter it is, to look at love through another man's eyes. Tomorrow, my heart will be heavy."

"Tomorrow, can't I play Rosalind?" asked Rosalind.

"I can no longer live by thinking," said Orlando. Besides, he thought, his feelings for Ganymede had become too confusing. Simply standing near the young man made his heart race.

"Believe then that I can do strange things," Rosalind told him.

She took a deep breath. What she was about to say was a lie, and yet there was some truth in it. "Since I was three years old, I have known a magician, and he has taught me many things…

and if your heart cries out for Rosalind, tomorrow, you shall marry her."

"You really mean it?" said Orlando.

"I do," said Rosalind. She grinned at Orlando. If all went well, he would soon have his heart's desire.

But not everyone in the Forest of Arden was as happy. Near Rosalind's cottage, there lived a shepherdess named Phoebe, who had fallen madly in love with a handsome young shepherd – called Ganymede. She kept sending him poems – endless verses that made Orlando's clumsy efforts seem like masterpieces.

Just after Rosalind had promised Orlando that he would marry his Rosalind tomorrow, Phoebe arrived, fell to her knees, and declared undying love for Ganymede.

It was not a moment that Rosalind enjoyed, and it was made even more awkward by the pained young man standing next to Phoebe. He was a shepherd called Silvius, who had loved Phoebe for as long as he could remember.

"Love Silvius," Rosalind advised Phoebe. "He worships you!"

But Phoebe ignored Silvius, gazing still at Rosalind.

"To love is to be full of tears and sighs – as I am for Phoebe," said Silvius.

"And I for Ganymede," sighed Phoebe.

"And I for Rosalind," echoed Orlando.

"And I for no woman," Rosalind said.

"To love," said Silvius, "is to be made of fantasy. And of all wishes, all adoration, humbleness, patience and impatience, all purity, all trial, all obedience – as am I for Phoebe,"

"As am I for Ganymede," said Phoebe.

"And as am I for Rosalind," breathed Orlando.

"Stop!" cried Rosalind. "It's like wolves howling at the moon!" She turned to Phoebe. "I would love you if I could," she said. "If ever I marry a woman, it'll be you. And I'll be married tomorrow."

The lovestruck Phoebe nodded. "I would marry you," Phoebe said, "even if I had to die that very hour!"

"If you refuse to marry me, in the end, will you marry your faithful Silvius?" Rosalind asked, and Phoebe nodded.

Next, Rosalind turned to Orlando. "I'll satisfy you, if ever I satisfied a man. And you'll be married tomorrow."

Finally she turned to Silvius. "I'll content you, if what pleases you contents you, and you'll be married tomorrow."

So they all vowed happily to meet the following day.

There was only one thing left for Rosalind to do. Still disguised as Ganymede, she went to find her father. Since she was going to be married tomorrow, she thought she probably should at least mention it to him.

In the forest, Duke Senior had found a life of sweet simplicity. Although it had pained him to be exiled, he didn't miss the flattery or lies of court politics. And when he heard Orlando's sad tale, it reminded him that others were far worse off than himself. "The world's wide theatre presents much sadder scenes than the one we're in," he remarked to Jaques.

"All the world's a stage, and all the men and women are merely players," Jaques replied. "They have their exits and their entrances; and one man in his time plays many parts. Here are the seven ages of man: first, he's a bawling infant; second, a whining school boy; third he's a singing lover; fourth, a proud soldier; fifth he's a wise, fat judge; sixth, he is a shrunken old man; and last of all comes a second childishness, and oblivion."

"All the world's a stage,
And all the men and women merely players."

Jaques, Act 2, Scene 7

As Jaques fell silent, two of these ages of man – the lover
and the old man – presented themselves. It was Orlando and his
faithful servant Adam, who had been invited to dinner.

Duke Senior welcomed them, and they sat down to eat.
The more the Duke got to know Orlando, the son of his dear
friend, the better he liked him. And so, when a young man called
Ganymede came along, asking whether he would approve of the
match between Orlando and his daughter, Rosalind, he didn't
hesitate to agree. "But where *is* Rosalind?" he said, filled with
longing to see his beloved, clever daughter again.

The youth smiled. "If I bring your Rosalind here tomorrow,
you will allow her to marry Orlando?" he asked again.

"I would," Duke Senior confirmed cheerfully, "and if I had a
kingdom to give with her, I'd do that too."

And so the stage was set.

The next day, Oliver and 'Aliena' were about to be married,
and Phoebe, Silvius and Orlando were all waiting nervously to
see if they would be able to marry their true loves, when Rosalind
appeared in her own clothes.

"If there is any truth in sight, you are my Rosalind," Orlando
said, marvelling at the sight before him.

"If there is any truth in sight, you are my daughter!" cried
Duke Senior, rushing to embrace her.

Standing next to him, Phoebe burst into tears. "If shape and
sight are true, then… love, adieu!" she sobbed.

But now Ganymede was gone forever, she found to her surprise,
that her love for him vanished as quickly as he had. She turned to
Silvius, and saw his pained, patient face as she had never seen
it before. "Let us be married," she said. "Your loyalty has won
my heart."

Just as the ceremony was about to begin, a messenger rode in, looking for Duke Senior. "Duke Frederick came to the forest, to kill his brother," he announced. "But on the edges of the forest, he met a monk who dissuaded him from his quest. Now he has given up his crown to his banished brother, and plans to spend the rest of his days in the forest as a holy man."

At these words, everyone leaped to their feet, cheering. Rosalind and her father looked at one another, their faces alight with joy. It meant they could, at last, go home!

"Come, brides and bridegrooms. Play music, and dance!" Duke Senior commanded. At this, the crowd cheered again – apart from Jaques, who despised dancing, and quickly bid everyone farewell. But before the music started up, Rosalind stepped forward.

"It is not the fashion for a woman to speak at a wedding, but it is no less handsome than a speech from a man. So, I say to all the women: please enjoy this feast as much you like. And to all the men: enjoy it as much as you like too."

Taking Orlando's hand, spun him round, and led him in a jig. As they whirled, more and more people joined in, until the whole forest was filled with the sound of music, laughter and love.

Henry IV

King Henry's kingdom is troubled by unrest. Rebellion threatens, led by his former friends, the Percy family. His own son Harry, better known as Hal, spends more time in the tavern than at court. Will Prince Hal step up to his role, for his father and for England?

King Henry IV

After taking the throne from Richard II, Henry IV is now dealing with the consequences. If only his son were as brave as Hotspur…

Prince Harry (Hal)

Henry's son and heir to the throne. No one thinks he's ready to be king, but maybe he can prove them wrong.

Sir John Falstaff

The laziest, most cowardly knight in all of England. He and Hal are great friends, but how long can it last?

Ned Poins

Hal's confidant and drinking companion. Together, they play jokes on Falstaff.

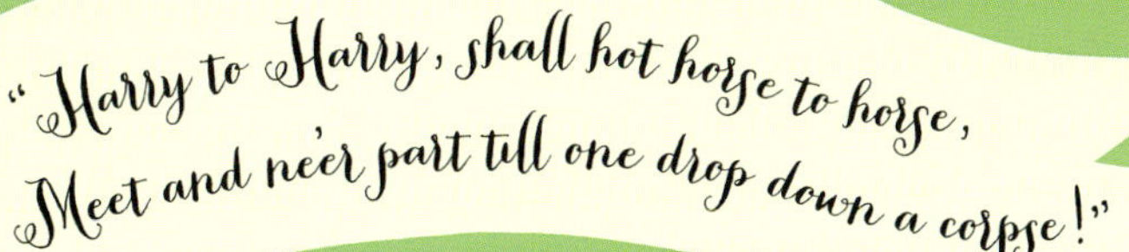

Harry Percy (Hotspur)

Son of the Earl of Northumberland. He's brave and honourable, so when he thinks the king has betrayed his family, he has to take a stand.

Lady Kate Percy

Hotspur's loving wife and Mortimer's sister. She wishes Hotspur were less interested in war…

Edmund Mortimer

Kate Percy's brother. After being captured by his Welsh enemy Glendower, he changes sides and marries Glendower's daughter.

Worcester

Hotspur's uncle, Thomas Percy, known as the Earl of Worcester. Helps Hotspur plot against the king.

Owen Glendower

The last Welsh prince. He's leading a rebellion against the English.

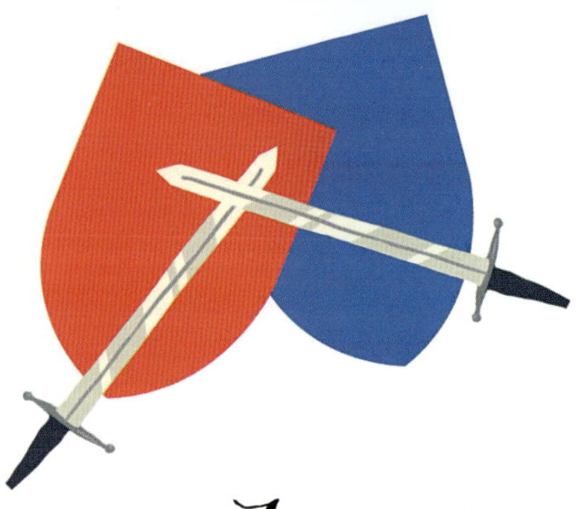

I NSIDE HIS LONDON PALACE, the new King of England, Henry IV, was meeting his advisors. "After many hard battles to decide who sits on this throne, we have, at last, a moment of peace," the king began. "You know my hopes… I want to send knights to protect Christians in the Holy Lands across the sea. We will put civil war behind us by forging an English army united in a common crusade. But first, we must discuss problems closer to home."

The Earl of Westmoreland stepped forwards. "A messenger from Wales has arrived, my lord, weighed down with bad news. The rebel commander, Owen Glendower, has captured our Lord Mortimer and butchered his troops. There's revolt in the North too," Westmoreland continued gravely. "Your gallant knight, Sir Henry Percy, or 'Hotspur' as his soldiers call him, attacked an invading Scottish army. I do not yet know the outcome, as my spy rode away before the battle ended."

"A dear and true friend has the answer," Henry smiled. "Sir Walter Blunt visited the site. Hotspur defeated the Scottish general, Douglas, and took many proud knights and noblemen captive."

"What great glory for the noble knight!" cried Westmoreland.

"Yes, and how I envy his father. He's blessed with a son who is bold, brave and beloved by everyone, whilst I, by comparison, see riot and dishonour stain the brow of my young Prince Harry." The king's own brow darkened. "I wish our boys had been swapped in their cradles so I could call Hotspur my own… But there is one

" …I by looking on the praise of him, . .·
See riot and dishonour stain the brow "
Of my young Harry.

thing about him that stings me. He has refused to send me his prisoners, owed to me by royal tradition."

"That will be his uncle's doing," replied Westmoreland. "You know the Earl of Worcester opposes you."

"Hotspur can explain it himself," said the king. "I have ordered him to Windsor Castle. I'll keep a cool temper and an open mind until then."

In another part of the capital, Prince Harry had only just woken up and was still getting dressed. He was startled when a mound of clothes reared up from the floor, and his tavern-friend, Falstaff, emerged. "What time is it, Hal?" Falstaff grumbled, rubbing his bleary eyes.

"Since when have you been fussy about the hour?" the prince laughed. "You'd only care if seconds were cups of wine to gulp, and minutes were roast chickens to chew on."

"That cuts close, Hal," replied Falstaff, scratching his chubby face. "When you are king you mustn't mock us knights of the tavern. I rest by day and quest by moonlight."

"You steal purses and fall down drunk, you mean," said Harry. "And it's usually me who pays the bill."

"You're a generous heir to the throne," Falstaff grinned winningly, picking something out from between his teeth, "and a friend to good thieves and free-thinking gentlemen like myself. When you're king, we'll have no more prisons."

"I'll make you judge," Harry snorted, "a thief to hang thieves, you wine-soaked rogue."

"It's my life's work, Hal. You can't blame a man for his calling."

Before the prince could answer, a shabby-looking figure entered. It was Poins, another of Harry's friends from the city's underworld of thieves and idlers, and he had a broad grin on his sharp face. "I've got a lovely job for us," he told them.

"Good day to you too, Poins," replied Harry. "This job of yours, is it honest work?"

"Honest as the gallows," Poins declared.

"I don't fancy that as payment," said Falstaff.

"Then how about gold instead?" hissed Poins. "Some rich traders are coming to town in a few days' time, so I heard. And we'll be waiting for them on a lonely road…"

"Count me in," Falstaff said.

"And count me out," said Harry.

"Get to the tavern, Falstaff," said Poins, giving Harry a sly look. "Let me have a private word with Hal."

Falstaff nodded. "It's thirsty work, all this planning. I'll keep a seat for you at the bar."

As Falstaff ambled out, Poins slipped his arm around the prince's shoulder. "It's all a trick, my lord," he explained. "We'll send Falstaff and his cronies to rob the traders, then put masks on and surprise them, stealing what they stole."

Harry shook his head. "I'm no thief."

"Imagine the look on Falstaff's face, and the tall story he'll tell."

"That'd be worth hearing," Harry chuckled. "Very well then, go and arrange it." Poins was out of the door like a flash.

The prince glanced down at his gold ring with its royal seal. "People scold me for living among these lowlife drunkards," he thought, "but when I choose to throw them off, I will appear as bright as the sun in comparison. I will dazzle everyone, like a diamond lifted from the dust. I'll outshine them all."

"You are testing my patience," snapped the king, hammering his fist on the arm of his throne. He stared down at Worcester, Hotspur and the group of other nobles and generals who had gathered at his castle in Windsor. "I see disobedience in your eyes, Worcester. You have my permission to leave – at once!"

While his uncle stormed from the room, Hotspur stepped forwards. "Sir, Worcester did not refuse you the prisoners. I am to blame. As I stood bleeding and exhausted, a sword still in my hand, some fool in fancy clothes rode up and began to pester me. He reeked of perfume and was worried that my soldiers might splatter his fine tunic with blood. This man demanded the prisoners, but in my rage at him I simply shook my head and walked away."

"Then where are my prisoners?" the king demanded.

"You may have them, sir," Hotspur said. "But I must first ask for help in raising the ransom for my wife's brother, Mortimer."

The king stared at Hotspur in cold fury. "Word has it that Mortimer, once captured, married our enemy Glendower's daughter! Should I empty my royal coffers to free a traitor? No, on the barren mountains let Mortimer starve. Give me my prisoners, Hotspur, or you'll learn what a king's wrath can be."

King Henry and his council marched from the throne room, leaving Hotspur seething. "If the Devil himself came for those prisoners," he spat, "I'd refuse him."

"Be calm," said Worcester, returning to Hotspur's side.

"We deserve better treatment," Hotspur said. "The Percy family fought to help crush King Richard, that sweet rose, and plant this thorn, Henry, on the throne. I am tired of bowing to a false king."

"Then listen," said Worcester. "I have a plot that will soothe your temper."

"Go on."

"You will hand your prisoners over…"

"To Henry?" cried Hotspur.

"No, back to their own commander, Douglas. Ask no ransom and make the rebel Scots your friends. I will send your father, the Earl of Northumberland, to York to rally support there. And in Wales, I'll recruit Glendower and Mortimer to our cause."

"That's a noble, broad plot," Hotspur grinned. "We'll have the

Scots, Glendower, York and my own forces to smash Henry's army. Oh, let the hours be short, till battlefields, and blows, and groans applaud our sport!"

Meanwhile, in the Boar's Head tavern, Prince Harry and Poins were sprawled at a table, drinking wine. They both looked up, trying not to giggle, as Falstaff crashed into the room. "A plague on all cowards," boomed the tubby knight. "Give me some wine, before I die of thirst."

"What's all this about?" asked the prince, winking at Poins.

"Where were you two for the robbery?" Falstaff asked them. "Too scared to join us? We took a thousand pounds from those feeble bumpkins."

"Let us see the spoils, then," the prince said.

"I can't," Falstaff confessed. "No fewer than one hundred foul thieves appeared from the shadows and snatched our gold away."

Poins snorted. "One hundred thieves?"

"It was a miracle I survived," Falstaff sighed, collapsing onto a chair. "I duelled with a dozen of them for at least two hours."

"It's down to a dozen already," laughed the prince.

"It was twice that at least," Falstaff cried indignantly.

"I pray you didn't murder any," said Poins.

"It's too late for praying," Falstaff told him airily. "I may be on the large side, but I'm as quick as a dart with a blade. I skewered two or more of them. But then another fifty thieves rushed in and my friends took fright and dragged me away. I'd still be there now if they hadn't, slashing away with my sabre."

"These lies are as large and silly as their master," the prince declared. "You idiot, Falstaff, it was me that robbed you, with the help of Poins. We put on disguises, rushed at you in the dark and saw you waddle away screaming."

Falstaff's swagger dissolved at once. "But – erm – of course," he said, rubbing his chin. "I recognized you immediately."

The prince wasn't letting him get away with it that easily. "Another lie," he pointed out sharply.

Falstaff just grinned. "How could I harm the heir to the throne?" he asked. "I told you that story so I wouldn't spoil your little joke. I'm a loyal subject, you see."

The prince laughed. "You're as smart as a fox, Falstaff."

"I *am* glad to hear you have the loot," replied Falstaff.

"I will hand that money in to the sheriff," the prince told him. "The joke was all I cared about."

"But that cash will come in handy in the dark times ahead," Falstaff wheedled. "A messenger called at your rooms to summon you to court. Hotspur, Glendower and Mortimer have raised a rebel army. The king's beard has turned white with the news."

"Here's a chance for you to be a brave soldier, at last," said the prince wryly. "I'll get you a command, Falstaff, with a company of infantry. And I'll see my father first thing in the morning."

The following morning, bright and early, Hal went to see the king in his royal quarters at Westminster. "Leave us," the king told his attendants. "I must talk privately with my son."

Harry kneeled before his father. "It has been a while since you asked me here," said the prince.

"It shames me to look at you," replied the king. "You have sunk so low, I can only think that the reason you were born was to punish me for my misdeeds."

"Many things they say about me are lies. As for the rest, surely they are not so bad that you cannot forgive me," Harry said.

"Let God pardon you," the king answered. "How can I forgive a drunken rascal son? If I had behaved like you I never would have taken this crown. Before my coronation I stayed hidden away, made myself as rare and special as a comet passing overhead, and never skipped with merry fools in the gutter. Living with commoners makes you common, Harry. That Hotspur looks more like a true prince than you, with more right to inherit this throne. See how he's raised an army against me, beating and then befriending Douglas and the Scots, and leading the rebel forces. Kingly stuff. But why do I waste my breath talking of enemies? You might be my worst enemy of all, turning on me and running off to be Hotspur's lapdog."

A fire had lit in Hal's eyes, and the king could see it well. "I'll win your forgiveness on the battlefield," Hal said boldly. "And the blood I shed will wipe away all past shame. I'll fight your gallant Hotspur and make him swap his fame and glorious deeds for my disgrace. I shall be the true prince. In the name of God, I promise it here."

"Then I'll give you command of my army, my son," the king said proudly. "The rebels are gathering around Shrewsbury; we'll march to meet them in battle."

While Hal rushed back to his rooms, his rival, Hotspur was in his castle, also making preparations for war. He strode briskly through the corridors, calling for his wife: "Kate, come say your farewells, I must leave within the hour."

"Leaving again?" said his wife, joining him in the castle hall. "For a fortnight now, I feel as though you have banished me from your side. Some secret has possessed you. Even in your sleep you shout battle orders, and the sweat breaks out on your brow like the bubbles in rushing water. I am your wife – I have a right to know what heavy business presses down on you. What is it that carries you away?"

"My horse, my lady," smiled Hotspur.

"You joke," replied Kate, sadly. "Yet I sense this is no joking matter. I fear that my brother, Mortimer, is up to something, and is leading you into danger. But I love you, my lord. Will you tell me you love me too?"

"As soon as I'm on my horse," Hotspur laughed. "Then I'll swear it to anyone who'll listen. But don't question me further, my lady. I must have my secrets, even from you, and what you don't know you can't tell. I'll go today, and you'll follow tomorrow, will that content you, my Kate?"

"It must," she sighed, "when I have no other choice."

"Where's that fat fiend, Falstaff?" roared the prince, striding into the Boar's Head tavern. "I've pleasant news for him."

"Over here, Hal, trying to lead a clean, virtuous life," Falstaff said, finishing off a glass of wine.

"I'd say the opposite was true," the prince scoffed.

"No, sir, I've been good," Falstaff told him indignantly. "I've stopped swearing, playing dice and visiting bars. At least, no more than five different taverns a day! Now, what sweet news do you have for me?"

"I've paid all the money back to those traders," the prince told him. "That's cleared your good name."

Falstaff almost sobbed. "I think I'd rather have the gold."

"And I got you those soldiers I promised," Hal went on.

Falstaff looked horrified. "You did?"

"Meet me on the road in the morning, armed and ready," the prince told him. "The country's on fire, and Percy's gaining the high ground. It's them or us: one side must be crushed down."

"I'd like to lie down and hide until it's over," Falstaff squeaked as he watched his friend stride away. "Off to war, he says. Well, I'm not going anywhere until I get a good breakfast."

At the rebel camp, Prince Hotspur was holding a war council, when a messenger ran into the tent. "I have a note from your father, my lord," he cried.

"Why did he not come himself?" Hotspur demanded.

"He lies in his sickbed," replied the messenger.

"We don't have the leisure to be sick," Hotspur snarled. "It will infect the very lifeblood of our enterprise." He snatched the letter and scanned it impatiently. "My father writes that he had no time to muster and send his forces. 'Fight on with what you have,' he says, 'for the king knows of your plans.'"

"The men won't like it," Worcester said doubtfully. "Some might say this sickness was brought on by fear."

"But it makes us look even braver," Hotspur replied, "fighting the might of the king when we're not even at full strength. And my father's troops will bring us fresh reinforcements later on."

"I have worse news," said another knight, pushing through the ring of generals to stand before Hotspur. "Glendower's forces will not reach us for a week or more. And the king is close by, with an army of thirty thousand men. Prince Harry leads the march, dressed in fine steel and looking every part a mighty warrior."

"Let him come," roared Hotspur. "I'll ride like a thunderbolt against this fine prince. Harry shall meet Harry, horse to horse, and we will not part till one drops down a corpse. Muster the men, we'll fight and die if we must."

On the outskirts of Coventry, Falstaff was leading a ragged band of men. He barked an order to one of his officers: "Gallop into town and fetch me a bottle of wine. I'm too embarrassed to parade this rabble of old men and farmhands into the city, so

"Harry to Harry, shall hot horse to horse,
Meet and ne'er part till one drop down a corpse!"

we'll go around, outside the city walls."

"Is that you, Falstaff?" called Prince Harry, riding up on a fine horse. "Why have you stopped? And who are these pitiful rascals with you?"

"My soldiers, Hal," replied Falstaff.

"Dressed in rags and starving!" the prince exclaimed. "I know what you've been up to, you rogue. You've taken bribes to let the good, wealthy soldiers return home, and filled the gaps by emptying prison cells."

Falstaff shrugged. "A man has to make a living."

"Let's hope they can fight, and that you can, too, my portly friend. Hotspur waits for us on the field," said Harry, and he galloped away.

On the green plain, in the bleak light before the dawn, the two sides met.

"We're outnumbered two to one," Worcester whispered to Hotspur as they rode between their men. "Too many of our allies have abandoned us."

"We will fight twice as hard," Hotspur answered defiantly. "Besides, even with these odds, the king fears defeat. Look, he's sending someone to negotiate."

Sir Walter rode across the plain from King Henry's side. "The king will hear your grievances," he said, halting before Hotspur. "He promises to pardon anyone that remains loyal."

Hotspur laughed bitterly. "We know the king's promises," he said. "It was the Percy family that gave him shelter when he was nothing but an outlaw. He made a vow to my father that all he wanted was to become a duke, but in his greed he saw a chance to kill Richard and seize the throne. Since then, he has refused to ransom Mortimer, my kinsman, claimed my victories as his own and dismissed my friends from court. He has broken too many oaths and has no true claim to the crown. Ride back to your false king, and sharpen your swords."

A blood-red sun rose over the hill as the two armies charged. After the first clash of cavalry, a cloud of dust rose from the battlefield, and knights stumbled and circled in deadly duels.

The fierce Scottish general, Douglas, circled Sir Walter. "Are you the king?" he said, raising his sword. The king was proving impossible to find, as many of his knights wore the same helmet, to confuse the enemy. "Yield to me as a prisoner!"

"I was not born to yield," cried Sir Walter, wheeling his sword in the air. But Douglas knocked him to the ground with a terrible, deathly blow.

Hotspur rushed over. "If you'd fought as hard when I met you last time," he shouted, "I'd never have defeated you. Fight on; we're winning."

"We've already won," Douglas replied. "The king lies dead before you."

"No," said Hotspur, examining the dead knight. "That's Sir Walter. They wear disguises to cheat us of Henry."

"I'll murder them all," Douglas bellowed in a rage, and he charged into a crowd of enemy knights.

Somewhere amid all the valiant knights, Falstaff was creeping through the gloom, looking for a place to hide. "I should never have left London," he whimpered. "I was safer there, with the thieves and cutthroats."

Prince Harry came at him out of nowhere. "What are you doing?" he barked. "This is no time for loafing, you lazy oaf. Lend me your sword."

"My pistol has more of a bite," replied Falstaff.

The prince reached down to Falstaff's pistol holster, and found

Hal, Act 5, Scene 3

a bottle of wine stuffed in there. He hurled it at Falstaff. "Don't joke with me, you fool," he snapped.

King Henry came running up. "My son," he cried, "You're bleeding. Harry, you must fall back to the tents and rest."

"I'll stay and fight on, my lord," said Harry staunchly. "God forbid a shallow scratch should drive any son of yours from such a field as this."

As he spoke, Douglas burst through the king's guard and raised his sword. "Are you another counterfeit?" he roared. "Or do I face Henry? True or false, I'll kill you to make sure."

But Prince Harry stepped in front of the king. "Look into my eyes, vile Scot," he shouted, scything his sword through the air. "I might be the last thing you see."

Douglas met the blade with his own but was soon forced backwards. As the ranks closed around the prince, Douglas retreated. "Rally the men," Harry called to his father. "I'll stay here and hunt for Percy."

"I can help you there," came a voice, and Hotspur emerged from the clouds of dust. "Your hunt, and your life, is over."

Hal faced him grimly. "Now we can decide," he said, "which Harry should rule England. Two suns cannot share the same sky."

The two princes smashed swords and shields together, oblivious to the battle raging around them.

Falstaff, unseen, was crawling through fallen bodies on the ground. He curled up, pretending to be dead, as warriors fought around him, and watched in amazement as his friend overpowered and cut down the famous Hotspur.

197

The prince stood over his fallen enemy, staring into Hotspur's dead, still face. "Goodbye, great heart," he said. "All mistakes will be buried with you. We will remember you for your heroic deeds."

He turned and saw Falstaff curled on the ground. "Are you dead too?" he cried. "My old tavern-friend, I swear I will bury you with banners flying over your grave. But now I must find my father." He staggered away into the murky light.

Glancing around to see if it was safe, Falstaff dragged himself onto his feet. "Bury me?" he muttered, "no need for that just yet. But if I am alive, perhaps that Percy is only pretending to be dead."

He went and bent over Hotspur's body. "He's gone all right," he said. The knowledge filled him with something like bravery and he puffed out his chest. "But if he had stirred, I'd have finished him off in a flash. I think that deserves a reward. I'll carry him to the king. His Majesty will make me an earl for this."

Unbeknown to Falstaff, Prince Harry had circled back in his search for the king, and was watching him through the haze. "I'm glad to see you alive, you rascal," he chuckled to himself. "You take your luggage to the king. If it brings you a prize I won't stand in your way. But I can hear our trumpets sounding the victory call. The battle's won. Now we'll count the cost, and see which friends have lived or died."

In the weeks that followed, the rebel leaders were called to task for what they had done. King Henry ordered Worcester to be executed for treason, but allowed Prince Harry to decide the fate of the captured warrior, Douglas. The prince showed mercy and sent the brave Scot home to his family.

Hotspur was dead and his army crushed – but the rebellion smouldered on across the land. Exhausted by the strain of the conflict, King Henry grew sick and died. The old monarch had worried to the end that his son would soon return to his old habits of drinking and gambling. But, when Harry was crowned King Henry V, he showed the world his kingly qualities. He rose to the challenge like a bright and glorious sun. He was just, and broke all ties with the tavern rogues and highwaymen he had once called his friends. Henry V dreamed of winning glory in distant lands, just as his father had. His courage inspired the people of England to unite and join him in a series of breathtaking victories…

But that is another story.

Julius Caesar

Caesar is celebrating his military victories with a procession through Rome. But comets, lightning and other evil omens hint at danger ahead. Who will the Roman people support in a time of war and treason – Caesar or his enemies?

Julius Caesar

A popular Roman leader. His ambition and increasing power have made him new enemies among the city's law-makers.

Cassius

The leader of a group of Roman senators plotting to bring down Julius Caesar.

Brutus

A respected senator. Cassius will need his support if the conspiracy is to succeed.

Calpurnia
Caesar's wife. Disturbed by all the evil omens, she begs her husband not to go to the Senate house on 15th March.

Mark Antony
One of Caesar's dearest friends and supporters. Could be an obstacle to the conspirators…

Lepidus
Allied with Octavius and Antony. But they do not regard him as an equal partner.

Octavius
Caesar's nephew and heir. He is a clever politician whose fortunes are on the rise…

YMBALS CLASHED AND TRUMPETS BLARED. The streets of Rome were thronging with people: nobles and commoners alike pressed forward, all of them straining to see Julius Caesar parade in triumph through the capital. His chariot glinted with gold and polished steel. His legionaries, fresh from victory in the civil war, proudly flaunted their battle standards. Caesar raised his arm to greet the crowds.

Then, through the din, a sombre voice rang out. "Caesar!" it called. "Tomorrow is the Ides of March: the fifteenth day. Beware the Ides of March!"

"Who is it in the crowd that calls to me?" Caesar asked, stepping down from his chariot. "Speak once again."

The crowd parted, and a soothsayer shuffled forward, leaning on a staff. "Beware the Ides of March," he repeated. "It's a day of evil omen for you."

Caesar paused at this warning, then shook his head impatiently. "He is a dreamer. Carry on!" With a flourish of trumpets, the procession continued, and the soothsayer was soon lost from view.

As Caesar's chariot turned into another square, two men hung back, frowning at the cheering crowds. They were Brutus and Cassius – high-ranking Roman law-makers, or senators.

"Caesar's power is growing day by day," Brutus mused. "I fear the people will choose him for their king,"

"You fear it? Then you must wish it not to be so," said Cassius.

"True, although I love him well," Brutus admitted.

"I know you're a man of honour," said Cassius, "and I love Caesar as much as you – but now he towers above the world like a Colossus. We senators are becoming little more than underlings. Is there only room in Rome for one man? Why should his name ring out more than yours? Brutus is a noble name too, and it's one to strike fear in tyrants' hearts."

"I think I know what you're getting at," Brutus replied thoughtfully.

The two friends parted, and Cassius watched Brutus go. "Brutus, you are noble," he thought, "but you can be seduced. Caesar hates me, but he loves you – and that may be his downfall!"

That night, a terrible storm lit up the sky. Thunder shook the heavens, and fiery meteors dropped through the clouds. Ghosts went gliding through deserted streets, and wild lions roared from the steps of the temples. In the flickering light of the storm, two figures met.

"Cassius, is that you?"

"Yes, Casca, it's me." The two senators greeted one another.

"What a dreadful night!" Casca exclaimed. "Who ever knew the heavens to be so menacing?"

"These strange sights are a warning, Casca. Can't you guess what tyranny provokes the skies?"

"Indeed I can," Casca replied. "They say the senators tomorrow mean to make Caesar a king."

"I know what I'd do with this dagger then," swore Cassius, drawing his weapon. "I'd bury it in my breast. I'd rather die than serve him. But you should know that, along with some of the noblest-minded Romans, I've made a secret plan for a bloody, fiery and most terrible deed."

"Well, you can count on me," said Casca firmly. "Now, if only we could win noble Brutus to our party! The people hold him in their hearts: whatever ills we do, will change in him to virtue and to worthiness."

"I'm on my way to see him now," replied Cassius. "He's three quarters on our side already. One more push will make him ours."

At that very moment, Brutus was pacing back and forth in his garden. "Since Cassius first set me against Caesar, I haven't slept a wink," he muttered. "I have no personal grudge against Caesar, but he wants to be crowned king – and who knows how that might change his nature? He's like a serpent's egg that, when hatched, grows dangerous. We should kill him in the shell."

There was a knock at his garden gate, and Brutus looked up to see Cassius and a small band of men whose faces were hidden in their cloaks.

"Here are the other conspirators, then," said Brutus. "Cassius, do I know these men?"

"Yes. They are fellow senators every one, and every one honours you," replied Cassius.

"Give me your hands, then, all." And one by one, the senators entered, revealing themselves to shake hands with Brutus.

"How shall we proceed?" one man asked. "Is Caesar the only one who should be touched?"

"I don't think Mark Antony, so well-beloved by Caesar, should outlive him," Cassius said. "He's a shrewd character, and could hinder our plans."

Brutus frowned. "It would seem too bloody to cut the head off and then hack off the limbs too – for Antony is really just a limb of Caesar. Let's be sacrificers, but not butchers! Let's kill boldly, but not wrathfully."

"Then let Antony live," the conspirators agreed.

"Will Caesar come to the Senate house today?" another senator asked. "Tonight's evil signs and omens may keep him home. And remember, the day that's dawning is the Ides of March."

"No, we will all of us be there to fetch him," said Cassius grimly. "Now, go your separate ways. Remember what you've said, and show yourselves to be true Romans!"

The senators slunk away as the first light began to dawn.

Close by, Julius Caesar himself was tossing and turning in his bed as the sun came up. "Neither heaven nor earth have been at peace tonight," he muttered, trying not to disturb his wife.

But Calpurnia was wide awake, listening to the weird storm raging, and the hooting of owls, and the roaring lions. "Caesar, you know I've never paid attention to omens," she said, "but now they frighten me. People have reported dreadful and uncanny sights: blazing comets, lionesses roaming in the streets, and clouds that drizzled blood. Please, don't go to the Senate house today. I am afraid for you."

Caesar frowned. "Cowards die a thousand deaths in their imaginations. The brave man only needs to face death once. It seems strange to me that men should fear the fate that, after all, will come when it will come."

Calpurnia kneeled by her husband's side. "Alas, my lord, don't go. Call it my fear that keeps you in the house, and not your own. We'll send Mark Antony to the Senate house, and he can say you aren't well today. Please, for my sake."

At this, Caesar started to relent. "Very well," he began – but just then, a servant knocked at the bedroom door.

"Caesar," the servant said, "Cassius is here, and the other senators, come to fetch you to the Senate."

"Tell them I won't be coming out today," Caesar replied.

Then came Cassius's voice: "But Caesar, the Senate has decided to grant you a crown today. Don't give the senators time to change their minds!"

"How foolish your fears seem now, Calpurnia," Caesar said.

"Cowards die many times before their deaths,
The valiant never taste of death but once."

Julius Caesar, Act 2, Scene 2

"Here's Cassius come to fetch me. Give me my robe, and I'll go."

Accompanied by Cassius and the other senators, Caesar made his way through the bustling streets. As he approached the Senate house, the soothsayer was waiting for him.

"The Ides of March are come," Caesar said to him.

"Ay, Caesar, but not gone," the soothsayer warned.

Shaking his head impatiently, Caesar strode on into the Senate house. In the great, column-filled hall, people were bustling about before the day's proceedings. One by one, the conspirators gathered around Caesar.

"Good morning, Caesar," said Casca on his right.

"A word with you, my lord," murmured Cassius to his left.

"My lord, a word," said Brutus, drawing close.

As they formed a ring around him, the senators all drew daggers from their cloaks. Casca struck the first blow, stabbing Caesar in the side. Blades flashed as each conspirator joined in. Caesar stumbled and fell to the marble floor, looking up to see Brutus thrust a dagger in his breast.

"You, too, Brutus? Then I must die," he gasped with his last breath.

"We've done it. Liberty! Freedom! Tyranny is dead!" one senator cried, waving his bloody dagger. People rushed from the hall to spread the news, and there was shouting in the street.

"Where's Antony?" Cassius asked. "He's still a danger."

"Here he comes," said Brutus.

Antony hurried into the Senate house and stood over his friend's dead body. "Oh, mighty Caesar," he cried, "are all your conquests, glories, triumphs, spoils, shrunk to this little measure? Brutus, Cassius, I don't know who else you mean to kill today. If I'm to die, there's no better time than this hour of Caesar's death, and no better instrument than those daggers of yours, made rich by his noble blood."

"Antony, don't beg us for your death!" Brutus replied. "We did this for Rome's sake, and bear you no ill will."

"We hope you'll be an ally," Cassius said, "when we explain to the people why we've done this deed."

Antony stared down at the blood beneath his feet. "I don't doubt your wisdom," he began. "Alas, I stand on slippery ground, and you must think me either a coward or a flatterer, but if you can give me good reasons for killing Caesar, I'll make peace with you."

"I knew you'd understand," said Brutus.

"As Caesar's friend, I hope you'll let me speak at his funeral," Antony added.

"Of course, of course," Brutus assured him.

"Brutus!" Cassius hissed. "Don't let him speak!"

"I'll speak first," insisted Brutus, "and show the reason for Caesar's death. Antony can speak after me."

With that, the senators went out to calm the crowds. Only Antony remained, his head in his hands, with Caesar's corpse. "Oh, pardon me, please, for being meek and gentle with these butchers. Woe to the hands that shed your costly blood! This I predict: soon, civil strife will sweep through Rome. And Caesar's spirit, raging for revenge, come hot from Hell, will then cry 'havoc!' and let loose the dogs of war – and this foul deed will lead to many more dead men's bodies groaning for burial."

Outside, a growing crowd of Romans buzzed with anger and confusion. Brutus stepped up to a podium and raised his hands for silence. "Romans, hear me! If you ask why I rose against Caesar, this is my answer: not that I loved Caesar less, but that I loved Rome more. If he were living, you'd all be slaves to his ambition.

And what true Roman would be happy as a slave? You? Or you? Or you?"

The crowd was silent, and Brutus continued. "I rejoiced in Caesar's good fortune. I honoured him for his valour. But I slew him for his ambition. In doing so, I set you free. Have I done wrong?"

"No!" the people cried. "He speaks truly. Long live Brutus!"

Satisfied, Brutus stepped down, and Antony took his place.

"Friends, Romans, countrymen, lend me your ears," Antony called. "I come to bury Caesar, not to praise him. The evil that men do lives after them; the good is often buried with their bones. Yes, Caesar was ambitious. Brutus says so, and Brutus is an honourable man. Caesar was my friend, faithful and just. He brought victories to Rome, and filled our coffers. When the poor cried, Caesar wept. But Brutus says he was ambitious, and Brutus is an honourable man. I won't argue with him, rather I will simply say what I know about Caesar."

The Romans looked at one another. "It's true," some whispered, "Caesar was bold and generous."

"Look," Antony continued, "here's a parchment closed with Caesar's seal. It's his will, and if you'd read it, you'd know how Caesar loved you. Shall I read it? No. I don't want to wrong those honourable men who murdered Caesar. Look – look, here's his cloak: see where Cassius ran his dagger through, where Casca ripped, where well-beloved Brutus stabbed. And that was the unkindest cut of all."

"Were they honourable men? Or were they traitors?" the

"Friends, Romans, countrymen, lend me your ears.
I come to bury Caesar, not to praise him."

people began to murmur.

"Read Caesar's will!" one Roman cried.

"Good friends, I don't want to start a riot," Antony continued. "The men that did these things are wise and honourable. I'm no great speaker like Brutus. I'm just a plain man who loved his friend. I have no power of speech – but if that eloquent Brutus were in my place, he could put a tongue in every one of Caesar's wounds, and they would speak to move all Rome to mutiny."

"Mutiny!" echoed the crowd. "Let's mutiny!"

"Read us the will!"

"Peace, peace. Here is the will. To every Roman citizen Caesar gives seventy-five silver coins. He leaves you all his lands on this side of the River Tiber, to be yours forever: to be your orchards, walks and parks."

"Most noble Caesar," the people cheered. "We'll avenge his death. Let's burn the traitors' houses!"

The crowd surged forward. Brutus and the other conspirators slipped through alleys and back streets away from the angry mob.

"Now mischief is afoot," Antony thought. "Let it take what course it may."

In the days that followed, civil war broke out. The conspirators raised an army among their supporters in the countryside. In Rome, three new rulers came forward to share power during the crisis: Antony, Lepidus, and Caesar's nephew, Octavius. They rallied their legions and marched out to confront the rebel troops. Skirmish after skirmish, battle after battle, the war ground on.

One night, in a makeshift camp by the side of a road, the war-weary generals Brutus and Cassius met to discuss their strategy.

"Our foes are nearing the town of Philippi," Brutus announced as Cassius joined him in his tent. "I think we should march and meet them in battle there."

"I've heard the same," said Cassius, "but wouldn't it be better if we stayed here and let the enemy seek us out, tiring their troops while we await them full of rest, defence and nimbleness?"

Brutus considered this. "I fear that if we wait, they'll recruit more troops and meet us with a heavier force. Our army is at its strongest. There is a tide in the affairs of men which, if you catch it when the moment's right, leads on to fortune. We're floating on such a sea right now, and I feel the tide is about to turn."

"Very well, then we'll meet them at Philippi."

Their decision taken, the two shook hands, and Cassius returned to his troops. Exhausted, Brutus slumped down into a chair and tried to read a few pages of a book. He could barely keep his eyes open, and the oil lamp on his table began to sputter and smoke. Suddenly, in the flickering light, Brutus saw that he wasn't alone: a dim shadow took form.

"Who comes here?" Brutus cried. "Are you some god, some angel, or some devil? Tell me what you are!"

"Your evil spirit, Brutus," said the shadow – and it spoke with Caesar's voice.

"Why have you come?"

"To tell you," the shadow continued, "that you will see me again at Philippi."

"What? What? What do you mean?" stammered Brutus, but the apparition was already gone.

The next day, the opposing armies arrived near Philippi. They tramped into position, facing off on an open plain surrounded by rocky hills. Antony, Octavius and Lepidus stood at the head of

"There is a tide in the affairs of men
Which, taken at the flood, leads on to fortune..."

BRUTUS, ACT 4, SCENE 2

their troops, and watched as Brutus and Cassius stepped forward holding a white flag of truce.

"Shall we go to speak to them?" Lepidus asked.

"You stay here," said Antony. "Octavius and I will go."

"Why don't you trust Lepidus?" Octavius asked, as he and Antony strode out from their lines. "After all, he's a tried and valiant soldier."

"So is my horse, Octavius," Antony replied. "And like my horse, Lepidus is a creature we tell to come and go, to stand or fight. He shares in our power to help carry our load, and will bear it like a donkey bears gold. Having brought our treasure where we will, we'll shake his ears and send him grazing in the commons."

"I see," said Octavius.

Brutus raised his hand in weary greeting as the two approached. "Words before blows. Is it so, countrymen?"

"We know you love words more than blows, Brutus," Octavius replied hotly.

"Good words are better than bad strokes," said Brutus.

"Where were your good words when your dagger hacked at Caesar?" demanded Antony.

"Come, let's away," Octavius said, turning on his heel. "Traitors, we defy you. Fight us if you dare."

Brutus and Cassius watched them go. "Cassius," Brutus said sadly, "this day must end the work the Ides of March began. And whether we shall meet again I know not."

"For ever and for ever farewell, then, Brutus."

The trumpets blared and, with a heavy tread, the armies moved into battle. The fight was long and gruesome, each side making advances in turn, and piercing the ranks of the enemy.

In the thick of the action, Cassius was surrounded by pressing walls of shields and darting spears. Swords hacked and flashed. He saw his troops falling one by one. The Roman legions were closing in on him from the left and right, and with a few surviving soldiers, he retreated up a nearby hill. From the top, he could see enemy reinforcements gathering, and now his capture seemed certain.

"Oh, I'm a coward to have lived so long," Cassius cried. Despairing, he turned to one of his companions and handed him his blade. "Come, Pindarus. My life has run its course. With this good sword that ran through Caesar, stab me in the breast. Here. Take the hilt."

Loyal and unthinking, Pindarus obeyed his master, and Cassius fell to the ground. "Caesar, here is your revenge," Cassius gasped with his last breath, and died.

Meanwhile, on the other side of the battlefield, Brutus too was retreating before Antony's men. Night was falling, and his army's ranks were shattered. Here and there, small bands of rebel soldiers resisted, clashing in the fading light, or fled, throwing down their shields and swords to make their escape.

With a handful of his soldiers, Brutus reached a sheltering outcrop of rock. They dropped to the ground to rest, and some, exhausted by hours of fighting, immediately fell asleep.

Brutus sat and spoke to one of his old companions, Volumnius. "Old friend, the ghost of Caesar has now appeared to me twice. Once in my tent, and once again tonight, in Philippi. I know my hour has come."

"Not so, my lord!"

"I'm sure of it. Our enemies have beaten us to the grave. It's better to leap in ourselves than wait for them to push us."

A trumpet sounded nearby, and the soldiers heaved themselves up from the ground to flee again. As one soldier jerked up from a deep sleep, Brutus grabbed his arm. "I beg you, Strato, stay, and do me this service: hold my sword for me."

"Give me your hand first. Farewell, my lord," Strato replied.

"Farewell, good Strato," said Brutus.

Strato held Brutus's sword firmly by the hilt, and with a few quick steps, Brutus ran, throwing himself onto the blade. Held in Strato's arms, with his last breath he whispered, "Caesar, now be still. I kill myself more willingly than I killed you."

The trumpet sounded again even closer. Accompanied by soldiers and torchbearers, Antony and Octavius approached to find their enemy dead among the rocks.

Antony kneeled by Brutus's side. "This was the noblest Roman of them all," he said. "He was the only conspirator who acted not from envy but for common good. His life was gentle. Elements combined in him in such a way that nature could stand up and say to all the world, 'This was a man'."

"We'll bury him according to his virtue," Octavius declared, "honourably, and like a soldier. So call the field to rest. Let's be away. It's time we shared the glories of this happy day."

At his command, four soldiers lifted the conspirator's body, and both the victors and the vanquished returned to the armies on the plain.

The Two Gentlemen of Verona

When one man falls for his best friend's beloved,
how far will he go to get what he wants?
Would he sacrifice friendship as well as the love
of the woman to whom he promised to be true?

Lance

Proteus's hilariously idiotic servant and his dog, Crab.

Speed

Valentine's amusing and quick-witted servant.

The Duke of Milan

Silvia's father wants what's best for her. Unfortunately, he thinks that's Thurio.

Thurio

Would-be beloved of Julia. Rich and rather clueless.

Silvia

A lady who knows what she wants and keeps her promises. She is clever, capable and true to her heart.

Valentine

Didn't believe in love until he went to Milan to seek his fortune and fell for Silvia. Unfortunately her father has other plans for her…

TWO YOUNG MEN SAT CHATTING in Verona's market square. They were best friends, and had lived in the little Italian town all their lives. But now one of them, Valentine, was leaving to seek his fortune in Milan.

"Proteus, stop trying to persuade me to stay," Valentine scolded his friend fondly. "I'd ask you to come too, if you weren't chained here by love."

Proteus sighed, "So you're definitely going. Goodbye then, dear Valentine. Think of me on your travels. I wish you every happiness in Milan."

"Same to you here. Write to me with your news," said Valentine, "and I'll write back with mine. Farewell, Proteus."

When Valentine had gone, Proteus sat back down, lost in thought. "There he goes, hunting honour. Here I stay, looking for love. He is leaving his friends – but in a way so am I… for love! Oh Julia," he sighed, "you've changed me, made me neglect my studies, lose my time…"

Just then, a man sprinted up and stumbled to a halt. It was Speed, Valentine's servant. "Have you seen my master?" he panted.

"He just left," Proteus replied. "Did you give Julia my letter?"

Speed scowled. "Yes I did. But she gave me sweet nothing in return," he grumbled.

"Did she say anything?" Proteus asked eagerly.

"No, not even, 'Here's a penny for your pains,'" Speed said pointedly, holding out his hand.

With a sour face, Proteus pressed a coin into it, and Speed dashed off to find his master.

The young lady in question was at that very moment sitting in her house only a few streets away, brushing her long, blonde hair.

"Should I fall in love with any of my admirers, or not?" she asked her servant, Lucetta. "Which one do you think is the best?"

"List them and I'll tell you," Lucetta replied.

"Sir Eglamour. He's handsome…" Julia began.

"A knight, and fine, but I wouldn't choose him."

"How about Mercatio? He's rich…"

"His money's good, but he's only so-so."

"What do you think of Proteus? He seems gentle…"

"I think he's the best."

"He doesn't declare undying love as much as the others…"

"Fire that's kept closest burns most of all… Anyway, he sent a servant with this." Lucetta handed Julia a letter.

Julia blushed. "How dare he send me a letter! And how dare you accept it! What will people think?" she protested.

She snatched the letter, glanced over it, blushed even brighter, then tore it to shreds and flung them to the ground.

Hiding her grin, Lucetta left. The moment she was alone, Julia gathered up the shreds and pieced them together, reading feverishly. "It says 'kind Julia' but I'm not kind, am I, flinging his words to the floor?… It says 'love-wounded Proteus'. Poor wounded name that I've torn to pieces." She folded the strips of paper, kissed them, and tucked them inside her dress.

A few days later, Proteus received a letter from Julia, declaring her love in return. Overjoyed, he sent a message asking her to meet him. When she agreed, he thought he would die of happiness.

By the time they met, however, his face was as long as a rainy Sunday. "My father is sending me to Milan," he moaned. "He thinks I'll benefit from seeing the world and spending time at court with the duke. Oh Julia! I promise to come back as soon as I can."

Julia took a ring from her finger and pressed it into his palm. "Take this to remind you of me," she said.

Proteus gave her a ring from his finger in return.

"And seal the bargain with a holy kiss," said Julia. Shyly, happily, they kissed.

With a deep sigh, Proteus said, "If I forget you for even a single hour, I hope something utterly hideous happens to me. I must go now, my father is waiting. Julia, farewell."

Proteus went down to the dock. His servant Lance came running after him, dragging a scrawny dog behind him on a piece of string. "My dog Crab is the hardest-hearted dog there ever was," he proclaimed. "Everyone wept at us leaving home: my mother, my father, even the cat – but this cruel-hearted cur has not shed a single tear."

"Hurry up Lance, or you'll have to row there," Proteus scolded. He said farewell to his father, and then he and Lance boarded the ship and set sail for Milan.

In Milan, Valentine was even happier than he had thought he would be, for he had unexpectedly fallen in love. The lady in question was the duke's daughter, Silvia.

He was so besotted with her, even his servant Speed had guessed it. "You have learned – like Sir Proteus – to relish a love song like a robin redbreast; to walk alone like one who had the plague; to sigh like a schoolboy that had lost his A B C..." he teased, "and you can't even see it. Love is blind."

Valentine sighed. "Last night she asked me to write a love letter to someone she loves."

"Ah, so did you make a mess of it to scupper their chances?" Speed asked.

"Not at all," Valentine protested. "I did it as well as I could... Hush! Here she comes now..."

Silvia, a pretty lady with shining auburn hair, walked by, and Valentine called to her, "Good day, my lady. I have written the letter you asked for." He handed her the beautifully penned paper.

"Thank you," said Silvia. "Was it too much to ask?"

"I'd do anything for you, but… it was tricky, not knowing whom it was for," Valentine faltered. "It might not be the best letter ever…"

"Then take it back," said Silvia abruptly. "Here. It's for you. If you don't like it, then it's not good enough."

Valentine took the letter back, looking dejected. "I will write a better one, and next time I'll make sure I'm moved by it before I give it to you," he promised.

"Good," said Silvia, smiling as she walked away.

Valentine turned to find Speed doubled up with laughter.

"What's the matter with you?" Valentine demanded.

"How can you have missed the joke?" giggled Speed. "Your beloved gave you a letter."

"The letter I wrote to her friend," said Valentine.

"Yes, and she delivered it. That's the end," Speed said.

Valentine looked at him blankly.

Speed rolled his eyes. "She has received many a letter from you, but was too modest to write one back," he explained. "So she got you to write one to yourself!"

The next day, Silvia, the duke and Valentine gathered at the dock to welcome Proteus's ship. Valentine had sung his friend's praises to the duke and his daughter, so they couldn't wait to meet him. As he stepped off the ship, Silvia's warm smile quite dazzled Proteus.

Later, when the two friends were alone, Valentine asked, "What's your news? How is your lady?"

"Tales of my love life will only bore you…" Proteus said.

"I've changed," said Valentine. "I'm in love too."

"With whom? The lady I just met?" Proteus asked, thinking

of the way beautiful Silvia had smiled at him.

Valentine nodded dreamily. "Isn't she divine? And she is mine! Silvia has agreed – in secret – to marry me," he confided. His expression darkened. "Her father has already promised her to another man called Thurio, whom he only prefers because of his wealth… We have decided to elope in the dead of night. Come and see me later, Proteus. I'll tell you everything."

After Valentine left, Proteus found himself wrestling with his feelings. "Just as one nail drives out another, so my new feelings for Silvia are driving out my feelings for Julia." He tried to pull himself together. "It's Julia I love, not Silvia," he told himself firmly. "Besides, what about Valentine? I couldn't steal my best friend's beloved."

Later that evening, Valentine confided his entire plot to steal away with Silvia, and Proteus tried his best to be happy for him. But as he went to bed for the first night in Milan, he thought to himself: "It's no good. If I am true to Julia and to Valentine, I can't be true to myself. I did adore a twinkling star, but now I worship a glorious sun: Silvia. I love her. It can't be helped. I will have to get Valentine out of the way… and then deal with Thurio."

At home, Julia was pining for Proteus so much she had decided to take action. She would disguise herself as a boy and travel to Milan to see him. That way she could travel alone without attracting unwelcome attention, and spend time with her beloved in Milan without causing a scandal.

Lucetta had made her some boy's clothes, and she tried them

"*At first I did adore a twinkling star,*
But now I worship a celestial sun."

Proteus, Act 2, Scene 6

on, tucking her long blonde hair inside the cap. "I'll call myself Sebastian," she told Lucetta, "and seek work in the service of a gentleman…" The thought filled her with nerves. "What will people think of me if they find out?"

"If you're worried about that, don't go," advised Lucetta. "What will Proteus think of you when you arrive?"

"That's the least of my worries," Julia assured her. "His words are his bonds… His love is sincere."

"I hope so, for your sake," Lucetta thought, waving goodbye.

Proteus, meanwhile, had told the duke all about Valentine's secret plot. "I feel it's my duty to tell you this, although I do not want to betray my friend's confidence," he lied.

The duke assured him he would make no mention of who had told him, then went to confront Valentine. Finding the story to be true, he exiled Valentine from Milan. He was to leave that very day.

Valentine was in his chamber when Proteus and Lance rushed in. "You are vanished!" Lance bawled. "We just heard!"

"Banished," Proteus corrected. "Valentine, are you all right?"

"No," said Valentine. "I am not."

Proteus bit his lip. His friend looked so utterly miserable he couldn't help but feel a pang of guilt.

"Does Silvia know?" Valentine asked.

"Yes. She is weeping and begging her father for mercy but it's no good. He threatened her with prison unless she sees sense…" Proteus said honestly, wincing at Valentine's devastated expression.

He couldn't bear it any longer; he had to get Valentine out of here. "Come on, I'll walk you to the city gates," he said, pulling Valentine to his feet. "You can write to her. Send letters to me. I'll make sure she gets them…" He had no intention of doing so, but it would help get Valentine out of the way…

"Lance, go and find Speed," Valentine said. "Ask him to meet me at the North Gate."

Lance nodded and watched them go. Then he sat down, pulled out a scrap of paper and studied it, scratching his head.

Speed came by and found him there. "How now, Lance?" he said. "What have you got there?" He snatched the piece of paper and started to read it out: "'She can milk; she brews good ale; she can sew and knit; she can wash and scour…' What's all this?"

"I'm in love. I won't tell you with whom, but this is a list I've written of her virtues. After those I've listed her vices…" Lance explained.

Speed read on: "'She can't be kissed because of her foul breath; she has a sweet tooth; she is slow with words; she has no teeth; she likes a drink or two… but she is rich.'"

"That's made up my mind: I'll take her," said Lance. "By the way, your master's waiting for you at the North Gate. He's been exiled."

"Wha–a–at? Why didn't you tell me that sooner?" Speed said. He thrust the list back at Lance and ran off.

Valentine and Speed left Milan. A little while later, they were passing through a forest, when a band of outlaws leaped out from the trees. "Hand over everything," they demanded.

"Friends—" Valentine began.

"We aren't friends, we're enemies!" one of the outlaws said.

"Quiet," said another. "Let's hear what he's got to say."

"I don't have very much with me, having just been exiled from Milan," Valentine said sadly. "It is all I have left in the world."

"Why were you exiled?" asked the first outlaw.

Valentine saw his chance. "I slew a man," he lied.

The outlaws looked impressed. "Then you can be our leader!" said one. "We're all gentlemen, banished for wooing the wrong ladies mostly… Come on, we won't take no for an answer."

THE DUKE OF MILAN, ACT 3, SCENE 2

After Valentine's departure, Proteus found the Duke of Milan talking to Thurio. The duke confided in his new friend: "I had hoped, with Valentine out of the way, that Silvia would see what a good match Thurio was."

"She spurns me," Thurio added gloomily, "and mopes all day."

"A little more time might melt her cold thoughts, and make her forget about Valentine…" said the duke.

Proteus agreed. "Yes – but she probably also needs to hear that Valentine is not so worthy… from someone she knows is his friend," he added slyly.

"Someone such as you…?" the duke ventured.

"I would not be much of a friend to speak ill behind his back…" said Proteus, feigning indignance.

"But Valentine is gone now – your words won't affect him either way…" the duke assured him.

"And while telling her how unworthy Valentine is, you can tell her how very worthy I am," Thurio suggested piteously.

"I can try," Proteus said. "But Thurio you need to do something too. Write love letters, saying you are sacrificing tears upon the altar of her beauty; serenade her with love songs…"

"Valentine was right about you," said the duke. "You are indeed a faithful defender of true love."

Nobody saw Proteus's cheeks grow red, nor the shameful way he looked down at his feet.

Proteus's plan had worked. From that moment on, the duke encouraged him to spend as much time alone with Silvia as he wanted – without suspecting a thing. But in another way it was not going well at all. Whenever Proteus tried to say something against

Valentine, Silvia accused him of betraying his friend. And if he paid her a compliment, she begged him to think of his beloved Julia.

And at the same time, he was having to help Thurio creep about under her window serenading her with terrible love songs. It was all becoming rather unbearable.

But Proteus didn't give up. He sent Lance with a pretty little dog as a present. But Lance lost it on the way, so offered his own mangy hound in its place. Unfortunately, when he dragged it into the lady's dining chamber, the dog stole the meat off her plate and cocked its leg on her tablecloth…

Unsurprisingly, she rejected the gift.

When a sweet, young man named Sebastian arrived at court, looking for work, Proteus asked to see him. "He looks a lot more sensitive than that oaf Lance," he thought. Little did he know that this boy was actually Julia in disguise.

"I have some delicate business you can help me with," he told her. "It's a matter of love." He pulled the very ring Julia had given him from his finger, and pressed it into her hand. "Give this to Lady Silvia for me, Sebastian. The lady who gave this ring to me loved me."

Julia stared at it, her face as white as a ghost. "Alas!" she cried.

Proteus stared. "Why do you say that?"

"I – I pity her," Julia stammered, trying not to give herself away. "She must have loved you just as much as you love this Lady Silvia."

Proteus looked uncomfortable. "Well, anyway… please give Silvia the ring and ask if she would give me the portrait of herself which hangs in her room," he said. "I'll wait here for you."

So off went poor Julia to do as she was told.

Silvia gave Julia the picture, but said, "Tell him from me I will not wear that ring. His false finger has worn it, but mine will not do his Julia so much wrong."

"Thank you!" Julia blurted. "I mean – she thanks you."

"Do you know her?" Silvia asked, looking at the young man before her with curiosity.

"Erm – almost as well as I know myself," Julia replied rather awkwardly.

"Is she pretty?" Silvia asked.

"She's been prettier. She's pale with weeping and the roses have faded from her cheeks," Julia said sadly.

"Poor lady. It brings tears to my own eyes. Here," she handed Julia a gold coin. "That's for being true to your mistress. Farewell."

Julia hurried out. "What a kind and beautiful woman," she thought. She stopped and looked at the painting. "I'd have scratched out your unseeing eyes to make my master love you less," she told it. "But now I'll treat you as kindly as your mistress has treated me. I just hope Proteus's love will grow cold…"

Later that day, Julia went back to Proteus's chamber and found him there with Thurio. She was just about to hand him the painting when the duke burst in. "Silvia is gone!" he cried. "The friar saw her with Sir Eglamour riding into the forest. She's gone after Valentine, I'm sure of it. Save her!"

Thurio and Proteus dashed out at once, with Julia behind them.

Deep in the woods, a band of outlaws watched from the shadows as a feeble knight and a beautiful lady galloped through the trees on horseback. As they slowed to cross a stream, the outlaws leaped out in front of them.

"Help!" yelled the knight and fled into the forest.

"Some escort he was," thought Silvia, looking after him.

"Don't worry," said one of the outlaws. "We won't harm you. We'll take you to our leader."

But as they were leading Silvia away, Proteus and Julia caught up with them. Proteus drew his sword and charged at the outlaws with a fierce roar. There was a short, sharp clash of steel, and soon the outlaws scattered and fled into the bushes.

"See what I did for you?" Proteus said to Silvia when the outlaws had gone. "Do I deserve a kind look at least?"

Silvia glared at him. "I'd rather have been a lion's breakfast than have had you rescue me. Go away!"

Proteus lost his temper. "If you won't willingly show me any love then I'll force you to," he said frustratedly, and grabbed hold of Silvia's arms to kiss her.

"Let go of her this instant!" thundered a voice, and a figure burst out from the trees. It was Valentine. He stopped in his tracks when he saw his friend. "Proteus!" he cried. "You traitor!"

Proteus let go of Silvia and sank to his knees. "What am I doing?" he thought. It was as if he were waking up from a trance, and all his wrongdoings fell on him like bucket of cold water. "Valentine, I could not be more sorry."

Valentine looked at his old friend's face and couldn't help but forgive him. "If Silvia is now yours…" he began.

"I am not!" interrupted Silvia.

There was a thump and they all looked around in astonishment to see that Sebastian had fainted to the floor. His cap fell off, and long, blonde hair spilled out…

"Julia…?" whispered Proteus.

Her eyelids fluttered open as he dived to her side. "Yes, it's me," she admitted. "I changed my appearance, which is rather embarrassing… but you did worse: you changed your mind!"

"I'm sorry," Proteus said. "I can't imagine why I ever did.

"It is the lesser blot, modesty finds,
Women to change their shapes
than men their minds."

JULIA, ACT 5, SCENE 4

What could I have seen in Silvia that is not there in you?" He gazed adoringly at Julia's face. Then he helped her to her feet and the roses bloomed in Julia's cheeks once more.

Just then, the duke and Thurio came galloping along on horseback. "There's Silvia. She's mine!" shouted Thurio, charging.

Valentine drew his sword. "Take one step closer and I won't answer for the consequences," he warned.

Thurio backed away. "I don't care for her *that* much," he said.

"What?" roared the duke, outraged. "You'd leave her just like that? You cowardly wretch! Valentine, I applaud your spirit. It seems I was wrong to think ill of you. If Silvia truly loves you, then I bless your union."

"I do love him," said Silvia, happily taking Valentine's hand.

Valentine smiled at her. Then he turned back to the duke. "May I ask one more thing? There's a band of outlaws in this forest, exiled gentlemen, who really have done very little wrong. Would you please pardon them so they may return to Milan?"

"Certainly," said the duke good-naturedly.

"Then let's all go back home," said Valentine. "We'll have a double wedding and all be happy at last."

And so they all rode back to the city of Milan, and everything was back as it should be.

Othello

With Cyprus in danger of being attacked, a general named
Othello is sent from Venice to lead its defence. But
tensions on the island are running high, and one soldier
is determined to ruin him. Slowly, Othello finds himself
eaten up by jealousy, madness and murderous intent…

Othello

A proud general, who
is also known as 'the
Moor'. Deeply in love
with Desdemona, but
trusts the wrong people.

Desdemona

Devoted wife of Othello,
who accompanies him to
Cyprus. Her kindness and
innocence are easily taken
advantage of.

Roderigo
A rich, foolish nobleman who is in love with Desdemona.

Iago
A scheming soldier who preys on the weaknesses of others. Angry that Othello has promoted Cassio ahead of him, he seeks his revenge…

Cassio
A handsome, inexperienced soldier, recently promoted to lieutenant.

Bianca
Loves Cassio, but her affections for him are not returned.

Emilia
Desdemona's loyal servant, unhappily married to Iago. Unaware of his schemes.

"I HATE HIM!" IAGO FUMED. "Othello, the Moor, has promoted Cassio to lieutenant over me!"

Roderigo tutted as he hurried alongside the soldier down a dark street. He was angry too – he'd just found out that Othello had secretly married Desdemona, the daughter of a wealthy Venetian. Roderigo had wanted to marry her himself. "This is her father's house," he said, slowing down.

Iago peered up at a window above and began to shout. "Awake, what ho, Brabanzio, thieves, thieves, thieves!"

A few moments later, an old man appeared at the window with a clatter. It was Desdemona's father, Brabanzio. "What is the matter there?" he croaked.

"You've been robbed!" Iago called up to him. "Your daughter and the Moor have run off together!"

"Oh, treason of my own flesh and blood!" Brabanzio gasped. He hadn't given his daughter permission to marry anyone – let alone Othello. "Find them! My daughter has been stolen from me – this is a matter for the Duke of Venice!"

It was the middle of the night, but the duke was in his palace discussing urgent matters of war. A fleet of Turkish ships was sailing towards Cyprus, an island in the Mediterranean under Venice's control. The Turks were preparing to attack.

Suddenly, Brabanzio burst in, dragging Othello and Desdemona with him. Iago and Roderigo slunk in behind.

"Whatever is the matter?" said the duke in surprise.

Brabanzio glared at Othello. "Oh, you foul thief! You have enchanted my daughter and married her behind my back!"

"What do you say to this, Othello?" asked the duke. Othello was one of his most trusted generals, and he valued his opinion.

Othello bowed. "It is most true that I have married her. But I used no magic. I only told her the story of my life: the battles and sieges, the travels and adventure."

The duke smiled. "This tale would win my daughter, too."

But Brabanzio was far from satisfied. "Desdemona, to whom do you owe the most obedience? To Othello or me?"

"My noble father," said Desdemona softly. "I am divided by my duties. I am your daughter, but Othello is my husband. I must show him the same duty that my mother showed you."

Brabanzio frowned at Othello. "She has deceived me, and may deceive you too," he said bitterly.

Anxious to return to matters of war, the duke cleared his throat. "Othello, our enemies, the Turks, are preparing to attack Cyprus. You must leave this very night and take charge of our castle there."

"Let me go with him!" Desdemona exclaimed, unable to bear the thought of being parted from her new husband.

Othello kissed her hand. "It would be safest if you wait until morning. My trustworthy soldier, Iago, will accompany you."

As the duke nodded in agreement, Iago and Roderigo quietly retreated out of the room. "Now I may as well drown myself," Roderigo wailed, once they were outside. "I'll never marry her!"

Iago rolled his eyes. "Why, you silly man! It won't be long before Desdemona goes off Othello." Then with a sly grin, he added, "If you give me enough money, I'll see to it that she does."

"Promise?" said Roderigo hopefully.

"You can be sure of me. Go, make money," Iago ordered.

As Roderigo scurried off, Iago smiled. "Rich fool," he thought. "I'll use his money for my own gain! I hate Othello, and I'd love to stir his marriage up… Cassio's a handsome man – maybe I'll make it seem that Desdemona is in love with him!"

Huge waves crashed onto the beach as Desdemona waited anxiously in Cyprus for her husband to arrive. Everybody had reached the island safely except Othello, whose ship had been separated from the rest by a terrible storm.

Finally, she spotted it on the horizon, and soon enough he was stepping onto the shore. "My dear Othello," she cried.

Othello hugged his wife, then turned to his soldiers. "News, friends," he announced. "Our wars are done. The Turkish fleet has been wrecked by the storm, and our enemies are drowned. Come, let us celebrate!"

With a cheer, Othello's soldiers began heading up towards the castle. Only Iago hung back. It was time to carry out the first part of his plan – to stir up trouble and get Cassio drunk, so that he would be stripped of his promotion.

"Cassio!" he called out, catching up with the lieutenant. "Have some wine with me. Let's drink to Othello's health."

"Not tonight, Iago," Cassio said warmly.

"Just one drink," Iago insisted.

Not wanting to offend his friend, Cassio followed Iago into a nearby tavern.

"Some wine, ho!" said Iago, filling up Cassio's glass.

"To the health of our general!" Cassio smiled.

Before long, the tavern was full of merry soldiers. Iago watched as Cassio grew drunker and drunker, and eventually staggered out of the door. After a few moments, he heard shouts coming from nearby, and he sauntered outside.

In the street, he found Cassio waving his sword at Roderigo. It was just as he had planned. He'd ordered Roderigo to come and provoke the drunken Cassio to a brawl.

"You rogue! You rascal!" slurred Cassio.

"God's will, gentlemen!" cried Iago, running over and standing between the two men. "Cassio, you're drunk."

"Drunk?" Cassio drawled. He tripped over himself and knocked into a passing soldier, who angrily drew his sword.

Just at that moment, Othello appeared. "What is going on here?" he bellowed.

Cassio froze and dropped his sword, while Roderigo managed to slip quietly away without being seen.

"Iago, who began this?" Othello demanded.

Iago sighed dramatically, looking at Cassio. "I'd rather not blame Cassio," he said. "Yet I must speak the truth. A fellow was crying out for help: Cassio was chasing him with his sword."

Othello's face was full of disappointment. "Cassio, I love you, but you may never more be an officer of mine," he said quietly.

A smile twitched at the corner of Iago's mouth – Cassio had lost his position as lieutenant.

Cassio hung his head in shame as Othello strode off. "My reputation, Iago! My reputation!" he lamented.

Iago put an arm around him. "I'm sure Othello will change his mind if you ask," he suggested, trying to look concerned.

"He'll tell me I'm a drunkard," Cassio sighed.

Iago moved in even closer, his eyes glittering. "Then ask Desdemona. She has a lot of influence over Othello."

A weak smile appeared on Cassio's face. "That's good advice." Straightening up, he wished Iago goodnight and left for bed.

Iago sneered. "Of course Desdemona will help, she has a kind heart," he thought to himself. "That kindness is the net I'll catch them in – her, her husband and the rest. While she pleads with

"So will I turn her virtue into pitch,
And out of her own goodness make the net
That shall enmesh them all."

Iago, Act 2, Scene 3

Othello to forgive Cassio, I'll poison the Moor against her. I'll convince him that Desdemona is in love with Cassio!"

The next morning, Cassio woke early and began looking for Desdemona. As soon as he found her, he explained everything and begged her to plead his case to her husband.

"I'll do everything I can to help you," Desdemona promised.

Spotting Othello and Iago walking towards them, Cassio thanked Desdemona and hurried off in the opposite direction.

"Was that Cassio?" Othello said, looking at Iago in surprise.

"Cassio, my lord?" Iago replied. "Surely not, I cannot think that he would hurry away so guiltily."

"My lord," Desdemona said, greeting her husband with a kiss. "Will you forgive Cassio? Call him back."

Othello laughed. "Not now, my sweet."

"Tomorrow at dinner, then?" Desdemona insisted.

Othello sighed before giving in. "I will deny you nothing."

Desdemona kissed her husband and left. Watching her go, Iago cleared his throat. "My noble lord, when you first fell in love with Desdemona, did Cassio know?" he asked casually.

"Yes," Othello replied. "He carried messages between us. Why do you ask?"

Iago tutted. "Men should be what they seem," he muttered.

"What do you mean?" Othello frowned.

"Beware, my lord, of jealousy," Iago said. "It is a green-eyed monster, which mocks the very meat it feeds on."

"What do you mean?" Othello was beginning to get angry – he could not understand what Iago was hinting at.

"Look to your wife," Iago continued. "Observe her well with Cassio. She did deceive her father, marrying you…"

Shocked, Othello grabbed Iago's arm. "My wife is virtuous," he growled, leaning in closely. "She had eyes and chose me."

Iago shrugged and looked away.

"I'll see proof before I doubt her." Othello's eyes flashed, and he dropped Iago's arm. "Leave me, Iago."

Dinner was announced, but Othello was nowhere to be seen. After searching all over the castle, Desdemona finally found him sitting in a corner, clutching his head.

"How now, my dear Othello?" she said, looking concerned.

"I have a pain upon my forehead," Othello groaned.

"Let me bind it." Desdemona pulled out a handkerchief.

"Let it alone!" Othello waved her hand away, knocking the handkerchief to the floor. "Come, let's go to dinner." He marched off to the dining hall, and Desdemona hurried after him.

Emilia, Desdemona's maid, had been standing nearby, and bent down to pick up the handkerchief. "This was Desdemona's first gift from Othello," she thought, looking at the handkerchief, which was embroidered with strawberries.

Her husband, Iago, had described that very handkerchief to her and asked her to steal it a hundred times. Unaware of any of his evil schemes, Emilia slipped it into her apron. "I have something for you!" she called out, spotting Iago in the hallway later on. She waved the handkerchief in the air.

Iago's eyes lit up and he snatched it from her greedily.

"What will you do with it?" Emilia asked.

"I have a use for it," Iago snapped, shooing Emilia away. Clasping the handkerchief in his hands, he began to think. "I'll drop this in Cassio's chamber and let him find it. When Othello sees him with the handkerchief, it will look as though Desdemona has given it to him. Othello will see it as proof that Desdemona is in love with Cassio!"

Later that evening, Othello paced back and forth restlessly. A seed of doubt had been planted in his mind, and he could not bear the idea that Desdemona could be seeing Cassio in secret. Furious, he stormed through the castle to find Iago.

"Villain!" Othello cried, grabbing Iago by the throat. "Give me proof that Desdemona has betrayed me. Or answer to my rage!"

"I'm sorry that I said anything," Iago gasped. "But if you must have proof…" He thought quickly. "Last night I slept in a bed next to Cassio. In his sleep I heard him say, 'Sweet Desdemona, let us be careful, let us hide our love.'"

"Monstrous!" Othello let go and staggered back in shock.

"And tell me this," Iago went on, advancing on Othello. "Does Desdemona have a handkerchief embroidered with strawberries?"

"It was my first gift to her," Othello answered.

"I saw Cassio wipe his face with it!" Iago said triumphantly.

"I'll tear her to pieces!" Othello cried. "Blood, blood, blood!"

Upstairs in the castle, Desdemona was rummaging through her chest looking for her handkerchief. "Emilia, have you seen it? I'd rather lose a purse full of gold coins than that…"

Hearing footsteps, Desdemona looked up to see Othello towering over her. He cast a dark shadow across her face.

"How are you, my lord?" she said softly, standing up to kiss him. Then, remembering her promise to help Cassio, she added, "Will you call for Cassio?"

"Lend me your handkerchief." Othello's eyes were cold. "The one which I gave you."

"I don't have it with me," Desedmona replied.

"That's too bad," Othello growled. "That handkerchief was given to my mother by an Egyptian charmer. There's magic in it. If it is lost or given away, terrible things will follow. Bring it to me!"

Desdemona stepped back nervously. She'd never seen Othello

in such a strange mood, and she could not recognize the look in his eyes. "Why do you speak so startlingly?" she whispered.

"The handkerchief!" Othello demanded.

Desdemona was confused. Could his anger be something to do with Cassio? He had angered her husband, that's for sure. But she'd promised to speak on his behalf… so she tried again. "Is this a trick to distract me? Please, will you speak to Cassio again?"

"The handkerchief!" Othello roared. Pushing Desdemona aside, he stormed out of the room, slamming the door behind him.

Emilia gasped. "Is he jealous?"

"I've never seen him like this before," Desdemona replied, her voice shaking. "I'm most unhappy to lose the handkerchief."

The following day, Cassio spotted something unusual on his chamber floor. It was a handkerchief embroidered with strawberries. Where on earth had that come from? Shrugging, he put it in his pocket and headed out to find Othello — it was time to speak to the general directly to beg for his position back.

On his way up to the castle, Cassio bumped into Bianca, a young woman who had been chasing his affections for some time. He pulled the handkerchief out of his pocked. "Bianca! Isn't this pretty?" he asked.

"I suppose it's a gift from a new girlfriend." Bianca pouted.

"You're jealous," he teased. "I found it in my chamber. I like the pattern very much — will you take it and have it copied?"

Bianca took handkerchief reluctantly. "When will I see you again?" she asked Cassio wistfully.

"Take it, and copy it. I can't stop now," Cassio told her. "I'm on my way to see the general."

Disappointed, Bianca blew him a kiss and walked away.

From an open window in the castle, Iago spotted Cassio walking up to the gate. He beckoned to Othello. "Hide yourself," he whispered. "I will make Cassio tell me where, how, and how often he has been seeing your wife, so you can hear for yourself."

"Oh, you are wise," Othello said, slipping into the shadows.

With Othello hidden by the window, Iago rushed downstairs to speak to Cassio. "I will question Cassio about Bianca," Iago thought, "but make it seem as if I am talking about Desdemona. Othello will go mad."

"Cassio!" Iago called out, catching up with the soldier. "How are you coming along with Desdemona?" He nudged him playfully, then spoke in a low voice so Othello couldn't hear. "Now if it was in *Bianca's* power, things would move more quickly!"

Cassio laughed. "Poor thing, I think she loves me."

Watching from above, Othello flinched. "Look how he laughs!" Othello was certain he was talking about Desdemona.

Downstairs, Iago questioned Cassio again. "She claims you shall marry her. Do you intend it?"

Cassio laughed even louder. "Ha! Marry her? Of course not!"

Othello bristled with indignation. Not only was Cassio courting his wife – now it seemed he was laughing at her too.

Just at that moment, Bianca reappeared on the street below, holding the handkerchief in her hand. Upset that Cassio was taking advantage of her, she had returned to confront him.

"What did you mean by this handkerchief you gave me?" she fumed, throwing the handkerchief in Cassio's face. "I was a fine fool to take it!"

Othello could not believe his eyes. If once he had doubted his wife's affair with Cassio, now the handkerchief was proof of it.

Iago returned upstairs, and found Othello simmering with rage. "Did you see the handkerchief?" Iago needled. "See how Cassio prizes your dear wife. She gave the handkerchief to him, and he has given it away to another woman!"

Othello's face twisted with jealousy. "Let Desdemona rot and perish tonight, for she shall not live. No, my heart is turned to stone. Get me some poison, Iago."

"Don't do it with poison," Iago said coldly. "Strangle her in her bed. I'll see to Cassio's doom myself."

Iago's plan was quickly escalating – if he managed to persuade Othello to murder his own wife, the general would never be able to set foot in Venice again. Othello's life would be ruined.

The sound of trumpets blasted across the castle. Lodovico, a messager from Venice, had just arrived. "Greetings!" He smiled at Desdemona and Othello. "The duke has sent me to bring you home, Othello. Cassio will take care of the fort here. How is he?"

"My lord and Cassio have fallen out," Desdemona told him. "I'd do anything to change it, for I care for Cassio."

As Othello listened to his wife, a shadow passed across his face. "Devil!" he spat, slapping Desdemona hard across the face.

Desdemona cried out in shock. Clutching her cheek, she fled the room in tears. Othello strode after her, muttering to himself.

Lodovico watched in horror. "Is he quite sane?" he asked.

Iago shook his head. "He is much changed," he said gravely.

Othello followed Desdemona into her chamber and grabbed her by the arms. "What are you?" he sneered.

"Your wife, my lord. Your true and loyal wife." Desdemona looked searchingly into his eyes.

"I took you for that cunning harlot of Venice that married Othello," Othello spat, before storming out of the room.

Back in the town, Iago was being cornered by Roderigo. "You're not dealing with me fairly," Roderigo complained. Still lovesick over Desdemona, he was angry that Iago hadn't kept his side of the bargain: he had promised to break up Desdemona's marriage to Othello, in return for money.

Iago sighed. "Othello goes home tomorrow, and will take Desdemona away. Unless he is stuck here by some accident…" He looked at Roderigo slyly. "The surest way is to remove Cassio."

Roderigo frowned. "How do you mean 'remove' him?"

"Why, knock out Cassio's brains and kill him," Iago said simply. He leaned in close, and began to explain his plan.

That evening, all was quiet in the castle. Upstairs, Emilia was helping Desdemona get ready for bed.

"Please help me put my special wedding sheets on the bed," Desdemona asked, looking paler than usual. Some strange sense of foreboding had overcome her. "If I die tonight, wrap me in these same sheets," she added.

"Come, come!" Emilia replied, puffing pillows anxiously.

Desdemona sat down and began to sing a sad song. It was about a woman sitting under a willow tree, deserted by her lover. "Sing willow, willow, willow…"

Lurking in the darkness outside the castle, Roderigo and Iago were waiting for Cassio. As his footsteps approached, Roderigo leaped out. "Die, villain!" he yelled, thrusting his sword.

But Roderigo missed, leaving time for Cassio to draw his own sword, which he thrust into Roderigo's side.

Roderigo fell to the ground groaning. Iago, seeing his plan failing, leaped out and stabbed Cassio in the leg from behind, then vanished back into the darkness.

"Help, ho! Murder! Murder!" Cassio collapsed to the ground.

A few moments later, Iago reappeared. "Who did this?" he gasped, kneeling down next to Cassio.

Cassio pointed weakly to the shadows where Roderigo lay.

"Oh, villain!" Iago cried. He crept over to Roderigo's bleeding body and, in the shadows, used his dagger to finish him off.

Desdemona was asleep in bed when Othello crept in. An eerie sense of calm had taken hold of him. "I'll not shed her blood," he thought, gazing at her soft, white skin and beautiful golden hair. He bent to kiss her once, and then again. "One more, and that's the last. For she must die. I weep, but they are cruel tears. My sorrow strikes where it loves most."

Desdemona's eyes fluttered open.

"Have you prayed tonight, Desdemona?" Othello stroked her face gently. "I will not kill you unprepared."

Desdemona's eyes grew wide and she tried to sit up. "You talk of killing?"

"You are on your deathbed," Othello said, holding her fast.

"I never offended you in my life!" Desdemona cried in terror.

"You gave Cassio the handkerchief that I gave to you," Othello insisted, as his wife struggled under his firm grip.

"I didn't! Send for him and ask!"

"It's too late," Othello whispered. He took a pillow and held it firmly over Desdemona's face. Pursing his lips, he watched as Desdemona struggled beneath him, before finally falling limp.

A knock came at the door, and Othello quickly covered Desdemona with a sheet. He walked over to the door to open it.

"Cassio has killed Roderigo!" Emilia cried, bursting in.

"But Cassio wasn't killed?" Othello was surprised – Iago had said he was seeing to that.

Then, a faint voice came from the other side of the room. "Oh, falsely, falsely murdered…"

Emilia instantly recognized it as her mistress's voice. She raced over to the bed and tore off the sheet. There was Desdemona, her skin deathly white.

"Help! Help! Oh lady, speak again!" Emilia cried, cradling the dying Desdemona in her arms.

"A guiltless death I die," Desdemona whispered.

"Who has done this deed?" Emilia sobbed.

"Nobody," breathed Desdemona. "Commend me to my kind husband." Then she closed her eyes for the last time.

"She's like a liar gone to burning Hell," Othello said curtly. "It was I that killed her. She loved Cassio. Ask your husband."

"My husband?" Emilia gasped in disbelief. "He's lying. Help! The Moor has killed my mistress! Murder! Murder!"

A group of soldiers rushed in, Iago among them.

Othello pointed at Iago. "Iago knows. Cassio confessed it. She even gave Cassio her handkerchief."

Emilia snorted. "She gave it to Cassio? No. I found it and I gave it to my husband."

Howling in anger, Iago ran at Emilia with his dagger. He plunged it into her side and then fled, closely pursued by soldiers.

Emilia fell to the floor. "She loved you, cruel Moor," she sighed, before she too died.

The horror of what he'd done slowly dawned on Othello, and he choked back a sob. Iago was the villain – Desdemona had been innocent all along. He ran to the bed and clutched his wife's lifeless body to his chest. "Oh, Desdemona! Dead! Oh! No!"

The soldiers returned, dragging a squirming Iago with them. Behind them, Cassio limped in with the messenger Lodovico.

"Devil!" Othello spat, glaring at Iago.

Iago shrugged casually. "What you know, you know. From this time forth I never will speak a word."

Othello turned to Cassio. "How did you come by that handkerchief that belonged to my wife?"

"I found it in my chamber," Cassio replied. "Iago has confessed to putting it there."

"We also found a letter in Roderigo's pocket," Lodovico added. "It was written by Iago, telling him to kill Cassio."

Othello buried his head in his hands. "Oh, fool, fool, fool!"

"Othello, your power is taken from you," Lodovico said. "From now on, Cassio rules in Cyprus, and Iago is his prisoner."

Othello looked up. "A word or two before you go," he said, steadying his voice. "Please, when you tell what happened here, hold nothing back. Speak of me as I am. Speak of one who loved not wisely, but too well… One not easily jealous, but who, worked up to a frenzy, threw away a pearl worth more than all the treasure in the world… And one who, when he met the foes of Venice, seized and struck them… like this." Before anyone could stop him, Othello pulled out his dagger and plunged it into his heart.

He collapsed onto the bed where Desdemona lay, and brushed her cold cheek with his lips. "I kissed you before I killed you. Now I'm dying while I kiss you again," he whispered.

And, with that, Othello was dead.

The room fell silent. Lodovico and Cassio stared speechlessly at the ghastly scene before them. Othello and Desdemona lay dead on the bed, with Emilia's body crumpled on the floor below.

"This is your work," Lodovico told Iago, finally breaking the silence. "And for that, you hellish villain, you will be punished." Then he turned to Cassio. "Lord Governor, it is up to you: the time, the place, the punishment. Oh, make sure you enforce it!"

Iago's lips tightened as the soldiers led him off. Whatever led him to carry out such a terrible plan, nobody would ever know. Noble Othello was dead, along with his loyal wife, Desdemona, her maid, Emilia, and her unfortunate admirer, Roderigo. But the scheming soldier who caused it all was never to speak again.

The Merry Wives of Windsor

Sir John Falstaff is running low on funds – but he has a plan. If he can woo Mistress Ford and Mistress Page, they might give him some of their husbands' money. Unfortunately for him (and for their husbands), these merry wives of Windsor aren't easily fooled.

Sir John Falstaff

A knight, also a greedy old trickster, always up for trouble – if it fills his belly or his purse.

Mistress Ford

A merry and clever woman married to Master Ford. She plans to teach Falstaff and her husband a lesson…

Mistress Page

Mistress Ford's best friend, and Master Page's wife. She is keen to help her friend turn the tables on Falstaff and the menfolk of Windsor.

Master Ford

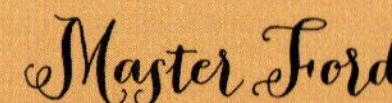

A jealous man, who suspects his wife, Mistress Ford, is up to no good. He's trying to catch her and Falstaff together.

Doctor Caius

A French doctor.
Mistress Page thinks
he would make a
good match for her
daughter Anne…

Master Page

Mistress Page's husband.
He quarrels with her about
their daughter's future
husband. He thinks it
should be Master Slender.

Anne Page

The daughter of
Mistress and Master
Page. She won't let
them decide whom she
should marry – she has
eyes only for young
Master Fenton.

Master Fenton

A poor gentleman, who
loves Anne Page – but
her parents won't even
let him visit her.

Master Slender

A dim-witted young
gentleman, whose wealth is
his most appealing quality.

HE GARTER INN, SO OFTEN THE SEAT of merriment in Windsor town, for once was sombre and still. Slouched among the empty benches, Sir John Falstaff glumly jangled the few coins left in his purse. "I'm getting dangerously poor," sighed the portly knight. "I'll need to live off my wits from now on. Either I come up with a crafty, gold-winning swindle, or I'll go hungry. Or, even worse, thirsty!"

Falstaff banged his empty mug down on the table. "Pistol! Nim!" he yelled. "Wake up, you rogues!" Beside him on the bench, a heap of rags stirred. It groaned, stretched, and divided into a pair of scruffy men. These were the knight's servants: two scrawny, part-time thieves.

"What is it, Knight?" yawned Pistol, rubbing his eyes.

"Why'd you wake us?" Nim complained. "It's barely noon!"

"Which of you know Master Ford and Master Page of this town?" Falstaff asked.

"I know them," said Pistol. "They're both wealthy fellows. Page has a beautiful daughter called Anne, and half the men in town are angling to marry her."

"More fool them," said Falstaff. "Daughters are nothing but trouble. But wives – wives are the thing. Now, listen: I've a plan, and I'll tell you the long and short of it."

"The *wide* of it's about two yards or more," sniggered Nim, pointing to Falstaff's more than generous belly.

"Yes, I'm a big man, two yards or so around the waist," Falstaff admitted. "But this isn't about waste. It's about thrift. I'm running low on cash, and I spy an opportunity in Ford and Page. Everyone says their wives control their riches. Well, I've seen those ladies around town. I've seen them giving me the secretive and loving side-eye, ogling my shapely calves, and amorously admiring my manly curves."

"Like sunshine gazing on a dunghill," chortled Pistol.

"In short," Falstaff continued, stroking his paunch, "I plan to woo them. They shall be my East and West Indies, and I'll trade to them both. And when they fall for my ample graces, their husbands' wealth will soon be mine."

Inspired by his own plan, the knight scrabbled about for paper, a quill and a pot of ink and began to scribble. He entirely covered two sheets with a black, looping scrawl that resembled a beetle's dancing progress. Then he unstoppered a tiny vial and sprinkled the pages with musky perfume. "Look boys," he crowed, "I've written two irresistible love letters: one to Mistress Ford, and another to Mistress Page. Your job is to deliver them."

Nim looked with distaste at the letter Falstaff had thrust in his hands. "What do you take me for – Cupid?" He handed it back to Falstaff.

"I've got a reputation to uphold," said Pistol, doing the same. "I'm no delivery boy."

"A reputation!" Falstaff scoffed. "That's the last straw! I'll give these to the scullery boy to deliver. And the two of you are fired – I can't afford you anyway, you lazy rascals. Get out! Vanish like hailstones. Trudge! Plod! Pack it up! Hit the road!"

The two ruffians tumbled out of the inn, cursing their former master. "That vile varlet," Nim spat. "I'll get my revenge!"

"With wit or steel?" asked Pistol, his hand on his sword.

"I know a way. I'll go and tell his plan to Master Ford."

"Good idea," Pistol grinned. "And I'll tell Master Page."

Later that day, a scullery boy from the Garter Inn knocked at the Pages' front door. When Mistress Page opened it, the boy gave her a sly wink, handed her a letter, and scampered off.

"What's this?" said Mistress Page, wrinkling her nose at the scent wafting from the paper. "Did I escape love letters in the days of my youth only to fall prey to them now? Let's see what it says…"

She giggled as she read: "'Dear Mistress Page, ask not why I love you, for whys don't matter, and love itself is unwise. You're not young – and neither am I. You are merry – and so am I. You like wine – and so do I. Let that be enough. Tell me you love me!

> By me, your own true knight,
> By day or night,
> Or any kind of light,
> With all his might,
> For you to fight,
> John Falstaff.'"

Mistress Page thought she would crease herself laughing. "How dare that worn-out knight play the young gallant with me – a married woman? What could I possibly have done to make him think I'd welcome his attention? I've only met him once or twice."

There came another rap at the open door. It was Mistress Ford. "Dear friend, I was just coming to see you," said Mistress Page. "How are you?"

"In shock," Mistress Ford giggled. "I've just received the most preposterous letter – here, you'd better read it for yourself." Mistress Ford handed her friend a familiar-looking letter. "Have you ever seen anything like it?"

"I have," said Mistress Page, sniffing the perfumed paper. "I have its twin brother right here!"

Each woman read the other's letter. "Why, these are identical – word for word!" exclaimed Mistress Ford.

"He's only changed the names at the top," agreed Mistress Page. "The scoundrel! How shall we get our revenge?"

"Revenged I will be, as sure as his guts
are made of puddings."

"I think the best way is to give him hope," decided Mistress Ford. "We'll lead him on, play him for the fool and let him stew in his own grease! Call Mistress Quickly. She's the town matchmaker, and she'll gladly be our go-between. Oh, but it would be a disaster if my husband saw this letter. You know he's famous for his jealousy, and he'd find support in this for all his wild suspicions."

As a matter of fact, their husbands already knew all about the letters, for Nim and Pistol had cornered them in the marketplace and revealed Falstaff's plan. "Take heed," warned Pistol, "there's mischief afoot!"

"The knight's a mighty Cupid," added Nim in a hoarse whisper, "awash with romance. He will woo you into woe!"

That afternoon, the husbands walked home together. "You heard what those knaves had to say?" growled Master Ford.

"Yes, but I can't believe that Falstaff would attempt it," said Master Page sensibly. "His accusers are scoundrels – servants filled with petty jealousies and keen to stir up trouble. And, even if the knight did want to woo my wife, I'd let him try. He'd get nothing from her but sharp words or worse!"

"You're much too confident," said Master Ford grimly. "It's not that I don't trust my wife… but I won't rest until I get to the bottom of this."

Master Page shrugged. "I've got more important things to worry about," he said. "My wife wants our daughter Anne to marry that fancy French physician, Doctor Caius. Anne only has eyes for penniless-but-dashing Master Fenton. But I want her to marry young Master Slender. He's far more suitable, with his three hundred pounds a year. In fact, here he comes now."

Master Ford took his leave, while Master Page rushed to greet young Master Slender, who was idly batting at the purple plume that dangled from his hat. "Have you thought any more about my proposal?" asked Master Page.

"Oh, ah, yes," said Master Slender, stuffing the plume behind one ear. "I'd be happy to marry Anne Page, if you want me to."

"But do *you* want to? Are you sure you love her?"

"I'm sure I *would* love her, within reason," Master Slender promised rather vaguely. "If you say so…"

Master Page rolled his eyes. "That's not exactly how love works." Then he took the young man's arm. "But never mind about that. Tell me more about your inheritance…"

That evening at the Garter Inn, confident that his plan would bring new riches rolling in, Falstaff spent his last shilling on a cup of wine. He sat among the barrels, warbling a romantic song. He was a little hazy about the verses, but he rolled out the chorus in a confident baritone. "Gree-e-eensleeves was all my joy, Gree-e-eensleeves was my delight…"

The innkeeper came in with his hands over his ears. "Sir John," he yelled. "There's a woman here to speak with you."

The woman, Mistress Quickly, bustled in past the innkeeper and curtsied to the knight. "Good evening, your worship," she said. "I've come from Mistress Ford."

"From Mistress Ford?" said Falstaff eagerly. "Good evening, good evening. What does she say?"

"My days above! You've certainly put the canary among the pigeons," Mistress Quickly began. "She has received your letter and, my word, she's all in a tizzy. I've known her many a year, I have, and never once—"

"Yes, yes, all right, but what's her reply?" Falstaff interrupted.

"She thanks you a thousand times, and wishes to say that

her husband will be safely away from home tomorrow morning between ten and eleven, if you wish to come and serenade her," Mistress Quickly told him.

"Between ten and eleven," repeated Falstaff gleefully. "Tell her that I'll be there without fail."

Mistress Quickly curtsied, and left the knight to his songs.

A few minutes later, the innkeeper interrupted him again. "Sir John," he said, "there's a gentleman to see you. He says his name is Brooke, and he's sent you a bottle of wine as a gift."

Falstaff's day was getting better and better. "Call him in! Any Brooke that flows with wine is welcome!"

A man entered, adjusting his rather large and somewhat crooked moustache. In actual fact, he was Master Ford in disguise.

But Falstaff did not have the slightest suspicion. "Master Brooke, what a pleasure," he said, opening his arms in welcome.

"Sir John, I've come to you for help with a delicate matter," Master Ford began.

"Those," Falstaff answered sagely, "are my speciality."

"There's a gentlewoman here in Windsor named Ford. People say she's an honest woman, and that she loves her husband – but I don't believe it. She's too merry to be true," Master Ford went on.

"That's so often the way," Falstaff agreed knowingly.

"Now, Sir John, as everybody knows, you're a gentleman of breeding and of courtly grace." Here, Falstaff bowed so graciously that he tipped wine all down his front. "If *you* pursued Mistress Ford with your, erm, *enormous* charm, I'm sure you could win a kiss from her. Will you try? If you succeed, it will prove to all of Windsor that these merry wives are not to be trusted."

Falstaff beamed widely. "You've come to the right man," he said. "My romantic charms are already working on Mistress Ford. In fact, I've promised to visit her tomorrow between ten and eleven, when her jealous rascal of a husband will be away. Come back tomorrow, and you'll hear how easily I've won that kiss!"

Master Ford was fuming as he left the inn. He tore off his false moustache in a fury. "Now I see what's going on behind my back! I would rather trust a Dutchman with my butter, a Welshman with my cheese, and a Scotsman with my milk jug than my wife with herself. She plots! She ruminates! She devises! Thank God for my jealousy, that made me find her out. Tomorrow – between ten and eleven – I'll catch her."

The next morning, Master Page was sitting in the sun outside the Garter Inn with Doctor Caius and the local parson. They were debating, as usual, the marriage of Page's daughter.

"Eet is as clear as ze days," said Doctor Caius, "Anne Page weel love me. Your lady wife 'az told me eet must be so."

"Yes, Doctor, you have my wife's support," admitted Master Page, "but I stand wholly by Master Slender."

"What do you think of young Master Fenton?" asked the parson. "He dances, he writes verses, he speaks well, and he smells of April and May. I think he'll win out in the end."

"Not if I have anything to do with it," insisted Master Page. "He may be a clever young fellow, but he's poor. He spent all his money in revels with his friends. I won't let him mend his fortunes with my wealth."

It was nearly ten o'clock, and with that fateful hour fast approaching, Master Ford came hurrying around the corner. "Come, all of you," he urged. "Come with me quickly to my house. In the past, you've all made fun of my jealousy – but we'll see who's laughing once you've witnessed what we find there today, between ten and eleven…"

At that very moment, the Fords' house was a flurry of activity. Mistress Ford's servants had brought in a massive laundry basket, carried between them on a sturdy pole. "Place it here by the door," Mistress Ford directed. "And remember, when I give the signal, come pick it up and take it straight down to the Thames. Empty it in the muddy end of the washerwomen's ditch."

"Quick!" hissed Mistress Page at the window. "He's coming!"

"Places, everyone!" commanded Mistress Ford. The servants retreated hastily to the kitchen, Mistress Page hurried out the back door and, a few moments later, the lady of the house showed in Sir John Falstaff.

"Have I caught you, my heavenly jewel?" Falstaff asked romantically, spreading his arms wide.

"Not yet," Mistress Ford laughed, dodging his embrace.

"Let me persuade you that I love you," Falstaff said. "I'm not one to say you're as fair as this, or as sweet as that, like some of these new-fangled lovers. But I love you, none but you, and you deserve it!"

"Well," replied Mistress Ford, "heaven knows how much I love you. And one day you'll find out!" She slapped away the hand that was creeping round her waist.

"I can't wait," said Falstaff, rubbing his stinging fingers.

Suddenly, there came an urgent rap at the door.

"Someone's here!" cried Mistress Ford. "Quickly, Sir John, hide behind this curtain."

Falstaff barely had time to arrange the folds of the curtain around his belly before Mistress Page burst into the room. "Mistress Ford," she cried, "what have you done? Your husband is coming this way with all the men of the town. He swears you've got a secret rendezvous planned. He means to catch you with your sweetheart and expose your wicked ways!"

"What shall I do?" wailed Mistress Ford, winking at her friend.

"There is indeed a gentleman visiting me!"

"Your husband's in a jealous rage," Mistress Page went on. "He's bound to search absolutely everywhere. You must get the gentleman out of the house. Look – there's a laundry basket. If he's of any *reasonable* size, he can hide in there, and your servants can smuggle him out."

"Oh, he'll *never* fit in that basket," Mistress Ford said, swallowing a giggle.

"Show me the basket! Show me the basket!" cried Falstaff, leaping out from behind the curtain. "I'll have to fit."

Together, the wives wedged the knight into the creaking basket. They squeezed and squashed him down until only his head stuck out. Then, they piled dirty socks and greasy shirts on top of him.

"Why, Sir John, I thought *I* was the one you loved," whispered Mistress Page to the laundry basket. She nudged her friend, who was holding her sides with silent laughter. "Didn't you send me a love letter just yesterday?"

"Yes, and I do love you, I do," the laundry basket whispered piteously. "Just help me escape and I'll prove it!"

Moments later, the front door flew open and Master Ford charged into the house, his friends at his heels. They found Mistress Page and Mistress Ford sitting innocently side by side. The servants had lifted the laundry basket and, straining under its considerable weight, were carrying it away.

"Halt!" commanded Master Ford. "Where are you off to?"

"They're taking our dirty washing to the laundress," said Mistress Ford. "Since when are you so interested in laundry?"

Master Ford let them pass. "Now," he said, locking the door, "let's search every room and cupboard. I promise you we'll find a fox in this henhouse!"

The men tramped about, peering behind doors and into corners. Master Ford even clambered into the attic, getting himself covered in dust. "He must – *achoo!* – be somewhere," they heard him cry. But there was no one to be found. At last, he came back down, and stood shamefaced before his wife and friends.

"Have I been led astray?" Master Ford wondered.

"Zees is too much jealousies," murmured Doctor Caius.

"Master Ford, don't you see you're in the wrong?" asked Master Page. "There's no one here visiting your wife!"

"I hope you're ashamed of your suspicious ways," Mistress Ford scolded her husband.

Master Ford hung his head. "I am," he admitted. "Jealousy is my biggest fault. I beg your pardon, my dear wife."

"Just who did you expect to find here?" asked Mistress Page. "What dashing Cupid did you think could sweep my friend here off her married feet?"

"Er… Sir John Falstaff…" Master Ford admitted.

There was a moment's silence, and then his wife and all his friends burst into laughter.

Mistress Ford took pity on her husband. "Oh, little do you know," she said, wiping away tears of laughter, "how close and yet how far from the mark you were. If you came searching for my sweetheart, you never would have found one – but you walked right past that fat, saucy knight. Look!"

Mistress Ford opened a window and pointed. Down at the end of the lane, everyone saw the servants struggling with the laundry basket. When they reached the washerwomen's ditch, they tipped the knight and all the washing into the muddy water.

"What means all zees?" asked Doctor Caius.

Mistress Page and Mistress Ford explained everything. They described Sir John's wooing and their plot to punish him. They showed the knight's twin letters, and described how they had squeezed him into the laundry basket.

"I hope you've learned from this," Mistress Ford concluded,

MISTRESS PAGE, ACT 4, SCENE 2

"that wives can be merry and yet honest, too."

Master Ford laughed. "My dear wife, from now on, do as you like. I would sooner suspect the sun of cold than you of trickery."

"I wonder if Falstaff has truly learned his lesson," said Master Page. "Shall we try to fool him one more time?"

Mistress Page thought for a moment. "There is an old tale," she said, "about a ghost called Herne the Hunter that haunts the trees of Windsor Forest. At midnight, he walks around an ancient, blasted oak, rattling and moaning. Some still believe in it. Let's tell Sir John to meet us there, disguised like Herne, with stag's horns on his head, and draped in iron chains."

"Then what?" asked Master Ford.

"Then all the children of this town will dress as fairies – my daughter Anne will be their queen. And when Sir John arrives at the oak they'll circle him, frighten him with songs, and poke and pinch him until he confesses his misdeeds. Then we'll jump out and mock him all the way back home!"

That afternoon, in the garden behind the Pages' house, someone else was receiving a forbidden visitor. Together, Anne Page and Master Fenton were strolling between the flowers.

"Sweet Anne, your father never will approve of me," said Master Fenton. "He objects to my wild friends and past expenses, and suspects that I'm seeking not your love but his wealth."

"And is there any truth in that?" Anne asked.

"No, as Heaven's my witness," Master Fenton promised. "I confess it was your father's wealth first drew me to you, Anne, but I found you of more value than his coins of gold or sums in heavy bags. You yourself are the riches I now pursue."

"Gentle Master Fenton, seek my father's favour," Anne advised. "And if all our persistence still has no effect, why then—"

An angry voice interrupted them. "Here now, what's all this?"

The two youngsters looked up to find Master Page glaring at them over at the garden gate. At his side, Master Slender was puzzling over a book of poetry.

"You wrong me, Master Fenton, by loitering around my house," growled Master Page. "I told you, my daughter has been promised to another."

"That dizzy young man is my father's choice," whispered Anne scornfully. "Oh, how a world of faults looks handsome when it's dressed in an inheritance!"

"Anne, you know Master Slender," Master Page began. "If you marry him, he can keep you like a gentlewoman."

"Oh! Ah, yes, that's right," Master Slender confirmed vaguely, his nose still in his book. "I'm about as rich as a poor gentleman, you know. I have three servants."

"And if he dies, you'd inherit one hundred and fifty pounds as his widow," Master Page added brightly. He glanced at Master Slender, who looked the picture of health.

"Father, let him woo for himself," Anne suggested. "Master Slender, what do you want from me?"

"Truly, for myself, little or nothing," the young man said amiably. "Your father has made me an excellent proposal, though. He can tell you all about it."

Anne rolled her eyes.

"Good Master Page," Master Fenton cut in, "I love your

"O, what a world of vile ill-favoured faults looks handsome in three hundred pounds a year!"

Anne Page, Act 3, Scene 4

daughter fiercely, and against all rebukes and refusals I will still advance my cause. Please give me your consent."

"I will not," Master Page declared. "Anne, if you don't marry Slender, your mother will make you marry Doctor Caius."

"I'd rather be buried to the neck and bowled to death with turnips," Anne cried in horror. "My darling Master Fenton, nothing will be decided here. We'd better part for now."

With that, she marched into the house and slammed the door.

That evening, Sir John Falstaff was again seated in the Garter Inn. But he was in no mood for songs, clever plots, romance or rendezvous. He was drenched and muddy from head to toe, with a wreath of weeds behind one ear.

"Never," he said to Mistress Quickly. "Never," he repeated to Master Ford, who had resumed his disguise as Master Brooke. "Meet them at Herne's Oak? Not a chance. Do you know what I've already been through for their sake? Not only was I packed into a basket full of greasy napkins and stinky stockings, not only was I half smothered, but by the time I was all hot and bothered and half-stewed, they tipped me into the Thames to cool off – like a red-hot horseshoe sizzling in a bucket! Think of that!"

"Poor fellow!" cried Master Ford trying not to laugh. He poured Falstaff some hot wine.

"Brave man," soothed Mistress Quickly. "They do lament it, truly they do. They long to make it up to you! I've just come from Mistress Page *and* Mistress Ford, and they say if you will only meet them in Windsor Forest tonight, they'll show you just how sorry they are, and how much they love you."

"Harrumpf," said Falstaff.

"And just think," said Master Ford, "this will be your chance to prove your charms, win their husbands' riches, and show that women can't be trusted."

"I *am* charming, aren't I?" said Falstaff, a smile creeping across his stubbly face. "Probably charming enough for two."

"You'll do it then?" urged Mistress Quickly.

Falstaff sighed. "Just find me some stag's horns and some chains, and I'll be there."

Late that night, dressed up in his ghostly disguise, Sir John Falstaff crept into Windsor Forest. His stag's horns tangled in the branches overhead; his chains caught on the roots of trees, but he struggled valiantly onward. At length, he came to a clearing where the moonlight fell on mossy banks. In the middle, there loomed the broken trunk of a mighty oak tree. Unbeknown to Falstaff, his neighbours were hidden all around in the shadows of the trees.

"Here he comes," Mistress Page whispered to Doctor Caius. "Remember what you and I discussed: when the fairies come out, you slip away with Anne and marry her. She'll be the one in the white dress. And don't let my husband see you!"

"That's Sir John there," whispered Master Page to Master Slender a few yards away. "Remember our secret plan: when the dancing begins, sneak out and take the fairy in the green dress by the hand. It will be Anne, and she'll be your wife."

"The Windsor bell has struck twelve," Falstaff declared. "The moment draws near. Oh, powerful love, that makes a man a beast! Here I am: a dashing knight transformed into a Windsor stag – and the largest stag, I think, in the forest. Where are my does? Hallo!"

But when Sir John approached the oak, the merry wives were nowhere to be seen. Instead, a dozen strange and sprightly forms sprang out of the shadows.

"O powerful Love, that in some respects makes a beast a man, in some other a man a beast!"

Sir John Falstaff, Act 5, Scene 5

They had pointed faces, long ears and flowing gowns, and they danced around Falstaff, poking and pinching him with sharp fingers. "We are fairies, green and white! Moonshine revellers! Shades of night!"

"Fairies!" quavered Falstaff, ducking in fear and covering his eyes. "Whoever sees them is doomed to die!"

The fairies twisted and turned about him, racing and laughing in the moonlight – and as they danced, a close observer would have seen not two but three couples slipping away in the darkness.

"What wickedness brings you to this magic place?" the fairies chanted, circling the terrified knight.

"Oh, Oh, Oh!" cried Falstaff, cowering on his knees. "I confess! I've snuck out here to woo the wives of Windsor!"

At this, the townspeople emerged, cheering, from their hiding places. The fairies stopped and pulled off their masks, revealing laughing children's faces. Mistress Page and Mistress Ford stepped out from the shadows.

"Well, Sir John, what do you think of Windor's wives now?" asked Mistress Page.

"You'll always be my *deer*," Mistress Ford chuckled, tugging Falstaff's antlers, "but you could never be my darling."

Master Ford joined his wife, and showed Falstaff his false beard and moustache. "Well, Sir John, do you recognize your old friend Master Brooke?" he asked.

"I perceive," said Falstaff humbly, removing his horns, "that you have made not a deer but an ass of me. I've been pinched, poked and mocked at and I do regret it – but I have only myself to blame."

"Take comfort, good Sir Knight," said Master Page. "I'll invite you home to dinner, and we'll laugh together at my wife, who is now laughing at you. Because by this time, Master Slender will be married to my daughter Anne!"

"Erm, no," said Master Slender, appearing at the edge of the clearing. "I must have got the wrong fairy – the fairy in the green dress was a boy! Indeed, it was the postman's boy."

"You fool," crowed Mistress Page. "Anne was dressed in white, and by now has married Doctor Caius!"

"No," said Doctor Caius, appearing at the other end of the clearing. "I too have run off wiz a boy! I have married ze scullery boy in white!"

"Then where is Anne?" everyone wondered.

"Here I am," said Anne, stepping into the moonlight with Master Fenton. "And here is my new husband. Forgive me, dear parents. When Mother suggested I wear white, and Father suggested I wear green, I suspected you were both up to something, and would try to marry me off. So I put on my blue gown instead, and slipped away with Master Fenton. We were married in town not ten minutes past."

"I hope our love makes up for our offence," said Master Fenton.

The thwarted parents stared, but Master Ford just clapped his hands. "There's nothing to be done," he cried. "In love, the heavens themselves decide…"

"I'm glad I'm not the only one who went wrong," Falstaff chuckled. "It seems that hunters in the dark can end up chasing all sorts of deer!"

Mistress Page smiled at her daughter and new son-in-law. "May Heaven give you many merry days! Let's go home, and with Sir John and all the company, we'll laugh this night away."

Macbeth

On returning, victorious, from battle, Macbeth hears a
prophecy that he will be King of Scotland. Easily persuaded
by his wife, Macbeth commits ever-more grisly crimes to
achieve his ambitions. But at what cost?

"Is this a dagger which I see before me,
the handle toward my hand?"

Macbeth

Strong soldier but morally
weak. His ambitions
dictate his actions, but his
conscience unhinges
his mind…

Lady Macbeth

Ruthless and greedy for
power. Persuades Macbeth
to seize the chance of
becoming king, no matter
what gruesome acts must
be committed.

Banquo

Receives a prophecy of
future greatness, but has
the moral strength to
remain loyal. Murdered by
Macbeth, and haunts him.

Duncan

The rightful King of Scotland. His murder throws Scotland into disorder.

Malcolm

Duncan's son and rightful heir. Helped by Macduff to regain the throne.

Macduff

Macbeth's enemy. Tries to unseat him after Macbeth steals the throne.

Three Witches

These cackling hags are dark and dangerous. But do their prophecies affect fate or merely tell what would have happened anyway?

O N A BARREN, EMPTY PLAIN, three witches met, greeting each other by strange, unearthly names. All around them, the thunder crackled and the lightning flashed. Not far off, a battle was raging.

"Where shall we three meet again?" asked the first witch.

"The heath," replied the second.

"To talk with Macbeth," said the third. "By then the hurlyburly will be done. The battle will have been lost and won." Then off they went, through swirling mists and fog, their chanting growing ever fainter on the wind.

At the battle camp, Duncan, King of Scotland, stood anxiously waiting for tidings. His country was at war. The Thane of Cawdor had turned traitor, joining with the King of Norway. Together their armies had marched across Scotland, seeking to defeat the Scottish king. What would be the outcome?

At last, a bloodied soldier brought the news. "We've won," he gasped. "The King of Norway begs for a truce. The traitor, the Thane of Cawdor, has been defeated."

"And what about our generals, Macbeth and Banquo?" asked the king.

"They fought bravely. That other traitor, Macdonwald, was killed by valiant Macbeth. He sliced him from his belly to his teeth and fixed his head on our battlements."

"Great news," cried Duncan. He turned to one of his men. "Ross, go and greet Macbeth and tell him he has a new title: Thane of Cawdor," he told him. "What Cawdor has lost, noble Macbeth has won."

Blood-stained and battle-weary, the two generals, Macbeth and Banquo, came trudging over the heath. It was wreathed in thick clouds of mist that pressed down on them, heavy and damp against their skin.

"So foul and fair a day I have not seen," said Macbeth.

"Nor I," replied Banquo. "But wait!" he called. Strange shapes were emerging from the mist, hunched over, with scraggly hair and outstretched claws, that beckoned them closer. "What are they?" Banquo whispered. "What are these wild and withered creatures?"

"Speak, if you can," commanded Macbeth.

"Greetings, Macbeth! Thane of Glamis!" said the first witch.

"Greetings, Macbeth! Thane of Cawdor!" cried the second.

And the third: "Greetings, Macbeth, our future king!"

"What's this?" whispered Macbeth. "I am Thane of Glamis, but not of Cawdor. And to be king… that is beyond belief. A dream, maybe, but we already have a king, and he has two sons. I have no immediate claim to the throne…"

"And what of me?" asked Banquo. "Speak, if you can look into the seeds of time."

"Lesser than Macbeth, and greater," chanted the witches. "Not so happy, yet much happier. You will beget kings, though you will not be one."

"Tell me more," begged Macbeth. But the witches vanished, like breath into the wind.

Then came footsteps. Two more figures appeared out of the mist.

"Who goes there?" called Banquo.

"Ross and Angus," came the reply. "We've come from the king," said Ross, "with praise for your bravery on the battlefield. And for you, Macbeth… the king gives you a great reward. He has made you Thane of Cawdor."

"Thane of Cawdor!" exclaimed Macbeth. And then, beneath his

breath, "Glamis and now Cawdor… The witch's prophecy has come true. And Macbeth as king? The greatest prize of all! I hardly dare to think, could that happen too?"

Banquo was watching him closely. "A word," he said. "Are you dwelling on the witches' prophecy? For they are instruments of darkness," he warned. "Their prophecies can only lead to harm."

But Macbeth stayed rapt in thought. "Oh, to be king," he murmured. "Stars, hide your light so I may keep my dark desires hidden; no one must guess. Could chance do it? Could chance make me king? For the only other way I see is murder, and the very thought makes my heart knock against my ribs."

Then, tearing himself away from his dreams, he addressed the other men. "Let us go," he said, "to the palace and our king!"

There, King Duncan welcomed them. "And tonight, Macbeth," he declared, "we will dine with you at your castle."

In haste, Macbeth wrote to his wife, telling her everything, and rode ahead to meet her.

In her curtained chamber, Lady Macbeth read her husband's letter and smiled. "The witches called him king!" she cried. "And he will be one. It has long been our dream. Only Duncan and his sons stand between us and power. I will *make* it happen. If King Duncan comes to our castle, then this is our chance, for only murder will make Macbeth a king. And yet… do I dare murder Duncan within our battlements tonight?"

Lady Macbeth rose and paced her chamber, her smile cold. "Yes, I dare…" she vowed. "But I fear Macbeth's nature. He's too full of the milk of human kindness. And too full of fear. How to persuade him? I'll use the courage of my tongue to crush any objection."

LADY MACBETH,
ACT 1, SCENE 5

She stiffened her spine and stood tall. "Come, spirits," she commanded. "Thicken my blood so I feel no remorse. Fill me from head to toe with the direst cruelty. No compassion shall keep me from my purpose."

That night, King Duncan, his servants and his sons feasted well at Macbeth's castle. Macbeth watched them, knowing what his wife had planned – to drug the king's guardsmen, leaving him free to kill the sleeping king and lay the blame on them. But now he was full of creeping, nagging doubt. He left the table and slipped away from his guests, while his wife followed close behind him.

"What's this?" she demanded. "Why are you leaving your guests? Everything is planned. Are you failing me?"

"We will go no further with this business," replied Macbeth. "Duncan is a humble, virtuous king. I am his kinsman and his subject. I should guard him from murder, not bear the knife myself."

"Coward!" spat his wife. "Find your courage and we'll not fail. I'll slip a potion in his servants' drinks. Then they'll be so drunk that you and I can do what we like to the unguarded king, and they will bear the guilt. We'll clamour and roar with grief so that no one shall doubt us. Promise me you'll be a man and do it."

She spoke with a voice of steel. Virtue fought with ambition, and ambition won. "I promise," vowed Macbeth.

He waited until everyone had gone to bed so he could walk the corridors alone. The night seemed thick with witchcraft as he made his way to Duncan's door.

And there, hovering in the air, was a dagger, the handle pointing towards his hand, and on its blade, great gouts of blood.

"Is this a dagger I see before me?" Macbeth faltered, staring at it. It looked every inch real, and yet how could a dagger hang, dripping with blood, in mid-air?

"It is just a vision," Macbeth told himself. "The bell tolls. It is time the deed was done."

All too quickly, Macbeth was in and out of Duncan's room, and now his skin was smeared with royal blood. He hurried back down the corridors and held out his hands to his wife.

"Look!" he said, in a voice that shook. "It is a sorry sight."

But his wife spared him no pity. "A sorry sight? What a foolish thing to say. I would have done the deed myself, except…" she hesitated, "except the king looked like my father as he slept. But why have you brought the daggers? Take them and smear the servants with Duncan's blood."

"I can't go back," cried Macbeth. "I'm too afraid to look on what I've done."

"I'll go, then. Give me the daggers."

When she returned, her hands were blood-stained too. "But see," she said, smiling, washing her hands until they gleamed white again, "a little water clears us of this deed."

That night, a storm raged and the air was filled with strange screams and howls. First light brought with it a hammering at the castle door. *Knock! Knock! Knock! Knock!* echoed around the castle walls.

"Wake Duncan with your knocking," thought Macbeth. "I wish you could."

The porter woke, the doors were opened and in came Macduff and Lennox, two of the king's men.

"Is the king awake?" asked Macduff.

"Not yet," replied Macbeth. "Let me show you to his room."

Macduff and Lennox went in. First out came Macduff, stumbling, his hands covering his eyes, crying, "Oh, horror! Horror! Horror! The king's been murdered."

The bells rang. Everyone came rushing – Lady Macbeth, the king's sons, Malcolm and Donalbain, all asking, "What has happened? What's amiss?"

"Your royal father has been murdered!" said Macduff.

"By whom?" demanded Malcolm.

"By his own servants, it would seem," said Lennox, as he joined them. "They are standing outside his room, their hands and faces covered with his blood – and I found daggers, unwiped, beneath their pillows. They stared at me in confusion…"

Macbeth let out a cry and rushed into the king's chamber. Not long after, he emerged, shaken, his face pale. "Forgive me," he said. "But in my fury I have killed the servants."

"Why did you do that?" Macduff asked him. "Now we have no chance to question them."

"How could I restrain myself, loving Duncan as I did? There he lay, his silver skin laced with his golden blood, and the murderers next to him, their daggers steeped in gore."

There was a cry and everyone turned as Lady Macbeth reached out and looked as if she would fall. "Oh! Help me!" she cried. "I cannot bear it any more."

In the uproar, the king's sons huddled close. "There's more to this than meets the eye," they whispered.

"Whoever killed our father could kill us next. Let's get away from here. I'll go to Ireland," said Donalbain.

"And I to England," said Malcolm. "Farewell."

With Duncan dead, and his sons fled, Macbeth could claim the throne. He spread the rumour that Duncan's sons had plotted to kill their father, and quickly had himself crowned king at Scone. The deed was done.

"He has it all," thought Banquo, pacing outside Macbeth's castle, "just as the witches promised. King, Glamis, Cawdor, everything… and yet I fear he got it by foul means."

"A moment, Banquo!" called Macbeth, striding out of the castle. "Will you dine with us tonight?"

"Yes, my lord, but first my son, Fleance, and I will ride."

Macbeth nodded. "Then I hope your horses are swift and sure of foot."

But to Banquo's departing back, he hissed, "What was it the witches said? They hailed him father to a line of kings. If no son of mine succeeds me, then it is for Banquo's sons that I have murdered Duncan and tortured my own mind. What is it to be king if I live in fear? And I fear only Banquo. Come!" he cried. And with a gesture, he summoned two soldiers, waiting in the shadows by the castle walls.

"Go after Banquo," he instructed. "As we discussed last night – rid me of him, and his son."

"We will, Your Highness," vowed the soldiers.

Out in the night, the murderers lay in wait for Banquo and his son. The sound of hoofbeats came nearer and nearer until, at the last moment, when it seemed as if the horses would pass right by them, the murderers struck out. With his last words Banquo cried out, "Oh, treachery! Run, Fleance, run!"

Fleance fled. Blinded by the night, the murderers were forced to let him go. "We've failed in half our mission," they said. "Let us return to Macbeth and tell him what we've done…"

The dining table was set. Around it gathered Lady Macbeth, Ross, Lennox, and other lords and ladies. Macbeth, with news of Banquo's death fresh in his mind, surveyed the scene.

"Come," said Lennox, "Grace us with your royal company."

"Here's an empty seat," added Ross.

Macbeth made his way to the seat then gave a strange cry. There sat Banquo's ghost, his head bloodied, his throat cut. Macbeth pointed, his hand wavering. "Don't shake your gory locks at me!"

The others turned to look, staring blankly. They saw no vision of a bloodied ghost.

"You are forgetting yourself," hissed his wife. She turned to her guests, who were half-rising from their chairs. "Fear not," she said. "His Highness is… not well."

"Get out of my sight!" Macbeth cried, his eyes still fixed on Banquo's ghost. "Your blood is cold. You stare at me with sightless eyes. Get out, you vile shadow!"

For a moment, Macbeth shielded his eyes and when he dared to look again, the ghost had vanished. He turned on his guests, who stared at him in fear and confusion.

"How can you see such things," demanded Macbeth, "and keep the rubies in your cheeks while mine are blanched in fear?"

"What things?" asked Ross. "There was nothing there to see."

"Don't speak to him," said Lady Macbeth. "He grows worse and worse. The king is unwell. Everyone, go at once."

As ordered, the guests rose from their chairs.

"Good night," said Lennox. "We wish you better health."

Lady Macbeth waited until she was alone with her husband. "What made you act so?" she demanded.

"I had Banquo killed!" Macbeth replied. "And yet I swear I saw him – his bloodied ghost – at that chair. But Fleance is still alive. I have scorched the snake, not killed it. And Macduff, Thane of Fife, did not come tonight. Is he against me, do you think?"

"Come," said his wife, "Do not think of this. You are making yourself unwell. You must sleep."

"There is no contentment to be had, even with this crown upon my head," Macbeth said. "Tomorrow I'll go to the heath again, to see if I can find the weird sisters there. I have to know the worst. I am now so steeped in this vast river of blood, there is no turning back."

In a cavern on the heath, the three witches were huddled around their cauldron. "Three times the tabby cat has mewed," said one.

"Three times the hedgehog has whined," said another.

"It is time," said the third.

As one, they began to chant, and as they chanted, they danced around the cauldron. "Double, double, toil and trouble: fire burn and cauldron bubble. Eye of newt and toe of frog, wool of bat and tongue of dog, adder's fork and blind-worm's sting, lizard's leg and owlet's wing… For a charm of powerful trouble, like a hell-broth boil and bubble."

They took from their pockets all kinds of slithering, greasy, feathery things and flung them in the pot, cackling all the while. Before them, the cauldron simmered and bubbled, belching out great wreaths of smoke.

"Secret and midnight hags," Macbeth called out, as he entered their cavern.

Not one of them turned. Instead they continued to gaze at their bubbling cauldron.

"Please," begged Macbeth. "Tell me what I need to know."

As he spoke, an apparition rose from the cauldron. "Macbeth! Macbeth!" it whispered. "Beware Macduff. None of woman born shall harm Macbeth. Macbeth shall never be defeated until Birnam Wood comes to Dunsinane Hill."

"Then I am safe!" cried Macbeth. "What need I fear from

Macduff or any man, if no one born of woman can hurt me? And who can command Birnam Wood to make the trees pull up their roots? No one! I will be king all my life. But tell me one more thing… will Banquo's sons ever reign in this kingdom?"

"Do not seek to know more," said the first witch.

"Deny me and I'll curse you," vowed Macbeth.

"Then show his eyes and grieve his heart," chanted the witches, and eight kings appeared before him, all golden-haired and wearing crowns, followed by Banquo's smiling ghost.

"So it's true? Banquo's sons shall reign?"

"It's true," laughed the witches, and vanished.

"It is a cursed hour! Who's there?" Macbeth called, hearing footsteps approaching on the heath.

"It's Lennox, my lord. I was told I could find you here. I come with a message. Macduff, Thane of Fife, has fled to England."

"Fled to England," muttered Macbeth. "So he has turned against me. Well, if I cannot get to him, I'll deal with the children and the wife he left behind."

Gripped with paranoia and fear, Macbeth seized the town of Fife, then raided Macduff's castle and had his wife and children murdered. His reign had turned into one of terror. But all the while in England, Malcolm and Macduff plotted to restore the throne to its rightful king.

A gulf opened up between Macbeth and his wife. He was possessed only by the desire to hold the throne at all costs; she was possessed by guilt… At Dunsinane Castle, Lady Macbeth paced the floor every night, her eyes open, even in sleep, muttering about the things that she had done. At last her maid, worried for her sanity, called for a doctor.

"You say she talks in her sleep," said the doctor. "What does she say?"

"I cannot tell you," said the maid.

"Ah!" cried the doctor. "Here she comes. She carries a candle in her hand."

"It stands by her bedside. She must always have a light by her. Those are her orders," the maid told him.

"She paces and she rubs her hands," remarked the doctor.

"She often does that," replied the maid.

"Here's a spot," cried Lady Macbeth. She stopped and started rubbing desperately at her hand.

"Hark!" said the doctor. "She speaks."

"Out damned spot! Out, I say. Will my hands never be clean? The Thane of Fife had a wife. Where is she now? Oh! Who would have thought the old man would have so much blood in him?"

"Ah!" said the doctor. "She's said something she should not. What secrets is she keeping? Ah. She speaks again…"

"Will my hands never be clean?" Lady Macbeth muttered. "And I still have the smell of blood on them. All the perfumes of Arabia could not sweeten this little hand. To bed, to bed, to bed."

"She carries heavy secrets in her heart. Will she go now to bed?" asked the doctor.

"She will," replied the maid.

"God forgive us all," said the doctor. "She needs a priest, not a doctor. Look after her."

The doctor found Macbeth busy with his troops under the shadow of the castle walls.

"How is my wife?" asked Macbeth.

"She is not ill," replied the doctor, "but she is troubled with visions that keep her from her rest."

"Well then," said Macbeth, "cure her diseased mind. And as for me… I need a cure for my country. Can you do that? You see I am dressed for war. Have you heard the news? My thanes, my men, are all deserting me. Malcolm has returned to Scotland, and he has brought with him English troops. Macduff marches at his side. But I am not afraid of death – not until Birnam Wood comes to Dunsinane…"

In Birnam Wood, Malcolm stood at the head of a vast army. "I want every solider to break off a branch and hold it in front of him," he declared. "That way we'll hide our numbers from the tyrant, Macbeth, until it is too late. The time has come. Armies march! Advance to Dunsinane!"

"Let them come!" cried Macbeth, when a messenger brought the news that an army was approaching. "Our castle is strong enough to laugh off their siege."

And then, from the battlements, came a strange, piercing cry, that seemed to hang in the air even after it had gone. "What was that?" said Macbeth.

A servant came running. "The queen is dead," he said, still panting for breath. "She has taken her own life."

Macbeth froze a moment, his face expressionless. "My wife should have died another day, for now there is not the time to think of it," he said starkly.

But it filled his thoughts nonetheless. "Oh! Tomorrow, tomorrow and tomorrow. The days creep along until the end

" Tomorrow, and tomorrow, and tomorrow,
Creeps in this petty pace from day to day
To the last syllable of recorded time:

And all our yesterdays have lighted fools
The way to dusty death. "

Macbeth, Act 5, Scene 5

of time and each one that passes only brings fools closer to their death. Each life is a candle, burning briefly, only to be snuffed out," he said to himself. "This life is nothing but an illusion – an actor strutting about the stage. It's a tale told by an idiot, full of sound and fury – meaning nothing."

But Macbeth only paused for a moment to dwell on his wife's sudden death, for now the messengers came thick and fast with news of war.

"My lord," said one. "I should say what I saw, but I do not know how to do it…"

"Speak quickly," replied Macbeth.

"As I stood on watch, I looked towards Birnam Wood, and I thought I saw it move."

"You're a liar!" cried Macbeth.

"You may punish me if it's not so," the messenger replied. "Three miles from here you can see it coming: a moving wood."

"If you lie, you can hang from the nearest tree. If you tell the truth, I care not if you do the same for me." The witches' prophecy rang in his ears: 'Macbeth shall never be defeated until Birnam Wood comes to Dunsinane Hill…' "And now the wood is coming," Macbeth muttered. "Is this, then, the time for fear?"

Aloud, Macbeth cried out, "Ring the alarm bell! Blow, wind! Come, ruin! At least we'll die with our armour on."

Macbeth waited at Dunsinane Castle as Malcolm and Macduff's

army marched on towards him. At the final moment, they threw down their branches and surged up the hill in full battle cry.

Macbeth's soldiers hated him and had no stomach for a fight, but Macbeth fought like a man possessed. The witches had promised him no man born of a woman could kill him. He believed himself immortal. One by one, he slew his enemies, until, at last, he faced Macduff alone.

"Get back!" said Macbeth. "I've shed enough of your family's blood already. I bear a charmed life. No one can harm me unless they are not born of a woman. So I am safe."

"Ha!" said Macduff. "I am not born of a woman. They cut me from my mother's womb before she could give birth."

Macbeth lowered his sword in fright. "I will not fight you."

"Then yield, coward."

"No!" cried Macbeth, filled with desperate courage. "I will not kiss the ground before young Malcolm's feet. Though Birnam Wood has come to Dunsinane and you are not born of a woman, I will fight to the last."

When the bloody fight was over, Macduff held Macbeth's severed head in his hand. He kneeled before Malcolm and cried out, "Hail, King of Scotland! We are freed from tyranny."

"My thanes and kinsmen," said Malcolm. "We will call home our exiled friends that fled from tyranny, and bring to justice those who served this dead butcher and his fiendish queen. Thanks now to everyone. I will reward each of you as you deserve. Come, I invite you all to watch me be crowned King of Scotland at Scone."

The Winter's Tale

When Leontes becomes convinced that his pregnant wife is having an affair, his jealousy tears his family apart. By the time he realizes the truth, it seems his wife, son and newborn daughter are all dead, and it's all his fault. But not everything is as it appears to be and, years later, fate plays a surprising hand…

Antigonus

Paulina's husband, a nobleman. He's given a terrible order by his king, but will he succeed in carrying it out?

Shepherd and his son

The shepherd finds a baby girl. He brings her up as his own, along with his son.

Autolycus

A pedlar, confidence trickster and thief, always on the lookout for opportunities to make money.

Perdita

Abandoned to die as a baby, she is rescued and brought up by a shepherd, not knowing her true identity.

Florizel

King Polixenes's son. He falls in love with Perdita, not knowing who she really is.

"My dear friend, I've been here for nine months! I really must go home. Bohemia needs its king." King Polixenes smiled apologetically at his friend, Leontes, the King of Sicily.

"But surely you could stay just a *little* longer," Leontes pleaded. "Just a week is all I ask."

It was a surprisingly warm and sunny afternoon for midwinter. Leontes, his heavily pregnant wife, Hermione, and his old childhood friend, Polixenes, were strolling in the palace courtyard, while the young prince, Mamillius, played happily in a corner.

"Hermione, why aren't you helping?" Leontes complained. "Say something to make him to stay!"

Hermione laughed. "Dear husband, I was only waiting for you to say the obvious – that Bohemia is doing just fine without him. Polixenes," Hermione turned to her husband's friend, "you can spare us just one more week, can't you?" She gave him her most winning smile, and taking him by the arm she gently steered him away from her husband. "Will you stay?"

"No, madam…" Polixenes began.

But Hermione wasn't going to take no for an answer, and she continued to wear him down. Eventually Leontes impatiently interrupted: "Is he won yet?"

"Yes, my dear, he's won." Hermione turned with a satisfied smile and, defeated, Polixenes sighed his agreement.

"Well done! I couldn't get him to stay. And yet you have…" The smile on Leontes's face suddenly faded and his expression was replaced by a far darker one. A terrible thought had occurred to him. How could his wife have convinced his best friend so easily, when he could not? Unless, unless… there was more to their friendship than met the eye. He was suddenly filled with doubt, then fear, anger and, finally, an intense and deadly jealousy.

"Too familiar, too close," he muttered, as his wife and Polixenes, hand in hand, continued to talk. "Look how they touch each other, the way they smile…" He shuddered and looked away.

His son, still playing quietly, suddenly caught his attention. "Mamillius, my boy!"

Mamillius came running to his father who ruffled his hair roughly. "You are *my* fine young fellow, aren't you?"

Glancing over, Polixenes noticed the sudden change in Leontes's mood. "Are you alright, my friend?" he asked.

"Fine," Leontes replied, a tight, thin smile on his face. "Mamillius and I are just going for a walk. But why don't you and Hermione stay and talk?"

Polixenes gave a little bow. "We'll be in the garden."

"Yes, do whatever you want. I'll find you," Leontes said airily, thinking, "I'll give them enough space to give away what they're really up to."

He shooed them away, his smile now so tight it almost cracked, "Off you go, the pair of you."

Leontes watched them as they walked away together, jealousy taking a stronger and stronger hold of his thoughts. Suddenly, everything they did – the way they moved, the way they smiled, *everything* – spoke of just one thing to him: treachery. By the time his old friend Camillo found him, the idea that Hermione was having an affair with Polixenes had become a fact in Leontes's mind.

"You must have seen it, Camillo?" Leontes hissed. "Surely it's obvious that she's unfaithful." For a moment Camillo was speechless. He couldn't believe such a thing of the queen. But he was even more shocked by what Leontes had to say next.

"You, Camillo, you're his cupbearer aren't you? You could put something in his drink…" Leontes's voice grew calmer and more cruel. "Something that will make that drink his last."

Camillo held back a gasp. He couldn't afford to let the king know that he disagreed with him, especially given Leontes's current, clearly irrational state of mind.

"I *could* my lord, although if I were to do this, I would give him a poison that would make it seem as if he'd died of natural causes," he ventured, playing for time. "But I still can't believe that—"

"Do you really think I'd make this up?" Leontes snapped. "That I'd put myself through all this, if it were not true?"

Camillo shook his head. "I believe you, sir. I'll do as you ask." What else *could* he say? Who knew what Leontes would do if he refused? Yet, if Camillo did this… he knew there was really only one thing he could do. Leave. Leave the palace, the country. Leave his life behind – or, in all probability, lose his life.

"Good day, Camillo." Camillo almost jumped out of his skin. He'd been so absorbed in this dreadful train of thought, that he hadn't noticed Polixenes approaching.

"Do you know what's wrong with Leontes?" Polixenes asked. "You'd think he'd lost part of his kingdom, the way he's acting."

"I dare not know, my lord," Camillo replied miserably.

"Dare not or *do* not?" Polixenes insisted. "What on earth do you mean, man?"

Camillo looked away. "There is a sickness, which makes some of us feel very ill. I cannot say what it's called, but it was caught from you, even though you are well."

"What do you mean? Oh, come on, Camillo. What's wrong? Will I catch it? What can I do to prevent myself from doing so?"

"Sir, I…" Camillo sighed, then blurted out, "The king has ordered me to murder you. He thinks you're having an affair with his wife!"

Polixenes was astounded. And horrified. How could the king possibly think such a thing of his best friend? But, Camillo soon persuaded him that it was no use trying to understand Leontes's madness, or trying to reason with him. Polixenes had to leave, and as quickly as possible. They agreed that he would set sail for Bohemia straight away, and that Camillo would go with him.

Hermione was in the garden with Mamillius, completely unaware of all this. It would not be long now until her baby was born. She'd never felt so happy.

"Come, Mamillius. Tell me a happy story," she said, patting the bench for her son to come and sit beside her.

"A sad tale's best for winter," Mamillius replied solemnly. But he'd barely begun his story when Leontes strode into the garden, with a group of lords hurrying after him.

"Was he here? Was Camillo with him?" Leontes barked.

"Yes, I saw them both," one of the lords replied. "They were making for the ships."

"Ha! I was right all along and this proves it. They were plotting to murder me!" Leontes cried. "Give me the boy," he said, seizing his son by the arm. "He may look like me, but he takes far too much after you for my liking," he said glaring at his wife.

Hermione's smile had faded. "What… what *is* this?"

"Take the boy away," the king ordered his lords. "I don't want him anywhere near her, or…" he pointed at Hermione's pregnant belly, a look of utter disgust on his face, "…that brat of Polixenes's. She has betrayed me. Take her to prison!"

"How could you say such a thing? It's not true!" Hermione cried out in disbelief. But Leontes had made up his mind. His wife was a traitor, and nothing Hermione or anyone else said could convince him otherwise.

Hermione was taken away to prison, where she was forbidden all contact with anyone but her maids. Even her friend, Lady

Paulina, was not allowed through the prison gates. She was standing outside them when she heard the news that Hermione had given birth, prematurely, to a baby girl. A maid brought the baby outside for her to see.

"So beautiful, so innocent," Paulina murmured, holding the little bundle in her arms. An idea came to her. She would take the baby to Leontes and make another plea on Hermione's behalf. "Surely seeing this baby will soften his heart," Paulina thought.

But she couldn't have been more wrong.

Leontes was in a foul mood when Paulina approached him. A foul mood made worse by the fact that he hadn't slept, and that his son Mamillius had been taken ill.

"Get her out of here," Leontes ordered. "Get rid of this… spy."

His look of pure hatred was terrifying. But Paulina was not a woman to but put off by Leontes's foul moods. "I am no spy," she said calmly. "I'm just as honest as you are mad."

"Traitor!" Leontes shouted. "Will no one get rid of her? Antigonus!" he turned to one of his lords, Paulina's husband, "Why can't you control your wife?"

"There is only one traitor here," Paulina said quietly, "and that is you. You are a traitor to your wife, to your son. And…" she laid the baby girl down in front of Leontes, "…to your newborn baby."

"That brat is not mine," Leontes spat. "It's Polixenes's. The baby and its mother should be burned alive. Now get out!"

Everyone gasped, but Paulina was not deterred. "All right, I'll go. But look at your baby, my lord. Look at her! *She is yours.*"

"Mine! Mine?" Leontes exploded. "Antigonus, take it away and have it killed!" he commanded, and then when Antigonus made no move to do so, "If you won't do it, I'll kill it with my own hands!"

But when Antigonus reluctantly picked the child up, doubt flashed across Leontes's face and he changed his mind. Instead of having the baby killed, he ordered Antigonus to take her to some remote place and leave her there. Perhaps by chance she'd survive. Perhaps she would not.

Antigonus was horrified, but agreed. After all, it was better than the alternative, wasn't it?

Antigonus had already left Sicily when news arrived that two servants had come back from Delphos in Greece. Leontes had sent them to consult the Oracle of the gods – to find out if Hermione really was guilty – and they'd brought back the answer on a sealed scroll. Leontes summoned Hermione and all the lords of the palace to hear what he was sure would be the proof of her guilt.

"Read the charges." Leontes's face was a stony mask of hatred.

An officer read: "Hermione, Queen of Sicily, you are accused of treason, of being unfaithful to the king and of plotting to have him killed."

"There is little point in my saying that I am not guilty," Hermione said, when the officer had finished, "given that whatever I say will not be believed. But you, my lord," she turned to Leontes, "know that in the past I have been as faithful and honest as I am now unfortunate."

"If you are bad enough to have committed this crime, you are bad enough to lie," Leontes snapped.

Hermione soon realized that there was nothing she could say to change her husband's mind. She hardly cared now anyway. Everything she valued had been taken away from her. So the scroll was brought forward and the seals broken.

"Read it," Leontes commanded.

The messenger read: "Hermione is faithful, Polixenes is blameless, Camillo honest, Leontes a jealous tyrant, the innocent baby is his child; and the king shall live without an heir if that which is lost is not found."

OFFICER, ACT 3, SCENE 2

For a split second, there was a stunned silence. Then, a general murmuring of relief, until Leontes burst out, "The Oracle is false! It's false, I tell you!" But he was interrupted by a servant rushing in.

"My lord!"

"What is it?" snapped Leontes.

"Oh sir, it's your son… your son is gone."

"Gone where?"

"He is dead," the servant replied.

Leontes let out a small cry, and Hermione fainted to the floor.

"You've killed her!" Paulina screamed.

"She's not dead. She's just upset." Leontes looked truly shaken. "She'll recover. Look after her…" As Hermione was carried away, the king dropped to his knees in remorse. "I will apologize to Polixenes," he said desperately, "I will woo my queen again. I will call the good Camillo back."

But it was all too late. Paulina rushed back, her face ashen with grief. "The queen is dead."

Meanwhile, Antigonus had already taken the baby to Bohemia. He'd had a dream in which Hermione had told him to leave her there. He gently laid the child on a bed of leaves in the forest, and placed a box beside her. The box contained gold and jewels, and a letter stating where the baby had come from, and her name – which, in his dream, Hermione had told him was Perdita.

It broke Antigonus's heart to leave the tiny baby, but he could not disobey his king. As he walked away from her, he heard a noise. Turning, he saw a huge bear. He started to run, but with a fearful roar it pursued him. "I am gone forever!" he cried out, fleeing further into the forest with the beast at his heels.

Not long after, a shepherd and his son arrived at the same spot. They didn't see the baby at first, but when she began to cry, the shepherd scooped her up, marvelling at his discovery. Only then did he spot the box. He couldn't believe his eyes when he opened it. He was rich! He decided to take the baby home and bring her up as his own, vowing to tell no one else about the box.

Sixteen long years passed. Perdita grew up happily, believing herself to be a shepherd's daughter. Her true father, Leontes, was still tormented by the guilt of what he'd done.

Camillo stayed with Polixenes in Bohemia, and the two became great friends. One day, Camillo received a letter from Sicily. It was from Leontes, begging him to return home. He had been feeling homesick, and so he broached the matter with Polixenes.

Polixenes did not want him to go. "I need you here!" he said. "And *please* don't mention the King of Sicily again." So Camillo agreed to stay – but from then on, his longing to go home grew.

In the meantime, however, there was a mystery to solve. Polixenes's son, Florizel, had been spending a lot of time away from the palace, and rumour had it that he was spending it with a certain shepherd's daughter, who went by the name of Perdita. Polixenes was determined to get to the bottom of the matter and had asked Camillo to help him.

One warm summer's day, not long after Camillo had heard from Leontes, a scruffily-dressed man was ambling along the road near the shepherd's cottage, singing cheerfully. His name was Autolycus and he was was a notorious cheat – a thief, a confidence trickster, a con man. His singing came to a sudden stop when he saw a young man approaching, and he flung himself to the ground.

"Help, help," he cried out pathetically. "I've been robbed!"

The shepherd's son came rushing over. "What happened?"

"They took all my money and my clothes and left me with these rags," Autolycus groaned pitifully.

"Let me help you." The shepherd's son leaned down to pull Autolycus up from the ground and, as he did so, Autolycus slipped his hand into the man's pocket and stole his purse.

"Who did this to you?" asked the shepherd's son. "I heard that that rogue Autolycus is up to his tricks in these parts."

Autolycus nodded thoughtfully. "Yes, it must have been him!"

"Well, if you're all right, I'll be on my way," the shepherd's son said. "I'm off to buy spices for a sheep-shearing celebration."

"He won't be buying any spices now he's has his purse stolen," Autolycus thought, smirking. But a sheep-shearing party. Now *that* sounded like an excellent opportunity to make some money…

At the shepherd's cottage, Perdita and Prince Florizel had stolen a little time for themselves before the festivities began. They'd first met when Florizel's hunting bird had flown across the shepherd's land. It had been love at first sight and, since then, Florizel had been visiting Perdita, disguised as a shepherd. She was the only one at the cottage who knew he was really a prince. She also knew how much his father, the king, would disapprove of their love for one another if he found out.

They were talking happily when the old shepherd burst into the cottage with two strangers. "Daughter, where are your manners? Come and welcome our guests," he cried.

The strangers were, in fact, Polixenes and Camillo, in disguise as farmhands. They had followed Prince Florizel to the cabin to find out more about his secret liaisons. Perdita greeted them graciously. She asked them to sit down and busied herself attending to them. Watching her, Polixenes and Camillo could not but help be impressed. The way she spoke, and the graceful way she moved, suggested that she was something more than just a simple peasant girl. And it was clear that she and Florizel were very much in love.

Once the celebration was in full swing, Autolycus slipped in among the guests. He was disguised as a pedlar, with a tray of ribbons and bangles suspended from his neck. As people flocked to buy trinkets off him, he cunningly set about picking their pockets.

Meanwhile, Polixenes had started chatting to Florizel, turning the conversation easily to Florizel's favourite topic: Perdita. Florizel just couldn't help himself. He'd soon told the 'stranger' how much he loved her and how they planned to be married.

"An engagement!" cried the shepherd, who'd been listening in. Tears of joy filled his eyes. "Our new friends can witness it!"

Polixenes and Camillo exchanged quick, worried glances.

"Now wait a minute. Does your father know about this?" Polixenes asked Florizel sternly.

"He does not, sir, and nor shall he," Florizel answered defiantly.

Polixenes frowned. "But surely this is not the behaviour of a dutiful son. Certainly, a young man should choose his own wife, but surely his father should be at least consulted on the matter." He was trying his best to sound reasonable, but he could feel the anger bubbling up inside him.

"I really can't tell him," Florizel replied.

The two argued until Florizel said in exasperation, "No, he really can't find out. Now please do witness our engagement, sir."

"*You* can witness your *separation*, sir," Polixenes roared, flinging off his disguise. "I hardly dare call you 'son'," he growled. "If you ever see this girl again, I'll disinherit you. You'll *never* be King of Bohemia. You," he turned to the shepherd, "are a common traitor! And as for *you*!" he said to Perdita, his face dark with anger, "If you ever see my son again, I'll come up with a punishment far worse than death!"

Polixenes stormed out of the cottage, consumed with rage.

"King of Bohemia!" the shepherd exclaimed, who had really not had any idea who Florizel was.

"I told you this would happen," Perdita wailed.

But Florizel was undeterred. "I'm sorry, rather than afraid. Our plans are delayed, but nothing has changed. I still love you and we will still be married."

Perdita looked doubtful, but Camillo had a suggestion to make. Throwing off his disguise, he told them his idea. They would sail to Sicily, and present themselves to Leontes. The king was so wracked with guilt about his treatment of Polixenes, he'd be bound to receive them with open arms. The pair agreed to the plan, and Camillo was delighted. Finally he had an excuse to return home.

While Camillo, Perdita and Florizel discussed the arrangements, Autolycus had wandered back into the room. He was feeling mighty pleased with himself. He'd picked the pockets of most of the people at the party, and would have picked them all if it hadn't been for the commotion Polixenes had caused.

Camillo saw Autolycus, and looked him carefully up and down. Florizel needed a new disguise, and this pedlar was just his size. They could swap clothes! Well, Autolycus wasn't going to say 'no' to a nice new set of smart clothes, so he quickly agreed.

The shepherd and his son were deep in conversation when Autolycus, dressed in his new finery, spotted them. They were debating how best to avoid punishment for Perdita's actions.

"Tell the king the fairies left her," the son was whispering to his father urgently. "See, you have the box and its contents as proof… She's got nothing to do with us, so we can't be punished, can we?"

Autolycus cleared his throat, making the two of them jump out

"I am but sorry, not afeard. Delayed,
But nothing altered. What I was, I am.

FLORIZEL, ACT 4, SCENE 4

of their skins. "Now then, you two." Autolycus put on his noblest accent. "Where might you be off to?"

"To the palace, my lord." Neither the shepherd nor his son recognized him in Florizel's clothes.

"Really? Why? What will you be doing there, and who with? I want your address, names and ages, and anything else I should know!" Autolycus barked. "And what's in that box?" He pointed at the bundle the shepherd was trying to hide under his arm.

"We're… we're just ordinary people, my lord. You're a courtier, aren't you, sir?" the shepherd's son replied in awe.

"I am indeed," Autolycus replied, puffing himself up. "And I demand to know what your business is!"

It didn't take much for Autolycus to get them to admit they were going to see the king, but the shepherd was determined not to say what was in the box. Clearly, a different tactic was required.

"The king's not at the palace," Autolycus said airily. "He's on a ship preparing to set sail. You must have heard about this business of his son marrying a shepherd's girl. He's in a *terrible* mood. Right now he's planning horrible punishments for the girl's brother and father…"

"We should ask him to speak to the king for us," the shepherd's son whispered fearfully to his father. "We could pay him with gold from the box." The shepherd agreed anxiously.

Of course, Autolycus graciously agreed to help them. He couldn't help smiling when they'd parted ways. It wasn't every day that he had foolish men pour gold into his lap.

In Sicily, Leontes and his lords were discussing the topic of his finding a new wife. The king needed an heir, his supporters argued, but Paulina was doing her best to dissuade him. It wasn't difficult – she only had to mention Hermione's death for him to reject the idea. Paulina reminded them all of the Oracle's prophecy too – that there would be no heir until the child that was lost had been found. Clearly remarrying was not the answer.

Just then, a servant entered the room. "King Polixenes's son, Prince Florizel, is here with his wife," he announced.

Leontes frowned. It seemed strange that the prince should arrive out of the blue like this. "And his wife, you say?"

"Yes, my lord. The most beautiful woman I've ever seen."

"Well, go and bring them in."

When the young prince and his wife entered the room, Leontes was immediately struck by how much Florizel looked like his father had at the same age… and was bowled over by Perdita's beauty. He realized, with a pang of sadness, how she must be about the same age his lost daughter would have been, had she survived.

"I am here to bring greetings from my father, who is too unwell to come himself," Florizel trotted out his well-rehearsed lie. "And this is my wife, the daughter of the King of Libya." Leontes felt a great rush of happiness, but it was tinged with sadness, as he remembered how he'd treated Polixenes. He was also intrigued by Perdita. There was something familiar about her…

But before he could work out what it was, a lord rushed in. "The King of Bohemia is here! He's come to fetch his son who's run away with a shepherd's daughter!"

A stunned silence fell upon the room.

"Where is Polixenes?" Leontes demanded, his voice trembling.

"In the city! I've just come from him," the lord replied.

"That wretch Camillo betrayed me!" Florizel cried out angrily.

"You can say that to his face!" a lord retorted. "He's here too!"

"What, Camillo's here?" Leontes asked, overjoyed.

"Yes indeed, sir, and the girl's father and brother, too."

"The heavens must be against us!" Perdita cried. "We are doomed never to marry."

"What! You're not married?" demanded Leontes.

"We are not. Nor are we likely to be now," Florizel said sadly.

"And is this," Leontes indicated Perdita, "really a princess?"

"She is," answered Florizel defiantly, "once she is my wife."

"That isn't going to happen, if your father has anything to do with it," Leontes said gravely. "I am sorry. Sorry that you have fallen out with him. And sorry that you have fallen in love with a woman whose status is not as great as her beauty."

"My dearest," Florizel said gently to Perdita, "luck seems to be against us, but nothing can change our love for one another."

To Leontes, he said, "I beg you, speak for us. If you ask, my father will grant you any request."

"I wish that were true," Leontes replied sadly. "Your precious princess reminds me of my own beloved wife… But yes, I will talk to him for you."

The news spread fast. Soon the whole town was talking about the course of events that had unfolded at the palace – events so incredible, they sounded more like a fairy tale than reality.

"You should have seen the king's face when he saw Lord Camillo again," one man said. "At first, the two of them looked as if the world was about to end. They were so emotional, you couldn't tell if they were happy or sad."

"Yes, and when the old shepherd showed them his box, and the letters that proved Lady Perdita was the king's daughter…" another chimed in, "Well, it all began to make perfect sense. How the young lady looked like her mother, and behaved like a princess. The king was overcome with joy. I've never seen so many tears."

"And when the king met Polixenes, well…" A third man had joined the little group outside the palace. "They hugged and cried and the king asked for forgiveness, and hugged his new son-in-law to-be, and kissed and hugged his daughter so fervently, you'd think he'd never let her go again. It was a sight for sore eyes."

"Of course, Lady Paulina was devastated to hear how her husband was killed by a bear," the first gentlemen added sadly. "Apparently the shepherd's son saw it all. Mind you, not that he's a shepherd now. The king has made him and his father lords!"

And so the prophecy had been fulfilled. The lost child had been found, the two kings were reconciled, and Florizel and Perdita were to get married. But this was not quite the end of the tale.

Paulina told the reunited families that she'd had a statue made of Hermione, which had only just been completed. Of course they all wanted to see it. So the two kings, their children and Camillo all set off for Paulina's house.

She took them into a room where the statue was kept behind a curtain. She drew back the curtain and everyone fell silent.

"She… she looks so natural," Leontes said after a moment. "But Paulina, she has more wrinkles than Hermione did in real life."

"Only a few," Paulina said, barely hiding a smile. "The sculptor carved her to look as she would if she were alive today."

"Oh, if only she were alive today," Leontes burst out sadly.

"You shouldn't look at it any more," Paulina said to him, "in case wishful thinking makes you believe it is moving…"

"But it is!" Leontes cried. "Doesn't she look as if she's breathing?" he asked the others imploringly.

"It's true," Polixenes said. "It really is amazingly lifelike."

"You'll think it's alive next!" Paulina said.

"Oh Paulina, let me think it, let me have that madness for a while," Leontes begged. "I shall kiss her."

"No! My lord, you must not! You'll spoil the paint on her lips. It's not dry yet," Paulina said. "I'll draw the curtain."

"No!" Leontes cried out.

Paulina looked at him thoughtfully. He looked so desperately sad, so full of regret… She came to a decision.

"In that case," she said slowly, "either leave, or be prepared for something astonishing. I shall make the statue move, and, indeed, step down from its pedestal and take you by the hand. But…" She paused for a moment, a twinkle in her eyes. "But you might think I have evil powers. Perhaps…"

"I don't care, Paulina. *Do* it!" Leonates begged.

Paulina smiled. "Very well…" She spoke to the statue. "Awake! It's time. Come down. Be stone no more."

The statue blinked and, very slowly, seemed to come alive. It stepped down from the pedestal and stood in front of Leontes.

"Don't startle her," Paulina warned Leontes. "And do not turn her away ever again. Give her your hand as you did when she was young. When you wooed her."

"She's warm!" cried Leontes, as he took her hand. Tears flowed down his cheeks as Hermione, come back to life, embraced him. Perdita rushed forward and Hermione flung her arms around her daughter too.

Paulina laughed to see their reunion, but there was sadness in her eyes as she thought of her dead husband.

Leontes called to Camillo. "Come, take Paulina's hand. We will all go somewhere more comfortable, where we can talk and begin to make up for the time we have all lost."

All that day and all the next, the little group laughed and cried, and laughed again as they caught up with all that they had missed of each others' lives over the years. There was so much to talk about, and a wedding to plan too. A winter wedding, and a new beginning.

Antony and Cleopatra

The Roman empire has three joint rulers: Antony, Caesar and Lepidus – but their alliance is crumbling. Antony has been spending all his time in Egypt with the beautiful Cleopatra. Now, with civil war brewing, he will have to choose between duty, power and love.

Mark Antony

A famous Roman general and statesman. But instead of ruling, he spends his days at lavish banquets with Cleopatra...

Cleopatra

Fabulously beautiful queen of Egypt, she is also Antony's lover. But to keep his heart she will need to compete with Rome itself...

Enobarbus

Antony's trusted advisor and lieutenant. Enobarbus is wise, dependable, and – so far – loyal.

Octavius Caesar

The second, and youngest,
Roman ruler. An ambitious
politician and Julius Caesar's heir.
He has no patience for Antony's
Egyptian love affair.

Lepidus

The third, and weakest, Roman
ruler. All he wants is for Caesar
and Antony to get along, but he
may not be able to keep the peace
between Rome and Egypt.

Octavia

Caesar's beloved sister.
A marriage between
Octavia and Antony could
ease the tensions between
him and Caesar.

Sextus Pompey

Leader of a pirate army that's
threatening Roman ships across the
Mediterranean. If left unchecked,
he might even topple Rome.

THERE WAS A GREAT FEAST UNDERWAY in the Egyptian royal palace in Alexandria. To the sound of flutes and cymbals, dancers wove among the columns of the banquet hall. Servants staggered under heavy silver platters of figs, roasted meats and rare Egyptian delicacies. On one side of the hall, two Roman soldiers stood guard, sweating in the summer heat.

"I can't believe we're stuck here," one of them muttered, "as if our spears were made to wave the flies from plates of meat."

"Our general is infatuated with the Egyptian queen," replied the other. "His eyes, that used to scan the ranks of battle-ready troops, now focus only on her foreign beauty. The man who rules one third of all the world has surrendered his heart to a woman."

"Hush, here they come!"

Antony, carrying Cleopatra in his arms, strode into the hall. The queen was laughing. Her arms were draped around his neck, her gleaming green eyes locked lazily onto his. In a voice like silk, she said, "If you truly love me, tell me how much."

"What value is there in love that can be measured?" Antony asked, setting her down on an embroidered couch.

"I could tell you how far your love should stretch," Cleopatra insisted playfully.

"You'll need to find new Heavens, new Earths to contain it," Antony vowed.

A servant approached. "My lord," he murmured, "some messengers have come from Rome."

"Ugh," said Antony, "is it important? Tell them to wait."

Jealousy darkened Cleopatra's expression as quickly as a cloud covering the sun. "Hear them, Antony," she snapped, her eyes narrowing. "Maybe that beardless boy, Caesar, has sent you orders: 'Do this, do that – or else.' Or maybe Fulvia, your wife, has called you back to Rome, and you'll be rid of me at last."

Antony turned her jealous face to his. "Let Rome melt into the River Tiber," he declared, "and let the empire's wide arch fall. Here in Egypt is my place, and the nobleness of life is this." He kissed Cleopatra. With a slow smile, she twined her fingers in his hair.

"Shame on you, you wrangling queen," he whispered, "how well each mood or passion suits you – whether you're chiding, laughing or weeping! Tonight I'll hear no messenger but yours."

Late the next morning, rumpled and bleary-eyed, Antony rose to meet the three Roman messengers. They spoke in the great hall, among the stacks of silver plates, the spilled wine and scattered cushions left over from the feast.

"Well, tell me the worst," said Antony.

"My lord, there's war in Asia," said the first. "Some few, undefendable provinces have fallen to invaders."

"You mean to say the provinces I *should have* defended. Speak plainly," Antony urged, "and taunt my faults with the power that truth brings to bear. Whoever tells me the truth, even if he brings fatal news, has flattered me. What else?"

"My lord," the second messenger began, "the pirate captain Sextus Pompey has taken command of a fleet of ships. His army rules the seas, and people are flocking to join him. He may soon be powerful enough to threaten Rome itself."

"My lord," said the third man, "your wife, Fulvia, is dead."

Antony looked up in shock. "There's a great spirit gone," he said mournfully. "It's true we never liked each other. I wanted to be rid of her – but now I almost wish her back."

Antony dismissed the messengers. "Since I've been in Egypt, I've neglected the affairs of state," he thought. "I must break off from this enchanting queen, or else my idleness will hatch ten thousand other ills to match what I have heard today.”

The Roman turned and called for his lieutenant, Enobarbus. The grizzled veteran, still groggy from the night's feasting, hurried to his side. “My lord?” he croaked.

“Enobarbus, I must visit Rome,” Antony said.

“Cleopatra's not going to like that,” Enobarbus warned. “And you know her tantrums – they aren't just sighs and tears. They're storms and tempests.”

Antony knew very well. “I sometimes wish I'd never seen her!” he sighed.

“But you'd have missed something wonderful,” Enobarbus said.

“That's true,” Antony agreed. “But now, let our officers know what's afoot, and I'll speak to the queen.”

Enobarbus hurried off to find the other Romans. A few moments later, Cleopatra breezed into the hall. She looked magnificent in a shimmering golden gown. Her handmaidens, Charmian and Iras, fanned her gently with ostrich plumes.

“I'm sorry to have to say this…” Antony began.

“Stop! I can tell from your face something's wrong,” Cleopatra said fiercely. “What is it – has your wife ordered you home? Well, she can't claim *I* kept you here. *I* have no power over you.”

“My dearest queen—”

“Oh, never was a queen so mightily betrayed!” She stamped her foot and her eyes glinted dangerously.

“Cleopatra—”

“Why did I believe that you could be mine and true, when you've been false to Fulvia?” Cleopatra stormed.

“My most sweet queen—”

“No, don't make excuses,” Cleopatra said. “Just bid farewell and go.”

Antony reached out to her, but Cleopatra turned away.

"*Then was the time for words: no going then. Eternity was in our lips and eyes*"

"Once you begged to stay with me," she said. "*Then* was the time for words. There was no talk of going then. Eternity was in our lips and eyes. But now I see your every word's a lie."

Antony couldn't tear his eyes from her flawless face. "Hear me, Queen," he insisted. "Italy is shining with the swords of civil war, and pirates raid the ports of Rome. These desperate events demand my services a while – but my full heart remains with you."

"So you say! But Fulvia—"

"She's dead, my queen."

Cleopatra turned back to him in shock. "Fulvia is dead?"

Antony nodded, and her fury seemed to falter and fade. "Oh, most false love," she said bitterly, "where are the tears you should be weeping? Now I see – I see, in Fulvia's death, how you'll behave when I am gone."

Her own tears were flowing freely now, and she let Antony hold her as she wept for her rival. They stood together for a long moment. At last, the Egyptian queen brushed away her tears. "Very well," she said. "Your honour calls you back to Rome. May all the gods go with you, and may they bring you swift success."

That same day, Sextus Pompey and his pirate captains met on the coast of Sicily. The time was right, they agreed, to make a bid for power. "The people love me, and the sea is mine," Pompey declared. "My strength is growing, and meanwhile, the three rulers of Rome do nothing but squabble. Antony wastes his days dining in Egypt; Caesar sends him endless angry messages from Italy; Lepidus flatters both, but neither cares for him."

"Together the three of them could raise a mighty army,"

warned Menas, one of Pompey's captains.

"True," Pompey admitted, "but I doubt that lovestruck Antony will strap on his helmet for such a petty war. We'd be in trouble if he did – he's twice the soldier the others are."

"Let's hope that together, Cleopatra and the skilled Egyptian cooks can keep him at the banquet table," Menas smiled.

"And that his quarrels with Caesar stay fresh," agreed Pompey.

The bad blood between Caesar and Antony was on everyone's mind a few days later when, in a stately villa in Rome, the three rulers gathered for an urgent meeting.

Caesar and Lepidus arrived first with their advisors. They paced back and forth in the marble-floored atrium.

"You see, Lepidus, what news we've had of him," said Caesar, holding up a sheaf of reports. "He feasts and drinks, and spends his nights in revelry."

"I wouldn't have thought there were evils enough to darken all his goodness," Lepidus replied.

"You're too indulgent," Caesar retorted. "Even if we could excuse his merriment, his absence has doubled the work we have."

They heard a swift step in the hall, and Antony strode in, followed by Enobarbus. They had just arrived from the coast, and the white dust of the roads still clung to their cloaks.

"Welcome, Antony," said Lepidus. "My noble friends, we three have combined to make a greater force – don't let a lesser quarrel tear us apart. Instead, let's gently air our differences."

Caesar waved him aside. "Antony," he began, "when you were revelling in Alexandria, you ignored my messengers. You broke your oath to lend me arms and aid when I required them."

"That which combined us was most great, and let not
A leaner action rend us."

Lepidus, Act 2, Scene 2

Antony looked Caesar squarely in the face. "Say rather that I neglected it," he replied. "I didn't know the severity of your need. I'll admit my faults to you, Caesar, but don't try to take advantage of my honesty."

Lepidus sighed. "If only there was a way to bind you two and save this friendship."

One of Caesar's advisors, clever Agrippa, softly cleared his throat. "I know a way," he said. "Caesar, you have a sister: the admired Octavia. And great Mark Antony is now a widower…"

"Be careful what you say, Agrippa. If Cleopatra heard you, you'd regret it!" Caesar said, glancing at Antony.

"Let's hear what Agrippa has to say," Antony said.

"To seal your friendship, make you brothers, to knit your hearts with an unslipping knot, let Antony take Octavia as his wife. Then all the little jealousies which now seem great will shrink away," Agrippa suggested.

"What does Caesar think?" asked Antony.

"What do *you* think?" Caesar replied.

"If Agrippa could persuade you, I'll go along with it," said Antony.

"Agrippa could," Caesar admitted.

"Then from this hour," Antony declared, "let the hearts of brothers govern us."

The two shook hands. "We should decide what to do about Pompey," Caesar said.

"Yes," Antony agreed. "We'll need to act quickly. If we can show him our united strength, I think he'll agree to negotiate."

As the three rulers pored over nautical maps and numbers of troops, Agrippa and Enobarbus strolled around the villa. "Welcome back to Rome, Enobarbus," said Agrippa. "Is it true what we've heard about your marathon banquets in Egypt?"

"You don't know the half of it," Enobarbus grinned.

"What about Cleopatra?" asked Agrippa. "What's she like? I suppose Antony will have to leave her now."

"Never," Enobarbus said. "Age cannot wither her, nor does her infinite variety ever grow stale. You should have seen her when she first met Antony, on the River Cydnus. She sailed in on a ship of beaten gold. Its silver oars kept time to the tune of flutes. Its sails were purple, and perfumed so that the very winds were lovesick with their scent. When she arrived, the city poured its people out to view her, and Antony, enthroned in the marketplace, was left alone, whistling to the empty air. That night, she invited him to dine with her, and for that meal he paid with his heart…"

Despite Cleopatra's unrivalled beauty, Antony's marriage to Octavia proceeded as planned. In Egypt, the poor messenger who delivered news of the wedding to Cleopatra felt lucky to escape with his life. But in Rome, the political benefits of the marriage were immediate. Caesar and Antony worked together as never before, and raised an army to counter Sextus Pompey's force. Soon, the pirate leader agreed to talks, and invited them to complete their negotiations with a feast aboard his galley.

The leaders and the enemies of Rome sat together on cushions on the deck, and servants passed around jugs of wine. "Pompey, you've read our proposal," Caesar said, "so tell us: do you agree? Will you lay down your sword, and take back to Sicily the brave young men that otherwise would perish here?"

"I will," Pompey agreed. "You give me Sicily and Sardinia, and I'll rid the sea of pirates, and pay a tax of wheat to Rome – and so our swords can rest securely in their scabbards."

The four men made a toast to peace, and so began a long night of celebration. Beneath the galley's gently swaying mast, the goblets were filled and emptied again and again. As the stars came out, Antony entertained the others with stories of life in Egypt. They chatted and joked almost like old friends.

Later, when the Roman leaders had departed, Pompey and Enobarbus talked. "I didn't expect to see Antony and Caesar united this way," Pompey admitted.

"Nor did I," said Enobarbus. "But I think you'll find the very bond that seems to tie their friendship up will strangle it. Sooner or later, Antony will return to his Egyptian queen, and poor Octavia's sighs will fan the fire of Caesar's rage."

A few weeks later, Antony sailed with Octavia to Egypt to resume command of his legions. The sea between the two brothers-in-law washed away the trust between them. Soon enough, their feud picked up where it had left off. Messengers and spies crossed back and forth, delivering ominous news. In Alexandria, they reported that Caesar's troops were skirmishing with Pompey in Sicily. In Rome, they described how Antony once again spent long nights feasting with the Egyptian queen.

"Your brother is slandering me in public," Antony complained to Octavia, "and he's broken our treaty and started another war against Pompey! I've even heard that he's thrown Lepidus in jail, accusing him of treachery. It's just a ploy to take more power."

"Oh, my good lord," said Octavia sadly, "a more unhappy lady never stood between two men. I pray for both of you, but each prayer undoes the other."

"Gentle Octavia, you may need to choose between us. Choose whoever most deserves your love," Antony told her.

"I'll try to make peace between you," Octavia decided, "for if you quarrel, our whole world would split – and only dead men then will solder up the rift."

"Go to Rome," agreed Antony, "and judge for yourself who's right – me or Caesar. For our faults can never be so equal that you love us equally."

But when Octavia arrived back in Rome, the prospect for peace had already worsened. "My dear sister," exclaimed Caesar as he welcomed her, "don't you know what your husband's up to? He's raising a foreign army to fight against Rome."

"I came to put a stop to all of this…" Octavia began.

"And he let you come because you stood between him and Cleopatra," Caesar said. "The two of them are partners now, in love and in war."

"Can this be true?" cried Octavia. "Oh, what misery!"

"I have my eyes on him," Caesar said. "Just days ago, he and his Egyptian queen appeared together in public, enthroned on seats of gold. Until now, your happiness held back my rage. But now I see how he's betrayed you, this war will carry on its destined course."

Soon after, civil war broke out across the Roman empire. Antony and Cleopatra, with their trusted captains and advisors, met in the throne room in Alexandria to discuss their strategy.

"Caesar's troops are here," reported Enobarbus, showing them a map of the Mediterranean, "and here are his ships. Shall we fight him on land or on sea?"

"He's challenged us to fight at sea," said Antony, "so we will."

One of Antony's soldiers frowned. "Sir, our sailors are unskilled compared to our foot soldiers. By sea, you throw away the advantage of your soldiership – your famous expertise. Don't put your trust in rotten planks. We used to conquer standing on the earth, and fighting foot to foot."

"I'll fight at sea," said Antony firmly.

Cleopatra agreed. "I have sixty ships to add to our fleet."

Soldier, Act 3, Scene 7

As they left the great port of Alexandria, their ships seemed to cover the horizon. The very sound of the waves was drowned out by creaking ropes, stamping feet and the cries of sailors. Antony commanded a heavy Roman galley, while Cleopatra lounged aboard the lavishly decorated flagship of the Egyptian fleet.

They met Caesar's forces in the Bay of Actium, off the coast of Greece. There, the rival fleets attacked. Propelled by rows of oars, the narrow ships rammed their opponents, crushing hulls and snapping keels. Javelins whistled through the air, smoke billowed from burning ships, and soldiers skirmished on the decks.

The battle continued for many hours. The outcome was still uncertain when, suddenly, Cleopatra's flagship raised its purple sail. Leaning over in the wind, the ship fled the battle, heading for the open sea. One by one, each of the remaining Egyptian ships followed suit.

Panic spread through Antony's fleet. Damaged galleys drifted helplessly side by side, their oars entangled. Sailors ignored the shouted commands of their captains. Men leaped into the sea, and tried to swim to shore. Although ships were burning and sinking on both sides, it now seemed that Caesar had the upper hand.

Soon, Antony's own flagship spread its sails and turned south, heading swiftly towards the coast of Egypt.

When he stepped ashore in Alexandria, the defeated general stumbled and sank to the ground. "The land itself is ashamed to bear me," he groaned.

Soon Cleopatra and her handmaidens came running down to the quay. The queen knelt beside Antony. "Oh, my lord, forgive my fearful sails," she cried. "I didn't think you would follow me."

"You knew too well my heart was tied to your rudder," Antony said bitterly, "and you towed me after. You knew your power over me! Now I must send Caesar humble treaties – I, who once could make or mar men's fortunes as I pleased, who ruled the bulk of half the world!"

"Forgive me!" Tears were rolling down Cleopatra's cheeks, and they splashed on Antony's knee.

The Roman looked down at his weeping queen and sighed. "No more tears. A single one of these is worth more than all we've won or lost. Give me a kiss – and even this repays me. Come," he said, lifting her to her feet, "Caesar will soon besiege Alexandria, but I'll oppose him. The next time I fight, I'll make death love me for my ruthlessness. I'll send to darkness all that try to stop me. My sword and I will earn our fame. There's hope yet!"

"My brave lord," said Cleopatra, smiling through her tears.

"Now," said Antony, "let's have one more wild night. Call to me all my sad captains. Fill our cups once more. Let's mock the midnight bell."

The lovers walked up towards the palace. Enobarbus followed, reluctantly. "In this mood, Antony would face down lightning – fight against all odds," he mused. "It isn't reasonable. I have to find a way out for myself."

Many hours later, after all the revellers in the palace had gone to sleep, two night watchmen were patrolling the streets of Alexandria. They strode through narrow alleys and the empty city squares. The only creatures that crossed their path were stray cats

"Let's have one other gaudy night: call to me
All my sad captains: fill our bowls once more:
Let's mock the midnight bell."

ANTONY
ACT 3, SCENE 13

flitting through the darkness. But as they turned a corner near the city gates, a strange, unearthly music welled up around them.

"Hark! What's that?" cried one.

"Music in the air," said the other.

"No, it comes from underground!"

The two men listened for a moment, wide-eyed, as the faint strains dwindled away.

"What does it mean?" asked one.

"It's the god Hercules, whom Antony loved," said the other man. "The god is leaving him…"

The next day dawned bright and clear. As expected, Caesar's forces had encircled Alexandria. Trumpets sounded, calling forth the troops on either side. Antony awoke with a smile, leaping from his bed. "Eros, bring my armour," he called to his squire.

"I'll help too," said Cleopatra, struggling to lift his breastplate. "What's this piece for?"

"It's upside down," Antony laughed. "But leave that cold steel – you're the armourer of my *heart*!"

"No, let me help," insisted the queen, turning the breastplate around and strapping it on. "Now, haven't I buckled this well?"

Eros came in, carrying his master's boots.

"Eros, you've been replaced," said Antony, chuckling, "and my queen's a squire more skilled than you! But never mind. Have you seen Enobarbus today?"

"Sir," Eros said hesitantly, "Enobarbus is gone."

"What's that you say?" Antony asked.

"He's gone to Caesar. He crept away, and left all his belongings and his treasure behind," the squire told him.

"Are you sure?" Antony said, amazed. He sighed. "Send his treasure after him, Eros, every coin, with a kind farewell from me. Say I hope he will never again need to change allegiances.

My fortunes have corrupted honest men," he mused solemnly. "Come, let's prepare for battle."

Antony's army took the field, and once again his ships sailed out onto the Mediterranean to face Caesar's fleet.

On the ground, Antony led his men with furious confidence. Agrippa's legions folded before him, and Caesar's men found themselves pushed back to their own camp. There, they fought among their tents, wondering at Antony's renewed daring.

However, the sheer force of numbers was starting to tell: for every soldier who fell before Antony, a fresh legion seemed to march into place.

At sea, the defeat at Actium seemed to be repeating itself. The Egyptian ships gave way first, fleeing before the Roman galleys. As the Roman ships sailed into the harbour, Antony finally gave way. Cursing his Egyptian allies, he retreated to the palace.

There were sounds of combat in the streets outside as Caesar's troops poured into the city. "All is lost," Antony raged. "Again, that Egyptian and her cowardly sailors have let me down."

Antony refused to see Cleopatra. "He's furious, and swears you should die for betraying him!" her handmaidens reported.

"Then let him see how he likes it," said Cleopatra angrily. "I'll lock myself in my chamber. Iras, go and tell him that I've killed myself, and that the last word I spoke was 'Antony'."

Iras bore her message to Antony.

"She's dead?" Antony gasped, stunned. At once, his anger drained away. "Oh, my heart, crack your frail case! Eros, the time has come. I won't bow to the victorious Caesar. Draw your sword and kill me."

"How can I do what the enemy, with all his spears and arrows, could not do?" Eros protested.

"This service is the greatest you will ever do for me," Antony assured him.

With tears in his eyes, Eros drew his sword. He raised the weapon, then lowered it. "My dear master, my captain, let me say, before I strike this bloody stroke, farewell." But instead of striking Antony, Eros plunged the blade into his own breast. "And so I escape the sorrow of Antony's death," he gasped, falling into his master's arms.

"Valiant Eros," Antony cried, laying his squire's body gently down, "you are nobler than myself. You and Cleopatra have showed me how to act. I'll do what I have learned from you."

Antony took Eros's sword and thrust it deep into his own chest. The bloody weapon clattered to the floor and Antony slumped to the floor after it. "How am I not dead yet?" he groaned. "I've failed even at death. Help! Won't anybody end what I've begun?"

Just then, Cleopatra rushed into the room with her handmaidens. "Oh, Antony, Antony! Help me, friends! Antony, I only meant to frighten you."

"Peace, my queen," said Antony, smiling faintly. "At least I die not by Caesar's hand, but by my own."

"So it should be," said Cleopatra, fighting back tears. She laid Antony's head in her lap, his blood spreading across her golden gown. "None but Antony should conquer Antony."

"I'm dying, Cleopatra, dying. But let me live until you've laid the last of a thousand kisses on my lips. Quick, or I am gone!"

Cleopatra bent and kissed him, and he closed his eyes.

"The great soldier dies," sobbed the queen. "Now there's nothing remarkable left beneath the moon."

"So it should be, that none but Antony should conquer Antony. But woe 'tis so!"

CLEOPATRA, ACT 4, SCENE 15

News of Antony's death spread quickly. Messengers raced from the palace through the city to Caesar's tent, where he was discussing the battle with his captains. Caesar sat down heavily. "Antony, dead?" he said. "The breaking of so great a thing should make a greater crack. The ground should shake. The death of Antony is not a single doom: in that name lay half the world."

His lieutenants looked on in silence as tears welled up in Caesar's eyes. "Look, sad friends, this is news to wash the eyes of kings. He was my brother, my competitor, my companion on the battlefield. And now our quarrel has destroyed him."

"It's strange," said Agrippa quietly, "how sometimes we regret what we've worked hardest to achieve."

"Now," said Caesar, standing again. "We must go to Cleopatra, seize the palace, and capture her. If we can secure her surrender, and bring her back to Rome alive, our triumph will be complete."

In the palace of Alexandria, Cleopatra had retired to her chambers with her handmaidens, Iras and Charmian. She was dry-eyed and resolute. "Iras, what do you think? You know as well as I do Caesar's plan. He'll make me his captive, carry me to Rome, and parade me through the streets to mark his victory. The onion-eating labourers will gawp at me, and the senators will scold me. They'll make up plays about me, and squeaking boys will act my part out on the stage."

"The gods forbid!" cried Iras.

Cleopatra lifted her chin in defiance. "I won't stand in chains, nor once be chastised by the sober eye of dull Octavia. Charmian, bring me my best robes and my crown. And Iras, please bring me that basket."

Dressed in all her gleaming and glittering finery, Cleopatra uncovered the basket Iras placed before her. Inside, a venomous snake – an Egyptian asp – writhed among purple figs. "I go to meet Antony," murmured the queen. "I have immortal longings in me. I am now only fire and air!"

She lifted the twisting serpent to her breast. "Come, deadly wretch," she said, "with your sharp teeth untie this knot of life."

"Oh, my queen," wept Charmian, "Oh, eastern star!"

"Hush," said Cleopatra, as the asp buried its fangs in her golden skin. "Don't you see this baby at my breast, that sucks its nurse to sleep? As sweet as balm, as soft as air, as gentle. Oh, Antony!"

The venom had done its work. Cleopatra's eyelids fluttered closed. Moments later, she was dead.

Caesar and his troops rushed into the palace and found her there, her handmaidens sobbing over her body. "It is as I feared," said the Roman conqueror. "Brave to the last, she took her own way. She shall be buried with her Antony. No grave on Earth shall hold a pair so famous."

The next day, true to his word, Caesar buried his rivals in solemn ceremony. His army lined the avenues of Alexandria to see the royal bodies carried to rest. Then, one by one, the legions boarded their galleys and sailed across the peaceful sea to Rome.

The Taming of the Shrew

Lots of men want to marry Bianca, but because her sister,
Kate, is older, her father says she needs to be married first.
The problem is that Kate is a 'shrew': a sharp-tongued
scold who scares men off. Unexpectedly, a brash gentleman
comes along who says he can 'tame' her…

Kate (Katherina)

Sharp-tongued and bitter,
even violent, Kate is difficult
to get along with. Is she too
embittered to love or be loved?

Baptista

Kate and Bianca's wealthy
father, who wants to marry
off his daughters.

Bianca

Kate's younger sister.
Apparently sweet and
innocent, she is seen as
real marriage material.

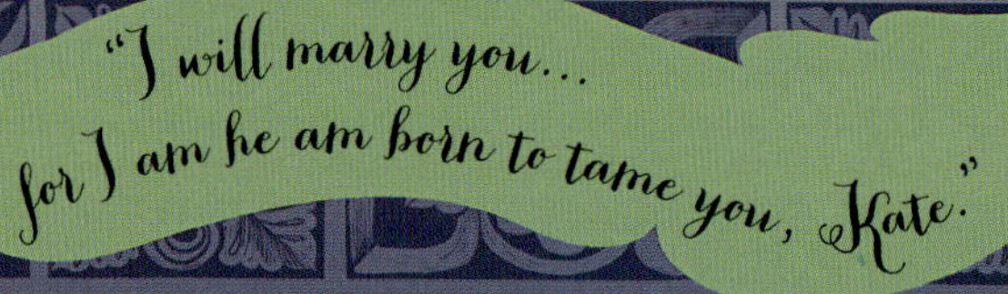

Petruchio

A brash gentleman looking
for a rich wife. He says he can
'tame' Kate. He proves himself
her intellectual equal on their
first meeting and gives her a
dose of her own medicine.

Grumio

Petruchio's
foolish and
comic elderly
servant.

The Taming of the Shrew is a play put
on to entertain these three characters:

Lord

Finds Sly, a drunken
tinker, and tricks
him into thinking
he's rich.

Sly

A drunken tinker,
who now thinks
he's a lord.

Page

The real lord's
servant, pretending
to be Sly's new wife.

Lucentio

A student, in love with
Bianca, who disguises
himself as a Latin tutor to
spend time with her.

Hortensio

Bianca's longstanding
suitor, who disguises
himself as a music teacher
to spend time with her.

Vincentio

Lucentio's father,
who comes looking
for him.

Gremio

A doddery old
suitor to Bianca.

Tranio

Lucentio's clever servant,
who swaps clothes with
his master and devises
a plot to win Bianca.

IT HAD BEEN A BIG NIGHT OUT FOR CHRISTOPHER SLY. He was snoring loudly when a nobleman came across him in the gutter outside the tavern. The lord decided to have some fun… "Let's play a joke on him," he said to his friend. "We can dress him up and put him in one of my best bedrooms. When he wakes up, we'll tell him he's a lord, and when he protests that he's not, we'll just tell him he's had a bad dream."

So Sly, still asleep, was washed, dressed and put to bed. And when, by chance, some actors arrived, the lord persuaded them to put on a play for 'Lord Sly'. Finally, he ordered his page to dress up as a woman, and pretend to be Sly's wife.

When Sly awoke, he was, of course, confused. But the lord's servants offered to attend to his every need, and everyone insisted so relentlessly that he was a lord, that Sly started to doubt himself. Before long, he began to warm to the idea – *especially* once he'd met his (admittedly somewhat boyish) 'wife'.

By the time the actors came into his room, he was more willing to watch their play as 'Sir Christopher', than he would ever have been as the lowly tinker, Christopher Sly.

And so the play begins…

"At last! Here we are in Padua," Lucentio grinned. "I can't *wait* to get started on my studies." He stared around at the great city he'd heard so much about, excited by the hustle and bustle.

"I hope you won't *only* be studying, Master," his servant Tranio replied. "Even the most serious scholars don't have to give up on fun, you know."

"Quite right, Tranio. Let's get settled, and then maybe make some friends. But what's going on here?"

Three men, one with a young lady either side of him, were approaching. The men were deep in conversation. One woman was smiling, the other scowling.

"Gentlemen, I am determined not to let my youngest daughter marry until I have a husband for her older sister," one of the men was saying, gesturing towards the girl with the scowl. "If either of you, Hortensio or Gremio," he looked hopefully at the two other men, "love Katherina, then I give you my permission to court her."

"*Cart* her, more like," Gremio laughed unkindly. "She's far too outspoken for me, my dear Baptista! What about you, Hortensio?"

The elder daughter flushed at her father's 'generous' offer. "Father, you're making a fool of me in front of these suitors."

"Suitors!" Hortensio snorted. "Not likely, unless you learn to curb your temper."

"No fear of *that*," Kate retorted. "The only interest I'd ever take in you would be to hit you over the head and paint your face."

"From all such devils deliver us." Hortensio rolled his eyes.

Lucentio listened in, intrigued. Intrigued, in particular, by Katherina's sister, who, standing on the other side of her father, had remained silent, smiling sweetly while they talked.

"Yes, Kate must marry first," the girls' father said. "Go inside, Bianca, there's a good girl. I hope this doesn't upset you, dear, because you know how much I love you."

"What a spoiled brat," Katherina sneered. "She'll probably make herself cry now," and she pulled a face at her sister.

"Don't worry." Bianca gave a saintly smile as she went inside, "I shall be *very* happy with my books and musical instruments."

"Now," her father said, "I really must find tutors for my dear Bianca. If either of you gentlemen know anyone suitable, please do let me know." And with that, Baptista went off to join Bianca. Katherina stomped after them, her face as dark as thunder.

Gremio and Hortensio were dismayed at this dreadful news. They were both in love with Bianca, and rivals for her hand in marriage. But if Katherina must be married first, their hopes were dashed. No one was going to want to marry *her*, were they?

Gremio was ready to give up, but Hortensio had an idea… "Gremio, I know we're not allies when it comes to Bianca, but if either of us is to stand a chance, we have to find Kate a husband."

Gremio barked a bitter laugh. "Only a devil would marry *her*."

"Tut, tut, Gremio." Hortensio shook his head. "I'm sure there must be *someone* out there who's willing to take her on."

Gremio wasn't convinced, but reluctantly agreed to join forces with his rival to try to find such a madman.

All the while, Lucentio had been listening in and, in those few minutes, he had fallen head over heels in love with Bianca too. She was so sweet, she was so pretty… He was so besotted.

"Tranio, she has the voice of a goddess," Lucentio sighed, a dreamy smile on his face. Tranio sighed too, for rather different reasons. He knew the signs. His master was in love.

"Oh! Her coral-pink lips… her very breath perfumes the air. I burn, I'm on fire, I'm in agony. I will *die* if I can't marry her."

Oh yes, his master was definitely in love, and it was pointless trying to talk him out of it. What they needed was a plan – a plan to enable his master to win the object of his love – and Tranio quickly came up with one: Lucentio would pose as a Latin tutor and offer his services to Bianca's father. That way, he could get close enough to Bianca to woo her. Meanwhile, people were expecting Lucentio's arrival in Padua, but no one actually knew what he looked like – so Tranio would take his place. Dressed as Lucentio, he could also speak to Bianca's father and win him over to the idea of a marriage between his daughter and Lucentio. What could be simpler? It was a plan that could not fail. Straight away, Lucentio and Tranio rushed to an inn to swap clothes.

Elsewhere in Padua, another visitor had arrived from out of town. Petruchio had come to visit his friend, Hortensio, and he was a man on a mission. He was here to find himself a wife.

"I don't care what she looks like, Hortensio," he declared. "Or how old or ugly she is. As long as she's rich, she'll do for me."

Naturally, one person immediately sprang to mind… "She's young, beautiful *and* rich," Hortensio told his friend, "but quite frankly, she's a shrew. She's argumentative and bad-tempered, and I wouldn't marry her for a whole mine full of gold."

Petruchio grinned. "You don't know the power of gold, my friend. I can't wait to meet her."

So the two set off at once for Baptista's house. They hadn't got far when they came across Gremio heading the same way, accompanied by a new 'Latin tutor' he'd found for Bianca. The tutor was, in fact, Lucentio in disguise.

"Only read books about love to her," Gremio was advising him.

"Who's *that*?" Petruchio's elderly servant, Grumio, asked, pointing rudely at Gremio.

"My rival in love," Hortensio frowned.

"And make sure you perfume her paper," Gremio continued, "for she is sweeter than perfume itself. Ah! Hortensio!" Gremio had finally spotted his fellow Bianca-admirer. "Guess what? I've found a tutor for my beloved."

"Oh, really?" Hortensio said casually. "*I've* met a music scholar who can teach her, so I'm no further behind in my duty to my beloved Bianca than you are." He was bluffing, and wondering frantically where to find a disguise so that he could pretend to be the music tutor himself.

"She's *my* beloved *too*, as my actions show," Gremio sniffed.

Hortensio bristled, then suddenly remembered Petruchio. "Gremio, this is no time for us to quarrel. I have good news. I've found someone who is prepared to woo Katherina. Meet Petruchio."

"Wonderful," Gremio said doubtfully, eyeing Petruchio. "You *have* told him about all her faults, haven't you?"

Petruchio laughed. "I know she's difficult and argumentative. But if that's all that's wrong with her, it's fine by me."

"Really?" Gremio said disbelievingly. "Well, if you think you can stomach her…"

At this point, the group was interrupted by yet another arrival: Tranio, in his master's fine clothes. "Good fellows, can you tell me the way to the house of Baptista Minola?" he asked.

Hortensio looked worried. "Are you a suitor to his daughter?" he asked suspiciously.

"What of it?" Tranio said, puffing himself up.

"Nothing, as long as you don't go to Baptista's house."

"Why shouldn't I?" Tranio asked indignantly. "The streets are free, aren't they?"

"Yes, but Bianca is not," Hortensio said, trying to look taller.

"She already has a suitor," Gremio said, and bowed.

"*And* another, even better suitor," Hortensio added, bowing too.

"Fair Bianca must be permitted more than a mere two suitors," Tranio replied. "I, Lucentio, intend to be one myself."

"Sir, have you ever *seen* Baptista's daughter?" Hortensio asked.

"No, sir, but I hear he has two. One is a nag, and the other famous for her modesty and beauty," Tranio replied.

"The first is mine," Petruchio interrupted. "And the second cannot be married until the first is."

"In that case," Tranio said, "if you do so, we'll all be grateful."

"Well said," Hortensio agreed. So the three of them decided that they should be friends until Bianca became available.

Back at Baptista's house, Kate was tormenting her sister. "So, which of your suitors do you like best?" she asked.

Bianca was trying wriggle free from the ribbon Kate had used to tie up her hands. "I haven't seen one I really like," she replied.

"You're lying. It's Hortensio, isn't it!" Katherina taunted.

"If you like him, *you* can have him," Bianca said scornfully. "I'll put in a good word for you. Now untie me!"

"Oh, so riches are more important to you than beauty. It's *Gremio* you like!" Katherina ignored her sister's plea.

"Oh, so it's *Gremio* you envy me for," Bianca mimicked. "Untie me, Kate. Ow!" Kate slapped her and Bianca started to cry.

"Kate, you wretched girl!" Baptista shouted, coming to the rescue of his favourite daughter. Released, Bianca ran off and Katherina flounced away upstairs.

Baptista was still grumbling to himself when Gremio, Tranio and Petruchio arrived, with two tutors for Bianca in tow: a Latin scholar (Lucentio, clutching a pile of books) and a music scholar (Hortensio, wearing a large, feathery hat and a rather itchy-looking orange beard so the others would not recognize him).

Petruchio, never one to beat about the bush, got down to business straight away. "You have a daughter called Katherina," he smiled at Baptista, "who is both fair and virtuous?"

"I have a daughter called Katherina," Baptista said cautiously.

"Good. I've heard so much about Katherina's wit, modesty and friendliness, and would love to make her acquaintance. And may I present you with this tutor," he said, pushing Hortensio forward, "who may instruct your daughters in music."

Hortensio bowed, and his wig nearly fell off.

"You are most welcome, sir," Baptista said, frowning. "But Katherina… she is not for you."

"Ah, I see you don't want to part with her," Petruchio smiled, "Either that, or you don't like me."

"No, not at all," Baptista said hastily. "Who are you?"

Petruchio started to introduce himself properly, but was interrupted by Gremio, who was eager to introduce his Latin tutor for Bianca. Tranio then introduced himself as another suitor for Bianca, offering books and a lute as gifts for her.

Baptista was very pleased with this promising new turn of events. He sent the two new tutors inside to meet his daughters, and sent Gremio and Tranio for a walk so that he could discuss Petruchio's proposed marriage to Kate in private.

"I don't have much time," Petruchio told him. "I've enough money to take care of her, but what can you offer me if we marry?"

The two quickly came to an agreement. All that remained, Baptista pointed out, was for Petruchio to win Katherina's love.

"Why that's nothing," Petruchio laughed. "I'm more than a match for her."

Petruchio didn't even seem bothered when Hortensio rushed outside, clutching his head, and crying, "Katherina hit me with the lute. All I did was say her fingers were in the wrong places!"

Petruchio roared with laughter. "What a spirited young woman! Now I like her more than ever. I can't wait to meet her."

Baptista was not so confident, but went to fetch her anyway.

"I will woo her with spirit," Petruchio said to himself. "Whatever she says, I'll say the opposite. And if she says 'no' to me, I'll simply say I'm looking forward to our wedding day. Ah, hello, Kate!" Kate had arrived with her usual scowl.

"My name," she replied icily, "is Katherina."

"Really? I think you're plain Kate," Petruchio retorted. "Plain Kate, pretty Kate, Kate known as a shrew, but the prettiest Kate in the world, Kate who'll be my wife, and I am driven to woo you."

Kate snorted. "Well, whoever drove you here can drive you right back again!"

The conversation that followed was not one for delicate ears, quickly sinking into a back-and-forth of insults…

"Come, come, you wasp, you're too angry."

"If I'm so waspish, you'd best beware of my sting."

"All I have to do is pluck it out."

"If a fool like you can find it."

…and so on, until finally, Katherina ran out of words and slapped her would-be husband across the face. Petruchio simply grasped her arms and pinned them to her sides.

"I'll have to hit you back, if you hit me again," he laughed.

"If you hit me, you are no gentleman!" Katherina spat.

"Oh, so you know all about family trees do you, Kate?"

"I know you have a fool on your family coat of arms," she retorted, a smile twitching at the corners of her mouth.

The duel of insults started afresh, until they were both flushed and out of breath. "I *will* marry you," Petruchio concluded. "for I am born to tame you, Kate, and turn you from a wild Kate into a conforming, common-or-garden, household Kate."

When Baptista returned, Petruchio told him that they'd agreed to get married. Kate's indignant protests went unheeded, and the deal was struck. "Kiss me, Kate, we'll be married on Sunday," were Petruchio's parting words as he went off to make the arrangements.

"That was quick," remarked Gremio, back from his walk. "Now, your other daughter," he smiled at Baptista. "I asked her first."

"And I love her most!" Tranio interrupted.

But Baptista had a different matter on his mind. "What can you offer her in terms of riches?" he wanted to know, and the two men began to make their offers as if they were bidding at an auction.

Back inside the house, Hortensio was tuning his lute and nursing his head. Instead of teaching Bianca Latin, Lucentio was whispering to her, telling her who he really was and how much he adored her.

Bianca seemed quite taken with him, and her tender looks convinced him he should tell Tranio to speak to her father about a marriage proposal as soon as possible…

Sunday arrived all too quickly. The wedding party was waiting nervously outside Baptista's house. They'd heard nothing from Petruchio since the day of the proposal, and now he was late.

"It's humiliating," Katherina complained. "I didn't even want to marry him, and now he's making a fool of me. I bet he's done this a thousand times: proposing, then not turning up on the day. He never had any intention of marrying me!"

Anyone would think that Kate actually *wanted* to marry him… Of course, if you'd asked her, she'd have said a hundred times 'no'.

"I wish I'd never set eyes upon him," Kate cried and, no longer able to hide how upset she really felt, ran weeping into the house.

"He's coming, he's coming!" a servant suddenly called. "But you should see what he's wearing. A new hat and an old jacket. Inside-out trousers, odd shoes and a rusty old sword. And he's riding a scruffy horse with a runny nose, cardboard reins and a strap with the initials of some woman written on it!"

"Where's Kate?" Petruchio asked as he rode up to the house. "And why is everyone staring at me?"

Baptista answered with as much dignity as he could muster. "It's your wedding day, sir. We were sad because we thought you were not coming. Now we are sad because you don't seem ready."

"Yes, well, I know I'm late, but I'm here now, and that's all that matters. Now where *is* Kate? I want to greet my bride and seal our bargain with a kiss!" Petruchio said.

"But you can't marry her looking like that!" Tranio protested.

Petruchio grinned. "Why not? It's *me* she's marrying, not my clothes!"

"He must be mad," Tranio muttered, as Petruchio went off to find Kate, with Baptista at his heels.

As the wedding party departed for the church, Lucentio went to find Tranio to discuss how the marriage proposal on his behalf was going. "Baptista has agreed that I, 'Lucentio', can marry Bianca!" Tranio told him. "So you are all set!"

Lucentio beamed.

"But he wants proof, first, that Lucentio has enough money..." Tranio added.

Lucentio groaned.

"But I've been thinking," Tranio said. "All we need to do is find someone to pretend to be your father and guarantee you have the money. Simple as that!"

The two were still discussing the matter when Tranio saw Gremio was hurrying towards them. "Have you come from the church?" Tranio asked, hoping he hadn't overheard them.

"I have, and I couldn't get away quickly enough," Gremio snorted. The wedding ceremony had not gone well. Petruchio had shouted and sworn and, in short, behaved atrociously. "And when he kissed the bride's lips it was with such a loud smack it echoed around the church! I couldn't bear to stay," Gremio said.

No sooner had he finished his account, than Petruchio and the wedding guests arrived back at the house for the wedding reception. But before the party had even begun, Petruchio announced that he and Kate had to leave. Her protests fell on deaf ears, and off they went on horseback to Kate's new home.

But the rest of the day did not go smoothly for poor Kate. On the way, she fell off her horse and landed in the mud, but her husband didn't lift a single finger to help her. Yet it was Petruchio who seemed to be in a bad mood when they arrived home.

When a servant brought Kate a bowl of water, he knocked

it flying, then told the servant off for being clumsy. He ordered dinner, but when it arrived, he sent it back, saying it was burned. Try as she might, Kate could not calm him down.

That night, the newly wedded couple retired to their bedroom hungry. There, Petruchio scolded his new wife all night long. He was so loud that the servants heard every word. Poor Kate, they concluded, was getting a taste of her own shrewish medicine.

Only when Kate finally fell into an exhausted sleep, did Petruchio allow himself a smile. "This is how I shall tame my shrew," he said to himself. It was all part of his cunning plan.

Meanwhile, Lucentio, still in disguise, was pursuing his quest to win Bianca's heart, and it seemed to be having the desired effect in more ways than one. Unknown to him, Hortensio and Tranio were spying on his Latin lesson.

"She's not worthy of me!" Hortensio declared, when he saw Bianca flirting with her tutor. "She obviously prefers a mere schoolmaster to a gentleman. I will not marry her."

He tore off his itchy beard and plumed hat in disgust. "Yes, it's me, Hortensio," he told a surprised Tranio. "I think I'll marry a wealthy widow instead. There's one that's been after me for years."

"I'll not marry Bianca either," Tranio said, "not even if she begs me!" It was true; he would not. He was, however, still hoping that his master, the real Lucentio, would. As luck would have it, Tranio had found an elderly merchant who agreed, for a fee, to pretend to be Lucentio's father. What could possibly go wrong?

Back at Petruchio's house, Katherina was becoming desperate. When would her husband come out of his terrible temper?
But then things seemed to take a turn for the better. Petruchio announced that they were going to visit her father. A tailor arrived with a new set of clothes for the visit. Kate loved her new outfit,

but to her dismay, Petruchio could only find fault with it and ordered it all to be taken away.

Of course she protested, but it was no use. Whatever she said, Petruchio pretended that she'd said the opposite or, worse still, he simply ignored her. It was infuriating, it was frustrating, it was demoralizing, but at least they were still going to her father's house, where she could get something to eat.

"It's almost seven now," Petruchio said patting her arm. "We'll be there by lunchtime."

"But it's nearly two o'clock!" Kate replied, bemused. "We won't be there before dinner."

"Kate, it's nearly seven. For goodness' sake, whatever I say, you contradict it! Well, never mind. We just won't go today! In fact, we won't go at all until you agree that it's the time of day I say it is."

And that was the end of that. Or so it seemed…

"How brightly the moon shines," Petruchio said loudly. It was some time later and they were *still* outside the house.

"It's not the moon, it's the sun!" Kate said, exasperated.

"I say it's the moon that shines brightly."

"I'm sure it's the sun," Kate replied, sounding less than sure.

"Now, Kate," Petruchio replied with a warning tone, "I know by my mother's son – and that's me, by the way – that it's the sun that shines brightly. Why am I *forever* being contradicted?"

Kate sighed. "Husband, I don't mind if you say it's the moon or the sun. If you want to call it a candle, then that's fine by me from now on. But *please* let us set off."

"It's the moon," Petruchio declared.

"I know it is," Kate replied obediently.

"You're a liar," he roared delightedly. "It's the sun!"

"Then it's the sun!" Kate cried. "But it's not the sun when you say it's not. Whatever you want to call it, that's what it is!"

"Well, in that case, let's go!" Petruchio laughed. "But wait a minute. Who's this?" An elderly gentleman was approaching them.

"Good morning, young Miss," Petruchio addressed him. "Have you ever seen such a beautiful young girl, Kate?"

"Never! What a lovely girl you are," Kate said to the man.

"Kate, are you *mad?*" Petruchio said. "This is a man!"

"Oh, I am so sorry, sir," Kate addressed the man again. "My eyes must have deceived me, blinded by the *sun.*" She smiled at her husband. Petruchio nodded and beamed back, then asked the bewildered gentleman where he was going.

"I'm Vincentio, from Pisa. I'm here to visit my son, Lucentio."

"What a coincidence!" Petruchio said. "My wife's sister is marrying your son."

Vincentio looked horrified. "Is this a joke?"

Petruchio assured him it was not. "Come, let us all go and see for ourselves," Petruchio suggested, and they all headed off for Lucentio's house.

Over at Lucentio's place, Tranio's trick seemed to have worked rather well. The pretend Vincentio had managed to convince Baptista that he could indeed guarantee that Lucentio was rich enough to marry, and they had drawn up marriage papers to seal the bargain. The only problem left, Tranio was thinking, was that of revealing that he was not, in fact, Lucentio at all, and to reveal the real Lucentio whom Bianca was supposed to marry.

However, when the real Vicentio arrived and introduced himself, chaos ensued. The imposter was so dedicated to his role that he was outraged. "Arrest the villain!" he declared. "He is clearly trying to cheat someone using my good name."

"Lucentio," Baptista said to Tranio, "whatever is going on? Who is your real father?"

"That's not Lucentio," Vicentio declared. He took Tranio by the scruff of the neck and shook him. "But he's wearing my son's clothes. What have you done with Lucentio?"

At that moment, to Tranio's immense relief, Lucentio arrived with Bianca. "Father!" Lucentio gasped in surprise.

Vicentio dropped Tranio and hugged his son. "You're alive!" he cried. "But why is this man wearing your clothes?"

"That's my servant, Tranio—" Lucentio began.

"What?" cried Baptista. "But he told me he was Lucentio! I've agreed to marry my daughter to him."

"I beg your pardon, dear father," Bianca said. "But *this* is Lucentio." She took the hand of the man her father thought was her tutor. "And, actually, we are married already."

Everyone fell silent while Lucentio and Bianca explained that they had decided to slip away and get married in secret, worried that her father would back out of the deal once he realized their deception. They finished and smiled hopefully.

But, almost immediately, another argument broke out – Baptista was furious that his daughter had married without his consent. It took a little while for him to realize that he had, in fact, agreed for her to marry the man she'd married.

Petruchio and Kate were standing apart watching it all.

"Do let's stay and watch this to end," Kate begged her husband.

"Only if you will give me a kiss," Petruchio smiled.

Kate was aghast. "A kiss? Right here in the street?"

"Are you ashamed of me?" Petruchio asked.

"Of you, no, but of kissing in the street, yes!"

"Then let's go home," Petruchio smiled.

"No. I'll kiss, you," Kate said, and she did. "Now my love, please let's stay," she said sweetly.

Petruchio's smile widened. "Come, sweet Kate, now isn't this good? Better late than never, for it is never too late to change."

Kate smiled back. Perhaps arguing wasn't always the best way to go about things after all.

One warm evening, not long after that day, three newly married men – Hortensio, who'd married the rich widow, Petruchio and Lucentio – were chatting with Baptista after a fine meal. Before long, the conversation strayed in the direction of their wives, and which was the most shrewish. Baptista said it had to be his daughter Kate, but Petruchio disagreed.

"Let's put it to the test," Petruchio suggested. "Let's each of us call for our wives and see which of them is the most obedient."

"What shall we bet?" Hortensio said confidently.

"I bet twenty crowns it's Bianca," Lucentio declared.

"I bet twenty times as much that it's Kate!" Petruchio laughed.

And so a servant was sent, first to Bianca.

"My mistress says she cannot come," was the reply that came back. "She's busy."

Hortensio sent the servant to fetch his wife, but she would not come either. "Let him come to me," was her reply.

"Oh *dear*!" Petruchio smirked. "Grumio, go and tell my Kate I want her."

"She won't come," Hortensio said decidedly. If the other two wives wouldn't, shrewish Kate most certainly would not.

But moments later Kate appeared. "You sent for me? What would you like me to do?"

"Where's your sister and Hortensio's wife, Kate?" Petruchio asked, a twinkle in his eye.

"They're chatting by the fire," Kate replied.

"Well, go and fetch them will you?" And off Kate went.

"It's a miracle," Lucentio declared.

"It is indeed. What on earth can it mean?" Hortensio asked.

"I'll tell you what it means," Petruchio said seriously. "It means love, peace and a quiet life. Everything that is sweet and happy."

"You have won the wager," Baptista said, clapping Petruchio on the back. "She's a new woman!"

"Come on, and kiss me, Kate."

"I've not finished yet," Petruchio laughed, as the three women came into the room. "Kate, that cap doesn't suit you, throw it on the floor!" he said impishly.

Kate looked her husband steadily in the eye and flung the hat to the floor. Bianca and Hortensio's wife gasped. They would *never* put up with that sort of treatment.

Kate managed to keep a poker-straight face when Petruchio winked at her.

"Katherina, tell these headstrong women what their duty is to their husbands and lords," Petruchio said.

Kate smiled. "Ladies…" she began, "rolling your eyes like that isn't attractive. Your husband cares for you, works hard for you, and in return, all he wants is that you love him and give him kind looks, rather than frowning all the time, and…" She cast a grin in her husband's direction, "to *occasionally* do what he asks. Is this all really too high a price to pay? After all, what does argument bring you? My spirit has been as proud as yours. I can match his every word in an argument. And his every frown, for that matter. I thought that was a good thing, but now I see that there is a better, more peaceful way."

"That's my girl," Petruchio beamed. "Come on, kiss me, Kate!"

And so Petruchio had won the wager spectacularly. As they left, Hortensio called after him. "You have tamed a shrew!"

"It's amazing," Lucentio added, "that she let you."

Petruchio and Kate simply exchanged amused glances, and headed happily home.

Henry V

England's King Henry V has a distant claim to the French throne, and starts a war with France. It all comes to a head on a muddy field near the town of Agincourt, where the English invaders, weary and outnumbered, face the might of the French army.

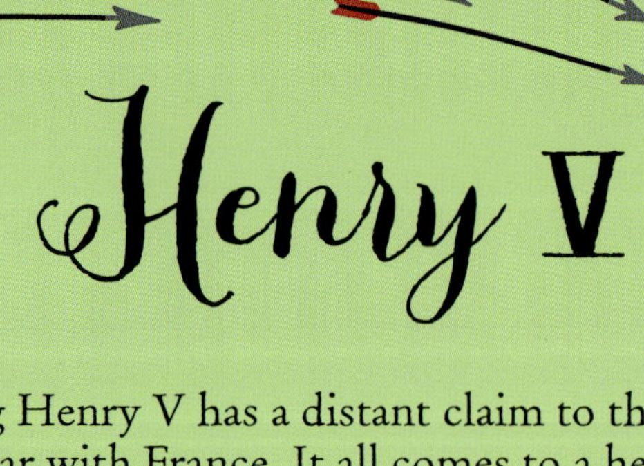

"Follow your spirit, and upon this charge Cry 'God for Harry, England, and Saint George!'"

King Henry V (known as Harry)

The young and warlike king of England, who is determined to claim the French throne as well.

The English noblemen

Dukes and earls allied with King Harry.

Earl of Warwick

Duke of Gloucester

Duke of Clarence

Duke of Exeter

Duke of York

Michael Williams

An English soldier who gives King Harry a piece of his mind.

The Dauphin

The French king's son and heir to the throne.

King Charles VI and Queen Isabel

France's rulers.

Princess Catherine

Daughter of Charles VI, she may have a role in bringing peace to France and England.

The French noblemen

Dukes and lords allied with the French king.

Captain Gower

An English captain in King Harry's army.

Captain Fluellen

A Welsh captain in King Harry's army.

Montjoy

A French herald charged with carrying messages between the warring forces.

ITH THEIR RED ROBES FLUTTERING behind them, two senior clergymen raced along the stone corridors of King Henry's court. "Make haste, my lord bishop," the archbishop puffed. "His grace King Harry commands our presence. We'll discuss his claim to the throne of France before he greets the French ambassadors."

"Our king is a true friend to the Church," observed the bishop.

"He's a worthy monarch," the archbishop agreed, "yet in his youth he was a wild offender. His companions were rude and rough and his hours were filled with riots, banquets and sport… But from the very moment his father died, his wildness seemed to die as well. Never was such a sudden scholar made: from under his veil of wildness emerged reason, wisdom and kingliness."

The two arrived at a massive oak door.

"Is it four o'clock?" the archbishop asked. "Then let's go in."

They stepped into the audience chamber to find the king speaking with his two brothers, the Dukes of Gloucester and Clarence, and his uncle, the Duke of Exeter.

"My lords," said Harry, greeting them, "can I with good conscience make a claim to France's throne? Please explain my right to it. Speak justly, and beware, since you may wake the sleeping sword of war. For two such kingdoms never quarrelled without a great fall of blood."

"Gracious sovereign," the archbishop replied, "there is no bar against Your Highness's claim. Your great-grandfather, Edward III, should have inherited the throne through his mother, but because she was a woman, he was denied. Unjustly denied – for it is written in the Bible, 'When the son dies, let the inheritance descend unto the daughter.' Gracious lord, stand up for what you own."

The Duke of Exeter nodded in agreement. "Everyone expects you to pursue your right."

"They know your grace has cause, and means, and might," added Clarence.

"Then by God's help and yours," the king declared, "France being mine, I'll bend it to my will – or break it all to pieces."

There was a knock at the chamber door, and the French ambassadors entered, rolling a heavy barrel between them.

"Welcome," said Harry. "I understand you bear a message for me from the Prince of France, the Dauphin."

One ambassador stepped forward to address Harry. "Your Highness has laid claim to certain thrones and dukedoms in France. In answer to your claim, our master the Dauphin says this: there's nothing in France that may be won with a dance. You cannot revel into dukedoms there. Instead of dukedoms, he sends you this barrel of treasure, much more fitting to your youthful temper."

Exeter lifted the lid of the Dauphin's barrel and peered inside. "It's full of tennis balls, my lord."

King Harry's eyes flashed with anger, but he spoke politely. "I'm glad the Dauphin is so merry with us. I thank you for his present. Tell him that, when we've matched our racquets to these balls, we'll play a set that shakes the courts of France. He mocks me for my youth – but tell him that his mockery will mock a thousand widows out of their dear husbands, mock mothers from their sons, mock castles down. Those not yet born will have cause to curse the Dauphin's scorn. His jest will seem poor wit when thousands more are weeping than did laugh at it. Farewell."

"*Some are yet ungotten and unborn*
That shall have cause to curse the Dauphin's scorn."

King Harry, Act 1, Scene 2

King Harry turned to his companions. "I have now no thought in me but France. Let every man prepare himself."

In the days that followed, the English noblemen prepared for war. The soldiers sharpened swords, and archers fletched their arrows. A fleet of ships assembled in the port of Southampton, and took on cargo for the invasion of France.

The French were making preparations, too. In the royal court at Rouen, King Charles VI met with his trusted advisors, the Dukes of Bourbon and Orléans, the Constable of France, and his son, the Dauphin.

"The English come with full power upon us," the king said. "We must look to our defences. Bourbon, go with Orléans and the Dauphin to inspect our cities and ready them for war."

"Father, it's right to prepare ourselves," said the Dauphin, "but we can do so with a light heart. For England has an idle king: her crown is worn by such a vain and giddy, shallow youth, that we need not fear her."

"Peace, Prince Dauphin," urged the constable. "You are much mistaken in this king. He's fearsomely resolved."

"Let's think King Henry strong, and strongly arm ourselves to meet him," King Charles declared. "Remember, he's descended from that bloody strain of Edward, Black Prince of Wales, who long ago beat us so badly at the battle of Crécy."

There was a flourish of trumpets outside, and a messenger announced the arrival of the Duke of Exeter.

"You come from King Henry of England?" the king asked.

"From him," Exeter confirmed, "and he greets Your Majesty: he asks, in the name of God Almighty, that you lay aside your borrowed glories and resign to him – the true challenger – your crown and kingdom."

"Or else what follows?"

"Blood and war," Exeter replied. "For if you hide the crown even in your hearts, with his sword he will seek it there. In a fierce tempest he is coming: with thunder and earthquakes, like a Greek god. And, if asking fails, he will compel."

The ambassadors went back and forth between France and England, trading threats and rejecting compromises, until at last King Harry's fleet set sail. The ships landed on the coast of France, and the army surrounded the port city of Harfleur.

English cannons began to batter the defences. Under a deadly rain of arrows, soldiers carried up seige ladders to scale the walls. Again and again they were beaten back – but gradually the guns began to breach the battlements, reducing parts of the walls to mere rubble.

King Harry himself, spattered with mud, his visor up, led each new charge. "Once more into the breach, dear friends, once more," he cried, "or close the wall up with our English dead. Now stiffen your sinews – conjure up your blood – disguise your gentle natures with hardened rage. On, on, you noblest Englishmen! I see you stand like greyhounds, straining at the start. The game's afoot. Upon this charge cry: 'God for Harry, England and Saint George!'"

With a roar, Harry's men rushed forward. "On, on, on! Up to the breaches, you dogs," roared the Welsh captain, Fluellen, beating stragglers with the butt of his pike. At the base of the city walls, the soldiers heaved up long seige ladders, and the English invaders swarmed up towards the battlements.

It was clear that the city wouldn't hold out much longer,

"Once more unto the breach, dear friends, once more,
Or close the wall up with our English dead."

and suddenly a white flag of truce was raised, fluttering, above the highest tower. The defenders sounded a trumpet, and Harfleur's governor appeared on the wall, calling to Harry to start negotiations.

"What say you?" Harry asked, still flushed with the heat of battle. "Will you give up? If I begin the assault again, the gates of mercy will be closed. Then soldiers, rough and hard of heart, shall rove your streets with bloody hands, with consciences as wide as Hell, mowing down your children like grass. Will you yield, and so avoid this tragedy? Or, still resisting, be destroyed?"

"Dreaded King," the trembling governor replied, "We yield our town and lives to your soft mercy."

Slowly, the city's battered gates creaked open. Harry turned with relief to Exeter. "Come, Uncle Exeter. Enter Harfleur and take command, but treat the citizens kindly. We'll rest tonight, and march on tomorrow."

As Harry and his troops advanced through France, the worried French king called together his bravest dukes and noblemen for a council of war.

More news had come of English victories, and the atmosphere in the room was grim. "Where have they found this bravery?" raged the Constable of France. "Is their English climate not foggy and dull? And yet they make our sun-drenched blood seem cold."

"We've got to face them, or our wives will mock us," groaned the Duke of Bourbon. "They'll call us dancers, say our grace is only in our heels, and call us lofty runaways."

The king struck the table with his fist. "Up, my princes! Make your spirits sharper than your swords. High Constable of France, you Dukes of Orléans, of Bourbon, and of Burgundy, my lords and knights, go and put an end to Harry of England, who now sweeps across our land with banners painted in the blood of Harfleur.

You by far outnumber him. With your full might, rush down upon his army, like the melted Alpine snows upon the valleys."

"My lord, we will," the constable swore, "and we will bring him captive in a chariot here to Rouen."

A few days later, Captain Fluellen and Captain Gower stood with King Harry beneath the bare, dripping branches of a tree. The day's fighting was coming to an end in a cold drizzle, and the men were discussing the campaign.

"The Duke of Exeter has held the bridge ahead," Fluellen reported, "and the French advance was driven off."

"How many men did he lose?" Harry asked.

"The French lost many soldiers, and the duke lost only one," Gower replied, "one man named Bardolph, who was executed because we caught him robbing a church."

"Quite right," the king declared. "Let nothing be taken from the villages unless it's paid for, and let none of the French be abused. When kingdoms are at stake, the gentlest player is the likeliest to win."

"It seems the French are gathering in force, Your Majesty," Gower said.

"Very well. The night approaches. March on to the bridge, and camp beyond the river. Tomorrow we will face the French. Remember, we're in God's hands, not in theirs."

That night, the French and English armies were camped so close together that each could see the other's cooking fires glimmering in the darkness. Through the long hours, each could hear the other's warhorses neighing and stamping, armourers hammering rivets, and sentinels tramping back and forth on patrol.

On the French side, King Charles's lords and dukes compared their finely polished armour and their high-stepping horses, and boasted about the deeds they would do in the morning. "It is now two o'clock," said the Duke of Orléans. "But let me see – by ten we shall each have killed a hundred Englishmen."

On the English side, King Harry's battered and weary troops huddled close to their fires. They knew they were outnumbered, and tomorrow's battle might be their last. Alone in his tent, Harry stripped off his royal armour. He threw a rough cloak about his shoulders and slipped out into the night.

In this disguise, he paced among the cooking fires and sleeping soldiers, unrecognized by his own men. Near the edge of the camp, three English soldiers leaned on their pikes, staring east to where the sun would rise. Harry paused to listen to their talk.

"Yonder we'll see the beginning of the day, but I think we'll never see the end of it," one said glumly.

"Now Williams," said another, "don't fret. At least we're in the king's company. His cause is just and his quarrel honourable."

"That's more than we know," grumbled Williams.

"And more than we need to know," added the third soldier. "It's enough for me that we're the king's subjects. If his cause is wrong, our duty to obey him wipes the wrong out of us."

"But if the cause is unjust," Williams said, "the king himself will have a heavy reckoning to make, when all those legs and arms and heads have been chopped off. For some dying tomorrow will leave poor wives behind, and some leave debts, and some leave sudden orphans. And those men's deaths will be a black matter for the king that led them to it. And yet we will obey, and I'll fight heartily for him."

King Harry left the soldiers to their talk, and strode on. "There you have it," he mused. "It all rests upon the king. They lay their lives, their souls, their debts, their fearful wives and children on the king. I must bear it all. Oh, what a hard condition, twinned with greatness: to be subject to the words of every fool who feels no more than his own interest! How much rest and ease must kings neglect that private men may enjoy? And what do kings have that private men have not, besides some empty ceremony? Ah, they know little of the struggle of the king to keep the peace – the peace whose hours the peasant most enjoys."

A pale strip of sky was now appearing in the east, and Harry spotted his brother, Gloucester, hurrying through the camp toward him. "Yes, yes, I know you've come to call the king," Harry sighed. "The day, my friends and everything depends on me."

The French camp, too, was soon stirring. "The sun is gilding our armour," the Duke of Orléans cried happily. "Up, my lords!"

"Mount your horses, gallant princes," commanded the Constable of France. "Just look upon the English there – a poor and starving band. There's hardly work enough for all our hands, and scarcely blood enough in all their veins to give each blade of ours a ruddy stain. If each man does but very little, all is done. Now let the trumpets sound! To the field!"

The sun was rising higher. The English had planted a row of sharpened stakes in the ground, and stood waiting behind this defensive line. Facing them across a narrow, muddy field, the French men-at-arms marched into position, hundred by hundred, in orderly squares. They were flanked by rows of crossbowmen, and, stretching into the distance behind them, were the dipping, jostling lances of the French knights and nobles on horseback.

A hush fell over the English army. "If only we had ten thousand more English troops," muttered Warwick.

King Harry whirled around around to face his men. "Who's he that wishes so?" he cried. "My cousin Warwick? No, fair cousin. I pray you, wish not one man more. The fewer men who fight today, the greater share of honour we'll receive."

Harry's voice rang out along the English line, and every weary soldier strained to hear his king. "This day is called the Feast of Crispin," Harry continued. "He that outlives this day and comes safe home will stand up straight when this day is named. He'll feast with his neighbours, and will roll his sleeves up, show his scars and say, 'These wounds I had on Crispin's day.' Old men forget – but when the rest is all forgotten, he'll still remember what feats he did that day. Then shall our names, as familiar in his mouth as household words – Harry the King, and Exeter, Warwick and Gloucester – be freshly remembered too.

"The good man shall teach his son this story, and Crispin's day shall never pass, from this day to the end of the world, without us being remembered. We few – we happy few – we band of brothers. For he today who sheds his blood with me shall be my brother. And gentlemen in England now tucked up in bed shall think themselves cursed they were not here to fight with us upon Saint Crispin's day."

A great cheer lifted from the English army – and, as if in response, from across the battlefield came the blaring of a hundred

"And Crispin Crispian shall ne'er go by,
From this day to the ending of the world,
But we in it shall be rememberèd;
We few, we happy few, we band of brothers."

King Harry, Act 4, Scene 3

trumpets. The vast French army slowly began to move forward. At the same time, a French herald with a flag of truce galloped along the English line and dismounted before Harry.

"My name is Montjoy, and I come from the Constable of France," he said. "Speak now, King Harry. If you will offer a ransom of gold and treasure, and retreat to England, you may yet be spared, and your followers may leave this field – where otherwise their poor bodies must lie and fester."

"I pray you," said Harry, "tell the constable: if he can kill me, he can sell my bones for ransom. No other ransom will he get. Tell him that."

"I shall, King Harry. Fare you well."

The herald mounted his horse and sped back across the field.

"Now soldiers, march away," commanded the king, "and how you please, dear God, decide the day."

As the French army charged across the battlefield, the English archers raised their longbows and filled the sky with arrows. Volley after volley rained down on the French. Arrows clattered off helmets and shields, struck horses, and found the chinks in armour. Injured men and animals fell underfoot, thrashing, churning up the mud, and tripping those who followed. With dense woods on either side of the narrow battlefield, there was little room to manoeuvre, and the French pressed straight on to the English line. The two armies met in a clashing of steel.

Hour after hour, hemmed in by the dead and dying, King Harry and his men fought against the French onslaught. The Duke of York was hacked down, along with the Earl of Suffolk, and they died side by side in the muddy field. The Duke of Gloucester was wounded in the leg, and fell beneath the swords of three French knights – but Harry stood firm over his brother and bravely held off his attackers.

At last, in the waning light, the rain of arrows ceased. No further waves of knights or men-at-arms crossed the battlefield. The French held back. King Harry and his men, muddied and bloodied from head to toe, regrouped.

"Here comes the herald of the French," said Exeter, and they watched as Montjoy approached, picking his way through the heaps of dead.

"What does this mean?" the king frowned. "Have you come again for ransom?"

"No, great king," Montjoy replied, kneeling before him. "I come to ask that we may wander on this bloody field to count our dead and bury them. To sort our nobles from our common men — for here lie many of our princes drowned in common blood. And here our peasants drench their limbs in princes' gore."

"I tell you truly, Herald," Harry said, "I don't know if we've won the day or not."

"The day is yours."

Harry gave a long, deep sigh. "We owe this victory to God, and not our strength. What is the castle called that stands nearby?"

"They call it Agincourt," said Montjoy.

"Then this will be the Battle of Agincourt," Harry declared, "fought on Crispin's day."

Montjoy departed, and the heralds criss-crossed the battlefield, going sadly from body to body. "Here was a royal fellowship of death," said Harry as Exeter read the final list of casualties. "In all, the French have lost ten thousand men — and most of them are princes, barons, lords, knights, squires and gentlemen. And we have lost but thirty men. When, on an open field of battle, was there ever known so great and little loss of life? The Constable of France is dead; the Dukes of Bourbon and of Orléans are prisoners."

Harry sighed. "Let all the credit go to God. Now let us go and perform our holy rites and enclose our dead in graves of clay."

Some weeks after the battle, King Harry and his advisors rode to the French court to discuss peace. In a lavish chamber draped with France's royal blue and gold, King Charles, Queen Isabel and Princess Catherine greeted the English invaders.

"Most worthy brother England, fairly met," said the French king, "and welcome, English nobles, every one."

"I hope," added Queen Isabel, "that this day will change our griefs and quarrels into love."

"We cry amen to that," said Harry.

France's chief negotiator, the Duke of Burgundy, stepped forward. "Great kings," he said, "what barriers remain preventing gentle peace from flourishing in this, our fertile France?"

"France must buy that peace by granting our demands," King Harry replied. "Go, Uncle Exeter, and Clarence, and Gloucester, and look over the articles with Burgundy and the king."

"I'll join them," said the queen. "A woman's voice may do some good."

The negotiators retired, leaving the English king and the French princess alone together.

"Fair Catherine," said Harry, "to cement the peace, we must be bound together as man and wife. Will you consent to teach this rough soldier words to touch a lady's heart?"

"Your Majesty shall mock at me," Catherine replied, blushing as she struggled with the unfamiliar English words. "I cannot speak your England."

"Oh, fair Catherine, if you will love me soundly with your French heart, I will be glad to hear you say it brokenly with your English tongue. Do you like me, Kate?"

"*Pardonnez-moi*, I cannot tell what is 'like me'."

"An angel is like you, Kate, and you are like an angel," said King

Harry, and he took the princess's hand. "I am glad you speak no better English, for if you could, you'd find me such a plain king that you'd think I'd sold my farm to buy my crown."

Catherine laughed. "Me understand well."

"I have no cunning, Kate. I speak to you as a plain soldier. A speaker is but a babbler, a straight back will stoop, a black beard will turn white and a fair face will wither – but a good heart, Kate, is like the Sun, for it shines bright and never changes. If you would have such a heart, take me. Take me, take a soldier; take a soldier, take a king. What say you to my love?"

"Is it possible zat I should love ze enemy of France?" Uncertain, Catherine began to draw back her hand, but Harry held it closer.

"No, Kate, but in loving me you would love the friend of France. For I love France so well that I will not part with a village of it; I will have it all mine. And Kate, when France is mine, and I am yours, then France is yours, and you are mine."

"I cannot tell what is zat."

"Can you not? I will tell you in your own language. *Je quand suis le possesseur de France, et vous avez possession de moi –* let me see, what then?" Harry laughed. His French was just as muddled as Catherine's English. "*Donc… donc votre est France, et vous êtes mienne.* It is harder for me to speak this much French, Kate, than to conquer the kingdom. But Kate, can you love me?"

"I cannot tell," said Catherine, but she was smiling. The king's persistence pleased her.

"Will you have me?"

"If it shall please ze king, *mon père.*"

"It will please him well, Kate."

"Zen it shall also content me," she said warmly.

King Harry took the princess in his arms. "Then I will kiss your lips, Kate."

"But eet is not ze custom!" protested Catherine pushing him away with a laugh.

"Oh, Kate, all customs curtsy to great kings," Harry said, kissing her.

The door to the audience chamber opened, and the French and English negotiators returned. "God save Your Majesty," said the Duke of Burgundy. "Are you teaching our princess English?"

"I wish to teach her how perfectly I love her," Harry replied, "and that is good English."

"King Charles has granted every article," Clarence announced, "and makes you his royal heir and son."

"Shall Kate be my wife?" Harry asked, taking her hand in his.

"Yes, fair son," said the French king, "and with that union let our quarrelling kingdoms cease their hatred, so that war shall never again bear its bleeding sword through England and fair France."

Queen Isabel reached out and took her daughter and King Harry's hands. "Let God, the best maker of marriages, combine your hearts in one, your realms in one. In hope that all the English may as French, and French as Englishmen, receive each other, let all say this: amen."

"Amen," the gathered nobles said.

"Now let's prepare our marriage," Harry said to Catherine. "Then you'll swear love to me, and I to you – and may our oaths be prosperous and true."

King Lear

Lear, the ageing King of Britain, wants to retire.
To decide how to divide up his kingdom, he asks his three
daughters how much they love him. When the youngest
refuses to give a flattering answer, Lear banishes her.
But he soon faces the folly of his decision, as he finds
himself cast out and wandering the wild heath.

King Lear

The King of Britain no longer
knows who to trust after he gives
up his crown. Has he lost his mind
as well as his power?

Lear's fool

The court jester goes
onto the heath with
Lear. He uses rhymes
and riddles to give Lear
honest advice.

Cordelia

Lear's youngest daughter is
loyal and honest to a fault.
Disowned by her father,
she agrees to marry the
King of France.

Regan

Lear's second daughter.
Regan and Goneril
inherit Lear's kingdom,
then turn against him.

Goneril

Lear's bitter and
callous eldest
daughter.

Earl of Gloucester
A loyal follower of Lear with family troubles of his own. He is convinced his elder son, Edgar, plans to kill him.

Earl of Kent
A straight-talking advisor to King Lear, Kent goes with Lear and the fool onto the heath.

Edgar
On the run on from his father, Edgar disguises himself as 'Poor Tom', a crazed beggar living in a hovel on the heath.

Duke of Cornwall
Regan's husband. He is cruel, violent and ambitious – just like his wife.

Duke of Albany
Goneril's husband. He is easily manipulated, but good at heart.

Edmund
Edgar's conniving half-brother, who turns Gloucester against Edgar to get his inheritance. But his hunger for power doesn't stop there…

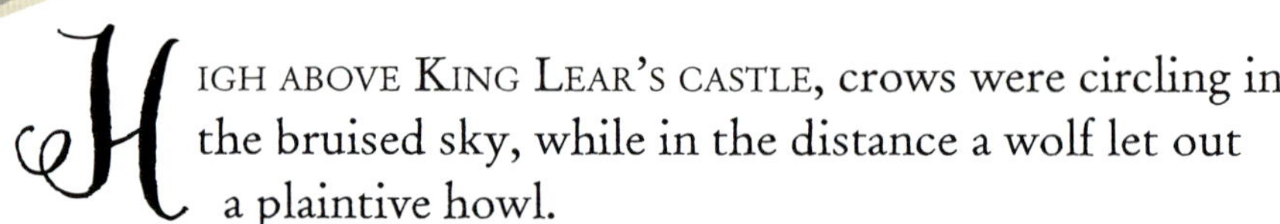

IGH ABOVE KING LEAR'S CASTLE, crows were circling in
the bruised sky, while in the distance a wolf let out
a plaintive howl.

Inside, Lear had gathered his three daughters and his chief
nobles in the main hall. "I have an important announcement to
make," he declared. "I am old and tired. It is my intention to shake
off the burdens of kingship, so I can enjoy what remains of my
advanced years in peace."

The king called his trusted advisor, the Earl of Kent. "Hand
me the map," he ordered. Kent ceremoniously handed over a scroll,
which Lear spread out on the table in front of him. "I have divided
my kingdom into three," said the king, sweeping his hand over
the map.

He turned to his daughters. "Tell me, which of you loves me
most? She shall have the largest share. Goneril, my eldest-born,
speak first."

Goneril stepped forward, clasping her hands and bowing her
head, as if in prayer. "Sir," she began, "I love you more than words
can say, beyond all that is precious, more than my health, more
than my beauty, as much as any child ever loved a father."

Lear nodded. "From here to here," he said, pointing at his map,
"with deep forests, rich meadows and plentiful streams, this land I
give to you and your husband, the Duke of Albany."

"Regan, my second daughter, wife of the Duke of Cornwall.
What say you?" asked Lear.

"I love you in every way my sister describes. Only… I find she
comes up short compared to my adoration of you, my dear father,
which goes beyond all other joys," Regan gushed.

"Very good," said Lear. "To you and your future heirs I give this portion of the kingdom to rule." He pointed at the map, then said to Cordelia, "Now, last but not least, my youngest child."

"Oh, what can I say?" Cordelia wondered. "Love and be silent? I'm sure my heart is more eloquent than my tongue."

Lear continued, "What will you say to gain a share more opulent than those I have given your sisters? Speak."

"Nothing, my lord," came Cordelia's reply.

"Nothing?"

"Nothing."

"Nothing will come of nothing," Lear bellowed. "Speak again."

Cordelia trembled. "I cannot heave my heart into my mouth. I love you as a daughter is bound to love a father. No more nor less. I am not yet married, but I shall never marry like my sisters to give all my love to my father and none to my husband."

"So young and so untender?" cried Lear.

"So young, my lord, and true," Cordelia insisted.

"Let it be so!" Lear raged. "Your truth is all you shall have. I disown you. From now on, you are nothing to me."

Kent stepped forward, nervously. "Your Majesty, I beg you think again."

"Silence, Kent!" Lear roared. "Do not come between the dragon and his wrath. The last third of my kingdom will be split between Goneril and Regan. From this moment, I hand over my power to them as queens. I will live a month at a time in each of their castles. All I wish is to keep a troop of a hundred knights, the title of 'King' and to be treated with the respect my age deserves."

Kent was horrified. "King, this is hideous rashness. You must have lost your mind to give up your kingdom to flattery," he protested. "Cordelia does not love you the least, but the most."

Lear's face clouded over, "No more!" he thundered. "You are banished. You have six days to leave the kingdom."

Kent bowed his head. "Then farewell, my king," he said. "May the gods protect you, sweet Cordelia. Adieu." And, with a heavy heart, he left the court that had been his home and where he had been a loyal servant.

Lear watched Kent leave the hall, then pulled himself upright in his throne to address the room. "Now then. We have a guest. The King of France is here to propose marriage to Cordelia. Your Majesty, do you take or leave her now she has nothing?"

The King of France bowed to Lear, then to Cordelia. What had just taken place had only persuaded him that Cordelia was a faithful daughter, who would be a loving wife. "Fair, honest Cordelia," he said. "If you will have me, I will happily take you to be the Queen of France."

"I will," Cordelia replied. Bitter tears welled in her eyes as she bade farewell to her sisters. "Look after our father."

"You cannot tell us what to do!" hissed Goneril. "We are in charge here now. Be gone!"

At the Earl of Gloucester's castle, Edmund, Gloucester's younger son, was pacing angrily. "Why should I inherit nothing from our father, just because I am younger than Edgar and have another mother? I'm just as clever and deserving," he fumed. Suddenly, an idea came to him. He sat down at his desk, dipped his quill pen in ink and wrote a letter. "Well, let's see how this letter changes things…" he thought with a smirk.

When Gloucester arrived home, his head was reeling with the shocking events he had just witnessed at King Lear's court. He tried to tell his son about it, but Edmund seemed distracted. "Is that a letter in your hand, Edmund?" he asked. "What is the news that agitates you?"

"Nothing, my lord," Edmund replied, making a show of stuffing the letter into his pocket.

Gloucester raised an eyebrow. "Nothing? If it is nothing, then there's no need to hide it from me, is there?"

"Oh, well it's from Edgar," said Edmund. "I have not read it in full, but I do not think it's fit for your eyes. I can only hope he wrote it as a test of my loyalty to you…"

"Give it to me. Let's see," said Gloucester. He snatched the letter from his son, straightened his spectacles, and read: "I've come to realize this reverence of old age keeps our inheritance from us until we ourselves are too old to enjoy it. If our father could be 'put to sleep', I would share half his fortunes with you. Come to me and I will tell you my plan. Your brother, Edgar."

Gloucester threw down the letter in disgust. "Conspiracy! How can a son be such a monster as to plot against his own father?"

Edmund assumed a soothing tone. "Father, let me speak to him," he said. "I'll find out for you what he means by this letter."

That evening, Edmund waited in the gloom outside the castle. He looked out at the wild heath that stretched all the way to the sea, watching for his brother to return home from a day's hunting. As soon as Edgar came into view, Edmund started wringing his hands and sighing, "Oh dear, oh dear…"

"What troubles you?" asked Edgar.

"Oh, Edgar. Our father is convinced that you are plotting to kill him. I tried to reason with him, but you know how he is when his mind is set…" said Edmund. "He has ordered his guard to kill you. You must fly this place now, while it is dark."

Edgar shook is head incredulously. "Some villain has done me wrong!" he said.

"Look! Torches!" cried Edmund. "Father's guard is coming. You must run!"

Edgar pulled his cloak tight around his shoulders and fled into the night. "There's an old, disused shepherd's hut out on the heath. I can stay there until I can find a way to resolve this matter," he thought. "And I will disguise myself as a crazed beggar. From now on, I am not Edgar, but Poor Tom."

Edmund watched his brother disappear over the horizon. "I will tell our father that I fought fiercely to defend him," he thought. Gritting his teeth, he took his sword and drew the blade across his arm. "A little blood should convince him…"

As intended, Lear spent the first part of his retirement at Goneril's castle. But it wasn't to be the leisurely decline into old age he had imagined. His daughter bossed him around, and her servants no longer bowed and curtseyed to him as they had when he was their king. For her part, Goneril seethed with resentment that Lear treated her home as his own and let his band of knights run riot. "I refuse to speak to the idle old man," she said. And she ordered her steward, Oswald, to ignore him too.

Unbeknown to Lear, his loyal servant, the Earl of Kent, hadn't gone into exile. Instead, he had disguised himself as a peasant and followed his master to Goneril's castle, determined to see that he did not come to harm. He was waiting at the castle gates when Lear came back from a ride.

"Take my horse to the stables, tell the kitchen staff to prepare my dinner and send my fool to entertain me," Lear ordered one of his knights. Then he turned to Kent. "How now! Who are you and what do you want?" he asked.

"I'm an honest-hearted fellow, and as poor as the king I wish to serve," said Kent.

Lear looked Kent up and down, but did not recognize his servant without his usual fine clothes. "Come in, talk with me and we shall see."

But inside, dinner had not been served. Lear called Oswald. "Where's my dinner and where is Goneril?" he demanded.

Oswald rolled his eyes and was about to turn his back on Lear.

"Don't you know who I am?" bellowed Lear.

"You're my lady's father," replied the steward. "I serve her and not you."

"How dare you speak to me like that, you rascal!" shouted Lear, slapping him across the face.

"I will not be struck!" cried Oswald, clutching his cheek. "Queen Goneril shall hear of this."

Just as Oswald bustled out of the hall, Lear's fool skipped in.

"Do you know the difference between a bitter fool and a sweet one?" riddled the jester.

Lear shook his head, looking intrigued. "No. Teach me, knave. This will be amusing."

The fool broke into a chant:

"The lord that has decided,
To give away his land,
Come place him here by me –
Let me take his hand.
The sweet and bitter fools
Will presently appear
In jester's costume here,
In royal velvet there. "

Lear's smile faded. "Are you calling me a bitter fool?" he asked.

The fool shrugged. "Indeed, Nuncle, you have given away all your other titles."

"This jester is certainly no fool," Kent remarked.

With a crash, the doors to the hall were flung open and Goneril burst in with her husband, the Duke of Albany, behind her. "Your rabble of knights treat my home more like a lowly tavern than a majestic castle," she snapped. "And now you have struck my most trusted servant. I will not endure this any longer. You must leave!"

"My lady, please. He is your father," said Albany. He tried to put a hand on the queen's arm, but she swatted him away.

"How hurtful it is to have a thankless child!" cried Lear. "Very well. Away, away! I have another daughter I can stay with. She will be furious when she hears how you have abused me."

Outside, there was a crack of thunder, and lightning ripped open the sky. Lear called to one of his knights, "Saddle the horses. We are going to Regan's castle." He turned to Kent. "You ride ahead and inform my good friend, the Duke of Gloucester, that we will break our journey with him."

Just as Lear was setting off, Regan and her husband, the Duke of Cornwall, were arriving at Gloucester's castle. They were appalled when he told them Edgar had been plotting to kill him.

Edmund showed them his wounded arm. "He tried to persuade me to help him," he said. "When I refused, he drew his sword and threatened to kill me… see, I have been cut… But when I vowed to defend our father, he fled onto the heath."

"I have disinherited him," said Gloucester. "My men will catch him, and bring him to justice."

"Of course, our men will help," said Regan.

They were interrupted by raised voices and the clash of swords ringing from outside the castle walls. Two of Gloucester's guards burst into the courtyard bringing Kent and Oswald with them.

"We found these men brawling at the gate," reported one of the guards.

"Who are you and what is all this about?" asked Gloucester.

Oswald stepped forward and scraped a bow. "Lady Regan, I bring you news from your sister," he said. "This ruffian tried to attack me."

"My lord, Gloucester, I bring news from King Lear," said Kent. "I drew my sword against this scheming knave, Oswald, because he has come here to discredit my master."

Regan was shocked. "That is no way to speak to Queen Goneril's trusted steward!" she cried.

"Lock him in the stocks!" joined the Duke of Cornwall. "Leave him overnight to learn his lesson."

The guards marched Kent over to the stocks – a rough wooden frame that Kent's legs were clamped into without ceremony.

Gloucester tried to intervene. "Please, you can't put this man in the stocks. He has behaved badly, but it is a grievous slight against a king to punish one of his servants in this manner."

"Then I will answer for it," said Cornwall.

"He is no longer a king," argued Regan. "It is far worse that Queen Goneril's man should be assaulted. Come, the light is fading. Let's go inside."

The crows had come in to roost, and the sun had dipped behind the battlements by the time Lear and his fool arrived at Gloucester's castle.

Shivering in the stocks, Kent called, "Hail King Lear, my noble master!"

Lear rushed over to his servant. "Who did this to you?"

"Your son Cornwall and daughter Regan are here," replied Kent. "Gloucester tried to stop them, but it was their order."

"No!" cried Lear. "How dare they treat my servant AND ME with such disrespect! Where is my daughter?"

"She is with Cornwall and Gloucester, inside," replied Kent.

Lear pounded at the castle door, but the guards did not dare let him in. "Vengeance! Plague! Death! Confusion! Let me speak with Regan!" he raged.

The door opened, and out strode Regan and Cornwall, with Gloucester cowering behind them.

"Did you put my man in the stocks?" bellowed Lear.

"I gave the order, yes," Cornwall replied. "But it was his own actions that put him there."

"Gloucester! Release my man at once!" ordered Lear.

Gloucester unlocked the stocks, saying quietly to Kent, "I am sorry, friend."

Lear turned to speak to Regan, but was interrupted by a fanfare of trumpets coming from the castle gates.

"Aha," said Regan. "It is my sister. She wrote to tell me she was coming."

The trumpets sounded again, and Goneril, Albany and their attendants entered the castle courtyard.

"Welcome, dear sister," cooed Regan, embracing her.

"Are you not ashamed to look upon me?" said Lear to Goneril. Then he turned to Regan. "How can you embrace her when she has so offended me?"

"How have *I* offended *you*?" demanded Goneril.

"Father, dearest, I cannot think my sister would fail in her obligation to you. I pray you, return to Goneril until the month is up," coaxed Regan. "My house is not yet prepared for your stay."

"Return to her? No, I would rather go without a roof, and wage war against the air!" roared Lear.

"Well, that's your choice," Goneril retorted.

A wild storm was raging outside, but it was nothing compared to the tempest that had blown up in Lear's heart. Seeing his two daughters united against him, he cried, "You unnatural hags, I will have such revenge on you both!"

Lear stormed out of the castle with his fool at his heels. "They do me wrong," he wailed. "My heart shall break into a thousand pieces, but I will not weep. Oh, I shall go mad!"

Out on the wind-blasted heath, the fool stopped to catch his breath under a tree that had been stripped of its leaves. "Oh, Nuncle, come away from the storm," he coaxed. "This cold night will turn us all into fools and madmen."

But Lear wouldn't listen. Instead, he stood in the open, his arms flung wide, and howled at the sky, "Blow, winds, and crack your cheeks. Rage, blow, you hurricanes, blow!"

Through the howling wind came a voice: "Who's there?" A figure took shape, and Kent emerged out of the gloom. He had followed Lear through the storm, and his threadbare peasant's costume was wet through. "Sir, this is no night to be without a roof over your head," he said. "Come. There is a hut nearby, where we can shelter from this foul weather."

Kent led Lear and the fool to a crumbling old hut. As they stooped to enter the low doorway, a moan came from inside. It was Edgar, disguised as Poor Tom. To convince them he was a harmless madman, he babbled, "Poor Tom's a-cold. O, do de, do de do!" but he offered to share his bed of straw and his blanket with the wanderers.

King Lear had just fallen asleep, and Kent and the fool were watching over him, when light appeared in the doorway and the Earl of Gloucester stepped in. "Oh, I'm so glad I've found you all!" he exclaimed.

In the dark corner of the hut, Edgar pulled up his blanket so his father would not see his face. But he listened as Gloucester told Kent how he had been turned out of his own castle by Goneril and

Regan, after objecting to their cruel treatment of King Lear.

"The queens are plotting to kill their father," said Gloucester. "I have brought my chariot for you to drive the king to Dover. Cordelia is on her way there with the French army to overthrow her sisters."

Edgar's heart swelled with love and pride for his father. "Poor Tom's a-help you," he said from his corner. He resolved to keep his disguise but to do whatever he could to help his father and the king.

Meanwhile, at Gloucester's castle, Edmund handed the Duke of Cornwall a letter he had found in his father's chamber. "As your most loyal servant, it is my duty to show you this letter from Cordelia to my father, though it gives me little pleasure to reveal his treachery," he said gravely.

Cornwall took the letter and read. "Cordelia is leading a French invasion to restore Lear to the throne, and Gloucester has promised to support them," he said. "Seek out the traitor and bring him to me!" he ordered his guards.

"Hang him instantly!" joined Regan.

"Pluck out his eyes!" hissed Goneril.

"Goneril, go and tell Albany to prepare your troops for battle," said Cornwall. "Edmund ride with her. Regan and I will deal with your father."

Edmund bowed to Cornwall and Regan. "I am your humblest servant," he said and he left with Goneril.

When the guards eventually returned with Gloucester, the punishment was swift and merciless. He was bound to a chair, and Regan restrained his head. "Out, vile jelly!" cried Cornwall, as he plucked out Gloucester's eyes.

"All dark and comfortless!" wailed poor, blinded Gloucester. "Where is my son Edmund? Why did he not defend me?"

"Ha! He is too good to pity you," Regan retorted. "It was he who informed us of your treason."

It was only then that Gloucester realized that Edmund had betrayed him and lied about Edgar too. "Oh, I'm a fool!" he cried.

Unable to bear the cruelty of what he had just witnessed, one of Cornwall's servants lunged at his master and stabbed him with a knife. Clutching his wound, Cornwall drew his sword and retaliated with a single, fatal blow.

As the servant fell, dead, to the floor, Cornwall called his wife, "I am hurt, Regan. Help me to my chamber." Then, to his remaining servant he said, "Throw out that eyeless villain. I want him gone from here."

Edgar, still disguised as Poor Tom, was waiting near the castle gates when Gloucester stumbled out. A kind servant had bandaged the old man's face, but the rags were soaked in blood. "Bless your sweet eyes, they bleed!" said Edgar, dismayed.

"Who's that?" asked Gloucester. "Your voice sounds familiar. Is it Poor Tom? Do you know the way to Dover?"

"Aye, Master," said Edgar.

"Then lead me there, and guide me to the brim of the highest cliff. From there I'll need no further leading…" said Gloucester. "What a time this is, when madmen lead the blind."

So the pair set off across the heath to meet their fate at Dover.

Edmund rode with Goneril back to her castle. He took her leave with a kiss and the promise that he'd be loyal to her to the death, then he rode on to prepare for battle. "Oh, he's so much more of a man than Albany, my milk-livered husband…" Goneril swooned, unaware that Edmund had already made a similar promise to Regan.

"'Tis the time's plague, when madmen lead the blind."

Gloucester, Act 4, Scene 1

Inside the castle, Albany's greeting was cold. He was appalled to hear how Goneril and Regan had treated their father. "You are not worth the dust the rough wind blows in your face," he told her.

"You're a fool," Goneril retorted. "Even now the French army is advancing and you're concerned with these trifles." Before she could complain further, a messenger arrived from Regan. Cornwall had died from the wound inflicted by his servant, and Goneril and Albany needed to head immediately to Dover with their troops.

The drums of war beat loud and fast as the opposing armies gathered on high ground near Dover. At the French camp, news of her father's plight reached Cordelia. She listened with sorrow as an attendant told her that Lear had arrived at Dover, but had lost his mind and was wearing a crown of weeds, and singing to himself that he was the King of Fools. "Search every field and meadow and bring him here," she ordered her guards. "Is there a way to restore his senses?" she asked her doctor.

"I can administer a sleeping potion that will bring his mind to rest," the doctor promised.

On the other side of the hill, two wretched figures made their way to a bare patch of ground in the middle of a meadow. "Poor Tom, are we nearly at the hill?" asked Gloucester.

"Why, can't you feel the slope beneath your feet? Listen, do you hear the sea below us?" Edgar replied. "We are there already."

"Then leave me here, at the edge of the cliff," said Gloucester. "Farewell." He kneeled down and prayed, "Oh you mighty gods! I now renounce this world. If Edgar lives, bless him!" And with that, Gloucester got to his feet and jumped. He landed flat on his face, on exactly the same patch of ground, and fainted.

When Gloucester regained consciousness, Edgar disguised his voice when he spoke to him. "Oh, sir!" he cried. "To fall all that way, either you must be as light as gossamer feathers, or the gods must wish to preserve your life."

"Have I fallen?" asked Gloucester, confused.

"Aye, over the cliff from a perilous height," answered Edgar. "Give me your hand, I'll help you up."

As Gloucester rose to his feet, Lear came weaving through the long grass. He was crowned in weeds and singing a strange song to himself, "No, they cannot catch me, for I am the King of… Look, look, a mouse! Peace, peace, this piece of toasted cheese."

"I know that voice," cried Gloucester. "Is that you, King Lear? Or do my ears deceive me?"

"Aye, every inch a king," answered Lear with a bitter laugh. He plucked a dandelion from his crown and held it up. The flower trembled in his grasp. "See how my subject quakes!"

Gloucester was dismayed at the change in the king's manner. "Do you not know me?" he asked.

Seeing his old friend, blinded and grief-stricken, brought Lear briefly to his senses. "But I know you well enough, Gloucester, my friend," he said.

"There he is!" came a voice, and three of Cordelia's men marched over to them.

Like a startled hare, Lear stiffened for a moment, then darted into the undergrowth. "If you want to catch me, you'll have to run!" he called over his shoulder. But he did not get far before the young soldiers caught hold of him. They wrapped a warm robe around the old king's frail frame and led him to safety.

Having become separated from his master outside Dover, Kent arrived at the French camp and was relieved to discover that Lear had already been brought there. Cordelia recognized him, despite his peasant's disguise, and greeted him as an old friend. She took him to the tent where Lear was sleeping under her doctor's care.

"Please, Your Majesty," said the doctor. "King Lear has slept long enough. It is time to wake him."

"Oh, my dear father!" said Cordelia. "Let this kiss repair those violent harms my two sisters have done to you."

As Cordelia bent down and kissed her father, Lear began to wake up. "Where have I been? Where am I?" he asked, rubbing his eyes. "I am a very foolish old man and I fear I am not in my perfect mind, but I think this lady is my child, Cordelia."

"And so I am!" wept Cordelia.

"But why do you weep?" asked Lear. "You have every cause to despise me."

Cordelia embraced her father. "There is no cause, no cause," she assured him.

The morning of the battle began in eerie silence, soon followed by a terrible cacophony of trumpets, murderous battle cries, the clash of swords and the thundering of horses' hooves. It seemed to be over no sooner than it had begun. The French were defeated, and men on both sides began the dreadful task of burying their dead. At Regan's insistence, Edmund had led her troops into battle. His soldiers had captured Lear, Cordelia and Kent. Now he marched them off to the British camp.

"Take them away and lock them up!" ordered Edmund. He beckoned one of his captains and surreptitiously handed him a letter. "Go after our prisoners and… deal with them," he said. "Follow the instructions in this note and you will be rewarded."

The captain nodded and went to carry out his mission.

Bruised and battle-weary, Albany returned to the British camp, where Goneril, Regan and Edmund were waiting. "Sir," said Edmund, "I have imprisoned Cordelia and the miserable old king. We will put them on trial tomorrow morning."

Albany snapped. "It is not your place to do such a thing!" And he sent his guards to release the prisoners.

"Too late for that…" thought Edmund.

Regan protested. "But Albany, I put Edmund in charge of my troops to act in place of my husband."

"But he is not your husband," retorted Albany.

"Not yet…" replied Regan.

"Not ever," spat Goneril. "He is promised to me!"

That was as much as Albany could bear. "Edmund, I charge you with capital treason," he said. "You will face trial by combat – with me."

But as Albany squared up to Edmund, a knight stepped forward. His sword was already drawn and his visor covered his face. "False to your father and brother, conspiring against the Duke of Albany… Edmund, you toad, you traitor," said the unknown knight. "I will fight you!"

The two men fought a tough duel. Edmund was bigger and stronger, but his opponent seemed able to predict and dodge all his best moves, as though they had sparred many times before. Eventually the knight struck Edmund to the ground.

Goneril howled in despair and Regan bent double in agony, crying "Oh, sick! I am sick." A servant took Regan to her tent, and Goneril hurried after them.

Fighting for breath, Edmund addressed the knight, "I am guilty of all that you have charged me with, and more besides. But who are you?"

The knight removed his helmet. "I am your father's son," he said. "Your brother, Edgar."

"Edgar!" exclaimed Albany. "But where have you been? And do you know what has become of your father?"

Edgar described how he had disguised himself as Poor Tom, and guided his blind father across the heath to Dover. Then he told how he had finally revealed his identity to Gloucester to ask his blessing before going into battle. "Sadly, his poor heart was too weak to support the extremes of grief and joy. He died, smiling."

A breathless nobleman came running, a stricken look on his face and a bloody dagger in his hand.

"What is this bloody knife?" asked Edgar.

"It has come from her heart. She's dead!" gasped the nobleman.

"Dead? Who's dead?" asked Albany.

"Queen Goneril, sir. She poisoned her sister then thrust this dagger into her own heart," answered the nobleman.

As he lay dying, Edmund felt deep remorse. "Despite all that I have done, I wish to do some good before I die. I sent my captain to kill Cordelia in prison and to make it look like her own last, desperate act. I hope there is time to stop him." With one, last gasp, Edmund died.

But his confession had come too late. Albany's guards had gone to release the prisoners and found Cordelia already dead. Now they trudged back across the camp with Kent to deliver the tragic news. A lone, broken figure stumbled behind them.

It was King Lear, holding Cordelia's limp, lifeless body in his arms. Exhausted, his legs crumpled beneath him and he wailed, "Howl, howl, howl, howl! She is gone forever."

Kent went to the king and kneeled down beside him. "My good master," he said softly.

Lear pushed him away without looking to see who it was. "A plague upon you, murderers, traitors, every one!" he cried. "I might have saved her. Oh, Cordelia, Cordelia! Stay a little. Have you no breath at all?" He kissed her and looked up, his eyes suddenly bright with hope. "But look! Look, her lips! She breathes." And with that brief moment of rapture, his eyes clouded over and his body slumped to the ground.

Edgar bowed his head. "He has gone," he said.

"The old man has been through such hardship, I can only wonder how he endured so much," joined Kent.

Albany called for the stretcher bearers. "Carry the dead, with due ceremony, to the castle. We will give them a grand state funeral," he said. "Our business now is woe."

"We must learn from this sad time, and the suffering of our elders," Edgar said, gravely, "to speak what we feel, not what we ought to say."

Edgar, Act 5, Scene 3

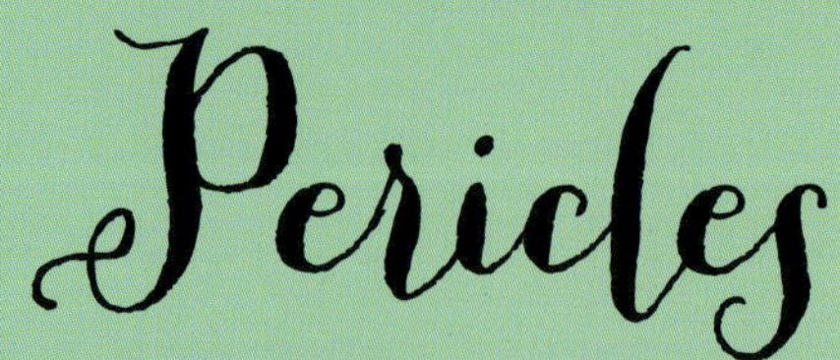

Pericles

Pericles of Tyre sets out to win the hand of Antiochus's beautiful daughter – but he soon finds out that all is not as it seems. He embarks on an unexpected journey in which he finds love, gains a daughter and then loses both. Can his travels ever have a happy ending?

Pericles

Clever, wise, handsome and just, Pericles is the ideal ruler of Tyre. But fate takes him far from home.

Cerimon

A lord of Ephesus and a doctor. He finds a princess in a coffin washed up on the shore.

Simonides

King of Pentapolis. He's holding a tournament for the hand of his daughter when Pericles arrives…

Thaisa

A princess as beautiful inside as she is on the outside. She falls in love with Pericles.

Cleon

Governor of Tarsus. After
Pericles saves the Tarsans
from starvation, Cleon owes
him a big favour.

Dionyza

Wife of Cleon. She has
one daughter for whom
she will do anything…

Marina

Pericles's only daughter.
Her father thinks she's safe
in Tarsus, but she ends up
on an adventure just as
perilous as his.

TARSUS

ANTIOCH

Antiochus

King of Antioch.
Prizes his daughter
so highly, he vows
never to let her go.

TYRE

Gower

A medieval poet
who narrates
the story.

ANCIENT GOWER, A STORYTELLER as old as the hills, used to tell this tale. Let us raise his spirit once more to tell it now. It is a tale of adventures across the seas, and the twists and turns of the stormy fate of one young hero, Pericles.

The story begins with Pericles, the noble young ruler of Tyre, seeking the hand of a princess in the nearby kingdom of Antioch. Her father, King Antiochus, was a most powerful and respected ruler. Years before, his beloved wife had died, leaving him with but one daughter. Consumed by grief and loneliness, Antiochus had sworn never to let his daughter leave him.

In time, however, his daughter became a woman. Tales of her beauty crossed the seas, and many a suitor came to ask for her hand in marriage. Strangely, none had yet returned home…

Fresh from his voyage and full of hope, Pericles entered King Antiochus's palace. "So, young Prince of Tyre," the king said. "You have something you wish to ask me?"

Pericles kneeled before him. "I do. It concerns your daughter."

Trumpets sounded, and into the room walked the princess, dressed in gleaming silk and glittering jewels. She was even more beautiful than the stories had told. Pericles gazed at her with adoration, drinking in her beauty with his eyes.

Antiochus frowned. "Her heavenly face may entice you to view, but that is all you may do," he said sharply. "You are aware of the danger of the question you are about to ask? Like Heracles, come to claim the golden apples, deathly dragons await you."

Pericles looked at him proudly. Like many young men before him, he was not deterred by the mention of peril. The idea made him bold, not afraid. He would prove himself and win the princess. He looked at the princess; she did not return his glance. But, out of a high window, something else caught his eye. Pericles felt his blood run cold, for, displayed in the courtyard outside, was a row of severed heads on stakes.

The king followed his gaze. "Famous princes like you have been here before, drawn by reports of my daughter's beauty, made adventurous by their desire. They warn you now, with their pale faces, with their speechless tongues. They advise you to desist."

"But what challenge did they undertake? I will not shrink from a hero's task to prove myself worthy…" Pericles began.

"Ask your question, then, if you must," said the king.

His eyes glittered dangerously, and suddenly Pericles understood. There was no heroic task for him to prove himself worthy. There was no way at all to win this king's daughter. Anyone who so much as dared to ask for her hand would die. "The book of a king's secrets is best kept shut," Pericles said carefully. "And so are my lips. I will not ask my question."

The king smiled but his eyes were cold. "Very well. But I insist you remain here as our guest. Make yourself at home." He swept out of the throne room, followed by the princess.

Pericles was afraid. "Knowing what I know, I'm certain he will not let me leave this place alive…" He told servants he was fetching gifts from his ship, and then slipped away and set sail for home.

When he found out, Antiochus was enraged. "I want Pericles dead!" he roared. "Send my assassin after him!"

When Pericles reached Tyre, he told his oldest, most trusted advisor everything. "Helicanus, I believe he will still want to have me killed…" he finished uncertainly. "But what frightens me more than that, is what he might do to my people if I remain here, and they try to defend me."

"You are right," the elderly lord agreed. "Antiochus is a tyrant and will kill you if he finds you. So, go, my lord, explore the world until he forgets his anger… or until destiny cuts his thread of life. You can trust me to manage Tyre in your absence."

Pericles embraced the elderly man. "Thank you. I will leave this very day and sail to Tarsus. I've heard they have fallen on hard times. I'll take a fleet of ships with me and deliver help."

So Pericles set sail from Tyre, leaving an ocean between him and Antiochus. When he arrived at Tarsus, his heart fell to see the pitiful state it was in. Once, Tarsus had been a most noble place. It had fine buildings, with towers so high their heads kissed the clouds. It had the finest food, with delicacies beyond measure. Poverty was unknown to its people. But now, any one of them would be grateful for a stale crust to eat. A blight had destroyed their crops, and hunger's sharp teeth gnawed at the civilized land.

Pericles went straight to the governor, Cleon. "I have come to help you. My ships are filled to the brim with corn," Pericles told him and his wife, Dionyza.

The pair fell to their knees in gratitude.

"I don't want your reverence," Pericles said humbly. "Just your love. And a harbour to rest in for a while."

"You are welcome here any time. Stay as long as you like," Cleon told him.

Pericles stayed, and his men helped restore Tarsus to some of its former glory. Before long, he received a letter from Helicanus, assuring him all was well in Tyre. No sooner had he left than an assassin had come looking for him, Helicanus wrote. He had made the right decision.

Anxious that the assassin might think to follow him, Pericles soon set off again, refilling his ships with supplies at the next port before sailing on. But out in the middle of the ocean, a terrible storm struck their fleet. All the ships were destroyed and everyone drowned – all except Pericles, who found himself tossed by the waves onto the shores of Pentapolis.

There, three fishermen found him. They gave him dry clothing and food, and told him all about their good king, Simonides, who that very day was holding a tournament. Every knight there would be vying for the love of his beautiful daughter, Thaisa.

"I wish I could fight in that tournament," Pericles sighed. "But my armour and everything else was lost at sea."

However it seemed his fortunes had turned again. That very moment, one of the fishermen found something heavy in his net. He dragged it ashore only to find it was a heap of rusty armour.

"It's mine!" Pericles cried in disbelief.

Promising the fishermen he would not forget their kindness, he put it on, and headed off to the tournament.

In the royal stand, Pericles saw King Simonides and, at her father's side, the princess. He was captivated by her strong green eyes, dark curls and quiet manner as she looked out at the games.

All day long, knights in fine, gleaming armour, riding handsome steeds, competed with each other – but Thaisa found her eyes drawn to the shabby stranger who, despite his poor appearance, easily defeated the rest.

The lords of Pentapolis sneered at his creaking, rusty armour, but the king silenced them by saying, "Only a fool would take the outer appearance for the inner man."

When the tournament was over, the king led his guests inside for a banquet.

"Opinion's but a fool that makes us scan
The outward habit by the inward man."

Before the feast began, Thaisa awarded Pericles the winner's garland, her heart fluttering in her chest as she placed it around his neck. Simonides watched his daughter closely. And, when she returned to her place, he gave her a nudge. "Why don't you offer a glass of wine to the good knight?"

Thaisa blushed. "I couldn't, Father!"

"Do as I ask, or I shall be angry!" Simonides said, but he was smiling. "Find out his name and where he came from too."

Shyly, Thaisa took a goblet to Pericles. "This comes from the king, my father. Please tell us who you are and where you're from."

Knowing his life was still in danger from Antiochus, Pericles thought for a moment before he replied. "I'm just a gentleman from Tyre," he told her. "My name is Pericles. I was looking for adventure on the high seas when my ship was wrecked and I found myself cast upon your shore."

Thaisa felt for the stranger, so handsome yet so lost and alone. "Well, you are welcome here," she said warmly. "Please stay with us in Pentapolis for as long as you would like."

The banquet went on late into the night, and Pericles and the princess found they had much to say to each other.

The very next morning, Simonides received a letter from his daughter. "She says she'll wed the stranger knight or never again view day nor light!" He laughed fondly: his daughter was so determined, she did not care whether he agreed or not. "It is just as well your choice agrees with mine," he chuckled.

At breakfast, he announced to the other knights that his daughter didn't want to marry for another year, and sent them home. But he called for Pericles. "What do you think of my daughter, sir?" he demanded sternly.

Pericles was taken aback. "She is good and noble…"

"And beautiful, too?" Simonides continued.

"Very beautiful," Pericles agreed.

Simonides threw the letter at Pericles's feet. "You have bewitched my daughter, Pericles! You are a traitor!"

Pericles gasped. "By the gods, I have not. And I am no traitor, even if a king tells me so," he replied fiercely. "I will defend my honour, if I must." He reached for his sword.

Just then, Thaisa entered.

"Princess, tell your father, I have never said a wrong word to you," Pericles urged her.

They both turned to Simonides and found him grinning at them. "Good. I've decided to make you man and wife!" he declared.

Thaisa and Pericles exchanged confused glances and Simonides broke into gruff laughter. "Well, are you pleased?"

"Oh, Father, you were joking!" Thaisa smiled delightedly and turned to Pericles, "If you love me…"

Pericles clasped her hands. "As much as my life…" he said.

Pericles and Thaisa were married with great ceremony. And soon, Thaisa became pregnant. They couldn't have been happier.

Months went by and, when the baby was nearly ready to be born, Pericles received a letter from Helicanus, telling him Antiochus had died. Pericles was free to return home. In fact, the letter begged him to return soon. The people needed their leader, and if he did not return immediately, they would crown Helicanus king instead. Helicanus said that was the last thing he wanted.

At last Pericles could reveal his true identity. All of Pentapolis was delighted to hear that Pericles was as royal as his wife.

Determined as ever, Thaisa declared she would accompany Pericles to Tyre, despite being almost nine months pregnant. And so, Pericles, Thaisa and her nursemaid set off in their best ship.

But Fortune is a fickle friend. Far out on the waves, the north wind threw a wild tempest at the ship.

Pericles stood on deck, the ship tilting and swaying beneath his feet as the waves washed over the sides and the wind tore at the sails. Below deck, his wife was giving birth. Her cries mingled with the howling wind and waves. Then he could hear her no more.

Thaisa's nursemaid appeared, cradling a tiny baby in her arms. "Take this last gift from your queen!" she cried over the raging wind and waves.

"What do you mean?" Pericles shouted back.

The nursemaid pushed the child into his arms. "The queen is dead, and all that's left is a little daughter. Take comfort in her."

"Oh, you gods!" Pericles cried in anguish. "Why do you make us love your gifts, then snatch them away?" He looked into his baby's face, tears mingling with the rain that streamed down his cheeks. "May your life be milder after this," he whispered to her. "No baby ever had a more blusterous beginning."

Two sailors appeared on deck. "Sir," the first cried, "We must throw the queen's body overboard: the sea shall not rest until this ship is clear of the dead!"

"That is mere superstition!" Pericles choked.

"Sir, we have seen it happen before," said the second sailor. "We know the customs, she must go overboard."

"My darling queen…" Pericles sobbed.

He went below deck and the sailors brought a casket for her body. He laid her in it, and filled it with precious jewels and sweet-smelling spices. He wrote a letter and put it next to Thaisa before sealing the lid.

They said prayers to their gods, and sent the casket overboard. Pericles watched desolately as it was taken away by the waves.

"Which coast are we near?" he asked the captain of the ship.

"Tarsus," the captain answered.

"My baby daughter will not survive the voyage to Tyre. Turn the boat and make for Tarsus," Pericles ordered him.

The next day, far away in Ephesus, an elderly doctor named Cerimon was sitting in his house, when there was a banging on the door, and three of his servants entered, struggling under the weight of a wooden casket that smelled of the sea.

Cerimon stood up. "What is that?" he asked.

"It washed up on the shore," one of the servants puffed.

"Then set it down and open it!" said Cerimon.

The servants cracked open the lid, and a sweet scent wafted out.

Cerimon peered inside, "What is this? A woman… A queen by the look of those gemstones."

He spotted the letter, and picked it up gently. "Indeed she was a queen," he said as he read. "But she must only just have died. She seems too fresh." He looked more closely. The queen's skin was still pink. "I think whoever put her overboard was too hasty. Light a fire and bring me my bag!"

The servants rushed around, and Cerimon began his work quickly. The fire warmed the queen's body, and soon Cerimon gasped, "Look, her eyelids are fluttering. She's alive!"

"Oh, Goddess Diana," Thaisa murmured, "Where am I? Where's my lord? What world is this?"

The servants eyed each other in disbelief.

"Stay calm, dear lady," Cerimon said soothingly to Thaisa. To his servants he said, "Let us move her to a bedroom to recover."

Later, when Cerimon asked Thaisa about the letters and jewels. she wept quietly. "They are from my husband, Pericles," she replied. "His ship must have been lost in the storm. Oh, I will never see him again! I can never marry another. Instead, I'll spend the rest of my life hidden away from the world."

Cerimon patted her shoulders kindly. "Madam, there is a temple of Diana here for just that purpose. And if it pleases you, my niece shall serve you there."

Thaisa nodded. "Thank you, sir."

Meanwhile, in Tarsus, poor, grief-stricken Pericles had returned to the house of Cleon and Dionyza with his baby daughter.

"This is terrible," Cleon shook his head. "Your poor queen."

"And my poor baby. I have named her Marina, for she was born at sea," Pericles said, rocking his daughter gently. "I cannot take her with me to Tyre. She is too young to survive the journey without a mother. I entrust her to you. When my kingdom is safe and settled, I shall come back for her."

"Of course," Cleon nodded, "I am more than glad to be able to help you now, especially after all you did for us."

Dionyza interrupted. "I have a daughter too, Philoten, who can be a sister to her. Your daughter will be as dear to me as my own."

"My thanks," Pericles said earnestly, "I will leave the nursemaid too, to help look after Marina."

With the urgency of matters in Tyre weighing heavy on his mind, Pericles said his goodbyes and sailed on to his kingdom.

Years passed, and Marina grew into a young lady, finely educated in words and music, and altogether so good and wise that wherever she went she was admired.

But the lovelier she grew, the more jealous Dionyza became. Dionyza's own daughter, Philoten, was the same age as Marina, but Marina outshone her at every turn.

When Marina's nursemaid finally died of old age, Dionyza hatched a dark plot. She ordered her servant Leonine to take Marina for a walk on the beach and murder her.

The two strolled along the windswept beach, as Leonine tried to summon up his courage to do the dreadful deed.

"I was born under a north wind. What wind is this?" Marina pondered out loud.

"South-west," muttered Leonine, peering darkly at the girl.

"My father is a king and a brave sailor, you know," Marina

remarked, looking out to sea. "Some day he will return for me."

"So I've heard," returned Leonine.

"And I was born in a terrible storm," continued Marina.

Suddenly Leonine spun around, revealing a knife in one hand. "Say your prayers!" he snarled.

Marina stumbled back. "What is this?" she cried.

"I'll let you pray, but then I must finish you," Leonine growled.

"You want to kill me?" Marina asked. "But why?"

"My lady ordered me to," Leonine told her.

Marina's green eyes clouded in confusion. "But why would she want me dead? I've never hurt a mouse nor killed a fly. And you, Leonine, you're too kind to do such a thing."

Leonine hestitated, but did not let the knife drop.

"I can see you do not want to do it. You have a good heart," Marina insisted.

Leonine's fist tensed around his weapon. "I have sworn."

At that moment, as fate would have it, a band of pirates rushed along the shore. "Stop!" shouted the first, waving a cutlass.

Leonine dropped the knife and fled.

"A prize, a prize!" yelled another, bundling up Marina in his arms. "Let's have her aboard!"

They scrambled back to their ship, carrying Marina with them.

From behind a rock, Leonine watched them go. "There's no chance she'll return," he said to himself, "I'll just tell Dionyza she's dead."

A few weeks later, the pirates led Marina into a murky tavern in the city of Mytilene. Inside, a hideous old man and woman sat at a dirty table littered with empty tankards.

The old woman fixed her eagle-eyed gaze on Marina. "She's pretty enough, but what are her qualities?"

A pirate pushed Marina forward. "She has a good face, speaks well, works hard and has fine clothes, too," he prattled.

"Hmm," the woman grumbled. "What's her price?"

"A thousand gold pieces," he replied.

The old woman waved a hand at the old man. "Take these pirates away and pay them."

She got slowly to her feet. "Now, let me look at you properly."

In Tarsus, when Dionyza revealed her terrible deed to her husband, Cleon, he was horrified. "Can it be undone?" he gasped.

His wife shook her head. "Nor should it be!"

"But what do we do when Pericles comes back for her?" Cleon asked desperately.

"We can tell him she died in her sleep," Dionyza replied. "We'll build a beautiful tomb. Who could doubt us?"

So, when Pericles finally returned to Tarsus to bring his beloved daughter home to Tyre, he was led to a tombstone. He broke down, desperate with grief, tearing his hair and ripping his royal robes. He changed his clothes for a sackcloth and set sail once more, swearing never again to wash his face nor cut his hair in mourning for his beloved daughter.

In Mytilene, word of Marina's beauty had spread so far that even the governor of the city, Lysimachus, had heard tell of her dark curls and green eyes. He went to the tavern to see for himself.

"How long have you worked here?" Lysimachus asked her.

Marina folded her arms. "I don't work here!"

"Come, come," chuckled Lysimachus. "Don't be coy!"

Marina rounded on him in anger. "I am a prisoner! I've been bought, like a slave. And you, supposedly the honourable governor, have done nothing to stop it. What honour do you have? Pah!"

Lysimachus had the good grace to blush a little.

MARINA, ACT 4, SCENE 6

"If you have any decency, show it now!" Marina went on. "I am an innocent girl, stolen from my home and brought here against my will. Oh, I wish the gods would set me free from this unholy place! Even if they turned me into a poor bird flying in the open air, it would be a better fate than this."

Studying Marina's earnest face and her passionate words, Lysimachus felt embarrassed for his shallow behaviour. "I did not think… I… I'm sorry. Take this gold." He pulled a purse from his pocket and pressed it into her hands.

Marina stared at the purse. With the money she could buy her freedom. "The gods preserve you!" she said gratefully.

"No," Lysimachus shook his head vehemently. "Thank you for making me see things differently. You are a true piece of goodness in this dark world."

Thanks to Lysimachus's gold, Marina was free. She became a teacher in Mytilene. She could sing and dance like a goddess and speak like a scholar. Moreover, goodness shone out of her like light from the Sun. The people of Mytilene flocked to learn from her, and she made herself content with her humble new life.

Her father, however, was consumed by sorrow. He did not speak, he hardly ate, and he showed no interest in the world outside his ship's cabin. Word was sent home to faithful Helicanus, who sailed out to join him. Realizing Pericles could not rule in such a state, he ordered the crew to sail across the sea away from Tyre.

As luck would have it, the ship dropped anchor in Mytilene for supplies. Lysimachus saw it and went to greet the visitors. He was welcomed aboard by Helicanus, who explained that his master, the king, was overwhelmed by grief, had not spoken for three months.

Lysimachus immediately thought of that good, wise young girl he had saved from the tavern, and sent his men to fetch her.

"I hope you can use your wisdom and goodness to aid this poor king's recovery," the governor told her, when his men brought her back to the ship.

Marina nodded solemnly. "I will try with all my heart. Let me be alone with him."

She entered Pericles's cabin where he sat with his head in his hands. "My lord, I am just a girl," Marina began, "but I have endured grief as strong as yours and fortune as terrible. I am of royal blood, but now live in servitude."

"Ha," Pericles laughed bitterly, "Grief as strong as mine? I doubt that. Come closer."

Marina stepped forward, and Pericles frowned. "You remind me of someone I knew once. Are you from these shores?"

Marina shook her head. "No, not from any shores."

Pericles couldn't stop staring at her. She was so like his wife. Those green eyes, the dark curls – even now, fifteen years after her death, he could see his beautiful Thaisa clearly, the image of the girl in front of him… Just as his daughter might have looked if she had lived. He shook his head quickly and, in a gruff voice, asked Marina, "Where is your family from?"

"If I told you, you'd think I was lying," she replied.

"You could never be a liar," Pericles said plainly. "Tell me who they are, and what your name is."

Marina looked back with a clear gaze. "My name is Marina. It was given to me by my father, a king."

Pericles jumped to his feet. "A king's daughter and called Marina?" he cried. "Are you flesh and blood? You're not conjured by fairies? Where were you born? Why are you called Marina?"

"I'm called Marina because I was born at sea," she answered.

"And your mother?"

"She was the daughter of a king, but she died when I was born, or so my nursemaid used to tell me."

Pericles trembled from head to foot. "Tell me your story, all of it, I won't interrupt you."

Marina was confused, but she told him everything of Tarsus and Cleon and Dionyza, of Leonine and the pirates, and of Mytilene.

"Why are you crying?" she asked gently when she had finished her tale. "You think I'm an imposter, but I'm not. I am the daughter of Pericles, if there is still a King Pericles in this world."

"Helicanus!" Pericles cried, "Helicanus!"

The old man hobbled in as quickly as he could, closely followed by Lysimachus. "My lord?" he asked breathlessly.

"My most noble counsellor, tell me, if you can, who this girl is and why I am weeping." Pericles clutched the lord's hands in his.

"I… I do not know, my lord, but this governor of Mytilene speaks highly of her," Helicanus said.

Lysimachus stepped forward. "She would never tell anyone here of her family or her history."

"Helicanus," Pericles said, his voice breaking, "this is Marina. Tell us your mother's name, Marina," said Pericles urgently.

Marina looked from one man to another and shook her head. She stared straight at Pericles. "First, sir, please, what is your title?"

Pericles pushed his shaggy hair from his face and tugged at his unruly beard. "I am Pericles of Tyre," he said slowly, "but tell me now my drowned queen's name. Become heir to my kingdoms and give new life to your father."

Marina fell to her knees. "Thaisa was my mother. She died giving birth to me."

Pericles bent and took her hands. "My child," he said softly, pulling her to him. "Not dead at Tarsus," he said to the others, tears of joy streaming down his cheeks. "She is your princess, Helicanus! Fetch me some fresh robes, I am wild to look upon!"

While Pericles washed and dressed, the others waited on deck. His manservant was trimming his beard when Pericles thought he could hear music. "How strange," he said. "Do you hear that?"

But the servant heard nothing unusual.

When the servant left Pericles alone, a strange thing happened: the goddess Diana appeared in his cabin. She told him to go immediately to her temple at Ephesus and tell his story to the priestesses there.

As soon as the vision faded, he dashed out of the cabin. "I planned to sail to Tarsus and seek justice, but now we will sail straight to Ephesus!" he declared.

Helicanus went to advise the captain of the ship of the new plan, and Lysimachus caught Pericles's arm, drawing him gently aside. "Sir, before you leave, I have a question," he said softly.

Pericles looked at him and understood right away. "You love my daughter? My dear sir, the choice is hers, but I think if you ask her to marry you, she may say yes. It seems you have been good to her. Is that what you meant?"

"With all my heart," Lysimachus said earnestly.

That evening Marina happily agreed to become Lysimachus's wife, and the whole family set sail to Ephesus.

They found the temple of Diana brimming with flowers and filled with incense. It seemed like a magical place to Pericles. Young priestesses lined each side of the aisle leading up to the altar, where the high priestess stood, veiled and solemn. Many Ephesians filled the temple, including the elderly doctor, Cerimon, leaning heavily on his servant's arm.

Pericles walked to the altar and fell to his knees in prayer. "Diana! I have come here to tell my story, as you commanded me.

I am the King of Tyre, who married beautiful Thaisa at Pentapolis. She died at sea giving birth to our child, Marina, who I left at Tarsus, where she was almost murdered. Her stars brought her to Mytilene, where I found myself, and finally she made herself known to me as my daughter."

The high priestess began to shake. "You are… you are Pericles?" she managed to croak before falling to the ground.

Pericles looked around wildly. "Help! Someone help! The priestess has fainted!"

Cerimon rushed forward. "Noble sir, if all you've said is true, then this is your wife!" He told Pericles everything he knew about Thaisa's arrival on his shore.

Thaisa's eyelids fluttered and her green eyes looked up to meet her husband's. "Oh, my lord, are you not Pericles? You sound like him; you look like him," she murmured.

"The voice of dead Thaisa!" Pericles cried in disbelief.

"When we left Pentapolis, my father gave you this ring," she pressed it into his hands. Pericles pulled her into his arms.

Marina ran forward. "Mother!"

Pericles drew her into their embrace. "Thaisa, this is your precious daughter, Marina."

And so, with the family reunited, the sands of this ancient story have run their course. When the Tarsians learned of Dionyza's dark plot, they rose up and overthrew their rulers. King Antiochus, of course, was long dead, and the pirates who captured Marina all drowned in a storm at sea. So the evildoers of this tale were punished, and those with good hearts were finally crowned with joy.

Sometimes Fortune can be fair after all.

The Comedy of Errors

Many years ago, two sets of identical twins were separated at birth. Now one of them, Antipholus of Syracuse, has arrived in the city of Ephesus, along with his servant, Dromio. He has no idea that his twin brother, also called Antipholus, lives here with *his* servant, Dromio. Life is about to get complicated…

Egeon

Father of the Antipholus twins. Hasn't seen his son, Antipholus of Syracuse, since the day Antipholus left to find his long lost twin brother…

Antipholus of Syracuse

Twin brother of Antipholus of Ephesus. When strange things start to happen in Ephesus, he thinks the city must be enchanted…

Dromio of Syracuse

Twin brother of Dromio of Ephesus, and loyal servant of Antipholus of Syracuse. Today, no matter how hard he tries, he can't get anything right…

Adriana
Married to Antipholus of Ephesus. When her husband claims he has no wife, she bursts into tears. Why is he being so heartless?

Luciana
Adriana's sister. Why is Antipholus suddenly being *so* friendly with her? He seems to have forgotten that he's married to her sister.

Antipholus of Ephesus
Twin brother of Antipholus of Syracuse. He can't understand why his servant Dromio is being such an idiot.

Aemilia
Abbess who claims she can cure Antipholus of all his mental confusion…

Dromio of Ephesus
Antipholus of Ephesus's servant. He has no idea that Antipholus has a twin brother and believes his master must have gone stark raving mad.

"In Syracuse I was born, and lived a happy man," Egeon began. "I had no idea how lucky I was!" The old man was standing in the town square in Ephesus, relating a sorry tale to the duke. "My wife and I had twin boys. One so like the other, you could only tell them apart by their names. That very same hour, a woman we knew gave birth to twin boys too. Because she and her husband were so poor, we took them on, to raise them as servants to our sons."

His eyes filled with tears as he remembered the next part. "One day, we were all aboard a ship, speeding across the sea, when a storm whipped up around us. As waves came crashing over the side of the ship, I ran to one of the masts, clutching one of my sons and one of the other boys. My wife raced to the other mast, and clung on for her life, holding the other two babies.

"In the distance, we saw two ships sailing towards our little boat. Our rescuers! But moments before they reached us, our ship smashed into a rock, and split in two. Then I saw – or I thought I saw – my wife being rescued by fishermen on one of the ships. A moment later, I was hauled onto the other ship, by sailors who took me home to safety, with two wailing babies in my arms.

"That was the last time that I saw my other son or my wife. Not sure which of the twins I'd ended up with, I guessed my son was Antipholus, and the servant baby Dromio. I raised them myself, hoping against hope that I would find the rest of my family again. But as the years went by, my hopes began to fade.

"Seven years ago, Antipholus left Syracuse in search of his long-lost brother, taking Dromio with him. He did not return. Five years ago, I set out to find him. Still my search goes on…"

That same afternoon, a young man came striding through the marketplace. He had just arrived in Ephesus. Antipholus was his name – he was the very same son that Egeon had been seeking.

"Dromio," he said to his servant, "take my money to the inn, where we're staying. I'll see you there for lunch. Till then I'll look around the town."

"Not a problem," said Dromio, grinning. "I'll take your money. Most servants would – you just wouldn't see them again."

Antipholus smiled. Dromio always cheered him up when he was out of sorts. Then he began to wander through the noisy streets of Ephesus, looking warily around, as he'd heard stories that Ephesus was full of magicians, witches and scorcerers. But as he watched the crowds pouring through the marketplace, something else tugged at his heart. Would he ever find his brother? Or his mother? And would he recognize them, if he did?

"I'm like a drop of water looking for another drop in the ocean," he thought. "In trying to find a mother and a brother, I could easily lose myself…"

He looked up, and was surprised to see Dromio standing in front of him. "Back so soon?" he said.

Dromio scowled at him. "Back so soon?" he repeated, "Back too late, you mean! The meat's burned, the roast is ruined, and my mistress is furious! She is hot because the meat is cold. The meat is cold because you didn't come home. You didn't come home because you're not hungry. And we are all sorry for it!"

"Enough!" said Antipholus. What on earth had got into Dromio? Suddenly he wasn't in the mood for one of Dromio's silly jokes. "Where's the money I gave you?" he demanded.

"I to the world am like a drop of water
That in the ocean seeks another drop"

Antipholus of Syracuse
Act 1, Scene 2

Dromio gave him a blank look. "You mean… the sixpence… that you gave me last Wednesday? I used it to pay the cobbler," he replied.

"Seriously," said Antipholus, "Where's the gold?"

"I beg you," Dromio replied, looking exasperated, "I've come from my mistress to tell you to hurry!"

Antipholus could feel waves of anger bubbling up inside him. "Tell me where you've put the gold, or I shall break that merry head of yours," he fumed.

Dromio took a deep breath. "Your wife, my mistress, asks that you come home to lunch," he repeated.

"Wife?" said Antipholus. "I have no wife!"

And then, as Dromio began to tell his bizarre story again, Antipholus decided that he had had enough. His first slap landed with a *SPLAT!* on Dromio's ear. His second – *SPLOT!* – landed on his chin. His third blow was aimed at Dromio's nose. And would have hit it too if Dromio hadn't ducked and run away.

"That scoundrel!" Antipholus thought furiously. "He was joking about stealing all my money. But now he actually has!"

Antipholus glared around himself. He didn't like this place at all. Then a thought occurred to him. They said this town was full of black magic. Could Dromio have been enchanted? Perhaps that was the reason for his odd behaviour. Despite the fact that he was searching for his long-lost twin brother, it didn't occur to Antipholus for a single moment that there could be another Antipholus and another Dromio in this very town…

In a nearby house, a young woman was pacing back and forth across the kitchen. The house belonged to a certain Antipholus of Ephesus, and the woman was frantic with worry because he wasn't there. "My husband still isn't back!" she said to her sister, Luciana.

"Let's just eat without him," Luciana suggested, "Look! Here comes Dromio! Perhaps he has news.”

Luciana smiled at Dromio as he came in, panting. As usual, Dromio couldn't help looking more than a little ridiculous, with the huge, lopsided hat he was so proud of.

Adriana crossed her arms. “So, is your master on his way?” she asked him. “Did he explain why he's over an hour late?”

“He gave my ear an explanation,” said Dromio miserably. He showed Adriana and Luciana his ear, which was now bright pink.

“But… is he coming home?” asked Adriana. (She wasn't too concerned about Dromio's ear. What did his pain matter compared to her distress about her missing husband?)

Dromio shook his head. “I said to him: ‘It's lunch time.’ He said: ‘My gold!’ I said: ‘Will you come home?’ He said: ‘My gold!’ I said: ‘The lunch is burned.’ He said: ‘My gold!’ I said: ‘But your wife.’ He said: ‘What wife?’”

Adriana clapped her hand over her mouth. This was worse than she'd thought. Not only was her husband late for lunch, he was pretending she didn't even exist.

“When I reminded him that he did have a wife,” said Dromio, “he rewarded me with a blow!”

By now Adriana was shaking. “You must fetch him and bring him home!”

“Can't you send some other messenger?” Dromio pleaded. “He's only going to use me as a punching bag!”

“Go,” hissed Adriana, “or I'll redden your other ear myself!”

So off Dromio went to find Antipholus, grumbling, “Here I go – being kicked from my master to my mistress, and back again. Before long, I'll turn into a football…”

In a street nearby, Antipholus of Syracuse had come across Dromio. (This time, it really *was* his servant Dromio).

“Here you are again,” said Antipholus. “What stories have you got for me this time? You received no gold? My wife wants me to come home for lunch?"

Poor Dromio stared at his master, utterly bewildered. "Erm… When did I say those things?" he asked.

"Just half an hour ago," said Antipholus.

"But I haven't seen you since you sent me to the inn, with the gold," he said.

"You villain!" said Antipholus. "You denied having the gold! You told me that I had a wife and lunch waiting for me!"

Dromio looked Antipholus up and down. "I'm glad to see you in a merry mood, although I'm not sure I get the joke."

"Joke?" said Antipholus. "This is no joke!"

Dromio, he decided, really needed someone to teach him a lesson. So he gave him a clout around the ear.

"Stop!" yelled Dromio. Luckily, Antipholus did stop, as he'd been momentarily distracted. Across the square, two beautiful women were waving at him.

"Who is this who beckons us?" Antipholus said.

"'Who is this', you ask?!" one woman exclaimed, bursting into tears as she marched up to him. Unbeknown to him, it was Adriana, the other Antipholus's wife. "You know," she said, "there was a time, when words weren't music to your ears unless I spoke them; when nothing pleased your eye apart from my glance; when no touch pleased your hand other than mine. What happened to turn you, my husband, into a stranger?"

Husband? Stranger? "It's true then, this town is full of black magic. This woman must be an enchantress…" he thought backing away from her. "I've only been in Ephesus for two hours so far!" he protested fearfully.

But now the woman was smiling at him. "Let's have no more of this," she wheedled. "I will simply take your arm…" She put her arm through his. "And we'll go home."

"This is like a dream!" Antipholus thought. "But perhaps it's not such a bad dream. It could be a wonderful dream…" The woman leading him along was rather good looking, after all. He might just have landed on his feet.

So away Adriana went, leading Antipholus of Syracuse down the street, convinced that he was her husband.

Following his master, Dromio wasn't so happy. "We're lost in Fairyland!" he muttered. He was sure the women they'd met must be witches in disguise. They could turn him into a beast at any moment! And one of them was staring at him strangely.

"Dromio!" Luciana said. "What are you doing, standing there, talking to yourself? You snail!"

Dromio gasped. "Have I been transformed?" he asked Antipholus. "What have they turned me into? I don't think I can be a snail. What am I? An ape?" he spluttered.

"No," said Antipholus, "you look the same to me."

"I think I am an ape!" wailed Dromio.

"If you're anything," scolded Luciana, "you're a silly ass!"

"Aargh!" shrieked Dromio, feeling frantically about on his head for ears. Perhaps the witches were about to turn him into a donkey. Perhaps the spell had already begun. But what could he do? He couldn't abandon his master now. He hurried along after Antipholus, until they reached a smart townhouse. Once they were inside, Adriana commanded him to keep the door locked. "If you open it for anyone," she said, "I'll break your head."

Dromio nodded. Whoever this woman was, she didn't look as if she was joking. Whatever else happened today, he had no intention of getting beaten up again.

A little later, Antipholus of Ephesus found his servant, Dromio, outside his house. But Dromio was acting very strangely. He kept claiming that Antipholus had hit him.

"Say what you will, sir," said Dromio. "But you beat me up at the marketplace. The evidence is right here!" He walked right up to Antipholus, showing him his bruised ear. "If my skin was made of parchment, and your blows were made of ink, your own handwriting would tell you what I think!" he declared.

Antipholus sighed. Why would Dromio make up such a strange lie? He must have got into a fight with someone. But Antipholus wasn't going to worry about that now. He was simply going to go inside and have lunch with his wife. He turned the handle of his front door. It didn't open.

"Dromio! Why is the door locked?" he said.

Dromio frowned. He hadn't locked the door. "Open up!" he shouted, thumping on the door.

"Go away!" a voice shouted back. Antipholus and Dromio looked at each other. Who on earth was inside?

"Hey – let us in!" called Dromio. "Who is that?"

"It's Dromio!" shouted the Dromio behind the door.

Dromio's eyes nearly popped out of his head "What?" he yelped. Dromio? But *he* was Dromio! "Dromio?" he shouted. "So you've stolen my job, and my name!"

Hearing the shouts, Adriana came to the hall. "Who's outside?" she called through the door.

"It's your husband!" cried Antipholus. "Let me in!"

"My husband?" Adriana replied. Her husband was sitting in the kitchen, finishing off a roast chicken. "I don't think so!"

"Fetch me a crowbar," Antipholus ordered Dromio. "I'll break down the door. I'll smash my way in!"

Dromio of Ephesus
Act 3, Scene 1

Dromio pictured the scene. It didn't seem likely to end well. "Why don't we have lunch somewhere else," he suggested, "and come back when Adriana's calmed down? If you break down your own front door, the whole town will know about it!"

"Fine!" fumed Antipholus. He didn't want to cause a scene. So he strode away, muttering angrily, with Dromio at his heels.

Inside the house, the lunch was not much of a success. Adriana's husband was acting very strangely. He kept saying he'd never met Adriana before. Soon, she was in tears again. Finally, Luciana dragged Antipholus outside to have a stern word with him.

"Why are you being so cruel?" she asked crossly. "If you married my sister for her money, well – think of the money! And if you don't love Adriana any more, then at least pretend you do!"

She stared at him, exasperated. Adriana had done nothing to deserve this cruelty. And now Antipholus was gazing at her with a very strange look indeed. He seemed almost drunk.

"Oh, sweet mermaid," he murmured, "your sister is no wife of mine! Do not sing for your sister. Sing for yourself!"

"Are you completely mad?" said Luciana.

"Not mad, but in love," replied Antipholus. "You are the Sun," he murmured, "and I am gazing at the sunbeams…."

"Keep your eyes to yourself," said Luciana, backing away.

"But, my love…" Antipholus implored her.

"Call my sister your love, you rogue!"

"No, it's you. You are my food, my fortune, and my sweet hope's aim…"

"You should be saying all this to my SISTER!" shouted Luciana.

"You have no husband," Antipholus said. "I have no wife. Give me your hand."

Suddenly, Antipholus was kneeling in front of Luciana, gazing at her with adoration in his eyes.

"I'm fetching my sister. Your WIFE!" Luciana yelled, before fleeing into the house. Moments later, Antipholus was still kneeling in a lovedrunk haze, when he saw Dromio arrive.

"Master!" said Dromio. He'd never been so happy to see Antipholus. "I am Dromio, aren't I?"

"Why wouldn't you be?" said Antipholus.

"I met a woman – a cook – who claims that I belong to her!" he said nervously. "She's covered in grease, and spherical, like a globe. I could discover whole countries on her. She called me Dromio, said that I was hers – and now she's haunting me. I didn't know her, but she knew me, down to the freckle on my left arm! I think she's a witch," he bleated. "Let's run away, before she finds me and turns me into a dog!"

Antipholus looked at his poor, trembling, terrified servant. Then he considered the strange occurrences from the last few hours. "There is no other explanation for it," he concluded. "This place is enchanted. That woman must have put me under a spell. I must plug my ears against her magic."

He stuck his fingers in his ears and told Dromio, "Go to the harbour. If there's a ship leaving Ephesus tonight, make sure we'll be on it!"

Dromio nodded. "Just as, from a bear, a man would run for his life, so I'll run from the woman that wants to be my wife!"

That evening, as dusk was falling, Dromio came racing back from the dock. "I found a ship!" he announced to Antipholus. "It leaves tonight, and is only waiting for us to step aboard."

To his horror, Antipholus looked at him blankly. "A ship?" he said. "Are you crazy? What ship is waiting for me?"

"Erm – the ship that you told me to find?" Dromio hazarded.

"You drunken fool, I sent you to fetch a chain! A gold chain! Where is it?" Antipholus roared.

Dromio looked quizzically at the man he thought was his master. "But… you sent me for a ship…" he began. But, as Antipholus drew back his fist, Dromio decided that the time for explaining was over. He ran away from his master, as fast as his legs would carry him. As Antipholus of Ephesus ran after him in hot pursuit, neither of them noticed Antipholus of Syracuse.

This Antipholus was frowning, deep in thought. Ephesus just kept getting stranger. Wherever he went, people greeted him, as if they'd known him for years. A goldsmith – who he had never set eyes on before – had forced him to take a gold chain, insisting that he'd ordered it. And then he had the cheek to say he wanted payment! He couldn't wait to get on that ship, and escape this strange, supernatural city. He breathed a sigh of relief when Dromio appeared.

"Any news of the ship?" he asked him.

"The ship?" Dromio said, his eyes all agog. "There *was* a ship. But when I told you about it, you told me you had no wish to set sail on it – so I went and told them to sail without us!"

"What?" How could Dromio possibly be so stupid? "Villain!" Antipholus cried, landing a punch on the end of Dromio's nose.

Meanwhile, Adriana was in a great deal of distress. Her husband had clearly lost his mind. So she had taken an extreme, but necessary measure. She had found a wizard to cure his delusions. Unfortunately, Antipholus had escaped from the wizard's clutches! So she and Luciana chased Antipholus and Dromio all the way across town, following them all the way to an abbey. Antipholus had fled inside it with Dromio. And to top it all off, the abbess refused to let Adriana in.

"I will not let him out until he is sane," the abbess said sternly, when Adriana explained what had happened. "He has sought sanctuary here, and I will cure him. Go home and leave him here."

But the thought of leaving her poor, deluded husband at the abbey horrified Adriana. "I will not leave him here. I should be his nurse. And you should not separate a husband and wife!"

"Be quiet and go! You shall not have him," said the abbess sternly. "For… I have many prayers to say," she finished. Then she slammed the door in Adriana's face.

Adriana turned to go home, utterly miserable. When would she see her dear husband again? And when would he come to his senses? Then she blinked, and stared. She knew her husband was *inside* the abbey. And yet – here he was, walking towards her, with Dromio by his side. She nudged Luciana, standing beside her. Was she seeing things? Could Luciana see them too?

Adriana wasn't the only person gazing in amazement at the two men. Walking behind them was an old man, with a look of wild delight on his face. It was Antipholus's father, Egeon – who had been following Antipholus and Dromio down the street. "Unless I have gone mad," he thought, "I can see my son and Dromio!" He was so happy he couldn't believe his eyes, and didn't dare speak to them, in case he was dreaming and speaking would wake him up…

Behind Egeon, another man was walking along the street. It was the Duke of Ephesus. Spotting the duke across the square, Antipholus of Ephesus stormed up to him. "You must punish my wife," he said. "She locked me out of my own house today."

"That's not true!" Adriana protested.

Adriana, Luciana, Antipholus and Dromio all started hurling accusations at each other. The duke listened to them all, increasingly under the suspicion that they must all be insane.

Finally, Egeon stepped forward. "You are Antipholus," the old man said, beaming with joy, "and that fellow is your servant Dromio. I know you well."

"Sir," Antipholus replied gravely, "I've never seen you before."

Egeon felt his son's words as if they were knives. "Grief has changed me since you saw me last," he said, "but tell me, don't you recognize my voice?"

"Not in the slightest," the bewildered Antipholus replied.

Egeon turned desperately to Dromio. "Dromio, don't you know me either?"

Dromio shook his head.

"Tell me you are my son, Antipholus," Egeon begged. "Seven years ago, you set out from Syracuse, to find your brother…"

"Syracuse!" Antipholus replied. "But I've never been there in my life!"

Poor Egeon. How could his son have forgotten everything about his former life? Egeon thought that losing half of his family was the greatest pain he would ever bear. But his own son denying his existence was far worse.

His thoughts were interrupted by Adriana, who let out an enormous shriek. The other Antipholus had just run out of the abbey, with Dromio beside him. They had stopped in their tracks each facing their twin brother. At last, the twins were all together — standing opposite each other like mirror images. They stared at one another, speechless in horror and disbelief.

"Unless my eyes deceive me, I see two husbands," Adriana said, staring from one Antipholus to the other.

"Which is the real man, and which is the phantom?" whispered Luciana. Then her eyes opened even wider as she realized there were two Dromios too.

The Dromios gawped at each other; shrieked; and then shouted in perfect unison: "I'm the real Dromio!"

They pointed at each other. "Send that one away!" they chorussed desperately.

Then Dromio of Syracuse's face lit up as he caught sight of Egeon. "My old master!" he cried.

But Egeon wasn't looking at Dromio. He was looking intently at the abbess, standing by the door to the abbey. It couldn't possibly be true. And yet… "Aemilia?" he said. She started at the sound of his voice. Then, very slowly, she walked up to him and looked deep into his eyes.

"Speak, Egeon, if you are the man who once married Aemilia, and had two fair sons. Speak to the same Aemilia!" she said.

"If I'm not dreaming, you are Aemilia," Egeon replied. "If you are, where is the son who floated away with you that fatal day?"

"That day," Aemelia said, "some fishermen rescued me. But I was separated from my dear son, Antipholus, and from the other baby, Dromio. Since that day, I have never seen them…"

Aemelia and Egeon fell into each other's arms. It had been more than thirty years since they had parted. They held each other tight, tears of pure joy streaming down their cheeks.

The two Antipholuses, meanwhile, stared at one another, amazed. After all this time, they had finally found each other. In one moment, each had found a brother, a father and a mother.

The two brothers embraced, and joined their mother and father in a tearful reunion.

Adriana examined Antipholus of Syracuse from all sides. "So…" she said finally, "you are not my husband?"

"No," said Antipholus simply. Now he turned to Luciana. "You called me brother," he said. "But it was not true. And what I said to you before – I hope to make it good."

He got down on his knees before her. "If this is not a dream… will you be my wife?"

Luciana gasped, then beamed. "Yes," she squealed with joy.

"For thirty-three years, my family was lost," Aemilia announced. "Today, I have found them all again. All of you, please come into the abbey. After so many years of grief, at last it's time for a feast!"

So they all went inside, even the duke, who had never witnessed anything so strange in all his time in Ephesus.

The two Dromios were the last to follow. In the almost empty street, they stood looking shyly at one another, and then slowly, very slowly, shuffled closer and closer together.

"I think you are a mirror, not a brother," said Dromio of Syracuse, when he plucked up the courage.

Dromio of Ephesus grinned. "Looking at you… I can see that I'm a handsome young man!"

"Shall we go inside then?" said Dromio of Ephesus.

"After you," said Dromio of Syracuse. "You're the older brother."

"Am I?" replied Dromio. "How can we decide?"

The two brothers both frowned.

"We could… toss a coin?" suggested Dromio of Syracuse.

"No," said his twin. "We came into the world as brother and brother. Let's go in hand in hand, not one before the other."

And so, hand in hand, they went inside to join the feast. They had a lot of catching up to do.

" *We came into the world like brother and brother;*
And now let's go hand in hand, not one before another. "

Dromio of Ephesus
Act 5, Scene 1

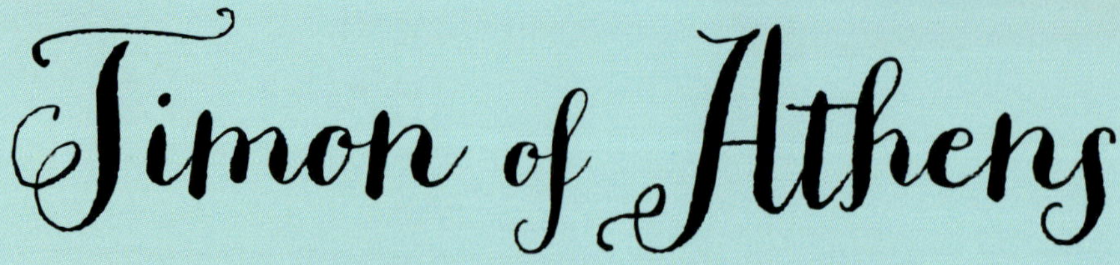

Timon of Athens

In all of Athens, there's no one more lavish
and generous than Lord Timon. Poets, painters and
jewellers flock to his house, and friends gather at his
table to receive his gifts. But what would happen if
Timon finally ran out of money?

Timon

A wealthy and generous Athenian
lord; a patron of the arts, who
showers his friends with riches.

Flavius

Timon's loyal steward, who
oversees his accounts, and
whose warnings go unheeded…

Ventidius

An Athenian lord put in
prison for debt. He appeals
to Timon for help.

Lucullus, Sempronius & Lucius

Timon's friends, always present
at his feasts, and first in line
to partake of his generosity.

Apemantus

A churlish and grumpy philosopher whose insults hold more than a grain of truth.

The Athenian Senators

These men rely on Timon to fund the city, and on Alcibiades to defend it. Their selfishness could put Athens in danger.

Alcibiades

A captain of the Athenian army. He has the power to defend or destroy the city if he so chooses.

The Creditors

These men are always happy to lend Timon more money – but some day they will want it back.

I N ANCIENT ATHENS, NO LORD OR NOBLEMAN was more generous than Timon. This kind-hearted soul owned lands that stretched all the way to the sparkling sea, and he used his vast wealth to entertain well-wishers in the banquet halls of his grand mansion house. Athenians from every walk of life flocked to Timon's parties, greedy for his fabulous gifts.

It was early evening, and guests were gathering in preparation for another of Timon's feasts, when an urgent messenger arrived. His master, a nobleman called Ventidius, had been imprisoned for not paying his debts.

"He begs your help, my lord," the messenger told Timon.

"Do not worry," Timon said warmly. "I am not the kind of man to shake off my friend when he most needs me. I will send money for his release right away."

"He will never forget your kindness, my lord," replied the messenger, before dashing away with the news.

The next moment, a crowd of men clustered around Timon. They were poets and painters, merchants and lords. Each greeted Timon with flattering words and broad smiles, hoping their host would press a gold coin into their outstretched hands.

"Get away, knaves," cried the philosopher Apemantus, shoving his way through the throng. Apemantus was one of Timon's regular visitors, known for his common sense and sharp tongue.

"Be calm, Apemantus," Timon protested, "you are too sour. Why do you call these good people knaves?"

"Are they from Athens?" Apemantus asked.

"Of course they are," Timon replied.

"Then my point is proved. If I could find an honest man in this city I'd knock his brains out," Apemantus growled.

"Our senators uphold the law here," Timon warned him. "They would hang you."

"But there are no honest men left for me to batter," Apemantus joked, "so I am safe."

A trumpet fanfare sounded from the stables and one of Timon's servants hurried to his master. "My lord," he panted, "your old friend, Commander Alcibiades, has arrived with twenty riders."

"Feed and entertain them all," replied Timon. "And bring more wine from our stores; we'll feast long into the night."

A man in a fine leather uniform entered the courtyard. He carried a battle helmet, streaked with dust from his long ride.

"Timon, you are a sight for my sore eyes," said Alcibiades. "Is there room at your table for a weary soldier?"

"Always," Timon replied, and he led his guests into the house.

Apemantus scowled as he watched them go. "All this courtesy and friendship," he grumbled, "and from such a pack of wolves. It's a good job I accept none of Timon's gifts, or there'd be nobody left in Athens to call him a generous fool."

Inside the hall, every table groaned under piles of roast meat, jugs of wine and platters of sumptuous treats. Timon moved about the room, followed by his chief steward, Flavius, who carried an open casket of jewels.

"My faithful friends," said Timon, stopping at a table where three men in rich robes were seated. "Lucullus," Timon continued, "my servants tell me you have offered to take me hunting. I accept, and in return for your kind invitation let me give you a gemstone ring for your finger. And you, Lucius, I overheard you admiring my white stallion earlier this evening. He is yours. As for you, Sempronius, I am grateful for all your advice on finances and loans. Please select any gem you desire from my coffers."

The three lords clustered around Timon, singing his praises and shaking his hand in thanks. When they had returned to their seats, Timon stepped towards another table, but Flavius touched his master gently on the arm, causing him to halt. "My lord," whispered Flavius, "I must speak with you."

"Is it urgent?" asked Timon.

"Very urgent, my lord. It's about your finances."

"This is no time for personal business," laughed Timon, "not when I am entertaining. It can wait for tomorrow. Now leave me."

"I bleed inwardly for him," thought Flavius, as Timon strolled away. "Every word and promise he speaks tonight binds him ever deeper in debt."

At dawn the following day, Lord Timon set out on the hunt, leaving Flavius fretting in the marble halls of the mansion. Flavius was a good and loyal servant. For many months, he had been trying to warn his master that he must spend less. Timon's tireless extravagance had cost him his fortune. All his lands were sold or promised to moneylenders. His chests of silver and gold were stripped bare, and every shelf and storeroom in his enormous house had been plundered to feed his insatiable guests. So Flavius was not surprised to see a noisy mob of people waving letters and bills gather at the main gate. At long last, Timon's creditors had sent their servants to call in their debts.

Flavius almost sobbed when, a few hours later, his master rode up to the gate. "What is your business here?" Timon shouted into the crowd. "You are blocking my way."

"I have overdue payments to settle," replied a man. "My master cannot wait; he wants his money today."

"Go to my steward," snapped Timon, spurring his horse into the courtyard. "Flavius," he called, as he swung down from his mount, "what's so wrong with this world that I am met by a riot outside my home?”

Flavius ran to the courtyard and quickly ushered the men towards another part of the grounds. “This is not the right time,” he explained, “just give me a chance to explain everything to my master.”

Inside his house, Timon was looking through the ransacked chests and sacks that had once bulged with riches. At last, he understood that his wealth was gone. “Am I poor?” he cried, as Flavius entered. “If you had only told me, I would have spent no more than what I owned, and been less reckless with my gifts.”

“I did try to tell you, my lord,” answered Flavius gently. “You would not hear me.”

“How bad is it?” Timon despaired. “Must I sell my lands to clear my debts?”

“Your estates are already promised to your creditors. What remains is less than half of what you owe.”

“All’s not lost, Flavius,” said Timon, recovering his hopes. “I am still wealthy in friendship. And it is time to test their good hearts. Send out my servants to Lucullus and Lucius, to Sempronius too. Before this day is over, you’ll see carts of gold coins arrive from these good men.”

Flavius was close to tears as he spoke: “My lord, forgive me. I have already done as you command. The moment I saw that crowd at the gates, I ordered messengers to all parts of the town. They have returned from your friends empty-handed.”

“They offer nothing?” Timon said incredulously.

“Not a penny, my lord,” answered Flavius. “They say the timing is unfortunate; they say you have only yourself to blame and that you shame them by asking for money.”

“Those ungrateful rascals,” snapped Timon. “At least I can rely on Ventidius. Go and remind him how I saved him from prison.”

“His answer was the same,” Flavius said quietly. “Nobody will help, not even Ventidius. Commander Alcibiades might have stood by you – but he has been banished from the city."

"For what crime?" Timon demanded.

"He quarrelled with the senators. They sentenced one of his soldiers to death, and refused all mercy – despite Alcibiades's pleas and despite his long and faithful service. They killed the soldier and banished Alcibiades. He can't help you now, and your other true friend, Apemantus, lives a modest life and has no money."

"I gave them everything," Timon groaned. How could his friends have been so false? "I sacrificed my wealth by spoiling them and they have abandoned me. Well, Flavius, we shall give them one last feast."

"My lord," cried Flavius, "there is nothing left, no food or wine. What will we give these jackals?"

Timon gave him a bitter grin. "Leave that to me," he said. "Go, invite them all, let in the tide of knaves once more."

That evening, Timon's courtyard was bustling with the same lords and merchants who had betrayed his friendship. Lucullus, Sempronius and Lucius chatted in the warm night air.

"It was a jest," laughed Lucius. "As soon as I heard about tonight's party, I knew his bankruptcy must be a joke."

"Of course," nodded Sempronius. "Timon's got more money than all of us, stashed away somewhere."

"Enter, my friends," called Timon, appearing at the doorway to his house. "Your feast is ready."

The lords filed into the banquet hall and stood gaping at the rows of covered food platters. "So many dishes," hissed Lucullus greedily. "This spread is going to be better than ever."

"Come, gather around me," said Timon, beckoning to his

guests. "You are welcome to this feast, and each of you has earned a taste of it. So uncover the plates, you dogs, and *lap it up!*"

Timon snatched a lid away, revealing a platter underneath filled with rocks and steaming water. "You reeking villains," he bellowed, "detestable parasites and smiling wolves, come and get a plateful."

Timon began to hurl the hot stones at his guests, who screamed and ran in panic. "Don't leave without your desert," Timon yelled, launching more missiles into the throng.

"Lord Timon's gone mad," shouted Sempronius, rushing from the house. "One day he gives us diamonds, and the next day stones. Call the city guards to protect us. Save us all!"

Timon's creditors showed no mercy. Within hours they had boarded up his house, seized his last possessions and turned their backs forever on their old friend. Destitute and mad with rage, Timon stormed away from the city, cursing the ingratitude and corruption of every man, woman and child in the world. "Your friendship was poison," he hissed at the high walls and watchtowers of Athens. "From now on, I'll live with the beasts in the woods and cut all ties with humankind. A pox on you all!"

Wearing only a rough blanket against the rain and cold, Timon lost himself in a wild forest. He set up home in a cave, scratching in the earth for bulbs and roots to eat.

But money, the root of evil, would not leave Timon at peace in his wilderness den. One morning, as he was digging close to the entrance of his cave, Timon uncovered a nugget of gold, glimmering in the dirt. He pushed more earth away and saw a great seam of gold buried around his camp. "What is this, gods?" he cried. "I prayed for roots for my breakfast and you give me the yellow slave, stuff that tempts all men and makes them monsters. I'll cover it up again."

As Timon buried the gleaming gold, he heard the roll of

a drum in the woods. A few moments later, the banished warrior Alcibiades emerged from the trees, dressed for war in his gleaming armour. The Athenian captain stared at the grimy creature scrabbling in the shadow of the rocks before him. "Who is that?" he asked. "Who is it that lives in this cave?"

Timon looked up, but seemed not to recognize his old friend. He scowled. "A beast lives here," he said, "a beast like yourself."

"Is that you, Timon?" asked Alcibiades, coming closer. "How did the noble Timon come to this change?" Timon looked so dishevelled and forlorn that his heart wrenched with sorrow. But his sorrow soon turned to anger. "Those wicked Athenians did this to you, didn't they?" he said, "They forgot your good deeds to their city. But I am your friend. I pity you."

Timon gave a bitter laugh. "You say you pity me," he said, "and yet you cause me pain just by standing there, by forcing me to look at another human being. I never wish to see another man again. They can't be trusted."

Alcibiades reached into his purse. "Take a little gold," he said softly. "Buy yourself some food and clothes. I can't give you much though – my army is waiting at the gates of Athens, and it costs me all I have to feed and arm them."

Timon waved his offering away. "Do you mean to attack the city?" he asked with interest.

"I will conquer it," Alcibiades promised. "And punish the wretches that banished us both."

"I like the sound of this," Timon said fervently. "And I have gold to help you. Use it to pay your soldiers, and command them to cut down every man, woman and child in Athens. Don't let your swords miss a single one."

Dropping to his knees, Timon pushed the dirt away and gathered up great handfuls of gold. He handed them to Alcibiades, who stared at the treasure in amazement.

"I'll gladly take your gold," Alcibiades said, "but not your advice. When I do take the city I shall rule it fairly."

Timon's expression soured. "Do as you wish," he snarled, "but get out of my sight. Here, take more gold. Use it to damn others, then let it damn you, too. I hope you die in a ditch. I have finished with human beings. I hate them all."

"I never did you harm, my friend," Alcibiades said mildly, "but I'll leave you be. I must return to my army and prepare for war."

Timon had many visitors over the following days. Some came out of greed, after hearing tales of his gold. When a gang of thieves visited, Timon loaded them with nuggets and urged them to keep on robbing and stealing. "This whole world is a crime," he laughed. "After all, even the Moon's a shameless thief: she steals her glow from the Sun."

Other men came to beg for Timon's help. The Athenian senators came, and pleaded with him to persuade Alcibiades not to attack their city. "Let Alcibiades be a plague on you," Timon shouted at them. "I don't care. I'll soon be free of this world."

Others came out of loyalty or friendship. Apemantus, the prickly old philosopher, had long warned Timon about men's ingratitude – but now he visited Timon's cave to reason with him.

"What do you hope to gain," he chided, "by living like a slave in the woods? Your hatred of men isn't even a proper philosophy. It's just a result of your grief and your bad fortune. Come back to Athens, and take a hint from all those rogues who sucked you dry: become a flatterer, and thrive again like those who ruined you."

Timon's eyes flashed with rage. "You threadbare thinker," he snarled, "what do you know about it? You were born as poor as a dog, and bred to suffer. No man has ever flattered you. You have never felt the tender clasp of Fortune's arm, and can't imagine what it's like to lose as I have lost. The world was mine. But now I'm like an ailing oak: the winter's blast has stripped me of my every leaf, and left me open, bare to every storm that blows."

"You sad, proud man," Apemantus replied, "you've only had the best and worst of human life. You've never known the middle of humanity."

"You tedious rogue," Timon exclaimed. "I *curse* humanity. I wish that you were clean enough to spit upon."

"You're too bad even for curses," Apemantus replied angrily, and he turned to make his way back to Athens.

Timon shied a rock at the philosopher's back. "I am sick of this false world," he said. "I'll go and prepare my grave, out near the sea, where salty foam can beat upon my gravestone."

But Timon had still one more visitor to come: his faithful steward, Flavius. Flavius greeted Timon with tears in his eyes. "Can this be my old, dearest master?" he wondered.

"Well, what if it is?" grumbled Timon.

"I beg you, my lord, accept my grief," Flavius replied. He kneeled in the dirt beside Timon, and held out a small purse of copper coins. "Please, while my poor wealth lasts, employ me as your steward once again, and let me comfort you as best I can."

Despite his bitterness and fury at mankind, this small act of kindness seemed to move Timon. For a moment he softened, the wall of anger letting in a chink of light. "Did I have a steward once," Timon said softly, "so true and just? Yes, I remember, you never took advantage of my bounty. So I proclaim there *is* one honest man. But don't mistake me – *only one*."

Timon showed Flavius the last heap of gold from the cave. "Here, take, take," he insisted. Timon pressed the heavy nuggets into Flavius's hands – but as he did so, the sight and touch of gold seemed to spark his rage again, and it consumed him once more. "You single honest man, you may live rich and happy, as I once did. But on this condition: you must hate all; curse all; show charity to none. Let the famished flesh slide off a beggar's bones before you would share a morsel with him."

 Flavius opened his fingers and let the gold trickle through them to the ground. His master was too embittered to listen to reason or to be comforted. Flavius rose and left him.

Timon's heart and mind had been broken by the cruelty of false friends. Death was his only ambition.

In Athens, war had broken out. Alcibiades and his army surrounded the city and, threatened with destruction, the Athenian senators were forced to surrender. Alcibiades was true to his word. He spared the Athenian people, and ruled according to the city's laws. When order was restored, Alcibiades sent a patrol to search for Timon and return him to his home in the city.

The soldiers found Timon's cave empty, and the seam of gold exhausted. They fanned out through the forest, calling Timon's name. At last, climbing the headland overlooking the sea, they discovered Timon's body lying in a shallow grave, cold and still beneath the dew. At his head stood a rough slab of stone, where Timon had carved for all to see a few, last, bitter words:

TIMON, ACT 5, SCENE 4

Richard III

The youngest brother of King Edward IV, Richard is driven by bitter hatred and dark ambition. He'll stop at nothing to seize the throne, even if it means killing those closest to him…

Richard

Duke of Gloucester, from the house of York. Born with a hunched back and withered arm. Fools people with his clever way with words.

Queen Margaret

Widow of King Henry VI, from the overthrown house of Lancaster. She curses the house of York, Richard's entire family.

Lady Anne

A widowed Lancaster, lured by Richard into becoming his bride.

Lord Buckingham

Richard's power-hungry follower, who helps him take the crown.

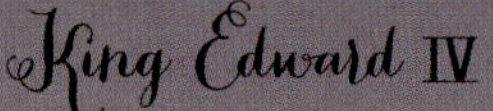

King Edward IV

Richard's eldest brother, from the house of York. The King of England when the story begins.

Duke of Clarence

George, Richard and Edward's middle brother.

Prince Edward

Next in line to the throne, Edward, Prince of Wales, has been living under protection in Wales.

Duke of York

The youngest prince. Lives with his parents, the king and queen.

Queen Elizabeth

Strong-willed wife of King Edward IV, but powerless to protect her sons.

Duchess of York

The king's mother is disgusted by the ambitions of Richard, her youngest son.

Earl of Richmond

A Lancaster and rival to the throne, he gathers troops overseas to challenge Richard.

Lord Hastings

Proud and rather too trusting, but a loyal follower of Edward IV and his sons.

Lord Rivers

The brother of Queen Elizabeth, and her greatest ally. He keeps a protective eye on Prince Edward in Wales.

AFTER A SERIES OF LONG, BITTER WARS between two branches of the English royal family, the house of York and the house of Lancaster, a resolution had finally been reached. Henry VI, of the Lancasters, had been overthrown and killed, and Edward IV, of the Yorks, had been crowned King of England. But, although the wars were over, many people were still unhappy – in particular, Richard, Edward IV's youngest brother.

"Now the bitterest winter of our discontent has been made into a glorious summer by my brother, the new king," Richard thought, mulling over the happiness that his family's victory seemed to have brought. As he limped down a street in London, he caught his reflection in a window and glared back at himself angrily. "Deformed and unfinished!" he spat. "Since I cannot be anyone's lover, I am determined to become a villain."

Richard, who had been born with a hunched back and a withered arm, was eaten up by anger and bitterness. He felt like an outsider in his own family, and while they were busy celebrating their victory, he had started making plans to stir up trouble…

He fell quiet when he saw his brother George, the Duke of Clarence, walking towards him, surrounded by guards. "Why are you waited upon by armed guards?" Richard asked innocently. Despite his expression of concern, he knew full well why Clarence was being captured, for he had devised the plot himself…

"King Edward, our brother, has ordered them to lock me in the

RICHARD, ACT 1, SCENE 1

Tower of London, where I will await execution," Clarence replied, his face full of despair. "He's been told a prophecy that states that 'G' will murder his children, the heirs to the throne. Because my name, George, begins with 'G', he thinks it's me!"

Richard looked horrified. "We are not safe, Clarence!" he gasped, reaching out to squeeze his brother's arm. "You won't be imprisoned for long – I'll make sure of it."

Clarence moaned pitifully. "Farewell, dear brother," he replied, before a guard pushed him onwards down the street.

"Stupid Clarence," Richard sneered to himself, watching them go. He had invented the prophecy himself to set his brothers against one another. "The king is ill, and will die soon. I'll have Clarence finished off in the Tower, and then I will begin my ascent to the throne," he thought with great satisfaction.

He decided to address the next part of his plan – to win himself a bride. A wife with royal connections of her own would help his rise to power, and he knew just the woman. He limped off towards Westminster Abbey.

Inside, there was a sombre scene. In the gloom of candlelight lay the coffin of the late King Henry VI, draped in cloth. Before it stood Lady Anne – Edward of Lancaster's widow, and the daughter-in-law of the late king.

"What black magician conjured you up, fiend?" Anne recoiled as she felt Richard's warm breath on her neck. She despised him – if it wasn't for him, her husband, Edward of Lancaster, would still be alive. It was a well-known fact that Richard had slaughtered him on the battlefield just a few months ago.

Richard sighed. "Sweet saint, I pray, do not curse me! Divine, perfect woman, give me a chance to explain myself."

"You can make no excuse now except to hang yourself," Anne replied, her voice full of scorn.

"I did not kill your husband," Richard declared.

"You are lying," said Anne, narrowing her eyes.

Richard moved in closer, ignoring Anne's shudder. "Well then, your beauty made me do it," he whispered, brushing a strand of hair out of her eyes. "Your beauty haunted me in my sleep. I would have killed all the world to have but one hour with you."

Try as she might, Anne could not tear her eyes away from his.

Richard fell to his knees. "If your vengeful heart cannot forgive me, I humbly beg for death," he declared. He drew his dagger and handed it to Anne.

With a shaking hand, Anne took the dagger by the hilt. Clenching her teeth, she willed herself to drive it into his chest. But she could not do it. The dagger dropped to the floor with a clatter. "Though I wish you dead, I will not be your executioner," she whispered weakly.

"Tell me to kill myself and I will!" Richard pleaded, seizing the dagger and pointing it to his own chest.

Anne looked at him numbly and shook her head. "I wish I knew your heart," she said. Was Richard the devil who killed her husband or not? He seemed now, on his knees, more like a pitiable cripple, filled with remorse and begging for her love.

Still holding her gaze, Richard reached into his pocket and pulled out a ring. "Please, take this," he wheedled, slipping it onto her finger. "Promise you will marry me," he whispered. "Let me live in hope...?"

"It's more than you deserve," Anne said, bewildered. She was not sure what to think, but she had no strength left to refuse him.

Richard knew he had won her. A cruel smile spread across his face as he watched her leave. "I'll have her, but I won't bother to keep her for long," he thought.

In the Palace of Westminister, Queen Elizabeth was talking anxiously with her brother, Lord Rivers, and their close friend,

Lord Hastings. Upstairs, her husband, King Edward IV, lay gravely ill in bed.

"What if the king dies?" Elizabeth looked to her brother.

"God has blessed you with two sons," Rivers soothed.

"But Prince Edward is young," Elizabeth replied. "If the king dies, Richard will become Lord Protector until Edward is old enough to take the throne." She dreaded to think what Richard would do if he was given a position of power.

There was a knock at the door, and Richard himself came in, followed by his loyal follower, Lord Buckingham. "You've done me wrong, and I will not take it," Richard said, glaring at Elizabeth. "Why have you complained to the king about me?"

"You are jealous of my position," Elizabeth retorted. "God grant that you never become Lord Protector."

"What!" Richard glowered. "I've shed my own blood to help your husband become the king!"

As the argument continued, Margaret, the late King Henry's widow, slipped unseen into the room. As one of the last remaining Lancasters, Margaret hated the Yorks for killing her husband and her son, Edward. "Hear me, you wrangling pirates!" she croaked, stepping out to stand before them.

Richard started in surprise. "Foul, wrinkled witch, why are you here?" he snarled.

Margaret's eyes flashed with anger. "You owe me a husband and a son," she hissed. "And you," she continued, pointing at Elizabeth, "a kingdom! Give way, dull clouds, to my quick curses!" As she spoke, the lamps flickered and the room grew dark.

Margaret prowled around Elizabeth like a hungry shadow. "May your son, Prince Edward, die young and violently, just as my son, Edward of Lancaster, did," she said. "May you die neither a mother, wife, nor England's queen!"

Then she turned to Lord Rivers and Lord Hastings. "Rivers,

Hastings, may you die unnatural deaths," she said.

"Finish your charms, you withered hag," Richard spat.

"And leave you out?" Margaret howled, spinning around to face him. "Stay, dog, for you shall hear me. May you never sleep, unless tormented by frightening dreams. You rooting hog… You son of Hell… You insult to your mother's womb!"

"Please, Margaret," Elizabeth said faintly.

"The day will come that you shall wish for me to help you curse this poisonous hunch-backed toad," Margaret retorted.

"That's enough!" Buckingham insisted.

"Buckingham, take heed of this dog," Margaret screeched, pointing at Richard. "When he flatters you, he's about to bite. And his poisonous bite will kill." Then she turned to the others a final time. "When Richard breaks your hearts with sorrow, say, 'Poor Margaret was a prophetess'."

Elizabeth shuddered as Margaret swept out of the room. "Let us go to His Majesty," she said.

As the others followed Elizabeth out, Richard hung back. "I must hurry and send a death warrant to have Clarence killed," he thought, pushing Margaret's words to the back of his mind. "Otherwise the king may change his mind and have him released."

Inside the Tower of London, Clarence lay in darkness waiting to hear his fate. At the sound of footsteps coming into the room, he sat up with a start and rubbed his eyes. "I have passed a miserable night," he moaned. "I dreamed I was on a ship with my brother Richard. He threw me overboard into the waves and I drowned."

As his eyes focused, Clarence could just make out the shape of two men looming over his bed.

"…take heed of yonder dog!
Look when he fawns, he bites…"

"In God's name, who are you?" Clarence cried.

"Your murderers," came the reply.

"H-h-how have I offended you?" Clarence stuttered.

"You've offended the king," said one of the men, lighting a lamp to reveal his ugly face.

Clarence whimpered. "I am the king's brother, and I love him," he pleaded. "If you're doing this for money, go to my brother Richard, who will reward you more for saving my life."

The two men laughed. "Richard was the one who sent us!"

The guards dragged Clarence out of bed. Within minutes he was dead, drowned in a barrel of wine.

"Clarence is dead?" The colour drained from the king's face as Richard told him the news. "But I sent an order to pardon him!"

Richard had been right – the king had sent a letter of forgiveness to the Tower, but Richard's men had got there first.

"He died, poor, dear man, by your first order," Richard replied, his face the picture of sorrow.

The king buried his head in his hands. "Oh, God, I fear justice will take hold on me," he wailed. "Poor Clarence!"

As the sickly king was helped back to his bed, Richard turned to the court. "This is what happens when reckless decisions are made," he said, solemnly.

The next evening, King Edward's mother, the Duchess of York, was dining with Lord Rivers in the banqueting hall. Suddenly the door was flung open, and Queen Elizabeth burst in. "Edward, my husband… your son… our king, is dead!" she wailed.

The duchess clutched her chest in pain. "There was never a mother that had so much loss," she cried.

"And now Richard is Lord Protector, and has been given guardianship of my two sons!" Elizabeth moaned.

Rivers stood up quickly. "Madam, send for your son, Prince Edward, in Wales. Let him be crowned immediately," he advised.

At that moment, a cough came from behind them – it was Richard, with Lord Buckingham at his side. "Sister, have comfort," Richard said. But his words sounded hollow and empty.

"I think a few courtiers should collect Prince Edward from Wales," Buckingham said smoothly, looking at Elizabeth.

Elizabeth nodded and turned to arrange it with Lord Rivers. With their backs turned, Buckingham leaned in to speak to Richard. "Let us be part of the party to collect Prince Edward. Along the way I'll separate him, and we'll send him to the Tower."

Richard's eyes glinted. "My other self, my most trusted advisor!" he whispered approvingly. "Towards Wales we'll go."

All was quiet in the palace, as Elizabeth and the duchess waited anxiously for Prince Edward's arrival. Unaware of the drama unfolding around him, the youngest prince, the Duke of York, sat at his mother's feet in front of the fire, playing with his toys.

Finally, a messenger arrived at the door, and Elizabeth jumped up. "How is my son, Prince Edward?" she asked eagerly.

"Well, madam, and in health," the messenger replied. "He is on the road to London with Richard. But I have the most distressing news…" He hesitated, biting his lip. "Your brother, Lord Rivers, who accompanied Richard and Lord Buckingham to Wales, has been taken prisoner and is waiting to be executed."

Horror filled Elizabeth's face. "Who ordered this?"

"Richard," came the reply.

Elizabeth crumpled into her chair. It was as she had feared – with the king dead, Richard was using his power as Lord Protector against her and her family. "Come, we will take sanctuary in Westminster Abbey," she said, nodding to the duchess who had taken the Duke of York's hand. "We are not safe here."

Trumpets sounded across the palace to announce Prince Edward's arrival from Wales. A group of courtiers and officials gathered in the courtyard to welcome him.

"God bless your grace with health and happy days," the Lord Mayor of London cried, kneeling at the young prince's feet.

Prince Edward smiled. "Where is my mother?" he asked.

Lord Hastings stepped forward. "I do not know why, but the queen and your brother have taken refuge in Westminster Abbey." His face was full of concern. "May I suggest…"

Before he could continue, Richard jumped in. "My lord," he said, wrapping an arm around his nephew and smiling pleasantly. "If I may suggest, spend a day or two at the Tower, where you will be safe before your coronation. Buckingham and I will tell your mother and brother to meet you there and welcome you."

The young prince nodded uncertainly as Richard's grip tightened. He looked up, but his uncle was still smiling widely.

"Seize the Duke of York from the abbey," Richard whispered to Buckingham, as he ushered Prince Edward into the hands of a guard. "Have him sent to the Tower, along with his brother."

Buckingham nodded. His eyes were on Lord Hastings, who was fussing around the young prince. "Do you think Lord Hastings will agree to help us put you on the throne?" he whispered.

"He loves the princes, and I doubt he will go against them," Richard replied quietly.

"Then what shall we do?" Buckingham asked.

"We'll chop off his head," Richard said, looking at Buckingham steadily. "Oh, and Buckingham? When I'm king, claim from me the earldom of Hereford, and all its possessions."

Buckingham's eyes lit up. "Of course," he replied.

The next day, a group of lords sat around a table for the first of Richard's council meetings. Richard had not yet arrived.

"Noble friends, we are meeting to discuss the prince's coronation," Lord Hastings announced. "When is the royal day?"

As the lords began to speak, Richard entered the room. "Good day, my noble lords," He smiled. "Buckingham, a word."

Buckingham stood up and followed Richard out into the hall.

"Did you find out about Hastings?" Richard whispered.

Buckingham nodded. "I visited him last night, and suggested that you should take the throne. He said he would rather lose his head than give consent to it."

"As I thought," Richard growled. "Watch how I make an example of him." Scowling, he stormed back into the room.

"Tell me, Hastings, how do you think a person should be punished for conspiring against me?" Richard said, quietly.

"I say they deserve death," Hastings frowned.

"Then see this – I have been bewitched!" Richard exclaimed, holding out his withered arm. He glared at Hastings. "You had your mistress do this to me – it is the work of witchcraft!"

Hastings took in a sharp breath. Everybody knew that Richard had been deformed since birth – it was not the work of witchcraft. "If she has done this deed…" he started.

"If? Talk you to me of 'ifs'? Traitor! Off with his head!" Richard bellowed.

The other lords watched helplessly as guards surrounded Hastings, and marched him away to his death.

With the princes locked in the Tower, and the late king's most loyal followers dead, the only person that stood between Richard and the throne was the Lord Mayor of London. With this in mind, Richard summoned Buckingham to his side.

"Go to the Lord Mayor and convince him that my brother Edward should never have been king," Richard demanded. "Tell him that our mother was having an affair when she fell pregnant with him. Convince him that the young princes are not true heirs to the throne. Use all your powers of persuasion."

Buckingham nodded. "I will do my best."

A few hours passed, and Richard waited impatiently for Buckingham's return. Finally, the was a knock at the door.

"He is on his way," Buckingham said, hurrying in. "Quick – try to look as godly as possible."

Richard grabbed a prayerbook and pretended to study it.

"Welcome," Buckingham crooned, as the Lord Mayor was shown in. "But I fear we will not be able to persuade Richard to become king."

"It is his duty to the people of London," the mayor replied. "It is only right, since the princes are not true heirs to the throne!"

Richard looked up from his prayerbook innocently. "Greetings, Lord Mayor, Lord Buckingham."

Buckingham bowed solemnly. "My lord, we ask if you will take on the charge of this land – not as protector, but as king."

Richard sighed. "Your love deserves my thanks. But I am not worthy enough to carry out your high request."

The mayor clasped his hands together, impressed by Richard's humility. "Your citizens need you," he implored.

Richard shut the prayerbook, and paused for a moment. "Since you request it, Lord Mayor, I suppose I must bear this burden."

"God bless your grace!" the mayor beamed.

"Long live Richard, England's worthy king!" Buckingham cried, falling to his knees. "Tomorrow you shall be crowned."

The next morning, Richard arrived at Westminster Abbey with his new wife, Lady Anne. After a short coronation, Richard was crowned King of England, and Anne, his reluctant queen.

Wasting no time, Richard summoned Buckingham to his side.

"It is a bitter shame that Prince Edward still lives." Richard tapped his fingers together. "I wish him and his brother dead."

Buckingham drew a sharp breath – to kill the royal children was Richard's most chilling request yet.

"Will you take care of it?" Richard asked.

"Give me a chance to think, dear lord," Buckingham replied.

Sensing Buckingham's hesitation, Richard narrowed his eyes. "He grows too clever," he thought. "I must have him killed, too."

Buckingham tried to change the subject. "My lord, now you are king, will you grant me your promise for the earldom?"

Richard snorted. "I'm not in the giving mood today," he said.

As Buckingham slunk away, Richard was already calculating his next move. "I'll have the princes killed," he thought. "And Anne, too. She's no use to me now. I'll make it known she's taken ill…"

Within a matter of days, Richard's plans were carried out. First, one of Richard's henchmen smothered the two princes in the Tower and buried them in a secret location. Then, Queen Anne quietly lost her life – murdered by another of Richard's men.

Elizabeth and the Duchess of York were in despair at news of the princes' deaths. They had tried for days to visit them in the Tower, but had been refused by the guards again and again.

They held one another and wept at the children's terrible fate. "My poor princes! My tender babes!" Elizabeth sobbed.

A sound of trumpets blasted through the corridor – it was Richard, striding towards them with noblemen on either side.

Elizabeth flew at him in a terrible rage. "You slaughtered the prince that owned that crown!" Elizabeth cried, pointing at Richard's head. "Tell me, you villain, where are my children?"

"You toad, you toad, where is your brother Clarence?" the duchess joined in, clawing at Richard's robe.

"Where is gentle Rivers?" Elizabeth sobbed. "And Hastings?"

Richard tried to back away, but the duchess moved in closer.

"Bloody, you are, and you will come to a bloody end!" she howled.

"ENOUGH!" Richard roared, angrily pushing the duchess aside. Then, pausing to compose himself, he carefully readjusted his crown. "You have a daughter, young Elizabeth," he said, turning to Elizabeth. "She is virtuous and fair, royal and gracious."

Elizabeth froze, afraid to hear what was coming next.

"With my soul I love your daughter, and do intend to make her Queen of England," Richard went on smoothly. "England's peace depends on our alliance."

Elizabeth looked away in disgust. She could think of nothing worse than for her daughter to marry the murderer of her two sons. "I'll give you her answer shortly," she replied, avoiding his eyes.

Richard leaned over and planted a wet kiss on Elizabeth's cheek. "Bear her my true love's kiss," he said, smiling.

But as the king's power increased, so did his enemies. The Earl of Richmond, from the Lancaster family, had begun gathering troops in France to challenge Richard for the throne. Buckingham, too, had revolted – fleeing to Wales to raise an army of his own.

When news was brought to the palace that Richmond and his troops had crossed the border of Wales into England, Richard ordered his army to prepare for battle.

Dark clouds gathered in the sky as Richard's army marched north to meet Richmond's. Trudging forwards into rain, Richard's men were filled with an uneasy sense of gloom.

"We'll pitch our tents here, in Bosworth Field," Richard ordered, when they came to a muddy field near the city of Leicester. "Richmond's army is less than a day's march away. We'll go to battle tomorrow."

Just then, a messenger arrived on a horse, bringing news to the king. "Buckingham has been captured, my lord," the messenger said, breathlessly. "His army has been dispersed."

Richard smiled. "Well then, send orders to have him beheaded. Tell me, how many traitors are left?"

"Six or seven thousand," the messenger replied.

Richard laughed. "Why, we have triple that amount of men. Besides, the king's name is a tower of strength!"

As Richard's troops began setting up camp, news came that Richmond's army were nearby, pitching their tents on the other side of Bosworth Field.

Darkness fell, and all was quiet. Alone in his tent, Richard fell into a restless sleep. Tossing and turning, he began dreaming about the ghosts of his victims.

"Let me sit heavy on your soul tomorrow. Despair and die!" the ghost of his brother Clarence wailed.

"Your nephews' souls bid you to despair and die!" moaned the ghosts of the two young princes.

Richard woke up with a start, beads of sweat on his forehead. "Oh cowardly conscience, how you trouble me!" he groaned. He lay back down, but did not fall back to sleep.

As dawn broke, the sound of drums beat faintly in the distance. Richmond's army was on the move, ready to attack.

"Upon them! Victory sits on our helms!" Richard shouted, as his army readied itself for battle. Rearing back on his horse, he waved his sword high in the air. Then, with a deafening thunder of hooves, his men surged forwards in a wave of red, blue and gold.

Just then, the mist parted to reveal Richmond in the distance, galloping towards them. Hundreds of cavalry were charging in tight formation behind him.

Before Richard's troops could react, a volley of arrows whistled through the air, and howls of pain rang out across the battlefield. Then, with a clash of swords, the two sides met.

“Fight, gentlemen of England, fight!” Richard bellowed, as the battle began.

Richard’s men fought hard, but Richmond’s troops advanced quickly and broke through Richard’s front lines, scattering them in confusion. Richard called for reinforcements, but it soon became clear that he had lost control of his officers, many of whom had retreated in panic.

In the chaos, Richard’s horse reared suddenly. Taken off guard, he tumbled to the ground.

“A horse! A horse! My kingdom for a horse!” Richard cried. Clambering up, he looked around, but nobody came to his aid.

Then, as if from nowhere, Richmond appeared, towering over him. Richard scrabbled for his sword, but it was too late. Richmond bore down on him. His blade flashed as he swung it, and King Richard sank back into the mud. Finally, the battle was over.

The clouds parted, and sunlight flooded onto Bosworth Field. “The day is ours,” Richmond declared to his troops. “The bloody dog is dead.”

A roar of victory swept across the battlefield. Richmond kneeled, and Richard’s crown was placed upon his head. Richmond was the new king, to be known as King Henry VII. “And now let young Elizabeth and I, the true successors of each royal house, be married,” he declared. “Peace shall live again.”

With Richmond as the new king, and young Elizabeth as his queen, the Lancasters and the Yorks would be united. The war between the families was over, and England was finally at peace.

Troilus and Cressida

The Greeks and the Trojans have been at war for seven years now, and both sides are tired and jaded. But in the city of Troy, young Troilus has fallen in love and he's forgotten about everything except Cressida. However, it looks as if his romantic bubble is about to burst.

Paris & Helen

She's said to be the most beautiful woman in the world, and he's the Trojan prince who stole her from her Greek husband. Their affair sparked the Trojan War.

Achilles

A famous Greek hero and their greatest warrior. But has his pride gone to his head? He's spending more time in his tent than on the battlefield.

Patroclus

Achilles's close friend and confidant.

Ajax

A famous Greek warrior, but not as great as Achilles. He is easily led.

Agamemnon

King of the Greeks and leader of the Greek armies. His brother is Helen's husband. He's getting old, and is sick of the war.

Ulysses

The wisest and wiliest of the Greek commanders. He can persuade anyone to do anything.

Diomedes

A handsome young Greek soldier.

JN ANCIENT TIMES, A YOUNG TROJAN PRINCE named Paris stole a beautiful queen from the Greek city of Sparta. That queen was Helen, whose beauty was famous the world over. Hot with rage, her husband raised an army to win her back. A thousand white sails crowded onto the sea. They landed on the beaches of Troy, and Greek warriors poured out to surround the city, determined to release Helen from its walls.

The beginning of our story leaps over seven long years to the middle of this great battle. But what will we find here? Something good? Something bad? The fortunes of war are never certain…

Prince Troilus stumbled back inside the gates of Troy, tugging off his helmet. "I cannot go on fighting when my own heart is under siege," he sighed to his elderly friend, Pandarus. "I'm too lovesick to raise my sword. The moment I think of Cressida, I grow weak as water. I can think of nothing else."

"She is as fair as Helen," agreed Pandarus. He was Cressida's uncle and naturally thought very highly of her. "But do not ask me to plead your case with her any more. I've had no thanks for my efforts. Cressida should have gone with her father when he deserted us for the enemy."

"Don't say that!" Troilus cried. "You know how I love her."

"All too well," Pandarus grumbled, leaving Troilus alone with his thoughts and the distant sounds of swords and battle cries.

"The Greeks and Trojans bleed for Helen," Troilus thought, "but I've got another prize to fight for. And my only chance of winning it is this bad-tempered uncle…"

Out in the field, the Trojan trumpeters sounded another charge.

"Hush," Troilus sighed, heaving his armour back on. "I hear you, and I'll do my duty. I'm coming."

That evening, Pandarus puffed his way up the stairs to Lady Cressida's rooftop garden. Despite all his complaints, he would once again try to play the matchmaker. He was greeting his niece when they were interrupted by a crowd, cheering in the streets below. "What are the people cheering for?" Cressida wondered.

"Hector, our champion, has come home from battle," a servant reported. "They say he fought like a lion today."

"Oh, him," said Pandarus. "Yes, he's brave." Then he added slyly, "but Troilus is braver, wittier *and* prettier. I've even heard Helen say so."

"Then perhaps Troilus should chase after Helen?" Cressida suggested, a smile playing on her lips.

"It's not Helen he loves," her uncle replied. "Look, our soldiers are returning. There's Aeneas, Antenor, Paris and Helenus. But the bravest of them all is Troilus, a real prince of chivalry."

"Some say that Achilles is the greatest man that ever lived," Cressida said innocently.

"He's a camel compared to Troilus," Pandarus snorted. "Can't you see Troilus is the best?"

Cressida grinned. "I see what you're up to, Uncle," she said. "But I won't let my heart be swayed by sweet words."

Troilus's servant came running, and called Pandarus away.

"All the praises he pours in my ear are nothing compared to my true feelings for Troilus," Cressida thought, watching her uncle hurry down the steps. "But men prize that which they do not possess – giving it even more value, perhaps, than it has. So, while my heart cries out with love, my eyes will give nothing away."

" Men prize the thing ungained…"

CRESSIDA, ACT 1, SCENE 2

In the Greek camp, inside a grand tent, King Agamemnon had gathered his generals. "Seven years of war," he said, "seven years of suffering, and still the walls of Troy stand firm. Even so, we should be proud: greatness only comes from hardship. But I see no pride or boldness on your faces, friends, only despair."

"Let me speak, my king," called Ulysses, his wisest and wiliest general. "It's not bravery we lack, it's unity and order. If we cannot work together, we will never smash those walls down. Troy lives on in our weakness, not her own strength."

"Wise words," said Nestor, the king's oldest advisor. "Ulysses understands your army's sickness."

"And the cure…?" asked Agamemnon.

"Our best warrior, Achilles, mocks us," Ulysses replied. "He thinks so highly of himself that he disobeys you by refusing to fight. Instead, he lounges in his tent with his friend, Patroclus, scorning our strategy and sneering at us all."

"We need him on our side," added Nestor, "him and his troops, the famous Myrmidons."

Before Agamemnon could respond, a trumpet sounded and a Trojan, Aeneas, entered the tent, escorted by Greek soldiers. "I have a message for kingly ears," said Aeneas.

"Then speak," Agamemnon said. "You stand before a king."

"Prince Hector's sword grows rusty," Aeneas declared. "He wishes to know if any Greek is willing to meet him tomorrow in single combat."

"If none volunteer, I'll go myself," Agamemnon roared. "Pass the word around," he commanded, "and make certain Achilles, in particular, learns of this challenge. Come, Lord Aeneas, and my generals, join me for supper."

As the king and his entourage departed, Ulysses beckoned to Nestor. "I have an idea…" he confided. "Let's teach Achilles a lesson. He's our best champion, but if he crushes Hector, his pride and insolence will swell to unbearable proportions. Yet, if he loses, the Trojans will snatch a great victory. So instead, let's call a lottery, and fix things so that it's Ajax who faces Hector. Ajax is mighty, too. When the glory of the duel falls upon him, Achilles will be shamed into taking up his sword again."

"A winning plan," said Nestor. "Let's tell the king at once."

Within the walls of Troy, King Priam sat with his sons: Hector, Paris and Troilus. They, too, were discussing the war. "So many have died," Priam said sadly. "All this time has passed, but the Greeks' demand never changes: deliver Helen and they sail home. What say you, Hector?"

Hector frowned. "We've sacrificed too many lives guarding a prize that is not ours – and every life was just as dear to us as Helen is. We should give her up. She is not worth the cost."

"No, brother," Troilus protested. "It's too late to change our course now. When Paris brought Helen to Troy, we all agreed she was more beautiful than the morning sky, and worth the cost of any war. She was precious enough to the Greeks for them to send a thousand ships. She's just as precious to them, and us, today."

A wail echoed from another room: "Cry, Trojans, cry."

"It's our mad sister, Cassandra," said Hector, softly.

The next instant, Cassandra dashed into the room. "Give me your eyes, Trojans," she cried. "I'll show them the future and fill them with tears. Paris will doom us all. Cry, cry! Let Helen go, or else Troy will burn." And she was gone, as quickly as she'd come.

"Do her mad warnings not trouble you, Troilus?" asked Hector.

"She may be mad, but we are not," the young man replied.

"We are right to fight on," Paris insisted. "Betraying Helen to the Greeks now, after these years of brave fighting and sacrifice,

"Cry, cry! Troy burns, or else let Helen go."

would only bring shame on us all."

"This is true," said Troilus. "We can win glory fighting for Helen's cause, or earn undying shame by giving her up."

"Bravely said," Hector agreed with a sigh. "I've news that might help our cause. I've challenged the Greeks to put up a champion to face me. I heard whispers that their champion slumbers in his tent, but I think my challenge will wake him."

While Hector described the details of his duel to his brothers, Agamemnon and his generals stood waiting outside Achilles's tent.

"Where is he?" the king barked at Patroclus.

"Achilles is unwell, my lord," Patroclus answered coolly.

"Again? You mean he won't see me. Go and tell him that I begin to have my doubts about this Achilles, the great fighter. What use is the world's best warrior, if he won't obey my orders?"

"I shall tell him," replied Patroclus, slipping inside the tent.

"He's not so special," snarled Ajax, approaching the king. "Is he any stronger than me?"

"No, good knight," replied Agamemnon, smiling. "You are just as strong, and loyal. Shall I send you to speak with him?"

Ulysses interrupted. "Please, no, my lord! We should prick Achilles's pride, not feed it. We need an army that fights together when you command it. Let's waste no more time on Achilles."

"Aye, let him sulk in his tent," said the king. "We've got a war to win."

He strode away to yet another council of war. Among the men present was a Trojan lord who had left his own side to fight alongside the Greeks. His name was Calchas, and it so happened that he was Cressida's father.

"Have I done you good service?" Calchas asked the king. "I hope you can see that I have, for it's cost me my good name, my home and my fortune – and yet I did it gladly. I wonder if now I may ask for something in return?"

"Name it, Trojan," said Agamemnon.

"You have a prisoner – Antenor is his name. Troy holds him very dear, and they would swap my daughter for him. Give me my Cressida, and I will forget all my other losses."

The king nodded. Turning to a soldier named Diomedes, he said, "Go and make this exchange. While you are there, tell Hector that Ajax will be waiting to duel with him on the plain."

When Agamemnon dismissed his lords, they strolled past Achilles, who stood at the entrance to his tent. Most of them ignored the great hero, snubbing him with their silence.

"Have they forgotten me so quickly?" Achilles asked Patroclus. "Just days ago, these same men fawned over me."

Ulysses, walking past, overheard him. "Time destroys everything," he said pointedly. "Most of all, a reputation."

"They must remember my many victories," Achilles insisted.

Ulysses smiled. "Things in motion catch the eye," he said. "But you've buried yourself in your tent as though it's a tomb, and refuse to move when the king commands it. The Greeks are talking about Ajax as their champion now, as though he's already defeated Hector. I'll leave you to your choices."

"I see my reputation is at stake," muttered Achilles. "My fame has been gored. But it's not too late to save it all…"

The sun was setting, casting long, red rays over the walls of Troy. The Greeks had retreated to their camp and the Trojans had shut the gates of their city for the night. Prince Troilus was waiting impatiently in an orchard outside his beloved Cressida's house. Pandarus had finally convinced his niece of the prince's true love.

The young lover paced up and down anxiously until, at long last, Cressida arrived with her uncle. She wore a veil, and when she lifted it Troilus could do nothing but sigh. "Your beauty robs me of words," he whispered.

"Actions count for more," Pandarus told him, "but swear the oaths to her that you have sworn to me."

"I will," promised Troilus.

"Come into my house, my lord," Cressida said to Troilus. "I confess I have loved you night and day, for many weary months."

"Yet you barely seemed to notice me," Troilus protested.

"I noticed, and from the first look I loved you. But I say too much; you will think me a fool," Cressida said.

"Never," Troilus replied, kissing her. "Fear not, I'll be true to you. When future poets search for words, they'll use my name: 'as true as Troilus', they will say."

"And if I lie," Cressida replied, "or am false in my love for you, let me never be forgiven, not before the end of time. I will be shamed with the terrible legacy, 'as false as Cressida'."

"I have witnessed this bargain," Pandarus laughed. "If either of you are false, let my name be cursed too. Lovers' go-betweens will all be known as Pandars."

"The deal is made," Troilus smiled.

"Go and be happy," said Pandarus. "May Cupid go with you."

The following morning, the lovers awoke in the pale dawn. "Go back to sleep, my dear one," whispered Troilus. "I must get ready for war. Let me slip away."

Cressida eyed him doubtfully. "Are you tired of me already?"

"No," Troilus laughed, "but the busy day has come, and the dreaming night can hide our joys no longer."

"You could wait a little longer," pleaded Cressida. "If I hadn't said I loved you, you would have stayed longer."

But before they could resolve their quarrel, there came a fierce, urgent knocking at the door to the street. The lovers hurried down, and found Aeneas and Pandarus waiting outside. Pandarus looked pale and glum. "What is it?" Troilus asked.

"Oh, Prince, your love's no sooner won than lost," said Pandarus. "Cressida has been called to her father's side!"

"Diomedes, the Greek, has arrived in the city with Antenor," explained Aeneas. "In exchange for Antenor's freedom, Cressida must return with him this very hour. King Priam has ordered it."

"Go over to the Greeks? I won't do it," sobbed Cressida. "My father means nothing to me. No kin, no love, no blood or soul means more to me than Troilus."

"And giving you up is like surrendering my own heart," cried Troilus. "We bought our love with thousands of sighs – must we sell it now so poorly in the space of a single breath? Time is stealing you away, fast as a robber… but I cannot disobey my king. There is only time for a single kiss, tainted with the salt of tears."

"Is the lady ready?" Aeneas asked. "We cannot delay."

"Be true to me, Cressida," said Troilus, seizing her hands in his.

"I'll be true, my true Troilus," Cressida vowed. "But when shall I see you again?"

"I'll bribe my way into the Greek camp and visit you disguised, I promise. Until then, take this as a keepsake," he said, taking a piece of cloth from his sleeve and pressing it into her hand.

"Here's my glove for you," Cressida said, giving it to him.

Troilus pulled her close. "Be true," he whispered urgently, "and don't be tempted away from me by some subtle Greek."

"Never," she promised.

"Here comes Diomedes," Aeneas warned.

"Diomedes, lead my lady to your camp," Troilus told the Greek.

"We two, that with so many thousand sighs
Did buy each other, must poorly sell ourselves
With the rude brevity and discharge of one."

TROILUS, ACT 4, SCENE 4

"Treat her well or you shall answer to me, and even great Achilles could not save you from my wrath."

"Be calm, Prince Troilus," said Diomedes smoothly, as he led away the weeping Cressida, "I always do as I think best."

Before Troilus could answer, the sound of trumpets and shouts rose up from the walls of Troy. Hector was preparing to ride out of the city gates to fight his duel.

The Greek army waited in full battle order before the city. Ajax stalked across the front line of soldiers, swinging his sword. "Sound our signal to our enemies," he roared, "to show I'm ready for Hector."

He pointed at a boy trumpeter. "You, crack your lungs!"

The boy blew his trumpet as hard as he could.

King Agamemnon arrived, flanked by his generals. "Here comes Diomedes," he said. "He is bringing with him Calchas's daughter, a real beauty…" As the pair rode up, he said, "You are most dearly welcome, Lady Cressida."

Cressida, with a frosty expression on her face, dismounted to greet Agamemnon. The elderly king kissed her on both cheeks.

"Let me take the winter from your lips, fair lady," said Achilles. He and the generals approached in turn, each kissing her gently.

"Let me save you from their warm welcome," said Ulysses, taking her hand and leading her back towards Diomedes.

"I don't mind their attention," Cressida said. She was smiling through her tears.

Moments later, Hector rode out of the gates of Troy with his brothers. Troilus cast a miserable figure, his face downcast.

"Who is that, who looks so sad?" asked Agamemnon.

"That is Troilus, one of Priam's brave sons," replied Ulysses. "All the best men of Troy are here."

"Then let the duel begin," cried Agamemnon.

Soon, the two noble heroes, Hector and Ajax, faced one another on the plain, surrounded by their armies looking on.

They gripped their swords and circled one another, then pounced like lions. There was a clash of swords and they sprang apart. They lunged and hacked, each as deft as the other, until eventually a trumpet blasted, and Aeneas shouted, "Enough. You have both earned your glory. There's no need for more blood and gore. I judge this duel a draw."

Hector agreed. "We are cousins, you and I, Ajax," he said. "I do not wish to kill such a brave warrior."

"I would fight on, but am proud to draw with Hector," answered Ajax, "a true champion. Will you come and feast in our tents? The Greek generals wish to meet you."

Hector walked side by side with Ajax, greeting Agamemnon and his war council. He swapped smiles and stories with each man, until he came to Achilles. For a moment, the best warriors of the rival armies gravely sized each other up. Then, Achilles stalked around tall Hector, prodding him with his finger.

"There? Or there? Or there?" he said. "Tell me, gods, in what part of this body will I make the wound that kills great Hector?"

"You proud man," said Hector angrily, "what god would deign to answer such a question? Know this: if ever you are brave enough to leave your tent, you'd best be on your guard."

"Today, we'll be friends," Achilles smiled, "but when I meet you tomorrow on the battlefield, I shall strike you down dead."

"Enough," cried Agamemnon, "no more threats. Come to my tent, good Hector, and eat with us."

As the soldiers melted away, Ulysses found himself walking with Prince Troilus who, he couldn't help noticing, looked anxious and sad. "My Lord Ulysses," said the Trojan, "could you guide me to the tent where Calchas rests?"

"I could," answered Ulysses. "He shares Menelaus's tent. Diomedes is invited there tonight as a guest, although he seems too distracted by Cressida to be interested in food and wine… Do you know this lady? She seemed so sad to be reunited with her father."

"I can explain why," sighed Troilus, "but only if you'll agree to take me there in secret, later, when it gets dark…"

It was close to midnight before Hector and his fellow generals returned to the high walls of Troy. Troilus lingered behind, until he saw Ulysses. "Follow me," whispered Ulysses, "Diomedes has already gone on ahead, and we'll tread softly after him."

The two knights tiptoed after Diomedes, not realizing that they too were being shadowed – by the Greek camp's crafty jester. "Look at all these proud knights creeping about like thieves," the jester chuckled. "They're all plain cheats and sneaks, really. Let's see what they're up to."

Ulysses arrived at the side of a huge tent and lifted the flap for Troilus. The two men entered, keeping to the darkest corner. "We must stay hidden," whispered Ulysses.

"There's Cressida," hissed Troilus, his heart racing as he stared into the torchlit heart of the tent. "She's welcoming Diomedes."

"She looks pleased to see him," the jester muttered to himself, watching from another shadowed corner.

"You promised me a kiss," said Diomedes, reaching out to take Cressida's hand. "Will you give it to me now?"

"I couldn't do that," replied Cressida.

"Music to my ears," thought Troilus.

"Then I'll waste no time on you," snapped Diomedes, turning.

"Don't leave in anger, my lord," said Cressida, softly.

"Oh, do," hissed Troilus.

The jester smiled. "He's not going anywhere."

"I have a token for you," said Cressida, pressing something into

Diomedes's palm. It was the piece of cloth Troilus had given her.

Troilus almost cried out. "Beauty, I'm betrayed," he thought.

"But wait," cried Cressida. She snatched the cloth back guiltily. "I loved him and swore to be true. This was a token he gave me…"

"But I'm here now," Diomedes said quietly, leaning so his face was almost touching hers, "and it's me you want."

Cressida hesitated. What was she to think? She'd barely had a single day with Troilus before they were parted. Now he might as well be a world away. She would probably never see him again.

Diomedes slowly pulled the cloth from her unresisting fingers. "I'll wear this into battle, and fight anyone who challenges me for it," he vowed.

"I'll be there to greet you," thought Troilus furiously.

"Shall I come and see you later?" Diomedes asked.

Cressida looked at his handsome face and sighed. "Yes, come," she answered. "I cannot lie. I want to see you again."

"Oh, Cressida," murmured Troilus. "You weren't strong enough to be true to me for longer than a day. But before tomorrow is over, I'll kill this Greek who tempted you."

"Come, good knight," said Ulysses, "we've seen enough, let me guide you back to your city gates."

The jester watched the two men steal away from the tent and laughed. "With them, it's all lust and war," he said, shaking his head. "They care for nothing more. Let the Devil take them all."

By dawn the following day, Hector was dressed for battle. His wife, his sister and his father, plagued by dreams and visions of his death, all pleaded with him not to leave the city. "Hold him fast," Cassandra told King Priam. "He is your crutch: you lean on him, and all of Troy on you. If he slips, we'll all fall together."

But it was no use. "I swore to fight the Greeks," Hector told them calmly. "I will not turn away from my duty."

The battle was soon raging once more. Blood soaked the ground, swords and axes clashed, and arrows flew through the air. Troilus and Diomedes came head to head, and fought like demons. "If you run from me," shouted Troilus, "I'll follow."

"Why should I run?" Diomedes laughed. "I'll win your horse from you and present it to my lady."

The pair crashed through the ranks of fighting soldiers, cutting each other with every lunge of their swords.

"We must rally together, Greeks," roared Ulysses, riding through the mass of men. "We've lost too many good warriors this day. Patroclus is dead. His body lies before Achilles's tent. Great Achilles is at last taking up his arms, vowing vengeance."

Consumed by grief at the death of his friend, Achilles tore into the battle like a furious god. Late in the day, he and his troops spied Hector standing alone in a quiet corner of the battlefield. Hector's sword was planted before him in the ground. "Now my day's work is done," he was thinking, "I'll take a breath. Rest, sword. You have had your fill of blood and death."

"The sun's about to set," Achilles said grimly, "and your life is done." In a moment, his troops had surrounded the Trojan prince.

"I'm unarmed, Greek," Hector protested. "Leave me be."

"Strike at him," Achilles ordered his men, "and then tell everyone that Achilles has slain the mighty Hector!"

Blood-soaked and exhausted, Troilus stumbled from the battlefield. He had lost sight of Diomedes in the tangle of men. But all thoughts of his rival in love were wiped from his mind by a horrifying sight: triumphant Achilles was driving his chariot in a wide circle around the walls of Troy – and dragging behind it,

"*Now is my day's work done; I'll take good breath.*
Rest, sword, thou hast thy fill of blood and death."

HECTOR, ACT 5, SCENE 9

for all to see, was the tattered, lifeless body of his poor, noble brother, Hector.

On all sides of the city, the clash of swords died down. The Trojans gaped, appalled, and drew back, while the Greeks burst into cheers.

Aeneas, caked in blood and grime, staggered up to Troilus. "Hector? Slain? How is it possible?" he gasped.

"Who will tell Priam?" Troilus said, his voice shaking.

"The news will break his heart," Aeneas said.

"And the heart of Troy," Troilus added. "This battle's over for today. Hector is dead… there is no more to say."

He turned and pointed his spear to the Greek tents in the distance. "But let the sun rise as early as it dares and I'll be armed again, searching for that coward, Achilles. I swear revenge on him. I'll haunt him like a wicked conscience. This war is far from over."

He stormed into the city. As he entered the gates, Pandarus hurried up to speak to him. When Troilus saw him, his heartbreak over Cressida welled up, and poured out in a torrent of rage. "Get out of my sight, you scheming shopkeeper," he roared. "I want no more of your shoddy goods."

He pushed past Pandarus and the old man was left alone.

"What did I do wrong?" old Pandarus wailed. "What a world this is? I did everything he asked and look how he rewards me. Weep for me, world, weep for poor old Pandar."

But nobody wept for Pandarus, and the battle raged on. It was many long years before the once-shining swords and helmets were finally laid aside. Troy was crushed, and Helen, the great love of Paris, was taken home to Greece. The war had tainted everything: love, honour and noble hearts.

The Tempest

Out at sea, a ship tosses and turns in a storm. A magician watches from a desolate island with a magical spirit at his shoulder, and his daughter at his side. The ship is full of his enemies and he plans to set things straight…

Prospero

Weaves his magic over everyone, drawing the characters into his master plan…

Ariel

A magical sprite, who serves Prospero.

Miranda

Prospero's daughter, who has lived with him on the island since she was three.

Prince Ferdinand

King Alonso's son, also shipwrecked on the island, who falls in love with Miranda.

Caliban

A strange creature that lives on the island and serves Prospero.

Stephano

A shipwrecked drunken butler.

Trinculo

A shipwrecked jester.

King Alonso

The shipwrecked King of Naples is grieving for his son, Ferdinand, who he thinks is lost at sea.

Gonzalo

Loyal old counsellor. He tries to comfort the king.

Antonio

Prospero's treacherous brother.

Sebastian

King Alonso's wicked brother, and Antonio's friend.

T HUNDER ROLLED AND LIGHTNING FLASHED. On the cliffs of a wild and windswept island, an old man and a girl stood watching a little ship tossing and turning out at sea. A giant wave crashed over the ship and it was lost from view.

The man's star-embroidered cloak billowed around him, and the girl hid her face in it. "Father, if it's your magic that has done this, please reverse it," she sobbed. "Save them."

The old man patted her arm, "Don't worry, there's no harm done," he said kindly. "Everything has been done with you in mind, Miranda… You know nothing of who we are; nor why we are in this god-forsaken place. It's time I told you more… "

He sat down, and beckoned to her. Miranda perched beside him. "You were only three when we came to this island," he began. "Do you recall how we got here?"

"No, Father."

"Twelve years ago, my dear Miranda, your father was the Duke of Milan."

"B-but *you're* my father," stammered Miranda.

"I am," Prospero assured her. "And I was a duke. But I was more interested in the study of magic, and so I entrusted my brother Antonio – your uncle – to run the state. But Antonio betrayed my trust. He paid the King of Naples to help overthrow me. Antonio opened the gates of Milan in the dead of night and let the king's soldiers in…"

"Treachery!" cried Miranda. "But why didn't they kill us?"

"They didn't dare," Prospero answered bitterly. "Our people

"Hell is empty and all the devils are here."

loved us. Killing us would have caused an uprising… Instead they bundled us onto a rotten little boat – without so much as a sail – and set us adrift at sea,"

Miranda gasped. "How did we survive?"

"My loyal old counsellor, Gonzalo, hid food and provisions – and my books – on the boat. Some great fortune brought us to this island before we perished."

"I wish I could meet that man…" said Miranda.

"Ah, yes, that reminds me," said Prospero, getting to his feet. "I have more to do." He peered at his daughter's alert, questioning face. "You look sleepy," he said. "Why not lie down?" Before she could protest, he stroked her forehead and instantly her eyes fell shut. She relaxed into his waiting arms and he lay her gently down on the ground.

Then Prospero turned, calling, "Ariel, come!"

A shimmering, silver-winged figure appeared in the air. "Here I am, Master!"

"Have you done as I asked?" said Prospero.

The sprite chuckled with glee. "Yes. I pulled the ship this way and that, and blew and burned, until every last passenger leaped into the sea in terror. Ferdinand, the son of the King of Naples, was the first to go. Before he jumped, he shouted, 'Hell is empty, and all the devils are here!'"

"Are they safe?" Prospero asked.

"I didn't harm a hair on their heads, Master. I have brought them ashore and spread them about the island. I pulled the ship into the harbour and hid it there. The sailors are all still on board, held captive in a charmed sleep."

"Well done, Ariel. But there's more to do now."

"More?" Ariel pouted. "When will I be free?"

Prospero frowned. "Ariel," he thundered. "Have you forgotten already how I freed you from the pine tree that the witch had trapped you inside?"

"No, I haven't forgotten," said the sprite sulkily.

"After the witch died, you would have been trapped for all eternity if I hadn't come along," Prospero went on. "Her misshapen son Caliban certainly wouldn't have freed you. And if you keep on moaning I could easily put you back!"

Ariel's manner changed completely. "I beg your pardon, Master," he said sweetly. "I will do everything you ask."

Prospero nodded, mollified. "Good. When we have finished everything, I will free you from my service, just as I promised."

"What shall I do next?" Ariel asked.

"Make yourself invisible to everyone but me. And after that…" Prospero gave Ariel the rest of his instructions.

"It shall be done, Master," said Ariel, and floated away in the air, fading from sight as he went.

Prospero turned to his sleeping daughter, bent down and took her hand. "Wake up, child." Miranda sat up and rubbed her eyes. "We need to go and see Caliban, to ask him to gather more wood."

Caliban lived in a dank cave near a larger one which Prospero had furnished as best he could, for himself and his daughter. As they approached Caliban's cave, he emerged – a miserable, misshapen creature, with a hunched, hairy back and dull, glowering eyes. "May a south-west wind blister you both all over," he spat at Prospero and Miranda. "The island is MINE. You took it from me when my mother died."

"Not that old line again," Prospero groaned. "Caliban you know full well how kind we were to you… until you tried to attack poor Miranda," he scolded. "We even taught you how to talk. Now fetch some wood or it'll be the worse for you."

"You taught me language, and now I can curse you: may the red plague take you!" growled Caliban, but he shuffled off to fetch wood all the same.

CALIBAN, ACT 1, SCENE 2

Prospero squinted down the hill and nodded to himself with satisfaction. Stumbling up from the coast came a handsome young man. Above him, Prospero saw Ariel, singing cheekily to lead him on. The young man was staring around bewildered, unable to see the sprite, but following the music.

Prospero called to Miranda. "What do you see down there?"

Miranda came to look. She had been trapped on the island since she was three years old, with her father and the misshapen Caliban as her only companions. Now, at fifteen, the sight of this handsome young man filled her with awe. "Something divine," she whispered.

Prospero smiled. Things were going to plan.

The young man stopped in his tracks when he saw Miranda. "Are you a goddess the music was for…?" he said in confusion.

Miranda laughed. "No, I'm just a girl."

"You speak my language!" cried the young man. "My name is Ferdinand. I have been shipwrecked, and my father, the King of Naples, I fear is lost."

"You are a prince?" Miranda asked.

"Yes, well, maybe a king now…" said Ferdinand looking troubled. Then, despite himself, he looked back at Miranda and smiled. "That means… I could make you my queen…"

The two gazed dreamily at one another.

"This is going rather too smoothly," muttered Prospero. "A prize won too easily can be taken too lightly. I must ensure this love is strong enough to last…"

He spun Ferdinand around to face him. "Hold on, you scoundrel! I'll bet you have come to take this island from me! I'll teach you! You'll carry logs for me instead."

Ferdinand drew his sword but, with a wave of the old man's arm, he found himself unable to move. Prospero moved his hand and he found himself sheathing his sword. Prospero beckoned, and he felt his legs propel him to follow. Prospero led the young man away to carry out his task.

"Father!" Miranda protested, running after them.

"This is the only man you have ever seen, Miranda, apart from your old father," Prospero told her sternly. "For all you know, all the others might look like angels compared to him!"

"But I have no ambition to find a better man than this one," Miranda protested.

Prospero swallowed a smile, and led the young man to the woodpile, closely followed by his daughter.

"Don't worry," Ferdinand called to her over his shoulder. "I'm happy being imprisoned if it's near you!"

Soon he was going to and fro, carrying logs to the woodpile and stacking them up. It was exhausting work, and Miranda accompanied him anxiously, while her father watched from the door of the cave. "Let me help," begged Miranda.

"I won't hear of it," said Ferdinand. "I'd rather break my back than have you do the work for me. As a matter of fact," he said dreamily. "I'd be happy to serve you to the end of my days."

"Do you love me?" Miranda asked innocently.

"I love and prize you more than anything in the world," Ferdinand replied.

Miranda's eyes filled with happy tears. "If you will have me, I will be your wife."

"I would gladly be your husband," said Ferdinand. Miranda put her hands in his, and they stared at each other. They looked the picture of happiness.

Prospero smiled to himself. "May the heavens rain grace on them." He came out, and said to Ferdinand, "I hope my punishment was not too severe. It was a test to see whether you truly value Miranda as much as I do."

"I couldn't value her more," Ferdinand replied, without an ounce of resentment.

"I live for my daughter… but I am happy to give her away to you… and gain a son," said Prospero.

He clapped his hands, and all kinds of magic began to weave its way through the air. Dancing nymphs appeared and showered the happy couple with flowers. Rainbows arched over them and enchanted music played to celebrate their love.

On the other side of the island, a miserable huddle of men was gathered on a beach. Alonso, the King of Naples, sat with his head in his hands on a washed-up trunk. His counsellor, Gonzalo, sat next to him. "Cheer up, sir. Sailors drown every day and yet we survived," the old counsellor urged.

"Quiet!" moaned the king. "My son is lost at sea."

"He receives comfort like cold porridge," jeered the king's brother, Sebastian.

Gonzalo struggled to think of a retort. Sebastian smirked, elbowing his friend. "Look, Antonio, he's trying to come up with a witty answer."

Suddenly a strange music filled the air. "I might…" Gonzalo began, and then suddenly his eyes closed and his head nodded onto the king's shoulder. He had fallen asleep in the middle of his sentence! What's more, the king was snoring too.

"They dozed off together as if by some agreement and now they lie there, helpless…" Antonio said. His eyes gleamed with sudden cunning. "Are you thinking what I'm thinking,

Sebastian?… Suddenly I'm imagining a golden crown on your head…"

"Go on…" said Sebastian, his interest piqued.

"Well, the king's son must be drowned, no doubt about it," Antonio said. "His heir is his daughter Claribel, who is miles away in Tunis, happily married, and knows nothing of all this… and the next in line is – well – *you*. Do you understand now?"

Sebastian's smile grew broader. "I think so."

"And your brother, the king, lies here sleeping helplessly…" Antonio put his hand on the hilt of his sword. "My sword could put him to bed forever," he hissed. "You could do the same to old Gonzalo – he'd only get in the way otherwise."

"And, in the same way you won Milan from your brother, Prospero, I could win Naples from mine! Draw your sword, friend," Sebastian said.

"Together!" said Antonio.

No sooner had they held up their swords, than strange music drifted all around them again, and they froze like statues. Ariel, unseen, was fluttering in the air above them, "My master sent me just in time," he said to himself. He flew over to the king and Gonzalo and shouted, "Awake!"

Gonzalo awoke with a start and, seeing Antonio and Sebastian with their swords drawn, he yelled, "Save the king!"

The king's eyes snapped open. "Why are your swords out?"

Antonio and Sebastian, suddenly finding themselves free to move again, were confused. They'd been caught red-handed but they weren't sure how. They racked their brains to think of a plausible explanation.

"We heard… erm…" Sebastian started.

"Bellowing…" Antonio chipped in. "From… erm… lions!"

"Really? We must search for my son," said the king.

"And save him from the lions," Gonzalo agreed.

The king and Gonzalo crept away from the beach with Sebastian and Antonio following behind.

Further around the coast, Caliban was gathering driftwood, when another shipwreck survivor came along. It was a jester, wearing a cap with bells, which jingled slightly as he walked.

Caliban had never seen a jester before. He squinted at him and scowled. "Is this another spirit my master has sent to torment me? I'll hide from it, and maybe it won't see me." He fell to the ground and curled up in a ball under his filthy cloak.

Trinculo, for that was the jester's name, nearly tripped over him. "What have we here?" he said, giving the bundle a poke. "A man, or a fish?" He wrinkled his nose. "It smells like a fish."

At that moment, thunder rolled. "Looks like rain. I'll get under its cloak and stay dry," the jester said. And he crawled under the filthy cloak and huddled up with Caliban.

Then along came a drunken butler, staggering along the sand with a bottle in his hand. "I shall no more to sea, to sea," he sang. He'd been shipwrecked too but had found himself on the shore with a cask of wine and some bottles. He'd drowned his sorrows in the wine and now felt rather more merry.

"Well, look at that," he said, swaying slightly as he stopped to stare at the bundle. "Some kind of sea monster with four legs. I'll give it a drink and tame it." He bent down and sloshed some of his wine into Caliban's mouth.

"I recognize that voice. Is that you, Stephano?" Trinculo called from under the cloak.

"There's a mouth at the other end too!" cried the butler.

Trinculo flung back the cloak. Seeing his old friend, he leaped to his feet and embraced him.

"Careful, I'm not too steady," Stephano said, staggering.

Caliban peered out from the cloak too, enticed by the wine, and said, "Are you a god? Did you drop out of the sky?"

"Yes, I'm the man in the Moon!" Stephano crowed.

"I've seen you up there!" cried Caliban, delighted. "I will serve you as my master. I can show you the island, and catch you the best fish. Come with me!"

"Let's drink to that!" Stephano chuckled, handing around the bottle as he staggered after the hunch-backed creature.

"I have a master on this island," Caliban confided. "A tyrant called Prospero. But you shall overthrow him! You can marry his daughter. Let's go and kill him while he is asleep!"

"And I shall rule!" Stephano agreed gleefully. "We'll go and fill this bottle back up first…"

After trawling the coast of the island, the king and his companions stopped to rest in a grove of trees. The king sat down glumly on a log, listening to the sigh of waves on the shore. "My son must have drowned," he said. "All the while we search on land, the sea mocks us."

Just then, they heard strange music. Through the trees, shadowy figures began to appear. They looked very odd: some flew on gossamer wings, some crept like shadows, some danced as if carried by a breeze. Between them, they carried a table and chairs. The men stared at them, wondering whether they were in a dream.

The strange magical creatures placed the table and chairs in the midst of the men. One waved its pretty fingers and a glorious feast appeared on the table: overflowing silver dishes and shining goblets brimming with wine. The men watched, open-mouthed, as the spirits bowed and faded away.

For a moment or two nothing happened.

Sebastian's stomach growled as he stared at the food. "Shall we eat?" he said.

Hesitantly, the king agreed. They sat down gingerly at the table. The food smelled delicious. The men started to reach for it when, with a thunderclap, a huge, hideous harpy appeared. It was Ariel. But he wasn't silvery and beautiful this time. He had black, tattered wings, and a twisted, hideous face. He crashed down on the table, his giant wings sending dishes flying.

The men leaped up, upsetting chairs, and drew their swords.

Ariel eyed the blades with scorn. "You may as well slice at the wind," he said, his voice ringing like struck iron.

Ignoring Gonzalo, he advanced on Sebastian, Alonso and Antonio, his eyes glowing like a demon's. "You are three men of sin," he roared. "Destiny has brought you to this island to repay you. You overthrew good Prospero in Milan, and set him adrift on the sea with his innocent child to die. For this foul deed, the sea and the wind have taken your son from you, King, and here on this island you will all suffer your *ruin*."

With another clap of thunder, he was gone. The food on the table had vanished with him. The strange spirits reappeared and carried away the table.

"Monstrous," muttered the king, his face was white as bone.

"I will fight those fiends!" cried Sebastian defiantly.

"And I," shouted Antonio.

They raced to the edge of the trees, and Gonzalo hobbled after them to stop them. "Enough evil has been done already," the old man protested. "Enough is enough!"

But when the two young men reached the trees, they suddenly fell back. "We cannot leave!" Sebastian called. He tried again to plunge forward, but some unseen force stopped him.

They were trapped, unable to do anything but wait for whatever terrible punishment the demon meant to bring them. They crept back into the middle of the grove and huddled there, whimpering with fear.

Just beyond the grove of trees was Prospero's dwelling, where Miranda and Ferdinand were still celebrating their engagement. Prospero had crept, unnoticed, into the trees to watch Ariel with the men. Now, he hurried back to the young couple. He waved his hand, and the spirits that were entertaining them vanished at once.

Miranda and Ferdinand blinked as if waking up from a dream. "Our revels are ended," Prospero said. "These actors were all just spirits, which have melted into thin air. Go inside, now. I'll come soon," he told them.

Too wrapped up in one another's love to dwell on how strange it was, Miranda and Ferdinand went into the cave. "Such is life," mused Prospero as he watched them go. "Everything will dissolve, just like those spirits, leaving nothing behind. We are such stuff as dreams are made of, and our little life is rounded with a sleep."

Ariel came flitting back and interrupted Prospero's musings. "Well done, Ariel, you played that part well!" he told the sprite as he appeared, once more his silvery self. "Now, where are the others – the jester, the butler and Caliban?"

"Plotting to overthrow you," Ariel laughed. "But I led them a merry dance into a pond behind the caves…"

"Let's deal with them now," said Prospero.

By this time, Trinculo, Stephano and Caliban were thoroughly drunk. They had found their way out of the pond and into the back of Prospero's cave, where they were trying on his clothes. "Look at me!" chortled Trinculo, trying on a velvet cloak.

"I'll have that," said Stephano, snatching it from him. He heaped clothes into Caliban's arms. "Hide these with my stash of wine, Monster."

Outside, Ariel and Prospero were casting a magic spell.

"There!" Prospero shouted, and at once a pack of phantom hounds burst into the cave.

Screaming in terror, Caliban, Trinculo and Stephano fled. Pursued by the phantom dogs, they hurtled out of the cave, past Ariel and Prospero, and away down the hill.

"It's coming together now," Prospero chuckled, as the sprite dashed off to spy on the trapped king and his companions.

"How are they?" Prospero asked when Ariel returned.

"Terrified," Ariel reported. "Gonzalo does nothing but weep, and the others quail and quake."

Prospero nodded, rubbing his hands and looking satisfied.

"They are in such a state now, in fact," added Ariel, "that I think you could pity them…"

Prospero looked at him thoughtfully. "Do you?"

"I would if I were human," Ariel replied.

Prospero sighed. "You're right," he said. "My aim was to make them regret what they did. If I've managed that, I should not carry it any further. Bring them here, Ariel."

Ariel fluttered away and led the four men back. They stood in a circle around Prospero as if in a dream. With a wave of Prospero's hand, they awoke from their trance and stood gawping in astonishment. "Are you a devil too?" whispered Gonzalo.

"No, dear Gonzalo. I am Prospero, whom you helped when he was set adrift," said Prospero. He glared at the others, "Here I stand, the wronged Duke of Milan."

"I beg you, forgive me, Prospero," King Alonso said immediately. "You shall have your dukedom back."

Prospero turned on Antonio. "You – my own brother – were the wickedest of all. But I forgive you."

Antonio stood gaping. He could think of nothing at all to say.

Miranda, Act 5, Scene 1

"But Prospero," said the king, "What's going on? What are you doing here? We were shipwrecked just three hours ago… and my dear son Ferdinand is lost," he added miserably.

To his bewilderment, Prospero smiled and said. "I lost a daughter in the tempest too."

"Why are you smiling? I wish we had died instead," Alonso burst out, "and our children were in Naples, happily married!"

"You have given me back my precious dukedom," Prospero said, "and now I can give you something even more precious." He beckoned them all to look into his cave. There sat Ferdinand and Miranda playing chess, clearly very much in love.

"My son!" exclaimed the king.

"Father!" Ferdinand cried, and ran to embrace him.

Miranda didn't recall ever having seen so many people, and she was astonished. "How wonderful mankind is. Oh, what a beautiful new world, that has such people in it!" she exclaimed.

Then stumbling into the cave, rubbing their sore heads, came Caliban, Stephano and Trinculo. They looked rather the worse for wear. Ariel propelled them forward.

"King of the island, eh?" Prospero said sternly to the butler.

"I would have made an awful king," Stephano admitted.

"Bring back the things you stole from me, and I will pardon you all," said Prospero.

He turned to his hovering helper, Ariel. "Fetch the sailors from the ship, Ariel. Then your work is done. You shall have your freedom. You've earned it."

"Did I do well, Master?" the sprite asked eagerly.

"Wondrously well," Prospero agreed. And then he added softly, "I shall miss you, my sweet Ariel."

> *"Now my charms are all o'erthrown,*
> *And what strength I have's mine own"*
>
>

PROSPERO, EPILOGUE

"Merrily, merrily shall I live now," sang the delighted sprite, "under the blossom that hangs on the bough." And he flitted away like a glimmer of light in the evening sun.

That evening, the sailors and the shipwrecked party celebrated in Prospero's cave, each telling the other their experiences, and marvelling over everything that had happened to them.

Prospero slipped out, alone, and stood on the cliff, staring out to sea. "Now all my magical charms are gone, without my Ariel. The only powers I have left are my own," he mused. "And they are feeble… But still, I have my dukedom back, and I've pardoned my enemies, so there is no need to stay on this bare island any longer. Tomorrow Miranda and I can sail back to Milan."

He picked up his magical staff, broke it in two and flung it far out into the waves. "Like Ariel and Caliban," he thought, "now, at last, I am free."

Stories told in brief

Henry VI

KING HENRY V IS DEAD. His son, Henry VI, is too young to be crowned King of England, so the Duke of Gloucester becomes Lord Protector of the kingdom. Trouble stirs up in France, as the French rebel against English control. Lord Talbot, General of the English troops, dies in battle trying to defeat the rebels. However, peace is finally agreed, and the leader of the French rebels, Joan of Arc, is burned at the stake.

In London's Temple Gardens, Richard Plantaganet, from the royal house of York, has an argument with the Duke of Somerset, from the royal house of Lancaster. Richard picks a white rose, the symbol of the Yorks, while Somerset plucks a red rose, the symbol of the Lancasters. Their disagreement marks the origin of the Wars of the Roses, a series of civil wars in England between the two royal houses.

When Henry VI is finally crowned, he marries a French noblewoman, Margaret of Anjou. Richard, now the Duke of York, begins to stir up a rebellion against him. Hoping to make peace, Henry makes York heir to the throne instead of his own son. But civil war breaks out, and York is murdered by Henry's wife, Margaret. Henry is taken prisoner in the Tower of London, and York's son, Edward, is crowned King Edward IV.

In the end, Henry is murdered by York's son, young Richard. Bitter and twisted with hate, Richard begins plotting for the throne himself… his story is told in *Richard III*.

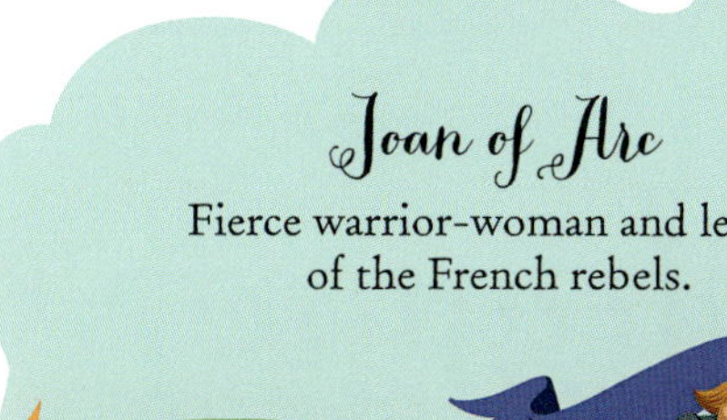

Joan of Arc

Fierce warrior-woman and leader of the French rebels.

Lord Talbot

General of the English troops in France. Noble, brave and loyal to the king.

Henry VI

King of England. Young to the throne and not a strong character, he struggles to control his warring nobles.

Margaret of Anjou

Henry's strong, determined French wife. She gradually begins taking power over the throne.

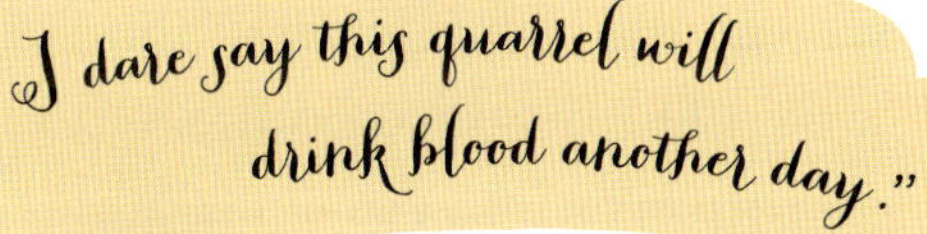

Duke of Somerset

Argumentative English lord, and a Lancaster. A fierce rival of Richard Plantagenet.

Richard Plantagenet, Duke of York

A York, who believes he is the rightful king. He makes it his mission to remove Henry from the throne.

Edward

Richard Plantagenet's eldest son. He becomes King of England after Henry VI dies.

Richard

Edward's younger brother, born with a hunched back. He has secret ambitions for the throne.

465

Measure for Measure

THE DUKE OF VIENNA HAS let law and order slip during his rule, so he appoints his strict deputy, Angelo, to rule the city in his place. The duke pretends to leave town, but instead disguises himself as an old friar so he can keep an eye on Angelo and his citizens.

Angelo immediately starts to crack down on crime. He sentences a man named Claudio to death because his girlfriend, Juliet, is pregnant outside of marriage. An old judge deems the punishment too harsh, but Angelo ignores him.

Claudio's sister, Isabella, pleads Angelo for her brother's life. Angelo offers to spare him on one condition: that Isabella becomes his mistress. Shocked, Isabella refuses.

The disguised duke, who has been listening to their conversation, concocts a plan to help Claudio. Under his direction, Isabella convinces Mariana – Angelo's abandoned fiancée – to visit Angelo in the dark, pretending to be Isabella. The trick works, but Angelo still refuses to release Claudio, demanding to see his severed head. A new plan is devised to send the head of another prisoner in Claudio's place.

Just in time, the duke throws off his disguise and everyone is forced to be honest. He frees Claudio, who marries Juliet. He orders Angelo to marry Mariana, and asks Isabella to marry him. Fair rule is restored to Vienna once more.

Duke of Vienna

Wise and caring ruler, but he reveals his manipulative side when spies on his citizens disguised as a friar.

Angelo

The duke's deputy. Harsh and hypocritical, he is happy to point out the faults of others, while hiding his own.

Isabella

A virtuous young woman who wants to become a nun. Should she do something against her principles to save her brother's life?

Claudio

Sentenced to death when his girlfriend, Juliet, becomes pregnant. It seems that no one but his sister, Isabella, can save him.

Mariana

Angelo's abandoned fiancée. She's talked into helping Isabella save Claudio's life.

Barnadine

A prisoner who narrowly escapes death when his head is offered up instead of Claudio's.

Juliet

Claudio's girlfriend, who is pregnant with his baby.

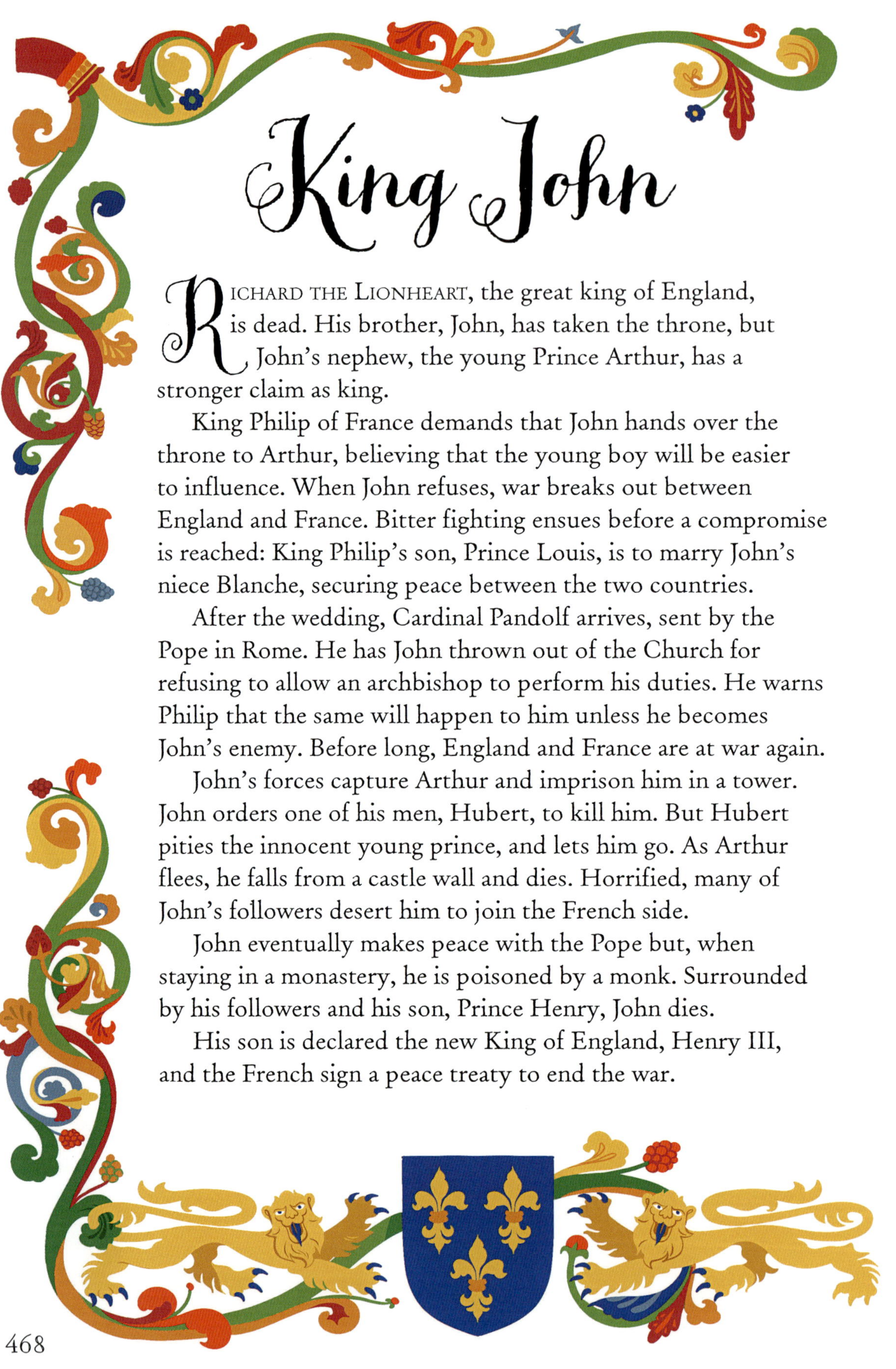

King John

RICHARD THE LIONHEART, the great king of England, is dead. His brother, John, has taken the throne, but John's nephew, the young Prince Arthur, has a stronger claim as king.

King Philip of France demands that John hands over the throne to Arthur, believing that the young boy will be easier to influence. When John refuses, war breaks out between England and France. Bitter fighting ensues before a compromise is reached: King Philip's son, Prince Louis, is to marry John's niece Blanche, securing peace between the two countries.

After the wedding, Cardinal Pandolf arrives, sent by the Pope in Rome. He has John thrown out of the Church for refusing to allow an archbishop to perform his duties. He warns Philip that the same will happen to him unless he becomes John's enemy. Before long, England and France are at war again.

John's forces capture Arthur and imprison him in a tower. John orders one of his men, Hubert, to kill him. But Hubert pities the innocent young prince, and lets him go. As Arthur flees, he falls from a castle wall and dies. Horrified, many of John's followers desert him to join the French side.

John eventually makes peace with the Pope but, when staying in a monastery, he is poisoned by a monk. Surrounded by his followers and his son, Prince Henry, John dies.

His son is declared the new King of England, Henry III, and the French sign a peace treaty to end the war.

King John

King of England.
Willing to go to any
lengths to hold on to the
throne – including going
to war with France.

King Philip

King of France. Locked in
a power game with King
John, desperate to take
back control of English
territories in France.

Cardinal Pandolf

The Pope's messenger.
He uses the power of the
Church to control the
relationship between
the two kings.

Blanche

King John's niece.
Her marriage to
King Philip's son,
Louis, encourages
peace between
England and France.

Prince Louis

King Philip's son.
His marriage to
Blanche gives him
more power over
English territories
in France.

Prince Arthur

John's nephew and
the rightful heir to the
throne. John has him
locked in a tower and
plots to have
him killed.

Hubert

An English nobleman.
King John orders
him to murder Prince
Arthur, but Hubert
lets him go.

Cymbeline

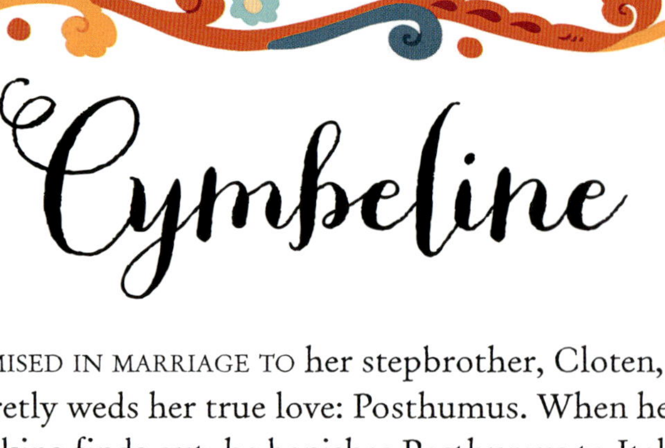

Promised in marriage to her stepbrother, Cloten, Innogen secretly weds her true love: Posthumus. When her father, the king finds out, he banishes Posthumus to Italy. There, Posthumus meets Iachimo, who bets him that Innogen will not remain faithful. To win the bet, Iachimo visits Innogen and then hides in her bedroom in a trunk. He returns to Posthumus and describes her bedroom as 'proof' he has had an affair with her. In a fit of jealous rage, Posthumus sends his servant to kill her. Instead, the servant helps her escape, disguised as a boy.

In Wales, Innogen is taken in by two men, Guiderius and Arviragus. Unbeknown to any of them, they are actually her brothers, who had been kidnapped as babies. When Cloten turns up, determined to possess Innogen, Guiderius kills him. Innogen takes some 'medicine' her stepmother gave her, and falls into a death-like coma. She awakes alone and, in despair, goes to work for the Roman army, which is attacking Britain.

Posthumus, filled with remorse for ordering Innogen's death, goes to war, dresses as a Roman and allows himself to be taken prisoner by the British. After a convoluted web of events, Posthumus and Innogen end up in Cymbeline's court, where the king recognizes them and they are reunited. The king is reunited with his long-lost sons, and the evil queen dies.

Cymbeline

British king who, enraged by his daughter's marriage to Posthumus, banishes the young lord.

The queen

Cymbeline's new wife and Innogen's wicked, scheming stepmother.

Princess Innogen

Cymbeline's daughter. She disobeys her father and marries Posthumus instead of Cloten.

Posthumus Leonatus

A poor but worthy lord who falls in love with Innogen and marries her.

Lord Cloten

The queen's son from a previous marriage. A brutal, dimwitted, odious fellow.

Jachimo

A dastardly Italian, bent on coming between Posthumus and Innogen.

Guiderius and Arviragus

Cymbeline's sons. Innogen's brothers. Stolen as babies, they reappear just in time to save Innogen from Cloten's clutches.

Titus Andronicus

AFTER TEN YEARS OF WAR between the Romans and the Goths, Titus Andronicus, a Roman general, returns home victorious. He brings with him Tamora, Queen of the Goths, and her three sons, as prisoners. In accordance with Roman customs, Titus has one of Tamora's sons, Alarbus, killed, in exchange for his twenty-one dead sons. Tamora is devastated, and swears to get her revenge.

To everyone's surprise, the emperor chooses Tamora as his bride. Suddenly powerful, Tamora begins plotting revenge with the help of her evil lover, Aaron.

The story becomes very grisly. First, she frames two of Titus's sons for murder, and they are beheaded. Next, she urges her own two sons to attack Titus's daughter, Lavinia, and cut off her hands and tongue.

In revenge, Titus has Tamora's sons baked in a pie, and feeds it to Tamora before killing her. He kills his own daugher to end her suffering. A vengeful bloodbath follows, in which nearly everybody dies, including Titus himself.

His son, Lucius, becomes the new emperor of Rome.

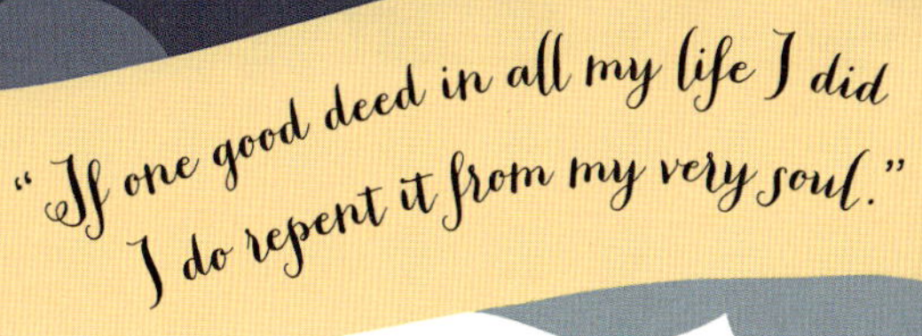

Titus Andronicus

A brutal and merciless general, he is finally stabbed to death by Emperor Saturnius.

Tamora

Queen of the Goths. She is stabbed to death by Titus, and her body is thrown into a pit of wild beasts.

Aaron

Tamora's lover. Truly evil character who ends up buried alive.

Emperor Saturnius

Tamora's husband. He is stabbed to death by Titus's son, Lucius.

Quintus & Martius

Titus's sons. They are framed for murder and beheaded.

Alarbus

Tamora's eldest son. Burned to death by Titus.

Chiron & Demetrius

Tamora's sons, who attack Titus's daughter, Lavinia. In revenge, Titus has them baked in a pie.

Lucius

The only son of Titus to survive. He is crowned Emperor of Rome.

Lavinia

Titus's daughter. She is brutally attacked by Tamora's sons and eventually killed by her own father.

King Henry VIII

POLITICAL INTRIGUE IS RIFE in the court of King Henry VIII of England. The king is surrounded by ambitious nobles plotting against one another to win power. Chief among them is Cardinal Wolsey, a church leader who seems to have the king wrapped around his little finger.

Wolsey persuades Henry that the Duke of Buckingham is a traitor. Buckingham is arrested and, although he speaks eloquently at his hearing, Henry sentences him to death.

Soon after, Henry meets Anne Boleyn and becomes infatuated with her. He asks the Catholic church in Rome to allow him a divorce from his wife, Katherine, so he can marry Anne. Wolsey pretends to support Henry, but secretly writes to the Pope opposing the plan.

Henry finds out about Wolsey's duplicity, and strips him of his power. He announces his marriage to Anne, and has Katherine demoted to 'Princess Dowager'.

Queen Anne then gives birth to their daughter, named Elizabeth, who the Archbishop of Canterbury predicts will have a long and glorious reign.

Cardinal Wolsey

An ambitious and scheming church leader who holds great influence over the king.

King Henry VIII

King of England. He decides he wants a divorce from Queen Katherine, so he can marry Anne Boleyn instead.

Duke of Buckingham

A loyal nobleman executed after Wolsey wrongfully accuses him of treason against the king.

Queen Katherine

Henry's first wife is the daughter of the King of Spain. She accuses Wolsey of plotting against her.

Anne Boleyn

A beautiful noblewoman. Becomes Henry's second wife and gives birth to their daughter, Elizabeth.

Thomas Cranmer

The Archbishop of Canterbury. He baptises Princess Elizabeth and predicts a glorious reign for her.

Princess Elizabeth

Baby daughter of Henry and Anne, who will one day become Queen of England – and Shakespeare's patron.

All's Well That Ends Well

AFTER THE DEATH OF HER FATHER, a great doctor, Helena is taken in by a countess in France. She falls hopelessly in love with the countess's son, Bertram. When Bertram goes to work for the King of France, who is suffering from a terrible illness, Helena follows him. She cures the king with a medicine made from her father's secret recipe. In return, the king asks her to choose anyone in his court for a husband. She chooses Bertram, and they are married.

Unfortunately, Betram does not love Helena. He flees his marriage to fight in a war in Italy, sending Helena a letter in which he says he will not be her true husband until she can take the ring from his finger and bear his child – which, of course, he thinks is impossible.

Helena goes to Florence, where she finds out that Bertram is in love with an Italian woman called Diana. When Bertram comes to spend the night with Diana, little does he know that Helena has swapped places with her. Thinking Helena is Diana, he gives her his ring. Helena gives him a ring the king gave her, and they spend the night together.

Eventually, Bertram returns to his mother's house in France. Diana and Helena arrive and reveal their trick. Helena tells everyone that she has Bertram's ring and is pregnant with his child. Finally, Bertram realizes Helena's true worth and accepts her as his wife.

King of France

Suffers from a terrible disease no one can treat, until Helena cures him with one of her father's medicines. He gives her a ring and grants her deepest desire.

Countess

Bertram's mother takes Helena in when she is orphaned. Sees Helena's worth and approves of the marriage to her son.

"Our remedies oft in ourselves do lie, Which we ascribe to heaven."

Helena

Orphaned daughter of famous doctor. Hopelessly in love with Bertram, and will go to great lengths to win him.

Bertram

Forced to marry Helena by his grateful king. Bertram cannot love her, so he runs away to war against Italy.

Diana

Italian young lady. Bertram tries to seduce her and visits her in the dark of night. Little does he know she's done a deal with Helena to trick him.

Parolles

Boastful, lying French soldier. His fellow soldiers, pretending to be the enemy, capture and blindfold him, tricking him into revealing his true colours in a comic, cowardly confession.

477

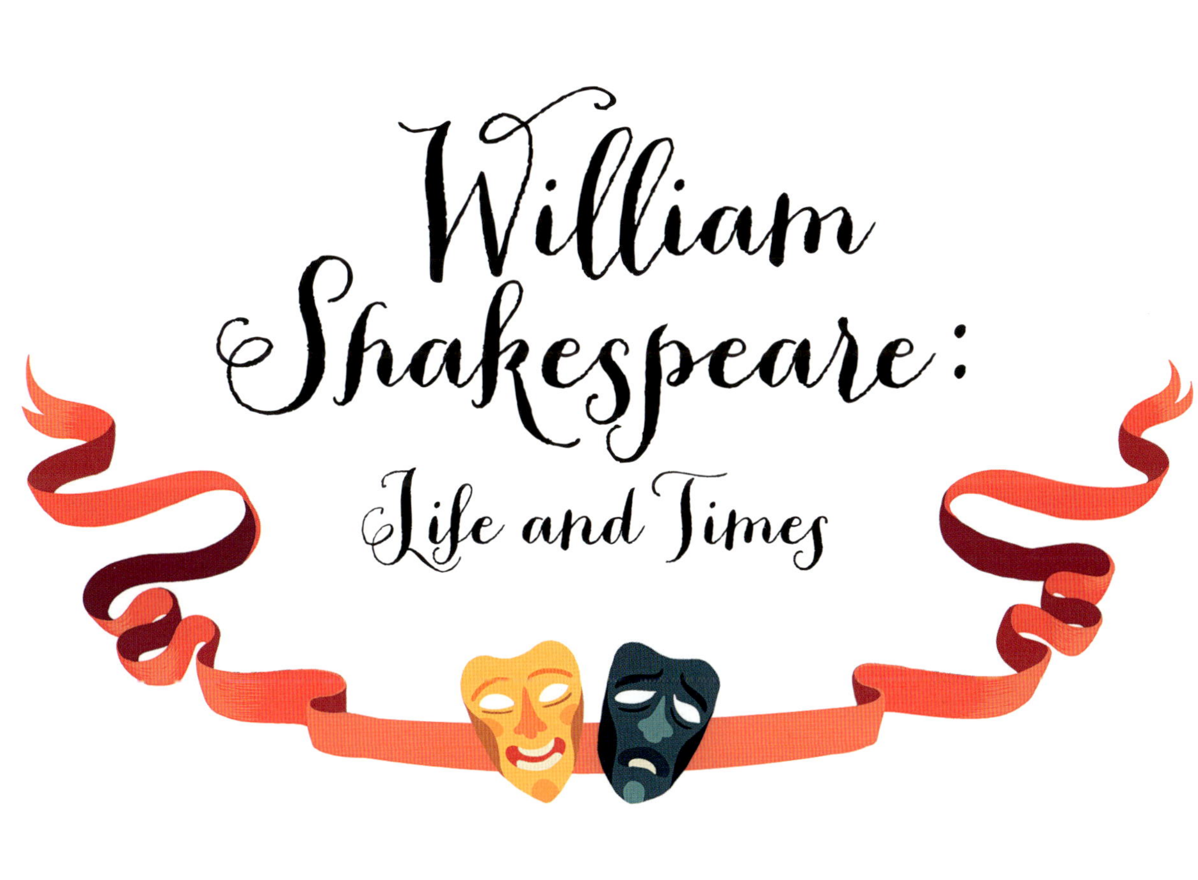

William Shakespeare: Life and Times

A Humble Beginning

WILLIAM SHAKESPEARE IS THE MOST FAMOUS, most quoted writer in the English language, yet we know more about some of the characters from his plays than we do of his own life. Court documents, bills and other surviving fragments provide us with the bare facts, enough to know that he was born in April 1564 in the British market town of Stratford-upon-Avon.

There was no particular hint of future greatness in his family background; his father was a glove-maker who also traded in wool and hides, and his mother's ancestors were farmers. William Shakespeare went to local schools, where he would have learned ancient Greek and Latin and studied ancient texts. At 14, he left school to help with his father's business.

When he was just 18, William Shakespeare married Anne Hathaway. They stayed in their home town of Stratford, and had three children (Susanna, Hamnet and Judith).

By 1592, when Shakespeare was 28, there are reports of him appearing on the London stage. Nobody knows how he got into the theatre. Perhaps he had been influenced by wandering groups of players (actors) who visited Stratford from time to time.

He and some fellow actors set up their own theatrical company, known as *The Lord Chamberlain's Men*. At this time, it was usual for the actors in a company to help write and adapt plays as they went along. Soon, Shakespeare was writing lines and speeches that dazzled people from every walk of life.

A Golden Age

SHAKESPEARE WAS AN EXTRAORDINARY WRITER, born into extraordinary times. The period, which saw great developments in arts, science and ideas, later became known as the Renaissance. There were new inventions, such as telescopes, enabling new perspectives on the world. People were gaining greater awareness of the wider world, with explorers such as Sir Walter Raleigh sailing to the Americas, and Sir Francis Drake sailing all the way around the globe in his ship *The Golden Hind*. Writers were beginning to explore the meanings and possibilities of this brave new world.

The wealth being generated by more global trade routes created a class of rich, educated people who supported the arts. Suddenly writers and painters could make a living out of their art, leading to an explosion in the creation and exchange of new ideas. Shakespeare was one among many famous writers from the period, which has become known as the Golden Age of English Drama.

Although literacy was increasing, not everyone was able to read. One way people could absorb new ideas or stories of their history was through theatre. Shakespeare's histories in particular were immensely popular, giving the audience insights into their past and their identity as a nation in the ever-changing world.

Religion played an important part in life in Shakespeare's time; you were fined if you did not go to church, for example. Christians were divided into Catholics and Protestants, and England was officially a Protestant country. Very strict Protestants, known as Puritans, thought plays were bad for people, and campaigned to close theatres. But luckily for Shakespeare, Queen Elizabeth I was a great fan of the arts – especially music, poetry and plays. So, with her support in particular, theatre flourished.

The Globe

As Elizabethan theatre flourished, crowds gathered in the first, purpose-built playhouses in London. Shakespeare's company of players was so popular it even built its own theatre called the Globe in 1599. Today, a reconstruction of it stands on almost the same site on the banks of the River Thames.

The atmosphere at the Globe was quite different to that of modern theatres. There was little or no lighting, so plays were staged in the afternoon under an open roof. The bulk of the audience gathered on three sides of a bare stage, standing throughout the performance and making the best of the weather. Richer patrons could pay a few pennies to sit on benches and hire cushions. Hawkers roamed through the crowd, selling nuts, gingerbread and beer.

City authorities believed acting was a disreputable profession, and it was illegal for women or girls to appear on stage. So male players took on female roles. Shakespeare would have known, and perhaps enjoyed, the confusion this might cause for his audience, and several of his plays feature girls disguised as boys, such as the character Viola in *Twelfth Night*.

The playhouses in Shakespeare's time were usually sited outside London's defensive walls, to avoid offending strict city politicians. But with the support of the aristocracy, courtiers and well-educated gentry, acting companies thrived.

Shakespeare would often give performances at universities and at the royal court, with special groups of actors. Some of his dramas, *Troilus and Cressida* for example, contain many references to Latin and scholarly texts, and might have been written with a highly educated audience in mind.

When James I came to the throne upon Elizabeth's death, Shakespeare's company changed its name to *The King's Men*, and continued to put on shows at court and occasionally go on tour to Oxford and other cities.

The Poet's Eye

IT WAS SHAKESPEARE'S ELOQUENCE AND POETIC genius that won over every audience. He was, at heart, a poet, and his language was rich enough to transport a crowd from the barren stage sets of the Globe to his imagined dramatic worlds: enchanted forests and ancient battlefields, haunted castles and the lavish banquet halls of Egypt. He wrote about great, historical figures, kings, queens and generals, but he gave each character human qualities, both good and bad, that everyone could – and still can – recognize and understand.

With his reputation and fortune made, Shakespeare bought a grand house in Stratford-upon-Avon, and from 1610 onwards, he began to spend more time with his family away from London's literary scene.

People often take one of his last plays, *The Tempest*, as an exploration of the power of theatre. The casting aside of Prospero's magical staff can be compared to Shakespeare laying down his pen. After this, he co-wrote two more plays (*Henry VIII* and *Two Noble Kinsmen*) with John Fletcher, before retiring for good.

He had every right to a long rest, having penned some 37 dramas and a series of famous poems called sonnets. But he died within a few years of leaving London, on 23 April 1616, aged 52.

Although his works were never published as books in his lifetime, many scripts survive from performances by *The King's Men*. A collection of his plays was printed in 1623, ranging across the dramatic forms and styles, from comedy to tragedy, and ending with his late, experimental works that include *The Tempest*.

The best of them are still staged today, and their representation of what it means to be human is still as striking and true as it was four centuries ago.

Words to tell the tale

THE LANGUAGE AND LAYERS OF MEANING in Shakespeare's writing might seem daunting to a modern audience or reader, but he would have expected the raucous crowd to follow each twist and turn in his dramas. Elizabethans were used to listening to stories being read aloud, and were fascinated by the wit and freshness of their changing language.

In Elizabethan times, English was rather looked down upon by other European nations. Many people dismissed it as lacking in expression when compared to Latin and French. It is one of Shakespeare's many triumphs that he proved the rich, descriptive magic of his mother tongue, borrowing and coining new words as it suited him, and presenting them in verse to a delighted audience.

Shakespeare created over 1,700 new words, and many phrases, commonly used today. This page shows just a few examples:

Internet links to find out more

For links to websites where you can find out more about the life
and times of William Shakespeare, and the plays he wrote, go to the
Usborne Quicklinks website at usborne.com/quicklinks and type in
the keywords 'Complete Shakespeare'.

Here are some of the things you can do on the recommended websites:

- See places where Shakespeare lived and worked
- Watch video clips of performances from some of
  Shakespeare's most famous plays
- See inside Shakespeare's Globe theatre in London, England
- Examine books of Shakespeare's plays called quartos,
  printed in the 17th century
- Try quizzes about Shakespeare, his plays and
  characters, and unusual words he invented

The recommended websites at Usborne Quicklinks are regularly
reviewed and updated but, please note, Usborne Publishing is not
responsible for the content or availability of any website other
than its own. We recommend that children are supervised while
on the internet.

Shakespeare consultant: Jakub Boguszak,
Research Assistant, Shakespeare's Globe

Editors: Anna Milbourne, Jerome Martin & Jane Chisholm
Managing Designer: Stephen Moncrieff

First published in 2016 by Usborne Publishing Limited, Usborne House, 83–85 Saffron Hill, London,
EC1N 8RT, United Kingdom. usborne.com Copyright © 2016 Usborne Publishing Limited.
The name Usborne and the Balloon logo are Trade Marks of Usborne Publishing Limited.

"If we shadows have offended,
Think but this, and all is mended,
That you have but slumbered here
While these visions did appear."

A MIDSUMMER NIGHT'S DREAM
ACT 5, SCENE 1